FREE CLINICS

FREE CLINICS

Local Responses to Health Care Needs

Edited by Virginia M. Brennan

The Johns Hopkins University Press
Baltimore

© 2013 The Johns Hopkins University Press
All rights reserved. Published 2013
Printed in the United States of America on acid-free paper
9 8 7 6 5 4 3 2 1

The Johns Hopkins University Press
2715 North Charles Street
Baltimore, Maryland 21218-4363
www.press.jhu.edu

Chapters 2–25 were originally published in the *Journal of Health Care for the Poor and Underserved* in the following volumes: chapters 2, 6, 18, 19, 21, and 24, vol. 20 (2009); chapters 3, 9, 11, 12, 15, and 20, vol. 16 (2005); chapters 4 and 17, vol. 17 (2006); chapters 5, 8, 10, and 14, vol. 15 (2004); chapters 7, 22, and 25, vol. 18 (2007); chapter 13, vol. 14 (2003); chapter 23, vol. 19 (2008).

ISBN-13: 978-1-4214-0884-2
ISBN-10: 1-4214-0884-8

Library of Congress Control Number: 2012948361
A catalog record for this book is available from the British Library.

Special discounts are available for bulk purchases of this book. For more information, please contact Special Sales at 410-516-6936 or specialsales@press.jhu.edu.

The Johns Hopkins University Press uses environmentally friendly book materials, including recycled text paper that is composed of at least 30 percent post-consumer waste, whenever possible.

Contents

Foreword

With ever-rising health care costs, access to health services has become a national priority. The increasing expense has a dampening effect on the growth of the U.S. economy, and inadequate health care access hinders the productivity and efficiency of the labor pool. With the growing burden of the uninsured, U.S. health care is facing another crisis. Like a strong ballast against the storm, free and charity clinics provide an ambulatory safeguard to the millions who would otherwise fall victim to this economic torrent.

The lay public and the government have recognized the importance of quality health care for the public good. With the passage of the Patient Protection and Affordable Act in 2010, the first steps to eliminating the insurance barriers to health care access have been taken. Perhaps the United States will move to a system designed not to maximize profits but to broaden the basic health care available to the largest possible segment of society. Until the act is fully implemented and the challenge of finding access to quality health care is no longer an issue, however, free clinics will still be needed to care for the economically disadvantaged.

In 2011, 46.3 million people were uninsured in the United States, about 15% of the population.[1] This figure was expected to rise by the end of 2012. For minorities, the figures are worse, with nearly 30% of Hispanics and nearly 20% of African Americans being uninsured.[1] Free clinics receive nearly 4 million patient visits a year.[2, 3] Without these clinics, the nation's emergency departments and public health clinics (including federally qualified community health centers) would have to absorb all these patients and the costs associated with their care.

The more than 1,200 free and charitable clinics nationwide play a crucial role in public health.[2,3] These clinics do so in the face of mounting pressures from both the for-profit sector and governmental forces. Both federal and state budgets are being trimmed, and funds to provide limited reimbursement to keep community health centers and free clinics afloat are being cut. Despite these threats, the services these clinics provide must continue, and this book explains why. Each chapter demonstrates some of the many reasons that free clinics are important to the overall health system, including descriptions of the strategies these safety-net clinics have developed to continue providing service in this challenging economic climate.

Free clinics stand on one of the transcendent pillars of medicine—doing good. This essential principle of benevolence drives societies' best and brightest to pursue careers in medicine, buttresses them through the rigorous education and training process, and sustains them until their matriculation. Although the promise of financial prosperity is attractive, generations of health professionals realize that a fulfilled career in medicine often pays dividends in nonmonetary ways. This cohort of health professionals is driven by purpose rather than profit. Out of these individuals' ideals and the obligation of the profession to serve the common good, free clinics were born and continue to thrive.

The second part of this book highlights the work done at various student-run free clinics. The student-run free clinic phenomenon traces its beginnings to the free clinic movement initiated by David Smith when he founded the Haight Ashbury Free Clinics in 1967 (see Weiss's history of the movement).[4] The concept of a free clinic was taken up by medical students, spreading across the country during the seventies and eighties. The academic medical establishment soon realized the value that student-run free clinics provided their enrollees and began to support them. These clinics provided a tremendous opportunity to instill the core values of compassion and commitment to helping the underserved that is crucial to the development of future physicians. Almost 50 medical schools operate about 110 student-run free clinics, which primarily treat underserved and uninsured populations. The Association of American Medical Colleges through its Group on Student Affairs has issued guidelines to help its members support students providing patient care abroad that are relevant for free clinic care by students as well.[5]

Student-run free clinics also speak to a larger problem that has echoed through U.S. health care since the first Haight Ashbury clinic opened. It is generally accepted that health is a right, not a privilege, and that the provision of public health services is a public good, yet it is still not required that everyone have the same access to basic primary health care. The public still becomes polarized around this issue in rancorous political debates. This book illustrates the central role that free clinics must continue to play in the health of the people as long as governmental authorities remain deadlocked in the politics of equal access to basic primary health care, a goal articulated by Dr. Smith over 40 years ago.

Charles Mouton, MD, MS
Senior Vice President for Health Affairs and
Dean of the Meharry Medical College School of Medicine,
Nashville, Tennessee

Notes

1. Centers for Disease Control and Prevention (CDC). Lack of health insurance and type of coverage. Atlanta, Georgia: CDC, released June 2012. Data source: CDC/NCHS, National Health Interview Survey, 2011, Family Core component. Available at www.cdc.gov/nchs/data/nhis/earlyrelease/earlyrelease201206_01.pdf.

2. Darnell J. What is the role of free clinics in the safety net? Med Care 2011 Nov; 49(11): 978–84.

3. Darnell JS. Free clinics in the United States: a nationwide survey. Arch Intern Med. 2010 Jun 14;170(11):946–53.

4. Weiss, Gregory L. Grass roots medicine: the story of America's free health clinics. Lanham, MD, and New York, NY: Rowman & Littlefield, 2006.

5. AAMC Group on Student Affairs Steering Committee. Guidelines for premedical and medical students providing patient care during clinical experiences abroad. Washington, DC: Association of American Medical Colleges (AAMC), adopted February 25, 2011. Available at www.aamc.org/download/181690/data/guidelinesforstudentsprovidingpatientcare.pdf.

Preface

This book opens with a comprehensive review—by Emily Rose Schiller, Michelle Ann Thurston, Zubair Khan, and Michael D. Fetters—of the literature on free clinics, nongovernmental organizations that strive to respond to a community's health care needs through health education, free preventive and diagnostic services, basic primary care, and a support network of peers and practitioners. Noting that free clinics form an important component of a health care safety net, the authors identify research areas to advance these clinics' effectiveness. Although free clinics vary greatly in their structures, missions, and services provided, all share seven major areas interventions might address: populations served; geography; epidemiology; funding, administration, and operations; approaches to care; health information technology; and volunteers. Improving free clinics could include adapting new models of care, creating or expanding electronic health records, improving screening for and assistance to clients who might qualify for government aid, eliminating barriers to care, and providing additional preventive and diagnostic screenings.

After this overview, the book is divided into two parts: "Free Clinics" and "Student-Run Clinics." The array of descriptions and reflections in these chapters illustrate the wide variety of measures that providers and community leaders have devised to respond locally to the problems of people who are uninsured.

Part I: Free Clinics
Providers

Part I begins with a short chapter by Richard C. Christensen, psychiatrist and long-time physician to people who are homeless. Christensen describes the core objectives of a street psychiatric outreach initiative to help people who are homeless in Jacksonville, Florida, by fostering relationship, reconnection, and recovery. Next, in chapter 3, Lois A. Wessel describes a typical week's work of one family nurse practitioner living in the Washington, DC, metropolitan area:

- providing primary care to uninsured immigrant patients on a mobile van,
- teaching an undergraduate nursing course entitled Community and Environmental Health Nursing at the Catholic University of America,
- screening Hispanic women for breast and cervical cancer through Celebremos La Vida (Celebrate Life) at Georgetown University's Lombardi Cancer Center, and
- leading continuing professional education programs for health care providers who work with the poor and underserved through the Pediatric Asthma Prevention Project and the Early Childhood Caries Prevention Project of the Association of Clinicians for the Underserved (ACU).

Chapter 4 maintains the focus on providers by reporting on a qualitative study of faith-based and secular urban community health centers. Farr A. Curlin and colleagues surveyed providers in Chicago about their motivations (religious and other) for working in clinics for the medically underserved.

Historical and descriptive accounts

The next three chapters describe individual clinics. Chapter 5 takes a historical perspective on nursing homes through description and analysis of the 100-year history of the Jane Dent Home, a home for the elderly in an African American neighborhood in Chicago. Susan C. Reed and Nancy Davis trace the rise and fall of community-created homes for the aged in the United States before and after the advent of Medicaid.

Next are two chapters describing academic–community partnerships in free clinics. First, Susan G. Pfefferle and colleagues describe the Nurses for Newborns Foundation in St. Louis, where a university-based researcher collaborated with the community-based organization to address depression in low-income new mothers who would not ordinarily have access to mental health services. Second, Mina Silberberg and her colleagues describe a clinic run by a federally qualified health center and Duke University in Durham, North Carolina. The clinic expands the community's primary care capacity, combining the advantages of big and small settings and of its dual affiliation. Survey data suggest the clinic prevents health care delays and lowers emergency department use.

Data-driven accounts

With the background established by the literature review and the individual descriptive accounts in place, this book continues with nine chapters that analyze data on one or more free clinics.

Stephanie Geller and colleagues at Brown University surveyed free clinics in seven midwestern states. Findings from this survey show that, in a single year, these 106 clinics provided medical, dental, and pharmaceutical services to over 200,000 patients, suggesting that free clinics nationwide are caring for a substantial number of our nation's uninsured. The next chapter concerns an attempt by one state, Delaware, to deal with the need for health care among the uninsured. James M. Gill and colleagues analyze the effectiveness of this state-level initiative.

What do patients at free clinics have in common? Rachel Mott-Keis and colleagues report on the characteristics of patients at three free clinics in central Massachusetts. Over 250 patients at the clinics responded to a survey over two months. Descriptive results showed that most free clinic patients are low-income, uninsured, and female. Many patients (62%) do not have a usual source of care, nor do they know where to go if the clinic is not open (61%). Most (82%) report using free clinics because they lack insurance or need prescription medication. Although free clinics serve an important need, they cannot provide comprehensive, continuous care, and this chapter provides specific evidence of that.

Free clinics often begin with the notion that they will provide episodic care but find they are the only option for many people. Jeffrey T. Kullgren and colleagues examine the early experience of a donated care program in southern Maine called CarePartners. Although such programs are often viewed as a short-term solution for those temporarily without health insurance, the authors find that CarePartners was a longer-term means for getting access to care for most enrollees.

Chapter 12, by Karen E. Lasser and colleagues, focuses on a common problem faced by community health centers as well as free clinics: missed appointments. Specifically, the authors ask to what extent language plays a role in missed appointment rates. They studied patients in four language groups (English, Portuguese, Spanish, and Haitian Creole) who were visiting a large local network of neighborhood health centers in the Cambridge Health Alliance (CHA), a Primary Care Practice–Based Research Network (PBRN) consisting of 25 primary care centers. The health centers predominantly serve a multicultural, low-income population in Cambridge, Somerville, and Everett, Massachusetts.

Mohan Nadkarni and John T. Philbrick describe the first five years of operation (1992–97) of the Charlottesville Free Clinic in Charlottesville, Virginia, a nonprofit organization staffed by volunteer health care providers. In chapter 14, Marie Soller and Lars Osterberg report on a survey of 210 patients at the Ann Arbor Free Clinic conducted over an eight-month period. While patients reported a high level of satisfaction, the authors are also able to identify numerous opportunities for improvement, specifically in the area of social work. In chapter 15, Robert Stroebel and colleagues from the Mayo Clinic College of Medicine report on their successful adaptation of the Chronic Care Model for use with uninsured patients in a free medical clinic staffed by volunteer physicians at the Salvation Army Free Clinic in Rochester, Minnesota. The final paper in this first part of the book concerns the increasingly common phenomenon of respite care for people who are homeless. Suzanne Zerger and colleagues from Salt Lake City, Utah, provide a comprehensive description of efforts to provide care to people who are homeless after they are released from the hospital but before they are able to return to the streets.

Part II: Student-Run Clinics

While professionals nationwide offer volunteer services at free clinics, another, smaller volunteer phenomenon also crops up again and again: student-run clinics. These clinics are generally small in terms of numbers of patients seen (much smaller than community health centers, and generally smaller than free clinics in the same localities). However, student-run clinics are training grounds for caregivers who may ultimately take up the challenge of careers devoted to the care of vulnerable populations. For that reason alone, they merit examination.

Ethics

The possibility lurks that the uninsured get care at student-run clinics but that this care is substandard. Conversely, many argue that it is of the greatest importance to engage students in care for underserved populations in order to ensure that some will subsequently choose to focus their lives in such settings. A professor from Rush School of Medicine and fellow from the Institute of Ethics at the AMA, David Buchanan and Renee Witlen, open this second half of the book by offering ethical guidelines for student-run clinics so that the first possibility is not realized while the second is.

Data-driven and descriptive accounts

The next eight chapters analyze care and student preparation at specific student-run clinics. Chapter 18 concerns diabetes care at the East Harlem Health Outreach Partnership (EHHOP) of the Mount Sinai School of Medicine in New York, a medical student-run, attending-supervised free clinic that offers primary care to the uninsured of surrounding East Harlem. Clinic rates of diabetes quality-of-care indicators ranged from 12% to 96%, and in most areas was comparable to or better than averages previously reported for uninsured populations, which is reassuring in light of the concerns raised in the preceding chapter.

In chapter 19, Brent Simmons and colleagues in Philadelphia report on their survey of first-year medical students about preparedness for work at student-run clinics, addressing patients' access to care, and social issues. In chapter 20, we see an example of training that might speak to the needs expressed by these students—in this chapter, Ellen Beck describes the closely supervised and highly collaborative work of students and faculty from the University of California, San Diego School of Medicine on the UCSD Student-Run Free Clinic Project.

Steven Bishop and colleagues describe the Charlottesville Health Access (CHA), an initiative to get people who are homeless into the health care system. A community homeless shelter worked with faculty and students from the University of Virginia Schools of Medicine and Nursing to create and run the program. Across the country in Los Angeles, Joseph Hastings and colleagues report on a man seeking care at the UCLA Mobile Clinic, illustrating and then discussing the challenges (especially mental illness and potential distrust of providers) of caring for people who are homeless. The authors conclude that student-run free clinics can be beneficial but further research must examine how well such clinics meet homeless patients' needs. In chapter 24, Vickie Mays and colleagues describe their work with undergraduates at UCLA, reporting how they engage undergraduate student groups to conduct outreach in medically underserved communities in an effort to counter racial/ethnic health disparities.

The Homeless and Indigent Population Health Outreach Project (HIPHOP) was founded in 1995 by medical students at the University of Medicine and Dentistry of New Jersey–Robert Wood Johnson Medical School (UMDNJ-RWJMS) in Newark, New Jersey, to add a community-based service-learning component to their curriculum. The goal of the Promise Clinic as it exists today (a project of an academic medical center and a local social services group) is to increase access to primary care for an underserved population while addressing deficiencies in medical education. Students manage common primary care problems, creating access for this mostly uninsured population. Manuel Jimenez and colleagues report on that project in chapter 23.

Finally, in chapter 25, Carmen Patrick Mohan and Arun Mohan report on a student-run program at several medical and nursing schools in Georgia to build a cadre of health professionals and health professionals in training to serve the underserved.

FREE CLINICS

Chapter 1

Free Clinics Stand as a Pillar of the Health Care Safety Net: Findings from a Narrative Literature Review

Emily Rose Schiller
Michelle Ann Thurston
Zubair Khan
Michael D. Fetters

Once you've seen one free clinic, you've only seen one free clinic.
—Slogan of the National Association of Free Clinics National Summit 2007

The Patient Protection and Affordable Care Act, signed into law by President Barack Obama on March 23, 2010, has been hailed as a great step forward for improving the U.S. health care system.[1,2] This legislation is projected to guarantee coverage and expand access to health care for 32 million more Americans.[3] Unfortunately, about 46 million people were uninsured or underinsured at the time of passage. The Congressional Budget Office estimates that by 2019, 23 million U.S. residents will continue to be uninsured under this plan.[4,5] About 7 million will be undocumented immigrants, a population explicitly excluded from government-supported care. The other 16 million without insurance will be citizens and documented immigrants. Details about this large population of the projected uninsured are beyond the purpose of this review, but suffice it to say that the need for the health care safety net is not going away.

The *health care safety net* refers to programs and providers that offer services regardless of ability to pay. Medically underserved and uninsured clients often rely on these services as their only options for health care. Free clinics stand as a pillar of the safety net because they aim to provide comprehensive, nonemergency care, with minimal funds, to those in need who cannot secure care through other

Emily Rose Schiller, BA, is a Health Disparities Fellow at the National Institutes of Health Academy in Bethesda, Maryland. *Michelle Ann Thurston, MBA, BS,* is the clinical research coordinator in the Department of Family Medicine at the University of Michigan, Ann Arbor. *Zubair Khan, JD,* is cofounder and partner in the Chicago law firm Rab & Kahn. *Michael D. Fetters, MD, MPH,* is a professor in the Department of Family Medicine at the University of Michigan, Ann Arbor, and director of the Japanese Family Health Program at Dominos Farms Family Medicine.

means. Scholars on free clinics mark the founding of the Haight Ashbury Free Clinic (HAFC) in San Francisco, California, as the beginning of a concerted free clinic movement.[6-8] In *Grassroots Medicine*, Weiss provides the most comprehensive study of the origins of the free clinic movement and traces the stories of activists and the emergence of free clinics from the 1960s until the first years of the next century.[6] Free clinics take on the challenge of serving diverse, uninsured, and underserved populations with high incidences of chronic illnesses and neglected health problems. To address these challenges, volunteers at free clinics structure creative and nontraditional approaches to care. In an effort to remove access barriers to care, a clinic might provide transportation, interpreter services, convenient hours, or free meals. In addition to providing medical treatment, many free clinics provide social welfare and health education programs. Free clinics can play a crucial role by acting as a social support service to help buffer isolation and create a support network.[9]

The current economic downturn has adversely affected health care and further strained the safety net. In 2009, it was estimated that 4 million Americans would visit 1,200 free clinics.[10] Statistics about the number of free clinics in the United States, however, are only rough estimates because national surveys cannot reach every clinic. The *Free Clinic Directory* (provided by the Free Clinic Foundation of America) lists only 365, and the incomplete membership limits generalizability of surveys using clinic directories.[11,12] Isaacs estimated that 1,718 free clinics in 49 states and the District of Columbia (concentrated in the most populous states) provided medical care to 2.5 million people in 2003.[13] Darnell provides a more recent snapshot of the structures and functions of 1,007 free clinics in 2010.[12]

Free clinics lessen the strain on other safety net components by preventing unnecessary emergency room visits and hospitalizations.[14-16] Crump et al. estimated that $6,500 worth of free clinic care saved a local emergency department a net $33,145.[15] Despite free clinics' crucial role in the health care safety net, however, the literature concerning them lacks a comprehensive review. Hence, we conducted a review of available sources to develop a more integrated picture of free clinics and to identify areas that merit further research.

Methods

For this project we conducted a narrative review.[17,18] To find relevant literature on free clinics, we conducted Boolean searches on PubMed, ISI Web of Knowledge, Proquest Business ABI/INFORM Global, and the Cumulative Index to Nursing and Allied Health (CINAHL). For all the databases, we used the search term "free clinic*," so that the results would include any mention of the terms "free clinic" or "free clinics."

Articles by authors who claimed they were studying free medical clinics were accepted for this study upon mention of treating clients regardless of insurance status for minimal or no fees. We specified the publication date range as January 1, 1990, to August 6, 2010, and limited the search to articles only in the English language. Additionally, in Proquest, we limited the publication type to scholarly journals, rejecting articles from weekly periodicals or lay magazines. We further limited the search to articles published in the United States. We excluded articles that merely mentioned free clinics as a part of the safety net but did not discuss free clinics in depth. Although Federally Qualified Health Centers (FQHCs) serve a larger number of uninsured clients than do free clinics, for the purposes of this review, we excluded FQHCs because, unlike free clinics, they receive governmental funding.[11] Thus, in the initial literature search, we identified 329 articles, and of these, 78 met criteria for inclusion. Through review of their bibliographies and suggestions from peers in the field, we found an additional 12 articles, for a total of 90 articles that were the focus of this review.

In addition to reading the articles multiple times and compiling notes on the major points of each one, we reviewed and analyzed the content of the papers qualitatively and developed domains of interest that emerged recurrently in the articles. Throughout the review, we sought to answer the following questions: What types of barriers do free clinics encounter in the United States? How do they overcome these challenges to provide health care for clients in their respective communities? What are future research areas?

To identify the most important articles, we created a four-tiered system of ranking: tier-1 articles were considered the most informative, tier-2 papers were moderately informative, tier-3 sources were minimally informative, and tier-4 documents contained no useful information related to the domain (table 1.1). Three authors (ES, MT, ZK) calibrated the coding scheme. Using the 4-tier system, we independently coded 10 articles initially and then discussed discrepancies to ensure consistent coding approaches. After we scored the remaining articles, agreement with the final consensus for all article ranking for reviewer 1 (ES) was 93%, reviewer 2 (MT) was 95% and reviewer 3 (ZK) was 92%.

Results

Based on our content analysis of the relevant literature, we identified seven major categories: (1) populations served; (2) geography; (3) epidemiology; (4) funding, administration, and operations; (5) health care approaches and quality improvement; (6) health information technology; and (7) volunteers. For each major category we developed related subcategories (table 1.2).

Populations served

We found 28 tier-1 articles, 19 tier-2 articles, and 42 tier-3 articles addressing populations served. These sources provide an overview of client statistics and experiences through interviews, quantitative data, surveys, case studies, and observations. Data consistently show that clients at free clinics are disproportionately low-income, female, uninsured, immigrants, or minorities.[11,19-21] Minorities often have more difficulty than Caucasians in communicating with their health care providers and understanding provided information.[22] Compared with clients who have health insurance, uninsured populations receive fewer services (preventive and diagnostic), delay seeking care, make more visits

Table 1.1

Categories addressed in the literature and source rankings

Category	Note numbers of citations Tier 1	Tier 2	Tier 3	Tier 4
Populations served	9, 11, 12, 19–26, 30–32, 35, 37, 38, 40, 48, 52, 55, 57–60, 88–90 (total 28)	7, 8, 27, 29, 33, 34, 39, 46, 47, 54, 61, 62, 72, 74, 75, 91–94 (total 19)	2, 13–16, 28, 36, 41, 42, 44, 45, 49–51, 53, 56, 63–65, 67–71, 73, 76–83, 95–103 (total 42)	104 (total 1)
Geography	11, 27, 40, 46, 73, 90 (total 6)	7, 8, 20, 21, 23, 25, 28–30, 32, 34, 35, 39, 41, 42, 44, 47–49, 51, 56, 58, 60, 71, 80, 89, 93, 104 (total 28)	2, 9, 12–16, 19, 22, 24, 26, 31, 33, 36–38, 45, 50, 52, 53, 55, 57, 59, 61–65, 67, 69, 70, 72, 75, 76, 78, 79, 81–83, 88, 91, 92, 94–103 (total 52)	54, 68, 74, 77 (total 4)
Epidemiology	7, 9, 32–35, 38–40, 48, 52–60, 92 (total 20)	8, 11, 20, 23, 26, 31, 46, 47 (total 8)	12, 13, 15, 16, 19, 24, 28, 37, 41, 50, 51, 62, 64, 67–71, 74, 75, 77, 79, 82, 88, 90, 91, 94, 95, 97–101, 103 (total 34)	2, 14, 21, 22, 25, 27, 29, 30, 36, 42, 44, 45, 49, 61, 63, 65, 72, 73, 76, 78, 80, 81, 83, 89, 93, 96, 102, 104 (total 28)
Funding, administration, and operations	2, 8, 11–13, 15, 20, 21, 23–25, 27, 28, 30, 32, 35, 36, 41, 42, 49, 50, 60–62, 64, 65, 74, 76, 77, 80, 81, 89–91, 95, 98, 104 (total 37)	7, 14, 19, 26, 29, 31, 33, 34, 39, 44–46, 48, 51, 53, 63, 67, 69, 71–73, 75, 78, 79, 82, 88, 92, 93, 101 (total 29)	9, 16, 22, 37, 38, 40, 52, 54–59, 70, 83, 94, 96, 97, 99, 100, 102, 103 (total 22)	47, 68 (total 2)

	Tier 1	Tier 2	Tier 3	Tier 4
Health care approaches and quality improvement	7, 11, 12, 20, 22, 24, 26, 29–33, 37–39, 45, 46, 48, 52–54, 56, 58–60, 62, 64, 74, 75, 79, 80, 82, 83, 89, 90, 92, 98 (total 37)	8, 9, 15, 19, 21, 23, 25, 27, 34–36, 50, 65, 73, 76, 77, 88, 91, 94, 97, 101 (total 21)	2, 13, 14, 16, 28, 40–42, 44, 47, 49, 51, 55, 57, 63, 67, 69–72, 74, 78, 81, 93, 95, 96, 99, 100, 103, 104 (total 30)	61, 68 (total 2)
Health IT	48, 56, 65 (total 3)	33 (total 1)	13, 21, 22, 24, 40, 44, 49, 52, 57, 58, 60, 67, 80, 88, 92, 94 (total 16)	2, 8, 9, 11, 12, 14–16, 19, 20, 23, 25–32, 34–39, 41, 42, 45–47, 50, 51, 53–55, 59, 61–64, 68–79, 81–83, 89–91, 93, 95–105 (total 70)
Volunteers	8, 11–13, 20, 26, 27, 36, 42, 44, 60, 68, 71, 72, 74, 77, 79, 90, 98 (total 19)	22, 25, 49, 50, 65, 70, 80, 89, 97, 99 (total 10)	9, 14–16, 19, 21, 23, 28–30, 32–35, 38, 39, 41, 45, 46, 48, 51–55, 57–59, 61–64, 67, 69, 73, 75, 76, 78, 81–83, 88, 92, 93, 95, 96, 100–104 (total 51)	2, 7, 24, 31, 37, 40, 47, 56, 91, 94 (total 10)

Note:

Tier 1 = Highly informative—detailed description

Tier 2 = Moderately informative—moderate description

Tier 3 = Minimally informative—minimal description

Tier 4 = N/A—not described in the article

Table 1.2
Overarching categories and subcategories regarding free clinics, based on literature review

Categories	Subcategories
Populations served	• Coverage under age extremes • Immigrant populations • Homeless populations
Geography	• State and regional organizations • Rural care • Urban care
Epidemiology	• Diabetes mellitus • Mental illness
Funding, administration, and operations	• Funding sources • Sustaining operations • Approaches to appointments
Health care approaches and quality improvement	• Quality and models of care • Chronic disease management programs • Complementary and alternative care • Preventive services • Education programs • Access to medication • General quality improvement
Health IT	• Client tracking and databases • Electronic records • Pharmacological management systems • Information technology and health promotion
Volunteers	• Faith-based volunteers • Volunteer backgrounds • Volunteer physicians • Student volunteers • Student-run clinics • Preparing students to volunteer • Altruism and medical students • Clinical skills and learning opportunities • Ethics of student participation

to the emergency room for preventable issues, and rarely see a primary health care provider regularly.[9,16,19,23–25]

The criteria for client eligibility influence the demographic profile of the patient population in each clinic. Some clinics will treat only uninsured clients or those at or below the federal poverty level. Other clinics will not turn away clients regardless of insurance coverage, immigration status, or care concurrently received elsewhere.[19,26,27] The latter clinics may serve insured clients who prefer the clinic because their insurance does not cover prescriptions or specific services or because of long waiting times elsewhere or physician referral.[19,27] Many clients at free clinics are employed or belong to working families but either do not receive employer-sponsored coverage or cannot afford the premiums.[14,23,28]

Coverage under age extremes. Because government programs offer coverage for many clients under 18 years and most 65 years and older, approximately 75% of the uninsured population are adults between 18 and 64 years.[23] Children and adolescents are more likely to be uninsured if their parents have no employer-based health care coverage or have insurance that does not cover dependents.[11,25,29] Free clinic efforts for young populations have included enrolling clients in the State Children's Health Insurance Program (S-CHIP), creating well-child programs, and designing child-friendly clinics, resembling private pediatricians' offices.[25,29,30]

Immigrant populations. Free clinics serving immigrant populations report additional barriers and needs facing their clients. Undocumented immigrants may feel safer using free clinics given fears of being identified through other hospital health care services.[19] Immigrant and low-wage workers, such as farm workers and garment workers, suffer disproportionately from occupational health hazards, such as chronic pain from musculoskeletal disorders.[31,32] Identified barriers to care include low wages, lack of employer-based health care coverage, legislation restricting health insurance to legal immigrants, lack of transportation, inability to take time off from work, linguistic barriers, and legislation preventing agencies from using federal, state, or county tax dollars to provide care for undocumented clients.[31,33]

Homeless populations. Homeless people are another subpopulation served by free clinics that faces many barriers to care, including the inability to store medication and syringes, poor nutrition, improper hygiene, and fear of asking for help.[34–36] About 45% of the homeless suffer from alcohol dependence, 33% suffer from mental illness, and many suffer from multiple illnesses; in one study clients had an average of nine diagnoses.[36,37] Free clinics have undertaken unique initiatives to serve homeless clientele needs, such as a joint soup kitchen–medical clinic and a mobile clinic.[35]

Geography

Our analysis yielded six tier-1 articles, 28 tier-2 articles, and 52 tier-3 articles addressing variations related to geographic location and its relevance to the kind of care provided. Geographic analysis reveals that cultural, political, and social environments can to some extent predict client demographic characteristics.[38] A few articles discussed care in specific demographic groups, such as rural or urban populations.[11,39] Although there are differences between rural and urban areas, the most common underlying determinant of not receiving health care remains being poor and living in a poor and underserved area.[9,40]

State and regional organizations. State and regional umbrella organizations, and some local and state governments, are able to provide partial funding for free clinic care. Large national or regional foundations do not usually support free clinics directly, although exceptions exist. Examples include the National Association of Free Clinics (NAFC, based in Washington, DC), the Free Clinics of the Great Lakes Region (FCGLR), and various regions under Blue Cross/Blue Shield.[13,27,28] Localized programs include the CITYNET Healthy Cities program, the Lone Star Association of Charitable Clinics, the North Carolina Association of Free Clinics, and the Health Care Access Network in Iowa.[41-45]

Rural care. Compared with the national population as a whole, residents of rural areas are more likely to be elderly and suffer from health issues resulting from physical inactivity, alcohol consumption, anxiety, depression, and higher smoking and obesity rates. Rural populations also have higher morbidity rates because of increased poverty.[46-49] Worsening matters, most physicians, especially specialists, tend to practice in populated, nonrural areas, where the clients are insured.[50]

Urban care. Cities in general offer better accessibility to health services than do rural areas. Such advantages in accessibility can be leveraged to support free clinic patients. Several specific initiatives address the needs of urban residents. In conjunction with free clinics, public and private teaching hospital emergency rooms are sometimes able to provide care at reduced cost. Free clinics in urban areas might also work with existing organizations such as homeless shelters or needle exchange centers.[35,51]

Epidemiology

We identified 20 tier-1 articles, 8 tier-2 articles, and 34 tier-3 articles pertaining to illness distribution, illness patterns, contributors to illness, and specific chronic disease programs (e.g., diabetes mellitus and mental illness). The literature shows that clients served at free clinics, depending on the location and populations served, have disproportionately high rates and multiple diagnoses of diabetes, hypertension, hyperlipidemia, cardiovascular disease, asthma, anxiety, depression, and musculoskeletal disorders.[11,20,32,33,35,38,40,52-57] Because of a lack of medical care, clients sometimes arrive at clinics in the late stages of an illness, with tertiary and neglected symptoms.

Diabetes mellitus. Diabetes is one of the most common problems discussed in epidemiology literature concerning free clinics.[39] Minority groups served at free clinics, including African Americans, Mexican Americans, and women, are more likely to develop diabetes at younger ages; have worse glycemic control (measured by hemoglobin A1c levels); suffer from coronary artery disease and strokes; and have higher rates of morbidity and mortality.[38,39,52,53]

Mental illness. Virtually all client populations at free clinics are affected to some degree by the psychological implications of poverty and surviving with limited resources. Major barriers to care include depression and anxiety, feelings of helplessness or hopelessness, and reluctance to ask for help.[9,34,35,47,58,59] Because poor patients often have comorbidities in physical and mental health, such as diabetes and depression, some free clinics have successfully integrated mental health services alongside physical health screenings.[37,59]

Funding, administration, and operations

We identified 37 tier-1 articles, 29 tier-2 articles, and 22 tier-3 articles concerning funding, administration, and operations. Free clinics vary greatly in structure and function, and these articles help to illustrate the diversity in funding sources, approaches to operations, and appointment systems in such clinics.

Funding sources. Obtaining start-up funds is easier than maintaining funding to sustain clinics.[28] Ongoing personnel costs associated with recruiting and retaining licensed physicians, maintaining a paid staff, and providing insurance coverage for volunteers can sap clinic resources.[13,28] Free clinics rely heavily on individual and corporate donors, such as churches, businesses, hospitals, charity foundations, and drug companies, while state grants and federal government funding provide minimal (if any) support.[11,25,28,60]

Sustaining operations. Although many free clinics charge nothing, some charge a small fee for services to raise funds, although fees may be waived or reduced based on a sliding scale.[11,12] Fundraising can include campaign drives, benefit dinners, concerts, dances, garage sales, or fitness activities.[60] Other ways to manage funds include referring patients to seek help elsewhere; some clinics maintain contact with a network of physicians or emergency rooms to which they can refer patients.[13,20,35,46,60,61] Free clinics sometimes help clients find care elsewhere by conducting client eligibility assessments and assisting with applications for government insurance aid programs.[61]

Approaches to appointments. In addition to traditional appointment and walk-in approaches, some clinics strive to use scheduling to care more effectively for clients. Group appointments encourage peer support and accountability and enable clinics to provide screenings and medications for multiple clients concurrently.[11,31,32,38,53] Clinics may also offer walk-in appointment times, weekly support groups, multicultural cooking classes, and supermarket tours.[35,53]

Health care approaches and quality improvement

We identified 37 tier-1 articles, 21 tier-2 articles, and 30 tier-3 articles concerning health care approaches and quality improvement. These articles address health care and clinical content (e.g., complementary and alternative medicine, preventive services, patient education programs), models of care (e.g., chronic care models, DM programs), and access to pharmaceuticals.

Quality and models of care. Various models of care have been studied extensively in hospital settings, yet the literature contains little on adapting these models to free clinics. Numerous obstacles to providing clients with care for chronic illness have been observed: lack of pharmaceuticals, nonadherence, insufficient funding, lack of volunteers, and extremely unhealthy client populations. Uninsured people are often unable to choose their provider and are much less likely to see the same health care provider consistently. Although the goal of many free clinics is to provide chronic illness care equal to that available in the private sector, gaps in funding and available services create a two-tiered system that makes reaching parity very difficult.[19]

Chronic disease management programs. The chronic care model (CCM) is a structured approach used in hospitals that has proved to be successful when adapted to free clinics. The CCM addresses cultural and linguistic diversity, client transiency, and volunteer challenges.[33] Successful programs for patients with type 2 diabetes, for example, must empower and educate patients to manage their disease. Systematic pharmacist-managed diabetes programs have also proved successful. By following standardized care and following algorithms diligently, participating pharmacists provide specific medications for clients based on test results.[52,53]

Complementary and alternative care. Alternative therapies can help people manage chronic pain. Despite the rising popularity of complementary and alternative medicine, two CAM therapies are cited as specifically underused among minority and low-income populations: chiropractic services and acupuncture.[24,40] This trend may be due to little cultural exposure, financial difficulties, or inaccessibility. Clinics offering alternative therapies are reported to treat referred clients effectively and address chronic pain and other health concerns.[20,24,40,62]

Preventive services. Most free clinics focus on prevention and health promotion to address most effectively the factors contributing to chronic disease and poor health. Health risk assessments (HRAs) have been used to educate clients about links between behaviors and health.[48] Useful preventive services in a free clinic setting include mammograms, Pap smears, colon cancer screenings, prenatal services, and immunizations.[11,57]

Education programs. Numerous articles discuss structured approaches to health education.[22,33,48,53,56] Characteristics of successful education programs include making materials that are accessible, easily understandable, and multilingual; that emphasize self-management; and that are not dependent on literacy.[22,33,48,53,56] A community partnership approach toward education can include hands-on community-building activities (e.g., cooking classes), a peer-support and mentorship system, or ensuring the availability of healthy food alternatives.[53]

Access to medication. Free clinics generally provide free or generic prescription medications whenever possible, and in the United States, these clinics are estimated to fill over 500,000 prescriptions annually.[63] Although providing free or discounted medication is critical for many clients, it can be very costly for clinics.[11,63] Free clinics obtain medications from donated samples, discounted bulk purchases, generic medications, the federal government's 340B discount drug program, or private companies' patient assistance programs (PAPs).[13,64] Completing the paperwork and adjusting to changing requirements of these sources is time-consuming and may require a full-time paid staff member.[13] Strict rules exist for pharmaceutical donations, and cumbersome administrative procedures can result in waiting periods of a few weeks before a client finally receives donated medication.[53]

The scale of pharmacy access is generally not well described in the literature. Of 53 free clinics examined in North Carolina in 2003, 25 were found to have pharmacies.[28] When individuals who receive initial care elsewhere are unable to obtain medications, they sometimes turn to a free clinic.[19,38] This can result in a suboptimal situation of two providers prescribing medication without full knowledge of the patient's prescriptions.[19] One clinic deals with clients who bypass other resources by dispensing pharmaceuticals one timeonly.[65] Two other solutions to common pharmacy barriers in free clinics are enrolling patients in medication assistance programs and prescribing generic alternatives.[64,66]

General quality improvement. Literature about free clinics devotes considerable attention to assessing the effectiveness of the care provided and implementing changes to improve outcomes. For our purposes, we examined articles for assessments of health care quality within free clinics. The quality might be evaluated with patient feedback surveys, through quantitative clinical markers, or by the number of patients served.[31,37]

Health risk assessments and patient satisfaction surveys are used to measure the success of and patients' opinions about free clinic services.[31,37,55] Surveys that address specific diseases, such as diabetes, have monitored ways in which disease status relates to quality of life.[38] Soller et al. used questionnaires to study missed opportunities within the Arbor Free Clinic in California and found that, although many clients surveyed desired health education materials or a meeting with a staff social worker, neither was offered to them.[22] Similarly, Foley et al. studied the effectiveness and existence of free clinic programs by using mailed surveys to assess the number of tobacco cessation services provided and if they adhered to the *Treating Tobacco Use and Dependence* guidelines set by the United States Public Health Service (USPHS).[45]

Health information technology

Within the health information technology (IT) section, we identified three tier-1 articles, 1 tier-2 article, and 16 tier-3 articles. Health IT applications, which encompass various computer technologies used in health care settings to maximize efficiency, are still developing in free clinics. Some examples identified in our research are electronic health records (EHRs); Internet access; printers for educational materials; data storage and management software; and electronic pharmacy tracking systems. With the growing pressure to use health IT in primary care settings, it is reasonable to expect health IT to become a critical part of free clinic organization and a potential area for advancement.

Client tracking and databases. Computerized systems can document new clients at arrival and track their progress. These systems help manage everything from simple client records to information about the clinic population's demographic characteristics, diagnoses, trends in acute and chronic illnesses, and on how and where clients receive health care.[33,57,67]

Electronic records. The existing literature provides few reports of EHRs in free clinics. One exception is a free clinic that implemented a disease management model and internally developed an electronic record-keeping system, called the clinical inquiry program (CLIQ). This program allows providers to enter information into an easy interface for recording progress notes, blood pressure, height, weight, and other relevant data.[56] Additionally, a free acupuncture clinic in a hospital successfully adapted the hospital's EHR system.[24]

Pharmacological management systems. Rosenbaum et al. found little literature about electronic pharmacy organization systems except one useful program at the Shade Tree Family Clinic.[65] The clinic used an innovative web-based pharmacy tracking system to streamline and manage clinic data and ensure proper inventory, documentation, and medication dispensing. Additionally, the program alerted volunteers when medications were running low.

Information technology and health promotion. Access to the Internet and printing capabilities can enable providers to give patients educational materials.[22] These materials might include printouts of HRA results along with brochures and handouts in multiple languages designed to reach clients with diverse diseases.[48]

Volunteers

Concerning volunteers at free clinics, we found 19 tier-1 articles, 10 tier-2 articles, and 51 tier-3 articles. The literature addresses volunteerism in general, trends in volunteering, incentives for volunteers, and specific categories of volunteers (e.g., faith-based physicians and students).

These studies show unequivocally that dedicated grassroots volunteers are committed to becoming involved in their communities, helping the underserved, and making free clinics successful. Although broad conclusions cannot be drawn about trends in volunteerism, one report from North Carolina raises concern about declining interest.[44]

Faith-based volunteers. Many articles discussed free clinics in partnerships or association with faith-based organizations.[8,49,60] Churches may contribute facilities, finances, or church volunteers while missionaries might serve as part of the clinic staff or "core-planning group."[8,49] The church basement, mentioned in four articles, becomes a metaphor for humble beginnings and grassroots efforts.[8,13,19,49]

Volunteer backgrounds. Engaging volunteers from diverse backgrounds and professions can be advantageous for free clinics. Both professional and nonprofessional volunteers are critical. Free clinics can use premedical and predental students as well as lay volunteers to work in clerical or administrative roles.[61] Physician assistant volunteers can contribute various skills to free clinics, including the ability to adapt and problem solve.[68] Many clinics are spearheaded by nurses, who are valued for their compassionate care, varied experiences and specialties, and thoroughness.[35,69]

Volunteer physicians. Physicians who want to volunteer may have concerns related to student loans, operating costs, and perceived risks of providing care for undocumented immigrants. Additionally, liability issues are complex. The Federal Tort Claims Act (effective 2004) covers volunteers at free clinics so that when there are alleged charges against a volunteer, a client sues the federal government instead of the volunteer.[13] Additionally, the Volunteer Protection Act and an amendment to HIPAA provide further protection for free clinic volunteers.[42] Still, obtaining protection is a tedious process, and not all clinics are covered.[13] Free clinic volunteering has a unique appeal for physicians and can be very rewarding for retired doctors.[70–72] In free clinics they have the freedom to provide the quality of care they deem appropriate and are not financially pressured to meet specific patient quotas.[72]

Student volunteers. Because inadequate numbers of licensed practitioners volunteer, free clinics provide medical and graduate students with opportunities to gain service-learning experiences and develop empathy, social awareness, and social and cultural competence.[20] Some clinics use high school and premedical college students to translate or to take on clerical tasks.[61,73,74] At the Arbor Free Clinic at Stanford, undergraduates assist with administrative and interpreter duties, business students assist with finances and maximizing efficiency, and law students provide legal assistance and draft formal agreements with providers.[67] A University of California Los Angeles mobile clinic expands clinic services by offering opportunities for students from many fields, including undergraduates and graduate students in business and law.[75] Still, recruiting and retaining student volunteers remains a challenge for free clinics.[36]

Student-run clinics. Free clinic volunteer programs have been incorporated into many medical schools to help students learn a humanitarian and socially aware approach to medicine.[50,76] A 2007 national survey, the first attempt to examine student-run clinics on a national scale, assessed success in achieving service and educational goals.[55] In another survey, Simpson et al. studied 111 student-run clinics at 49 schools in 25 states.[74] Almost certainly, free clinic experience helps to sustain students' values and remind them why they initially chose to practice medicine.[76]

Preparing students to volunteer. In some programs, medical student volunteering is supplemented by a mandatory or optional class that teaches students how to interact with medically indigent clients. Clinic experience can change medical students' attitudes and break harmful stereotypes, but adequate preparation is necessary so as not to reinforce prejudices.[77] In two institutions, students are required to take a class about community advocacy that aims to produce volunteers and prepare them for clinic immersion.[20,78] Simmons et al. found that medical students at the JeffHope clinic in Philadelphia often did not have enough knowledge or experience to deal with medical issues. Consequently, the clinic initiated an orientation and a lecture series about managing and providing care.[51]

Altruism and medical students. The Association of American Medical Colleges (AAMC) cites altruism as a crucial characteristic for students upon graduation from medical school. In response to the need to care for the poor and underserved, the AAMC also determined that medical school graduates must be *dutiful.*[77] Many medical schools may not adequately address social issues and underserved populations in medicine; contact with medically indigent populations exposes medical students from financially stable families to have first-hand experience with real poverty.[76] Davenport et al. demonstrated that student volunteers learned to see clients in a "contextualized psychological and social environment."[79] Clinic experience can allow students to take on leadership roles as mentors or advisers.[80] Some authors feel that reflection with a preceptor after the clinic visit is essential for student volunteers.[76,80] Some studies suggest that student volunteering may predict continued practice in primary care or work with underserved populations in the students' futures.[81]

Clinical skills and learning opportunities. Free clinic experiences can provide opportunities for students to acquire clinical skills (e.g., smoking cessation counseling[26] and client education skills in glycemic control[39]). Pharmacy students can also learn how to care for clients with chronic diseases by emphasizing self-care management using over-the-counter medications.[66] At a clinic in Minnesota, students from nursing, physical therapy, and physician assistant programs gained field experience while learning how to screen for substance abuse, offer intervention, and refer clients to useful resources.[82] Systems-based practice (SBP), a required competency for medical students to enter residency, can be learned during free clinic rotations.[83]

Ethics of student participation. There are potential ethical concerns about student-run free clinics. Student education must not compromise client care. Furthermore, without adequate supervision, students may develop bad clinical habits.[84] Some free clinics operate under conditions that would be unacceptable in hospital settings, such as inadequate privacy or supplies. Uninsured clients are vulnerable because they have few or no options and cannot choose to see another provider.[77] Additionally, care in student-run free clinics can be suboptimal because of limited resources, limited operating times, and high turnover of students and physicians. Of 111 clinics surveyed, each clinic had a supervising physician as mandated by law, though their attentiveness varied and students performed certain tasks without supervision (e.g., organizational and administrative tasks).[55] Although the ethics of student-run clinics has been weighed, existing literature predominantly supports student-run free clinics for responding to an overwhelming need.

Future Research

The number and locations of free clinics nationwide must be continually evaluated because a conclusive estimate is elusive; many clinics are not registered with the National Association of Free Clinics.[19] Additionally, the relationship between free clinics and other safety net providers should be studied further in terms of geography and demographics (for example, the extent to which free clinics exist in proximity to other safety net providers, such as community health centers).[27]

Given the increasing national movement to achieve health care indicators for chronic diseases, such as diabetes, hypertension, depression, and anxiety, more research in free clinics is needed to link chronic diseases with health outcomes (table 1.3). Although there is some descriptive literature on geographical variations and interventions, more research should focus on specific interventions related to the geographic area, such as early depression screening in rural locations.[47] Additionally, decreasing the number of missed visits and adapting models of care should build on previous efforts; both integrative acupuncture and a modified chronic care model have proved effective in a free clinic.[24,33,36,52]

Although much research has recently focused on EHRs in primary care settings for the insured, free clinics are not yet an integral part of any health care strategy to improve health care quality, safety, and efficiency and to reduce health disparities.[85] Although information about IT capabilities in free clinics is limited, its value in managing patient medications and pharmacy inventory has already been exemplified by free clinic programs.[65] Since the implementation of health IT

Table 1.3

Future research for free clinics

Domain	Future research
Population served	• Researchers should aim to develop a consistent and updated national survey of free clinics to determine demographic information and success rates[27]
	• The relationship between free clinics and other safety net providers should be studied further[27]
	• Patient demographics at free clinics need to be consistently defined and described[19,58]
	• Comprehensive interviews might be useful to assess how patients' perceived social support networks are related to health behaviors and biological stress marker data[9]
	• Relation of occupational health and safety to low-wage immigrant workers[32]
	• Ways to improve enrollment in programs like S-CHIP / Healthy Start, which can enable children in low-income families to have access to medical care[29]
Geography	• In rural free clinics, routine screening for symptoms of depression might help in early identification of at-risk patients[47]
	• Relationship between geography and health conditions and behaviors
Epidemiology	• How diabetes care at free clinics compares to national standards, including education, staffing levels, and prescription fill rates[38]
	• Research to decrease the number of uninsured diabetic patients[52]
Funding and approaches to care	• Implementation of the Chronic Care Model needs further study, with the inclusion of controlled and randomized trials[33]
	• What is the effectiveness of acupuncture and its appeal among uninsured populations?[24]
Health IT	• Implementing and monitoring the use of health IT[85]
	• Ways in which Health IT can be used to keep track of patients' medications and pharmacy inventory[65]
Volunteers	• The ability of student-run free clinics to meet the needs of homeless populations[75]
	• Effectiveness of smoking intervention programs in student-run free clinics[26]
	• Relationships between student participation in free medical clinics and interest in careers in family practice and care for the medically underserved[76]
Quality of health care	• Can maintaining better records enable providers to adequately allocate resources for prevention programs?[45]

is costly, researchers must closely examine cost effectiveness and implementation in systems with day-to-day and long-term variation in providers, changing contact information for clients, and switching between insured and uninsured systems by clients as coverage changes.

Because specific patient demographic characteristics correspond to particular health needs, the scope of patients treated at free clinics, the services they require, and especially how needs are met merit further study. The need for registries and tracking suggests the opportunity to meld quality improvement and health IT initiatives.

Discussion

Much literature posits that free clinics exist as a short-term solution to serve victims of a failing health care system, but even the most successful clinics cannot provide a viable long-term solution to disparities in health care. Nadkarni et al. estimated in 2001 that free clinics served only about 650,000 of America's 41 million uninsured.[57] Although Virginia has more free clinics than any other state, less than 5% of the uninsured there were served via the free clinic system in 2003.[11]

Issues involving underserved and uninsured populations require government and nonprofit organizations to work together to achieve health care goals. Funding is a constant concern at free clinics, but a stronger free clinic network could lessen the strain on emergency department use.[15,16] There has been optimism that President Barack Obama's recent efforts as part of the American Recovery and Reinvestment Act of 2009 (ARRA) will provide clinics with necessary government funds to reach more uninsured clients. More funds have been allocated for community health centers, however, than for free clinics. The ARRA will also provide additional funds to community health centers for the adoption of EHRs (primarily as Medicare and Medicaid reimbursements), or will help clinics upgrade their existing technology to organize health records more effectively.[86]

Recent health care reform may provide some funding for free clinics, but this will not eliminate the need for clinics or eliminate their challenges. For example, the health care system in Canada is mostly publicly funded, yet its safety net is still struggling.[87] In the current debate about health care reform, considering the need for a coherent and calculated policy that includes both health care system reform and the safety net is critical.

Limitations. Since the structure and funding of free clinics vary greatly, the classification of a free clinic remains arbitrary and open to interpretation. The selected literature provides us with a snapshot of these clinics, but we do not know the extent these articles accurately reflect the current and changing reality given the shifting sands of the current economy. The important role of free clinics—together with the incredible paucity of research on the epidemiology of illness, populations served, geographical differences, viable financial models, use of health IT, and quality improvement—underscores the need for collaborative research efforts. Significant funding, such as that possible from the National Institutes of Health, is needed to conduct the rigorous, systematic research necessary to understand and enhance the enigmatic free clinics system. Many articles do not compare a free clinic population to an insured one, for example, and this lack of a control group limits the ability to assess system performance. Use of standardized National Committee for Quality Assurance (NCQA) benchmarks, if funding were available, would allow for more consistent comparisons.

This research identifies concerns and challenges commonly faced by free clinics. The findings from this literature review reveal an approach among committed volunteers to identify problems and experimentally implement a model of care or structural changes within the free clinic. Thankfully, state and federal laws protect physician volunteers from some forms of liability.[42] By weaving together individual articles to provide a more comprehensive understanding of free clinics on a national scale, our findings elucidate key elements for the research agenda. There are numerous disparities in care and gaps in research. More extensive research in this field is necessary to fill those gaps and to promote equal care for all.

Notes

1. United States Senate. The Patient Protection and Affordable Care Act immediate benefits. Washington, DC: U.S. Senate, 2010. Available at http://dpc.senate.gov/healthreformbill/healthbill64.pdf.

2. Gibbs RD, Gibbs PH. Free clinics: a personal journey: comment on "Free clinics in the United States." Arch Intern Med. 2010 Jun 14;170(11):953–4.

3. Government Relations Staff. The Patient Protection and Affordable Care Act: new protections and opportunities for practicing psychologists. Washington, DC: APA Practice Organization, 2010. Available at www.apapracticecentral.org/advocacy/reform/patient-protection.aspx.

4. Mertens M. Some will remain uninsured after reform. Menlo Park, CA: Kaiser Health News, 2010. Available at www.kaiserhealthnews.org/Stories/2010/March/24/Some-Will-Remain-Uninsured.aspx.

5. Elmendorf DW. Letter to U.S. House Speaker Nancy Pelosi. Washington, DC: Congressional Budget Office, 2010. Available at www.cbo.gov/ftpdocs/113xx/doc11355/hr4872.pdf.

6. Weiss GL. Grassroots medicine: the story of America's free health clinics. Lanham, MD: Rowman & Littlefield, 2006.

7. Smith DE, Seymour RB. Addiction medicine and the free clinic movement. J Psychoactive Drugs. 1997 Apr–Jun;29(2):155–60.

8. Reynolds HY. Free medical clinics: helping indigent patients and dealing with emerging health care needs. Acad Med. 2009 Oct;84(10):1434–9.

9. Cadzow RB, Servoss TJ. The association between perceived social support and health among patients at a free urban clinic. J Natl Med Assoc. 2009 Mar;101(3):243–50.

10. Associated Press. Free clinics hit with more patients, less funding. MSNBC, 2009 July 20. Available at www.msnbc.msn.com/id/32011901/ns/health-health_care/.

11. Nadkarni MM, Philbrick JT. Free clinics: a national survey. Am J Med Sci. 2005 Jul;330(1):25–31.

12. Darnell JS. Free clinics in the United States: a nationwide survey. Arch Intern Med. 2010 Jun 14;170(11):946–53.

13. Isaacs SL, Jellinek P. Is there a (volunteer) doctor in the house? Free clinics and volunteer physician referral networks in the United States. Health Aff (Millwood). 2007 May–Jun; 26(3):871–6.

14. Reed K. Free clinics and Iowa's uninsured: the last safety net. Iowa Med. 2007 Mar–Apr;97(2):23.

15. Crump WJ, Fricker RS, Crump AM, James TE. Outcomes and cost savings of free clinic care. J Ky Med Assoc. 2006 Aug;104(8):340–3.

16. Semonin-Hollerin R. Here is one example that is working! J Emerg Nurs. 2009 May;35(3):182.

17. Collins JA, Fauser BC. Balancing the strengths of systematic and narrative reviews. Hum Reprod Update. 2005 Mar–Apr;11(2):103–4.

18. Green BN, Johnson CD, Adams A. Writing narrative literature reviews for peer-reviewed journals: secrets of the trade. Journal of Chiropractic Med. 2006 5(3):101–17.

19. Keis RM, DeGeus LG, Cashman SC, Savageau J. Characteristics of patients at three free clinics. J Health Care Poor Underserved. 2004 Nov;15(4):603–17.

20. Beck E. The UCSD Student-Run Free Clinic Project: transdisciplinary health professional education. J Health Care Poor Underserved. 2005 May;16(2):207–19.

21. Gertz AM, Frank S, Blixen CE. A survey of patients and providers at free clinics across the United States. J Community Health. 2010 Jun 8.

22. Soller M, Osterberg L. Missed opportunities for patient education and social worker consultation at the Arbor Free Clinic. J Health Care Poor Underserved. 2004 Nov;15(4):538–46.

23. Gerber R, Charpentier M, Tecun S, Massi M, Diaz J, De Groot AS. A place to be healthy: blueprint for a new free clinic for the medically uninsured of Rhode Island. Med Health R I. 2008 Apr;91(4):105–8.

24. Highfield ES, Barnes L, Spellman L, Saper RB. If you build it, will they come? A free-care acupuncture clinic for minority adolescents in an urban hospital. J Altern Complement Med. 2008 Jul;14(6):629–36.

25. Wera TJ, Cochrane J, Hadden JC, Letson GW. The Larimer County Children's Clinic. A public-private partnership to provide medical care to indigent children. Arch Pediatr Adolesc Med. 1994 Jun;148(6):572–7.

26. Der DE, You YQ, Wolter TD, Bowen DA, Dale LC. A free smoking intervention clinic initiated by medical students. Mayo Clin Proc. 2001 Feb;76(2):144–51.

27. Geller S. Free clinics helping to patch the safety net. J Health Care Poor Underserved. 2004 Feb;15(1):42–51.

28. Fleming O, Mills J. Free clinics in North Carolina: a network of compassion, volunteerism, and quality care for those without health care options. N C Med J. 2005 Mar–Apr;66(2):127–9.

29. Brown AM, Glazer G. Enrollment success in state children's health insurance program after free clinic referral. J Pediatr Health Care. 2004 May–Jun;18(3):145–8.

30. Bauer S. Community clinic offers access to care. A system and a city collaborate to care for an immigrant population. Health Prog.1993 Oct;74(8):42–4, 65.

31. Heuer LJ, Hess C, Batson A. Cluster clinics for migrant Hispanic farmworkers with diabetes: perceptions, successes, and challenges. Rural Remote Health. 2006 Jan–Mar;6(1):469.

32. Burgel BJ, Lashuay N, Israel L, Harrison R. Garment workers in California: health outcomes of the Asian Immigrant Women Workers Clinic. AAOHN J. 2004 Nov;52(11):465–75.

33. Stroebel RJ, Gloor B, Freytag S, et al. Adapting the chronic care model to treat chronic illness at a free medical clinic. J Health Care Poor Underserved. 2005 May;16(2):286–96.

34. Wilson CR. Nurse-managed free clinic fosters care connection for homeless population. Rehabil Nurs. 2009 May–Jun;34(3):105–9.

35. Carter KF, Green RD, Green LA, Dufor LT. Health needs of homeless clients accessing nursing care at a free clinic. J Community Health Nurs. 1994;11(3):139–47.

36. Moskowitz D, Glasco J, Johnson B, Wang G. Students in the community: an interprofessional student-run free clinic. J Interprof Care. 2006 Jun;20(3):254–9.

37. Krautsheid L, Moos P, Zeller J. Patient and staff satisfaction with integrated services at Old Town Clinic: a descriptive analysis. J Psychosoc Nurs Ment Health Serv. 2004 Nov;42(11):32–41.

38. Garcia AA. Clinical and life quality differences between Mexican American diabetic patients at a free clinic and a hospital-affiliated clinic in Texas. Public Health Nurs. 2008 Mar–Apr;25(2):149–58.

39. Ryskina KL, Meah YS, Thomas DC. Quality of diabetes care at a student-run free clinic. J Health Care Poor Underserved. 2009 Nov;20(4):969–81.

40. Stevens GL. Demographic and referral analysis of a free chiropractic clinic servicing ethnic minorities in the Buffalo, NY, area. J Manipulative Physiol Ther. 2007 Oct;30(8):573–7.

41. Adams CJ, Flynn BC. Establishing an indigent health care clinic in an Indiana "healthy city." Am J Public Health. 1996 Dec;86(12):1818–19.

42. Conde CC. Shield the volunteers: state, federal laws protect physicians from liability. Tex Med. 2009;105(3):37–41.

43. Finke M. Free clinics. Iowa Med. 1997 Oct;87(8):314–16.

44. Darrow M. Practioner volunteerism at free clinics: a critical need. N C Med J. 2007 Sep–Oct;68(5):374–5.

45. Foley KL, Sutfin EL. Availability of tobacco cessation services in free clinics. N C Med J. 2008 Jul–Aug;69(4):270–4.

46. Fletcher CW, Slusher IL, Hauser-Whitaker M. Meeting the health care needs of medically underserved, uninsured, and underinsured Appalachians. Ky Nurse. 2006 Oct–Dec;54(4):8–9.

47. McCrone S, Cotton S, Jones L, Hawkins TA, Costante J, Nuss M. Depression in a rural, free clinic providing primary care: prevalence and predictive factors. Arch Psychiatr Nurs. 2007 Oct;21(5):291–3.

48. Scariati PD, Williams C. The utility of a health risk assessment in providing care for a rural free clinic population. Osteopath Med Prim Care. 2007; 1:8.

49. Grimes WR. Starting a free clinic in a rural area. People in a small Kentucky town pool their talents to solve the access problem. Health Prog. 2004 Mar–Apr;85(2):23–5, 51.

50. Bennard B, Wilson JL, Ferguson KP, Sliger C. A student-run outreach clinic for rural communities in Appalachia. Acad Med. 2004 Jul;79(7):666–71.

51. Simmons BB, DeJoseph D, Diamond J, Weinstein L. Students who participate in a student-run free health clinic need education about access to care issues. J Health Care Poor Underserved. 2009 Nov;20(4):964–8.

52. Davidson MB, Karlan VJ, Hair TL. Effect of a pharmacist-managed diabetes care program in a free medical clinic. Am J Med Qual. 2000 Jul–Aug;15(4):137–42.

53. Soto NI, Bazyler LR, O'Toole ML, Brownson CA, Pezzullo JC. Starting a diabetes self-management program in a free clinic. Diabetes Educ. 2007 Jun;33 (Suppl 6):166S–71S.

54. Bibeau DL, Taylor ML, Rife JC, Howell KA. Reaching the poor with health promotion through community free clinics. Am J Health Promot. 1997 Nov–Dec;12(2):87–9.

55. Cadzow RB, Servoss TJ, Fox CH. The health status of patients of a student-run free medical clinic in inner-city Buffalo, NY. J Am Board Fam Med. 2007 Nov–Dec;20(6):572–80.

56. Horswell R, Butler MK, Kaiser M, et al. Disease management programs for the underserved. Dis Manag. 2008 Jun;11(3):145–52.

57. Nadkarni MM, Philbrick JT. Free clinics and the uninsured: the increasing demands of chronic illness. J Health Care Poor Underserved. 2003 May;14(2):165–74.

58. Burman ME, Petrie J. Depression and anxiety outcomes at a free clinic in a rural state. J Am Acad Nurse Pract. 2008 Jul;20(7):359–66.

59. Bowser DM, Utz S, Glick D, Harmon R, Rovnyak V. The relationship between diabetes mellitus, depression, and missed appointments in a low-income uninsured population. Diabetes Educ. 2009 Nov–Dec;35(6):966–77.

60. Smego RA Jr, Costante J. An academic health center–community partnership: the Morgantown Health Right free clinic. Acad Med. 1996 Jun;71(6):613–21.

61. Niescierenko ML, Cadzow RB, Fox CH. Insuring the uninsured: a student-run initiative to improve access to care in an urban community. J Natl Med Assoc. 2006 Jun;98(6):906–11.

62. Breuner CC, Barry PJ, Kemper KJ. Alternative medicine use by homeless youth. Arch Pediatr Adolesc Med. 1998 Nov;152(11):1071–5.

63. Gebhart F. Pharmacy board to oversee med distribution at West Virginia free clinics. Drug Topics. 2008 October;152(11):18.

64. Wiesner AM, Steinke DT, Vincent WR, 3rd, Record KE, Smith KM. National survey of pharmacy services in free medical clinics. J Am Pharm Assoc (2003). 2010 Jan-Feb;50(1):45–51.

65. Rosenbaum BP, Patel SG, Guyer DL, et al. The pharmaceutical management system at Shade Tree Family Clinic: a medical student-run free clinic's experience. Inform Health Soc Care. 2008 Sep;33(3):151–7.

66. Morello CM, Singh RF, Chen KJ, Best BM. Enhancing an introductory pharmacy practice experience at free medical clinics. Int J Pharm Pract. 2010 Feb;18(1):51–7.

67. Yap OW, Thornton DJ. The Arbor Free Clinic at Stanford: a multidisciplinary effort. JAMA. 1995 Feb 1;273(5):431.

68. Davis A. Physician assistant volunteers belong in free clinics. JAAPA. 2005 Apr;18(4):16–7.

69. Massengill L. Filipino nurses open a free clinic for the uninsured. Fla Nurse. 2007 Sep; 55(3):25.

70. Archambault D. Free clinic volunteers find they experience the joy of medicine. Mich Med. 2009 Mar–Apr;108(2):14–16.

71. Milles GA. Physician volunteers. Md Med J. 1999 Jul–Aug;48(4):182–3.

72. Wilson LB, Lester L, Simson SP. Assessing the involvement of retired health professionals in meeting the needs of underserved populations. Nurs Outlook. 2000 Jan–Feb;48(1):34–9.

73. Pi R. The Asian Clinic at UC Davis: serving a minority population for two decades. JAMA. 1995 February 1;273(5): 432.

74. Simpson SA, Long JA. Medical student-run health clinics: important contributors to patient care and medical education. J Gen Intern Med. 2007 Mar;22(3):352–6.

75. Hastings J, Zulman D, Wali S. UCLA mobile clinic project. J Health Care Poor Underserved. 2007 Nov;18(4):744–8.

76. Haq CL, Cleeland L, Gjerde CL, Goedken J, Poi E. Student and faculty collaboration in a clinic for the medically underserved. Fam Med. 1996 Sep;28(8):570–4.

77. Buchanan D, Witlen R. Balancing service and education: ethical management of student-run clinics. J Health Care Poor Underserved. 2006 Aug;17(3):477–85.

78. Steinbach A, Swartzberg J, Carbone V. The Berkeley Suitcase Clinic: homeless services by undergraduate and medical student teams. Acad Med. 2001 May;76(5):524.

79. Davenport BA. Witnessing and the medical gaze: how medical students learn to see at a free clinic for the homeless. Med Anthropol Q. 2000 Sep;14(3):310–27.

80. Clark DL, Melillo A, Wallace D, Pierrel S, Buck DS. A multidisciplinary, learner-centered, student-run clinic for the homeless. Fam Med. 2003 Jun;35(6):394–7.

81. Campos-Outcalt DE. Specialties chosen by medical students who participated in a student-run, community-based free clinic. Am J Prev Med. 1985 Jul-Aug;1(4):50–1.

82. Martin PM, Pilon-Kacir C, Wheeler M. Interdisciplinary service learning and substance abuse screening in free clinic settings. Subst Abus. 2005 Dec;26(3–4):49–52.

83. Colbert CY, Ogden PE, Lowe D, Moffitt MJ. Students learn systems-based care and facilitate system change as stakeholders in a free clinic experience. Adv Health Sci Educ Theory Pract. In press.

84. Poulsen EJ. Student-run clinics: a double opportunity. JAMA.1995 February 1;273(5):430.

85. Shields AE, Shin P, Leu MG, et al. Adoption of health information technology in community health centers: results of a national survey. Health Aff (Millwood). 2007 Sep–Oct; 26(5):1373–83.

86. The White House, Office of the First Lady. First Lady Michelle Obama announces release of $851 million from Recovery Act to upgrade & expand community health centers, to serve

more patients. Washington, DC, 2009. Available at www.whitehouse.gov/the_press_office /First-Lady-Michelle-Obama-Announces-Release-of-851-Million-from-Recovery-Act-to -Upgrade-and-Expand-Community-Health-Centers/.

87. Taylor TB. Threats to the health care safety net. Acad Emerg Med. 2001 Nov;8(11):1080–7.

88. Smolski L. The Rhode Island Free Clinic: access to health care for the uninsured. Med Health R I. 2006 Oct;89(10):339–41.

89. Barone TL. Culturally sensitive care 1969–2000: The Indian Chicano Health Center. Qual Health Res. 2010 Apr;20(4):453–64.

90. Bibeau DL, Howell KA, Rife JC, Taylor ML. The role of a community coalition in the development of health services for the poor and uninsured. Int J Health Serv. 1996; 26(1):93–110.

91. Levin L. History of need. A 102-year-old health center adapts to serve the uninsured in a growing Hispanic community. Healthc Exec. 2008 Sep–Oct;23(5):54–5.

92. Pell T, Feller ER. A collaborative management model for mental health care at the Rhode Island Free Clinic. Med Health R I. 2005 Aug;88(8):265–7.

93. Sundstrom W. Free clinic serves uninsured (letter to the editor). WMJ. 2006 Mar;105(2):4.

94. Program improves Latino population compliance. Patient Education Management. 2006 Nov 1.

95. Powell E. Nurses reaching out to the working uninsured: one clinic's experience. Ky Nurse. 2005 Jan–Mar;53(1):10.

96. Wood FG. The free clinic as a service learning opportunity. Nurse Educ. 2001 Jan–Feb; 26(1):4.

97. Lenehan G. Free clinics and Parish Nursing offer unique rewards. J Emerg Nursing.1998; 24(1):3–4.

98. Meah YS, Smith EL, Thomas DC. Student-run health clinic: novel arena to educate medical students on systems-based practice. Mt Sinai J Med. 2009 Aug;76(4):344–56.

99. Fordham H. Burton Free Clinic: a point of light for Flint's indigent population. Mich Med. 1993 Oct;92(10):51–2.

100. Collins AC. The Hahnemann Homeless Clinics Project: taking health care to the streets and shelters. JAMA. 1995 Feb 1;273(5):433.

101. Korrow C. Free clinics and the San Francisco Community Clinic Consortium. Life Liberty and the Pursuit of Happiness. 2006 11(43):16–7.

102. Hills S. Free clinic helps underserved. Nursingmatters. 1999 Nov;10.

103. Nursing at the Rhode Island Free Clinic. Rhode Island Nurse. 2009 Feb–Apr.

104. Leavitt PT. NP-managed free clinic finds a new home. Nurse Practitioner World News. Vol 14. Jamesburg, NJ: NP Communications Group, 2009; 7.

105. Smith T, Moore EJH, Tunstall-Pedoe H. Review by a local medical research ethics committee of the conduct of approved research projects, by examination of patients' case notes, consent forms, and research records and by interview. Br Med J. 1997; 314:1588–90.

Part I **Free Clinics**

Chapter 2
Psychiatric Street Outreach to Homeless People: Fostering Relationship, Reconnection, and Recovery

Richard C. Christensen

Individuals suffering the devastating effects of serious and persistent mental illnesses constitute a profoundly vulnerable segment of the homeless population in this country. Although methodological limitations may constrain attempts to count precisely the number of people who are chronically homeless and also contending with mental illness, several investigations provide reliable estimates. The most recent study conducted by the U.S. Conference of Mayors, for instance, estimated that 26% of the homeless population in this country suffers from a serious mental illness.[1] Other data from over the years support a range between 22 and 33%.[2–4]

Homeless individuals living on the street dealing with the symptoms associated with illnesses such as schizophrenia, bipolar affective disorder, and posttraumatic stress disorder differ in a number of respects from homeless people who are temporarily domiciled within a shelter system or service agency. Mentally ill people who are unsheltered tend to be older, are more likely to be male, have high rates of psychotic disorders, and have spent extended periods of time being literally homeless before.[5] Because of greater levels of functional and social impairment in comparison with their shelter-based counterparts, unsheltered individuals may be less likely to receive services for a number of reasons.[6] First, since they do not reside in a shelter or facility of any kind, they do not have immediate access to medical and psychiatric care.[7] Second, a very recent qualtitative study carried out on the streets of New York City found that the common reasons expressed by unsheltered homeless people for not pursuing medical or mental health care involved a pervasive mistrust of the outreach workers and a lack of confidence that the services provided would be of personal benefit.[8] Hence, in order to substantively engage the most severely impaired and most medically underserved individuals in our communities, providers must offer empathetic, patient-centered psychiatric street outreach informed by a well-founded understanding of what to expect among the people for whom they seek to care.

For nearly a decade I have been engaged in a transdisciplinary street outreach initiative operated collaboratively by my academic institution and a large service

Richard C. Christensen, MD, MA, is affiliated with the University of Florida College of Medicine and its Community Psychiatry Program.

center for homeless people based in urban Jacksonville, Florida. The most recent census undertaken in our city estimated the number of homeless people on any given night to be 3,000. Taking into account that there are only 600 shelter beds available citywide, it comes as no surprise that a very large segment of the homeless population in our community is made up of street dwellers. Moreover, our outreach records show that the most chronic of these individuals (i.e., those people who have been homeless for one year or longer or who have been episodically homeless multiple times over the past three years) are also the most seriously mentally ill and/or addicted. Psychiatric street outreach is an essential piece in our center's attempt to expand health care access to this radically marginalized population.

Our transdisciplinary team comprises four case managers who have training in the areas of addictions and housing, a nurse, and a psychiatrist. This model of care differs from the traditional multidisciplinary and interdisciplinary health care team approaches in a number of significant ways. First, it takes the view that all members of the treatment team actively share responsibility in the assessment and ongoing treatment of the individual clients we engage. This requires that outreach team members be in close communication and seek ways to integrate their knowledge and skills with one another's and those of other community agencies. Second, our street outreach approach endorses a treatment model where distinctive professional roles and responsibilities overlap and lead to clinical decision making that is open, informed, and fully shared. In a positive sense, a transdisciplinary team will encourage the blurring of role-specific activities as members share in the integrated care of the individual. For example, the addiction specialist understands the spectrum of housing options for a mentally ill person, while the case manager whose specialty is housing has a grasp of the types of treatment modalities most appropriate for the person who is actively abusing substances while on the street. The psychiatrist oversees the integration of all these services and gains perspective on medical case management through the skills and knowledge of the outreach nurse. The overarching goal is to provide comprehensive, integrated, and holistic care for homeless individuals whose health care and basic needs are extensive and complex.

Specifically, providing psychiatric care to individuals on the street requires ongoing clinical practice adaptations and an evolving understanding of physician-patient roles. From experience, I know well that people with chronic mental disorders who are living on the street seldom have images and memories of psychiatrists that are shaped by past experiences of benevolent and welcoming care. Rather, for most, their involvements with the public mental health care system (e.g., overcrowded crisis units, detoxification facilities, forensic hospitals, and jails) have left them with psyches scorched with painful recollections of involuntary hospitalizations, coercive treatment, and less than compassionate, recovery-oriented mental health care. After introducing myself to someone our team has located and identified as being new to the streets, I rarely hear something akin to, "Wow, am I glad to see you, Doc." On the contrary, the usual reactions are shot through with unbridled suspicion and pervasive mistrust.

Over the years, I have learned to take no offense during initial encounters, in part because my clinical perspective has undergone a significant transformation through my work with our outreach team. When I began doing street outreach 10 years ago, my approach was still shaped by my experience of interacting with people who willingly came to my community-based psychiatry clinic. Within that conventional medical setting, a traditional set of expectations was shared: patients came looking for treatment and I was there to help provide it. It took very little time to realize that those are not the realities when conducting street outreach.

On one of our team's initial forays years ago, we made contact with a woman living on the street who was floridly psychotic, filthy from head to toe, malodorous, and fairly agitated. After I told her who I was and what I did, she totally and completely ignored me. Staring off into the distance, she pressed on with a monologue that made sense only to her. I remember being flustered because I was unable to interrupt or otherwise get her attention. Looking for any hook to engage her, I said something along the lines of, "You know, Ms. Virginia, I could give you medications that would make you feel better." At that moment, she stopped her psychotic soliloquy in mid-sentence, looked me full in the eyes, and replied, "Hmmm . . . Ya think? Well, *I* think giving me medication would make *you* feel better, but it sure as hell won't make *me* feel better!"

Since that time I have come to recognize more fully that meaningful psychiatric street outreach is based not upon developing a diagnosis, formulating a treatment plan, or dispensing medication. At the risk of sounding blasphemous in this era of evidence-based medicine, it is not solely about measurable clinical outcomes. Rather, effective psychiatric street outreach, regardless of the city or the composition of the transdisciplinary team, is based squarely upon promoting three core, interrelated objectives: **R**elationship, **R**econnection, and **R**ecovery.

Relationship

First encounters with people who are living under a shroud of a serious mental illness, while trying to slug out life on the streets, must be intended solely to cultivate a relationship. Our only goal is to ensure that the person before us will be open to seeing me—or another team member—the next day or the following week. We provide food, water, and clothing, offer a shelter bed, and, above all else, listen deeply. We seldom mention and never discuss treatment plans. As a psychiatrist, I simply want this person to be receptive to having a conversation with me, or another person on our team, the next time we meet. I have come to learn that no other transformational change can occur unless the person is willing to enter into a relationship that recognizes the dignity and worth we each possess.

Reconnection

Chronically homeless, street-dwelling people are the most isolated, disaffiliated individuals in our communities. For those with distorted thinking, pervasive mistrust, and the sometimes extreme resulting behavior, the palpable estrangement from the human community is extreme and not easily bridged. In so many ways and for a wide range of reasons, these individuals have lost a connection to the web of relationships that define not only a social community but, more important, a community of caring. Hence, central to meaningful street outreach is the promotion of a reconnection to a community of welcoming compassion and overt caring.

Linking individuals to opportunities for social inclusion should be a central focus of every street outreach initiative, since the healing needed for those who suffer the effects of extreme ostracization can never occur in isolation. The outreach team must always look for ways to promote a person's reconnection to a system of care *and* caring (e.g., a shelter environment and its residential staff, a housing program and its cadre of specialists, or a medical home that is staffed by competent and compassionate primary care and mental health providers). The act of reconnecting to a community of care provides the basic supports needed for the person to begin navigating his or her way out of a state of homelessness. Above all else, a *reconnection* to a community of care signals that the person has once again established a tether to a social network that had previously been ruptured but is crucial for continued healing and inclusion. James Withers, MD, an internist with a longstanding commitment to providing medical care through street outreach in urban Pittsburgh, echoes these sentiments when he says, "It seems unreal in a city with the world's most advanced medicine that we are surrounded by those with frostbite, with maggots in their wounds, those who die alone, but more important those who have been lost to our 'community.'"[9]

Recovery

Meaningful street outreach has as its goal the recovery of the individual who often has spent years in fearful isolation, disconnected from family or community, tormented by a disordered mind. Recovery for a person who has been living on the streets will be reflected in movement toward greater self-direction and self-care. Collaborating in treatment and taking part in the healing process, which includes growing independence and enhanced social relationships, will be essential components of the recovery process for the person working with the street outreach team. Active participation in directing one's psychiatric care, willingness to enter substance abuse treatment, desire to pursue relationships or reestablish family ties, and, most important of all, passage into stable housing can all be seen as meaningful measures of recovery. The street outreach team should play less and less of a role as the person recovers his or her unique identity, an identity that is no longer based upon labels such as *homeless* or *mentally ill*.

Postscript

Four years after my initial encounter with Ms. Virginia, and after many, many street "house calls" where medications were never again brought up, Ms. Virginia agreed to move into safe housing. Today she is fully participating in her recovery from a devastating mental illness and is actively directing her own care. I fully believe that her long journey out of homelessness, like that of so many others before and after her, began with the compassionate practice of the three R's of transdisciplinary medical street outreach: **R**elationship, **R**econnection, and **R**ecovery.

Notes

1. The United States Conference of Mayors. Hunger and homelessness in America's cities, a 25 city survey. Washington, DC: U.S. Conference of Mayors, 2008 Dec. Available at: http://www .usmayors.org/pressreleases/documents/hungerhomelessnessreport_121208.pdf.
2. Susser E, Struening EL, Conover S. Psychiatric homeless men: lifetime psychosis, substance use and current distress in new arrivals at New York City shelters. Arch Gen Psychiatry. 1989 Sep;46:845–50.
3. Breakey WR, Fischer PJ, Kramer M, et al. Health and health problems of homeless men and women in Baltimore. JAMA. 1989 Sep;262(10):1352–7.
4. McQuistion HL, Gillig PM. Mental illness and homelessness: an introduction. In: McQuistion HL, Gillig PM, eds. Clinical guide to the treatment of the mentally ill homeless person. Arlington, VA: American Psychiatric Publishing, 2006; 1–8.
5. Lam JA, Rosenheck R. Street outreach for homeless persons with serious mental illness: is it effective? Med Care. 1999;37(9):894–907.
6. Nyamathi AM, Gelberg L. Sheltered versus nonsheltered homeless women: differences in health, behavior, victimization and utilization of care. J Gen Intern Med. 2000 Aug;15(8):565–72.
7. Gelberg L, Andersen RM, Leake BD. The behavioral model for vulnerable populations: application to medical care use and outcomes for people. Health Serv Res. 2000 Feb; 34(6): 1273–302.
8. Kryda AD, Compton MT. Mistrust of outreach workers and lack of confidence in available services among individuals who are chronically homeless. Community Ment Health J. 2009 Apr;45(2):144–50.
9. Withers J. The human element: house calls to the homeless. Health Prog. 1994 Sep; 75(7):71–2.

Chapter 3

Nurse Practitioners in Community Health Settings Today

Lois A. Wessel

During a typical week as a family nurse practitioner, I provide primary care to uninsured immigrant patients on a mobile van, teach an undergraduate nursing course entitled Community and Environmental Health Nursing at the Catholic University of America, screen Hispanic women for breast and cervical cancer through *Celebremos La Vida* (Celebrate Life) at Georgetown University's Lombardi Cancer Center, and lead continuing professional education programs for health care providers who work with the poor and underserved through the Pediatric Asthma Prevention Project and Early Childhood Caries Prevention Project of the Association of Clinicians for the Underserved (ACU).

As a family nurse practitioner, I am trained for a variety of practice settings, including primary care, teaching, research, and management. It is this flexibility and variety of work that I thrive on and that allows me the opportunity to be part of many exciting public health projects, while still having time for my family and community. This varied skill set allows me and other nurse practitioners to take on multiple roles in the evolving health system.

The ACU is a nonprofit, transdisciplinary organization of clinicians, advocates, and health care organizations united in a common mission to improve the health of America's underserved populations and to enhance the development and support of the health care clinicians serving these populations. The ACU defines transdisciplinary care as a holistic approach to patient assessment and treatment through a highly collaborative team of health care professionals.

This approach allows health care professionals other than physicians increased decision-making powers in patient care; furthermore, through continuing cross-disciplinary education and regulated overlapping roles, greater efficiency in patient care can be achieved. This collaboration is beneficial to patients and could be a cost-effective way to improve the U.S. health system and to expand it to treat those who currently go without regular health care. Furthermore, for people living with long-term illnesses such as HIV, hypertension, and diabetes, nurse practitioners (NPs) can help provide long-term patient education and preventive care.

Lois A. Wessel, RN, CFNP, is the associate director for programs and adjunct professor for the Association of Clinicians for the Underserved, Georgetown School of Nursing and Health Studies, in Washington, DC.

The Training and Roles of Nurse Practitioners

An NP is a registered nurse (RN) with additional training, usually at the master's level. (Some NPs have certificates, but those programs are being phased out.) The graduate training builds on nursing roles in patient advocacy and education and incorporates physical assessment and diagnostic skills, along with management of acute, chronic, and episodic diseases. This includes taking a patient history, performing a physical exam, ordering and interpreting laboratory tests, providing medication, referring to specialists, and promoting healthy lifestyles.

The first NP program dates back to 1965 in Colorado, where nurses were trained to provide pediatric care to underserved populations. In 1996, there were estimated to be over 40,000 NPs, and by 2000 that number had climbed to over 62,000.[1] In 2011, the United States had 180,233[2] nurse practitioners.

Some NPs specialize in areas such as women's health, pediatrics, school health, psychiatry, neonatology, and oncology, while others seek a broader focus in family medicine. While NPs work in specialty private practices and in-patient units, this chapter focuses on roles and opportunities for NPs in the community health setting.

Like members of many other professions, NPs are regulated by the state, in accordance with state laws, and through certification with national credentialing organizations. Some states allow NPs to practice completely independently, others require a collaborative agreement with an MD that defines the scope of practice for that work site, while others do not recognize practice by NPs at all. While the level of prescriptive authority also varies by state, NPs have prescriptive authority in most states, including the opportunity to apply for a Drug Enforcement Agency (DEA) number, allowing them to prescribe controlled substances. One of the many policy issues NP organizations are focusing on is that of allowing managed care patients to choose an NP as their primary care provider.

Nurse practitioners, along with physician assistants (PAs) and certified nurse midwives (CNMs), are often referred to as midlevel providers or physician extenders. Some NPs and PAs object to these terms, arguing that they imply the NP, PA, or CNM occupies a lower position than a physician. However one resolves such concerns, few would disagree that there is a role for every person in the complex health system, including physicians, nurses, social workers, pastoral care ministers, and NPs and PAs. In a recent *Wall Street Journal* article, Ann O'Sullivan, an NP at University of Pennsylvania, is quoted as saying that NPs and doctors collaborating with one another achieve the best outcomes. The example she uses is a patient who needs to stop smoking: the physician explains the physiological problems with smoking while the NP looks at the psychological factors in smoking and the personal barriers to smoking cessation.[1] On a transdisciplinary team such as this, all providers function as equal partners, each with his or her own strengths and skill sets. Patient satisfaction studies have shown NPs to be rated with high favorability.[3]

The most effective role of the NP in the primary care setting is that of a provider who combines medical knowledge, diagnostic ability, and prescriptive authority with education regarding disease management and lifestyle modifications, and works in a team with others. Nurse practitioners are in a favorable position to develop an ongoing relationship and to build on patient strengths, taking into account real life demands of the patient. While medical training focuses on diagnosis and treatment, NP training builds on nursing's foundations in care and prevention. For patients with chronic diseases, ongoing education and reinforcement in the management of the disease is important. By empowering patients to take care of themselves, make lifestyle changes, and prevent acute exacerbations of disease, NPs help in the prevention of expensive hospital visits, which will be financially beneficial to the medical system and personally beneficial to the patient.

One example of this is in the treatment of patients with elevated cholesterol levels. As an NP, in addition to providing cholesterol-lowering medications to patients, I talk to them about their diet and exercise routines. On the mobile van I primarily treat Latino patients, having become fluent in Spanish and having learned about Latin foods and cooking styles during a 10-year postcollege prenursing career stay in Central America. This gives me the unique opportunity to discuss the high amount of fat in the diet and make culturally acceptable alternative suggestions. As for exercise, it is unlikely that most of my patients will be able to afford a gym or an exercise machine, yet I know that dancing is a favorite pastime of many patients, and going to church is an important weekly activity. Therefore, I suggest dancing at home to CDs or the radio two or three times per week and parking far from the church or getting off the bus a few stops early, to increase physical activity. I can usually make other dietary suggestions that are culturally acceptable, as well.

Several of my physician colleagues are also adept at providing individualized patient-centered care. I have had the opportunity to work with and learn from many of them. However, the focus on prevention and empowerment through teaching is a particular strength of NP training. Many physicians come to it naturally, but others do not, and it is far less strongly emphasized in MD training.

My own path to becoming a family nurse practitioner started when I visited Mexico through an American Friends Service Committee (Quaker) youth project as a college student majoring in political science. I became aware of the serious health needs in the community where I lived and wanted to gain concrete skills to help prevent disease and malnutrition. Upon graduating from Oberlin College, I wanted to go back to Latin America and work in public health. As a Jew, I was reluctant to work with an organization based in a Christian church, and having seen firsthand the effects of the United States–backed wars in Central America, I did not want to work through the U.S. government in the Peace Corps. I eventually landed a job at the National Assembly of Nicaragua during the years of the Sandinista Revolution. While I wasn't working directly in a health capacity, I was able to see how a country could attempt to bring about social changes in health care and education. After several years in an office setting, I started a job at a Nicaraguan nonprofit organization that offered participatory education sessions on a variety of subjects, including breastfeeding, malaria prevention, and family planning, to peasant groups throughout the country. Later, I worked with the Department of

Maternal-Child Health in the Ministry of Health on women's health projects. After almost a decade of working in a country making clear attempts to improve the health and welfare of its population, in spite of economic and military pressure against it, it was time for me to return to the United States to figure out which direction to take next.

I considered a variety of options, including public health school, medical school, physician's assistant school, and nursing school. While I knew I wanted to work in a community health setting, either in the United States or Latin America, I didn't know if I wanted to do research, teaching, direct service, or management. I chose nursing school, in part because I could add a clinical or a public health degree to my training at a later point.

After receiving my bachelor's in nursing degree from Johns Hopkins University, I worked as a labor and delivery nurse and considered pursuing training as a nurse midwife. By the time I was ready for graduate training, I realized that in order to continue my commitment to the underserved, I wanted to be in a community health setting and not a hospital. Most of the local birthing centers in my area catered to the wealthier, insured population. Furthermore, I had received a National Health Service Corps (NHSC) scholarship to fund my graduate education, and I knew that midwifery placements in the two-year community service payback were scarce, so I chose to become a family nurse practitioner. I wanted broad skills to work with larger populations, and the idea of working with entire families and understanding how an illness in one member affects the entire family appealed to me. During my rotations in NP school at Georgetown University, I sought local community health settings, where I could work with the kinds of populations I would work with after graduation.

I vividly remember working with an internal medicine physician at Upper Cardozo Community Health Clinic in Washington, DC. I kept asking him why he wasn't putting his patients on the drug of choice, as I had learned it in pharmacology. Even in those days, before personal desk accessories were in the pockets of most clinicians, he could spout off the costs of all the major medications he put his patients on; often, the drug of choice according to the pharmacology textbook was out of the economic reach of the patients. This was an important lesson in community health medicine for me: the treatment of choice is often limited by the economic situation of the patient.

I completed part of my NHSC payback in a large community health clinic in Baltimore and helped set up a satellite clinic serving the Latino population. The other part of my payback was as director of primary care at the Washington Free Clinic, a free clinic serving the uninsured. In both of these settings, I learned substantial management skills and became aware of many realities of provision of care where there are limited resources. (In addition to short funds, these realities include suboptimal buildings, inadequately trained staff, and the absence of common technological systems, such as computerized scheduling.) The transdisciplinary model became key for me in both these settings, as I was usually the only clinician fluent in Spanish and could work with a physician to convey the treatment and medication regimens for a patient in the patient's primary language.

After the birth of my second child, the demands of work at a clinic with evening hours proved to be too much, so I took a job in the Department of Psychiatry at Georgetown University, on a research project to study interventions for depressed low-income women. I was one of several clinicians, both NPs and psychologists, who worked as a transdisciplinary team with a psychiatrist, treating low-income depressed women with pharmacological agents and cognitive behavioral therapy. The objective of the randomized controlled study was to determine the impact of an intervention to deliver guideline-based care for depression, compared with referrals to community care, for low-income and minority women.[4] It was exciting to be working with nationally accepted guidelines and low-income women, instead of offering them the cheaper, but not necessarily best, treatment plan for a problem. In addition, most women I had seen clinically were also suffering from depression and were not appropriately screened or treated for it. Through this project, I developed primary care skills for treating depression, worked in community-based research, and again was part of a transdisciplinary team.

Presently, working with ACU, I am able to combine all the skills and experiences gained from these positions as an educator to providers who work with the underserved. In ACU-sponsored projects focused on the reduction of early childhood caries and acute asthma attacks, I combine my history of management, teaching, research, and clinical experiences to educate other providers who work with the underserved. Additionally, I maintain my clinical skills by working in a variety of community health settings. These broad NP skills allow me great flexibility and job satisfaction.

NPs in the Future

New areas on the horizon for NPs include a growing number of independent NP-run practices, increases in the number of health insurance companies that permit NPs to be primary care providers, and the use of NPs in "minute clinics," or outpatient rapid clinics housed in drugstores, where NPs can quickly treat a variety of episodic diseases, such as urinary tract infections and conjunctivitis. The danger in these clinics, though they provide exposure for nurse practitioners to the general population, is that patients tend to be referred back to their primary care provider if the NP finds a more complex problem, yet often the patients have no primary care provider. Success for patients of these clinics will depend on the local community health resources available to meet their needs and the NP's knowledge of those resources.

Additionally, some nursing schools and boards of nursing are looking at a four-year doctor-of-nursing-practice program that would incorporate evaluating clinical studies and setting up independent practices into the NP training. As the baby boomers age, NPs will play an increasingly important role in geriatric care as well.

An NP is an essential part of a transdisciplinary health team. The combination of medical skills and nursing care provide a unique role that can fill gaps in many primary care settings and improve patient outcomes.

Notes

1. Blackman A. Personal health treatments—is there a doctor in the house? Perhaps not as nurse practitioners take on many of the roles long played by physicians. Wall Street Journal, 2004 October 11; R4.

2. Kaiser Family Foundation. United States: Total nurse practitioners, 2011. State health facts. Available at www.statehealthfacts.org.

3. Mudinger MO, Kane RL, Lenz ER, et al. Primary care outcomes in patients treated by nurse practitioners or physicians: a randomized trial. JAMA. 2000; 283: 59–68.

4. Miranda J, Chung JY, Green B, et al. Treating depression in predominantly low-income young minority women: a randomized control trial. JAMA. 2003; 290:57–65.

Chapter 4

Following the Call: How Providers Make Sense of Their Decisions to Work in Faith-Based and Secular Urban Community Health Centers

Farr A. Curlin
Karen D. Serrano
Matthew G. Baker
Sarah L. Carricaburu
Douglas R. Smucker
Marshall H. Chin

The recruitment and retention of well-trained, motivated health care providers in underserved communities is a well described, longstanding, and refractory problem.[1-5] In 1998, Singer and colleagues reported that the median tenure of primary care practitioners in federally funded community health centers (CHCs) is three years, regardless of National Health Service Corps obligations.[1] Provider turnover exacts substantial tolls on the health care safety net. Patient care suffers from loss of continuity and trust,[1,6] and it has been estimated that CHCs lose $150,000 to $300,000 in revenue and recruitment costs every time a provider position turns over.[6] In response, some have argued that improving provider retention is essential to the stability and long-term missions of CHCs.[1,7] Toward that end, researchers and policymakers have sought to understand the motivations for work among the underserved and to adjust the characteristics of these work settings in order to lessen the persistently high attrition rate.

Farr A. Curlin, MD, is a co-director of the Program on Medicine and Religion, an associate professor of medicine, and an associate faculty member of the MacLean Center for Clinical Medical Ethics, University of Chicago. *Karen D. Serrano, MD,* is a clinical assistant professor of medicine at the University of Wisconsin–Madison School of Medicine and Public Health, Department of Emergency Medicine. *Matthew G. Baker, PA-C,* urology, is a physician assistant at Medical and Surgical Specialists, in Galesburg, Illinois. *Sarah L. Carricaburu, MD,* is a family practice physician at Southern Albemarle Family Practice in Esmont, Virginia. *Douglas R. Smucker, MD, MPH,* is an adjunct professor at the University of Cincinnati College of Medicine, Department of Family Medicine. *Marshall H. Chin, MD, MPH,* is the Richard Parrillo Family professor of medicine, associate chief and director of research, Section of General Internal Medicine, director of the Chicago Center for Diabetes Translation Research, and director of Finding Answers: Disparities Research for Change, at the University of Chicago Medicine.

Prior studies have noted that providers who practice in underserved communities bear costs that are often similar in type, but greater in magnitude, to those they would encounter elsewhere. For example, work in underserved settings often carries with it lower salaries,[1] fewer academic opportunities, diminished professional prestige,[4] decreased control over the work environment,[1] increased bureaucratic interference, and little free time.[8] These costs are part of what the work-orientation literature describes as *external*[9] and *objective*[10,11] work characteristics. To the extent that providers see their work as merely a job, as merely a means of accruing material benefits,[10] such characteristics will have to be balanced by other, more valued external characteristics (such as loan repayment and flexible scheduling) in order for the provider to continue that work.

Yet, researchers have noted that some fraction of workers relate to their work more as a calling than a job.[10,11] For these, the work has meaning not merely as a means to material gain but also as an end in itself, and the most important characteristics of the work setting may be the way it invites or at least allows them to craft their work in ways consonant with their own expectations and values.[9] In this light, prior studies notably have found that providers often explain their work in underserved settings by emphasizing subjective, intangible rewards such as making a difference in society, caring for the poor, and developing meaningful relationships with patients.[8,12] For example, regarding rural physicians, Pathman and colleagues note that provider retention depends at least partially on providers developing a sense of belonging in their work settings and being able, within that setting, to realize their "personal hopes and aspirations" (p. 375).[8] In an earlier qualitative study, Li and colleagues found that providers valued the unique possibilities found in underserved settings for joining with like-minded colleagues to practice a form of medicine that is consonant with their core values. They wrote, "By having a positive impact on patients' lives, providers reinforce their sense of self and live as the selves they most want to be" (p. 130).[12]

The term *calling* is now used in the meaning of work literature to refer broadly to work done with a sense of inner direction and aimed at improving the world, but it originally expressed the religious notion of divinely inspired discernment of and commitment to morally meaningful work.[11,13] Many religious traditions call their followers to serve the poor and to be present to and to seek the healing of those who are sick. Yet, in spite of many references to the ways that practice among the underserved emerges from providers' hopes, aspirations,[8] beliefs, personal values, and basic orientations to humanity,[12] no prior studies have examined the relationship between religious characteristics of providers, religious orientations of health centers, and providers' decisions to work in underserved settings.

At the same time, governmental agencies such as the Bureau of Primary Health Care (BPHC) have begun to examine and facilitate the part that religiously oriented social service providers, often referred to as *faith-based organizations*, play in providing health care and other social services in low-income communities.[14] In the year 2000, the BPHC provided a grant to the Christian Community Health Fellowship (CCHF), a national organization of Christians providing health care to underserved communities, in part to investigate the best practices of its member

CHCs. In meetings to plan the research component of the project, leaders from multiple member CHCs noted that their levels of provider turnover are lower than the national average[1] and credited this to the religious motivations of their providers. However, others noted that in their faith-based context, providers continue to struggle with dissatisfaction in their work. In light of the experiences of these stakeholders, we set out in this study to explore the ways that providers from a sample of CCHF-affiliated faith-based CHCs, and those from otherwise similar secular CHCs, explain their decisions to work among the underserved. Our purpose was to begin to build theory regarding whether and in what ways faith-based CHCs present a distinctive setting in which providers work out a commitment to care for the underserved.

Methods

Participants

We conducted one-to-one, semistructured interviews with 49 providers (28 physicians, 15 nurse practitioners, 6 other providers) from six faith-based and four secular urban CHCs in California, Illinois, Indiana, and Texas. All faith-based CHCs were identified through referral from CCHF and therefore had Protestant Christian affiliations. Five of the six were federally funded; the number of annual patient visits ranged from approximately 3,000 to 90,000; and all health centers had predominantly minority patient populations. We did not ask participants to identify their race or ethnicity, but post hoc we asked health center leaders to describe the racial/ethnic characteristics of their health center's providers. At the time of this research, most providers in these health centers were White, non-Hispanic (range from 40% to 83%), but they also included non-Hispanic Black (0–36%), Hispanic (0–30%), and other races/ethnicities (0–20%). Secular health centers were identified by asking key informants at the faith-based CHCs to identify CHCs nearby that were similar in size and structure but were not faith based. Providers were asked by telephone or letter to participate in interviews to explore "providers' perspectives on their decisions to work in underserved settings." No providers directly refused participation, and our sample represents those who were able to participate within the period of data collection. Table 4.1 lists the characteristics of the participants.

Interviews

Interviews were conducted during the summers of 2001 and 2002 by seven health profession students as part of summer research internships sponsored either by CCHF or the University of Chicago. The students were trained in qualitative interview theory and techniques by two of the investigators (FC and DS) for three days before entering the field. They were also given regular feedback throughout the summer via telephone and e-mail by one investigator (FC). Interviews followed a guide centered on open-ended *grand tour* questions designed to "elicit

Table 4.1

Provider characteristics, n=49

Participant characteristics	Community health centers	
	Faith-based	Secular
Mean age, years (SD[a])	40.4 (8.6)	39.4 (6.3)
Mean tenure at CHC[b], years (SD)	4.4 (4.5)	2.7 (2.5)
Gender		
Female	24	10
Male	12	3
Physicians		
Family medicine	8	5
Pediatrics	4	1
Internal medicine	7	2
Medicine—pediatrics	1	—
Nurse practitioners	12	3
Nurses	3	—
Physician assistants	1	1
Optometrists	—	1
Total	36	13

[a]SD=standard deviation
[b]CHC=community health center

narratives detailing the informant's conception of the identified domains" (p. 96).[15] Over the course of the data collection period, the interview guide was revised for clarity and cogency; the ultimate formulations of the four grand tour questions are listed in table 4.2. Follow-up probes and questions were not structured but sought to clarify and explore physicians' ideas further.

Data analysis

Interviews were tape-recorded and transcribed verbatim. Transcripts were analyzed by employing an iterative process of textual analysis informed by the principle of constant comparison.[16] After the first several interviews, three of the investigators (FC, KS, and SC) independently coded the full transcripts by identifying and labeling discrete units of text that referred to one or more concepts relevant to the study purpose. Those investigators subsequently met with one another to develop consensus and to create a working codebook of categories, subcategories, and concepts. When new concepts emerged, addenda to the codebook were made. During the second year of data collection, qualitative analysis software[17] was used to code all prior and subsequent transcripts according to the codebook formulations. At various points throughout the study, an inductive approach to the data was employed to identify emergent themes and to identify relationships and patterns

Table 4.2
Grand tour probes

1. Describe how you came to work at this health center.
2. What are the rewards of working here?
3. What are the challenges of working here?
4. Some providers say they work in this setting partly because of religious convictions. Is that true for you? How?

between the themes. Finally, representative quotations were chosen to exemplify the themes identified.

To strengthen the trustworthiness of our findings, multiple investigators (FC, KS, and MB) immersed themselves in all of the data in the process of analysis and interpretation. In addition, an experienced qualitative researcher (DS) systematically reviewed and coded a portion of the transcripts to assess the consistency and fidelity of the analysis and to look for competing conclusions. The process of bringing to bear multiple perspectives in data collection, analysis, and interpretation, which is known as investigator triangulation, strengthens the credibility of the analysis. In addition, we conducted interviews until we reached theme saturation (the point after which subsequent interviews produced no substantial new themes). The University of Chicago Institutional Review Board approved this study.

Results

By design, the content of the interviews focused on four domains of the decision to work among the underserved: career trajectory, rewards, costs, and synthesis and meaning. Overall, we found that many themes were common to providers from both faith-based and secular CHCs, particularly regarding the costs of their work. However, providers from faith-based centers consistently used religious language to describe their career trajectories and the rewards of their work as well as how they synthesize rewards and costs and find meaning in their decisions to remain at CHCs. A minority of providers from secular health centers used similar language, but most described their intrinsic motivations in nonreligious terms.

Career trajectory

Providers in faith-based health centers consistently described a career trajectory on which they had pursued medicine as a means of *ministry*. Many entered medical training with the idea that their future medical practice was to be an expression of their Christian faith: "I went to medical school with the idea that it was a ministry. That's always been in my plans. So when I finished residency, I was interested in mission work" (interview 46). Several providers described their current work as a prelude to or substitute for their original goal of practicing medicine overseas as a missionary: "I had always wanted to be an overseas missionary because I wanted to work in places that were needy. During my residency, I began to realize that there is a lot of need in inner cities" (31). At some point along the way, fellow students, roommates, church contacts, or representatives of the National Health Service Corps informed these providers about the existence of Christian CHCs providing health care to the underserved. These contacts stimulated providers to consider a vocational calling to practice in low-income communities and later recruited them to particular health centers.

For providers from faith-based and secular health centers, the decision to work in their current settings was catalyzed by clinical rotations during medical training in which they gained firsthand experience of health care among the underserved.

> I did my rotation in a community clinic . . . and I liked what they stood for and the kind of population they served. So I decided that is where I wanted to practice. (6)

> I was a fourth-year medical student and had a one-month elective rotation. I wanted to try a Christian setting, and I'd heard so much about this place, so I came here for my elective, and I had a fabulous experience. (40)

The most prominent theme that emerged from and was largely unique to our interviews with providers in faith-based CHCs was that they believe they are responding to a Christian vocational calling. Some articulated the concept of *calling* as a specific and personal experience of divine guidance: "It seemed like God wanted me here. The most meaningful [thing to me] is knowing that this is where God wants me to work. That this is part of God's plan for me" (34). Others expressed the idea in terms of a conviction that they should care for the poor as an expression of their faith. By working in their current settings, they were living out what they viewed to be their Christian responsibility: "It just always seemed to make sense—like, if I read scripture and thought about social justice and how we're supposed to respond as Christians" (45).

Rewards

Providers from all health centers repeatedly mentioned a number of intangible rewards found in their work among the underserved. To begin, providers talked about the value of connecting with patients and making a difference by helping them gain access to adequate medical care.

> One of the rewards is that you are helping a community that doesn't have ready access to health care, and that always makes you feel good at the end of the day. You know you helped somebody who would have been shut out from a lot of other places. (22)

Providers also mentioned the satisfaction they experience in being part of a community with a shared vision and commitment in which they find mutual support and encouragement.

> The highlight of working at this center is definitely the community of people who are my colleagues, who share the same vision and calling and passion for what we're doing. It is being shoulder to shoulder with people . . . saying, "Our lives are gonna be spent

somehow—why not spend them the way that we know we should and do so among those who can enable us to do it, within the context of love." (33)

Providers also noted that they are able to provide a uniquely holistic form of care because CHCs have other staff, such as case managers and outreach workers, who are able to provide or help patients to access resources for housing, employment, education, finances, and spiritual care. This holistic, team-based approach decreased the load on the providers and affirmed the sense that their work in the CHCs was indeed making a difference.

> We were able to attract more resources to add some of the support things. And that helps a lot. I think I would have burned out a long time ago if we didn't have those extra services to be able to send them. Because you just realize, well, yeah, I can take care of the high blood pressure, but what about all this other stuff that's really just as important if not more important? (41)

Providers in faith-based CHCs related the health care team's shared vision and commitment to shared religious convictions. They talked about the faith-friendly elements of their work environment, particularly the freedom to express their Christian identities in interactions with patients and colleagues. A few mentioned their appreciation of scheduled devotions or prayer time among clinic employees, noting that such activities had a positive effect on staff morale. Some spoke of their freedom to pray with patients or staff. Others said they felt at home in an environment where they could address spiritual concerns with patients.

> I think there's a lot more to health care than diagnosing and prescribing, and a lot of that big component is the spiritual realm. And I want to be in a practice setting where I'm free to address that spiritual realm as it comes up. (13)

Although they emphasized them less than the intangible rewards, providers in all health centers also mentioned other, more tangible rewards of their employment. Such rewards included working with Spanish-speaking patients, receiving loan repayment benefits, having more flexible work schedules, seeing an interesting variety of clinical issues in their patients, and being in a desired geographic location.

Costs

Despite the many rewards that providers credited to practicing in their current settings, they also identified core elements of their work that they found difficult and frustrating. These costly elements were remarkably similar among providers from faith-based and secular CHCs and generally related to the stress of meeting overwhelming needs with inadequate resources.

To begin, providers described systemic problems that disproportionately affect the underserved and create barriers to health care in the communities in which these health centers are located. For example, providers said they find it difficult to gain access to the medications, clinical tests, and specialists that their patients (particularly those from immigrant communities) need.

[There are] not enough resources for what people need. Even if we try to send them over to specialty care, a lot of times they're denied, or it's deferred so far off in the future that it doesn't solve the problem. (3)

While providers attributed most of their frustration to a broken health care system, they also attributed some to the characteristics of the underserved population itself. Several suggested that patients' low educational levels lead to medical nonadherence.

There's constant patient education. It's just total repetition all the time. I think a lot of it has to do with culture and just not understanding. That's basically with both the hypertensive and diabetic patients; you see a lot of noncompliance. (9)

In addition, several providers voiced frustration with their health centers' administrative leaders. Some felt the administration was not sensitive to the providers' concerns, while others complained that they were required to see large numbers of patients to ensure the financial survival of the clinic. The common theme was that more was expected of them as providers than they thought possible.

Probably the most stressful thing is the expectation to maintain the patient volume, and yet still try to give holistic care. If I saw too many patients per hour, I wouldn't be giving the quality of the spiritual or emotional care that I would want to give. . . . The struggle is trying to find the balance. (32)

Providers expressed frustration at having inadequate nursing and administrative support. They often found themselves burdened by clerical tasks, nursing duties, and phone responsibilities that might be handled by support staff in other settings.

The providers on staff have to do a lot of secretarial work and extra work that you wouldn't necessarily do at a private practice. Everybody knows that coming in, but I think you're still overwhelmed with it once you get here. (44)

Some also found it difficult to work with staff whom they described as either poorly trained or not adequately motivated by and committed to the health center's mission. In addition, tensions in some workplaces seemed to be heightened at times by racial differences between the providers and other staff. The following excerpt from an interview with a provider is an example. (The research team did not record information about the race and ethnicity of providers, so that information is not available.)

I hear a lot from the African American staff that we don't understand them. And yet I don't think that any of us feel like we're prejudiced. We acknowledge that we don't understand . . . but there's still a barrier to some extent that you feel. . . . There's distrust, and getting across that is difficult. (15)

A few providers in faith-based CHCs said that differences of ideology among providers also detracted from their work. Two noted that, because federally funded CHCs cannot discriminate based on religion in hiring, team unity is at times eroded because some providers do not share the Christian commitments of other colleagues. Another noted that she had been frustrated by what she saw as the rigid and judgmental treatment by fellow Christian providers.

> Christians come to this health center with their own quote "religions." And I've found that you cannot violate those respective systems of thought and belief. . . . It actually makes interpersonal relationship more difficult in the sense that whenever things go awry they say "Well, you're supposed to be a Christian doctor," and "Why did you say that?" or "Why did you do that?" (16)

One provider with a long history of work in a faith-based CHC summed it up in the following way:

> I think sometimes you come with the idea that in a Christian setting everybody's gonna get along with each other . . . it took me a while to get over that and just realize that people are people and, and, you know, it's nice that we have our faith—that can help us through some difficulties—but it doesn't mean we're not gonna have interpersonal conflicts. We're not all perfect with each other. (42)

Finally, some providers noted that the relatively low pay was a drawback to working in their current location.

> I took a pay cut to come here. You know, that was kind of understood that this was more of a mission field rather than a professional field thing. (15)

Synthesis and meaning

When it came to reconciling the competing costs and rewards of their work, providers in faith-based health centers often referred to their religious convictions and sense of calling to make sense of their decisions to press on despite the challenges of their work.

> Yes, I've thought about leaving, just because it's so incredibly demanding, but my vision is to be in ministry. And I really specifically feel that God did call me here, so I can't leave without him telling me that I can. . . . If you don't have a sense of calling or the feeling that this is really what you want to do, then the demands and the needs of your patients can sweep you over. (49)

Providers in secular health centers spoke repeatedly of the deep satisfaction they experience in making a difference in the lives of patients who might otherwise go without adequate medical attention.

> It fulfills a need. I've always wanted to work with the underserved. . . . I just enjoy it. I just get a lot of self-satisfaction from it. (22)

Overall, it appears that many providers believe that the balance between costs and rewards is ultimately tipped by the rewards of working with colleagues who share their convictions, toward an end that they value, in a way they believe is consistent with their core values.

Discussion

We should note right away that our study has several basic limitations. First, because of its purposive sampling and qualitative design, we cannot use any statistical inference to predict how the themes we found are distributed in the broader population of physicians who work among the underserved. We did not collect data regarding participants' race and ethnicity, and it may be that providers of different ethnicities had different perspectives. Most CHCs are not faith based. Among those that are, this study only included ones associated with CCHF. In addition, this study's primary sponsoring agency, and most of its study personnel and authors, are also from the Christian tradition. Protestant Christianity is the most common religious background of both physicians and the general public in the United States,[18] but there are many other religious traditions that emphasize the importance of providing health care to the poor. Although this study builds theory regarding faith-based CHCs affiliated with one tradition, studies of CHCs affiliated with Catholicism, Judaism, Islam, Hinduism, Buddhism, or Native American religions are needed and may find somewhat different themes.

Finally, all semistructured interviews like these are forms of what have been called *introspective causal reports,* which are limited to the extent that individuals are not able to perceive their own motivations fully; furthermore, the descriptions provided by those interviewed of their motivations are not always accurate. For example, we found that providers in secular CHCs did not mention religious motivations as often as those in faith-based CHCs. Yet, we cannot tell from our data whether the providers in secular CHCs had motivations that were less religious or whether providers in faith-based CHCs selectively emphasized their religious motivations over others. Perhaps providers in explicitly faith-based CHCs are primed to describe their work in religious terms; this would not be surprising given the fact that the characteristics of a work setting, in this case its explicit religious orientation, influence the ways in which people craft and attach explicit meaning to their work.[9] Alternatively, providers in secular health centers may be more likely to understand their callings in secular terms. Others have observed that "a set of [religious] beliefs is neither a necessary nor a sufficient condition for having a calling" (p. 161).[11] In light of such interpretive ambiguities, Pathman and Agnew have argued that "it is more appropriate to understand studies using introspective causal reports as a type of descriptive study rather than one demonstrating causal connections" (p. 204).[19]

Yet, Pathman and Agnew agree that such a design is well suited for the two purposes for which the present study was carried out, "1) to clarify how people understand the reasons for their own behaviors (i.e., beliefs) and 2) to generate hypotheses, later to be confirmed through stronger research designs" (p. 207).[19] To show how this study accomplishes both, we will relate our findings to Herzberg's two-factor theory of work motivation.[20]

Herzberg argued from his analysis of the attitudes of a sample of accountants and engineers that there are two sets of factors that must be taken into account to understand worker satisfaction and motivation. First, there are basic objective workplace characteristics (termed *hygiene* factors) that, if inadequate, lead to employee dissatisfaction and demotivation. Many of the costs mentioned by our participants are of this type. Similar to prior studies, we found that those who work in underserved settings say they struggle with inadequate resources to accomplish their work,[12] and they note frustrations regarding administrative needs for such things as secretarial and nursing support.[3,7] Indeed, our findings suggest that some providers in both faith-based and secular CHCs at times experience dissatisfaction and demotivation as a consequence of what Herzberg would have called inadequate workplace hygiene.

Such findings lead us to hypothesize that CHCs will mitigate provider dissatisfaction to the extent they are able to mitigate and provide buffering resources for the adverse hygienic factors that seem to be part of practice among the underserved. Community health center leaders might consider ways to use resources judiciously to provide increased administrative and other supports to providers and to provide improved training for the support staff on which the providers depend. They might find ways to give providers greater control over their schedules and even augment providers' salaries where possible. Such efforts may attenuate and dissipate the demotivating pressures that providers experience when standing in the gap between unlimited needs and limited resources.

According to Herzberg, while adequate hygienic factors are necessary to prevent worker dissatisfaction and demotivation, what is needed to generate deeper worker satisfaction and motivation are what he called *motivators*—factors that take into account and respond to a worker's need for personal growth and self-actualization. Motivators lead the worker to value the work as an end in itself, or in the language of contemporary work-orientation theory, to enact the work as a calling rather than merely as a job.[9–11]

In this study we found that providers in CHCs strongly emphasize subjective and internal rewards of their work as the motivators that explain their practice among the underserved. We found, like others,[5,21,22] that providers who work in underserved settings are likely to have begun medical training with that orientation already in place. Most of the providers from faith-based CHCs, and some of those from secular CHCs, described their work as a calling defined in overtly religious terms. Those who did not mention religious concepts still emphasized the meaning of their work as a calling to "make a difference" for the underserved. These findings are consistent with Davidson and Caddell's earlier observation that workers with higher levels of religious salience were more likely than others to view their work as a calling but that belief in the importance of social justice was an even stronger predictor of work as calling than was religious salience.[13] Other researchers have found that "the source and experience of a calling can be of either a religious or a secular, inner-directed nature" (p. 162).[11] Whereas a person who enacts a religious calling typically apprehends and finds meaning in God's plan for her or his life through a process of spiritual *discernment*, those who enact secular callings find meaning through a process of self-exploration and personal fulfillment.[11] Davidson and Caddell conclude that religion leads some to see their work as a calling rather than a career and leads others, who may already find intrinsic meaning in their work, to think of that work in sacred rather than just secular terms.[13]

The centrality of intrinsic motivations leads us to hypothesize that CHCs will improve provider motivation and satisfaction (and subsequently recruitment and retention) to the extent that they provide environments that invite and provide opportunities for providers to craft their work into callings.[9] Wrzesniewski and Dutton note that workers with intrinsic motivations typically engage in more extensive job crafting, a process in which they "locally adapt their jobs in ways that create and sustain a viable definition of the work they do and who they are at work" (p. 180).[9] Consistent with these researchers' predictions, we found that providers say they collaborate with like-minded colleagues to frame the meaning of their work in ways that affirm the identities they want to sustain. Therefore, leaders of CHCs may be able to improve motivation and satisfaction by encouraging and empowering providers to collectively envision and craft forms of medical practice that are congruent with their hopes and aspirations.

We further hypothesize, on the basis of what we learned in this exploratory study, that faith-based CHCs provide a particularly attractive setting for some providers who seek to craft their work into an explicitly religious form of vocation or ministry; indeed, we found some evidence of this. For example, we found that providers in the faith-based CHCs believed they had responded to a sense of Christian vocational calling and that they had embraced and fostered a faith-friendly environment in which their core values coincided with those of their colleagues and with the mission of the CHC. For such providers, faith-based CHCs appear to provide distinctive opportunities for the fulfillment of their religious aspirations. If so, leaders of faith-based CHCs may want to foster environments that are explicitly organized around its religious vision.

In summary, this study generates several fruitful hypotheses that should be tested in future research. Future studies of the recruitment and retention of providers in underserved settings should, where relevant, include measures of providers' religious and other motivational characteristics. As Davidson and Caddell argue, "Researchers examining the ways people think of work ought to give their respondents opportunities to describe work in both secular and religious terms, and should incorporate religious as well as secular factors into the theories they use to explain different orientations toward work" (p. 145).[13] We hope to employ a longitudinal survey research design with broader sampling to quantitatively examine the association between physicians' religious characteristics, CHCs' religious or secular orientations, and the outcome of provider retention in underserved settings. Ultimately, future studies should also consider whether these factors have any influence on measures of health care quality and patient satisfaction.

We found that providers in CHCs make sense of their work by reference to subjective and intrinsic values that are realized by enacting their work as a form of calling, whether secular or religious. Providers struggle to meet overwhelming demands with inadequate resources, and the lack of Herzberg's hygienic factors in their work threatens to demotivate and dissatisfy providers. Yet, underserved settings also appear to have unique characteristics that motivate and satisfy providers by giving them an opportunity to live "as the selves they most want to be" (p. 130).[12] The apparent challenge for leaders of CHCs is to attenuate the costs of work in their settings and nurture the rewards that intrinsically motivated providers seek, so that providers do not discover a calling to work elsewhere.

Acknowledgments

We would like to acknowledge Greg Barker, Heather Harris, Leslie Gee, and Ellen Kennedy for their assistance in data collection, and Josie Bines and Jerry Stromberg for their assistance in the coordination and administration of this study.

This study was funded by the Bureau of Primary Health Care through the Christian Community Health Fellowship Best Practices Project, Grant #U30 CS 00207-03, Technical Assistance to Community and Migrant Health Centers Program. It was also funded through the Robert Wood Johnson Clinical Scholars Program (Drs. Chin and Curlin) and the Steans Family Foundation, Chicago (Ms. Carricaburu).

Prior presentation: (Partial data) Following the call: self reported rewards and costs of current employment for providers in two faith-based urban community health centers. American Public Health Association National Meeting. Oral presentation. November 12, 2002. Philadelphia, Pennsylvania.

Notes

1. Singer JD, Davidson SM, Graham S, et al. Physician retention in community and migrant health centers: who stays and for how long? Med Care. 1998 Aug;36(8):1198–213.

2. Weissman JS, Campbell EG, Gokhale M, et al. Residents' preferences and preparation for caring for underserved populations. J Urban Health. 2001 Sep;78(3):535–49.

3. Pantell RH, Reilly T, Liang MH. Analysis of the reasons for the high turnover of clinicians in neighborhood health centers. Public Health Rep. 1980 Jul–Aug;95(4):344–50.

4. Paxton GS, Sbarbaro JA, Nossaman N. A core city problem: recruitment and retention of salaried physicians. Med Care. 1975 Mar;13(3):209–18.

5. Porterfield DS, Konrad TR, Porter CQ, et al. Caring for the underserved: current practice of alumni of the National Health Service Corps. J Health Care Poor Underserved. 2003 May;14(2):256–71.

6. Blume S. Retaining physicians in a changing health care environment. Illinois Primary Health Care Association—Health Source. 2001 Jun;4(6):12.

7. Dievler A, Giovannini T. Community health centers: promise and performance. Med Care Res Rev. 1998 Dec;55(4):405–31.

8. Pathman DE, Williams ES, Konrad TR. Rural physician satisfaction: its sources and relationship to retention. J Rural Health. 1996 Fall;12(5):366–77.

9. Wrzesniewski A, Dutton JE. Crafting a job: revisioning employees as active crafters of their work. Academy of Management Review. 2001;26(2):179–201.

10. Wrzesniewski A, McCauley C, Rozin P, et al. Jobs, careers, and callings: people's relations to their work. Journal of Research in Personality. 1997;31(1):21–33.

11. Hall DT, Chandler DE. Psychological success: when the career is a calling. Journal of Organizational Behavior. 2005 Mar;26(2):155–76.

12. Li LB, Williams SD, Scammon DL. Practicing with the urban underserved. A qualitative analysis of motivations, incentives, and disincentives. Arch Fam Med. 1995 Feb;4(2):124–33; discussion 134.

13. Davidson JC, Caddell DP. Religion and the meaning of work. J Sci Study Relig. 1994;33(2): 135–47.

14. National Center for Cultural Competence, Georgetown University Child Development Center. Sharing a legacy of caring: partnerships between health care and faith-based organizations. Rockville, MD: Bureau of Primary Health Care, Health Resources and Services Administration, 2001 Winter.

15. Crabtree BF, Miller WL. Doing qualitative research. 2nd ed. Thousand Oaks, CA: Sage Publications, 1999.

16. Janesick VJ. The choreography of qualitative research design: minuets, improvisations, and crystallization. In: Denzin NK, Lincoln YS, eds. Strategies of qualitative inquiry. 2nd ed. Thousand Oaks, CA: Sage Publications, 2003; 46–79.

17. Muhr T. ATLAS.ti 4.1—short user's manual. Berlin: Scientific Software Development, 1997.

18. Curlin FA, Lantos JD, Roach CJ, et al. Religious characteristics of U.S. physicians: a national survey. J Gen Intern Med. 2005 Jul;20(7):629–34.

19. Pathman DE, Agnew CR. Querying physicians' beliefs in career choice studies: the limitations of introspective causal reports. Fam Med. 1993 Mar;25(3):203–7.

20. Herzberg F. The motivation to work. 2d ed. New York: John Wiley & Sons, 1959.

21. Rabinowitz HK, Diamond JJ, Markham FW, et al. Critical factors for designing programs to increase the supply and retention of rural primary care physicians. JAMA. 2001 Sep 5;286(9):1041–8.

22. Pathman DE, Steiner BD, Jones BD, et al. Preparing and retaining rural physicians through medical education. Acad Med. 1999 Jul;74(7):810–20.

Chapter 5
The Jane Dent Home: The Rise and Fall of
Homes for the Aged in Low-Income Communities

Susan C. Reed
Nancy Davis

When the Jane Dent Home opened its doors in 1893 as a home for the aged in Chicago's African American community, other ethnic communities in the city were establishing similar institutions to protect their elders from neglect, loneliness, and, ultimately, the poorhouse. When the doors of the Jane Dent Home were closed for good in 1975, many other ethnically based homes for the aged had also closed their doors, but there were some that had moved into new neighborhoods of the city or out to the suburbs. Over the course of the intervening century, the neighborhoods that were once served by not-for-profit homes for the aged increasingly housed for-profit nursing homes. In the process, care for the elderly and disabled shifted from a community endeavor to a business. Scholars have debated for 40 years whether quality of care suffered with changing ownership of long-term care facilities. The story of the Jane Dent Home is told as a case study of (1) the effect of economic segregation on the location of not-for-profit homes for the aged in Chicago and elsewhere; (2) how the passage of Medicaid inadvertently encouraged the displacement of not-for-profit homes for the aged by for-profit nursing homes; and (3) how these important changes in the nursing home market affect access to long-term care for the poor today.

Crucial to the story of the Jane Dent Home are the racial and economic changes that occurred over the course of the century within the African American community that housed and supported the home. Early in the twentieth century, the neighborhood of Grand Boulevard, where the Jane Dent Home was located, was racially segregated but relatively diverse economically. Working adults contributed to the Home financially and gave of their time whenever needed. But by the 1960s the community became economically as well as racially segregated, as a high per capita poverty rate settled in. Similar demographic changes have challenged communities of color in cities throughout the country.[1]

In addition to the effects of the demographic changes in communities like Grand Boulevard, the passage of federal legislation creating Medicaid in 1965

Susan C. Reed, PhD, is an associate dean of curriculum instruction and assessment and an associate professor in the School for New Learning at DePaul University, Chicago. *Nancy Davis, PhD,* is an associate professor in the School for New Learning at DePaul University.

required participating facilities to meet new standards of care. Both Medicaid, which covered nursing home care for the indigent, and Medicare, which covered only a limited number of days of skilled nursing care, established new criteria for eligibility.[2] Many homes for the aged, both proprietary and nonprofit, were forced to close because they were unable to comply with the stricter regulations.[3] On the other hand, the passage of Medicaid encouraged the growth of long-term care beds by covering construction and investment costs for new facilities.[2] Much of this new construction was of for-profit facilities located in poor communities of Chicago so the owners could profit from Medicaid-reimbursed care for the poor.[4]

After 1965, not-for-profit homes for the aged, once established to serve an immigrant population, became the preference of middle-class elders, leading to class differences between the residents of nursing homes by ownership type. Nationally, research suggests that residents of not-for-profit nursing homes have higher incomes than residents of for-profit nursing homes. The most recent study of patient sorting[5] found that those with the greatest need (as measured by disability, diagnosis, and age) and those with the greatest range of long-term care options (as measured by family income and college education) reside in not-for-profit nursing homes. This study confirms previous research that has found that not-for-profit residents have higher incomes and are more likely to pay privately, rather than with Medicaid, than residents of for-profit nursing homes.[6-9] (Some studies have found no such relationship between ownership and source of payment.)[10] Class differences between the residents of for-profit and not-for-profit homes is a health policy concern if the care that the poor receive in for-profit homes is of a lower quality.

In fact, more than 30 years of research comparing the quality of for-profit and not-for-profit homes has found higher mortality rates and cited deficiencies in for-profit homes using statistical techniques designed to ensure that differences between residents are not confused for differences between homes. With the publication of mortality data by the Health Care Finance Administration in the 1990s, several studies compared death rates of nursing homes by ownership type.[6,11,12] Aaronson, Zinn, and Rosko[10] used a simultaneous equation model and found lower adverse outcomes among not-for-profits in Pennsylvania. Likewise, Spector, Selden, and Cohen[5] found a higher likelihood of death in for-profit homes using risk-adjusted outcome measures in the analysis of data from the 1987 National Medical Expenditure Survey. The most recent study of quality differences[7] sought to address possible local market variation by analyzing quality inspection data for nearly every nursing home in the country. After controlling for the functional severity of residents, investor-owned facilities accrued a higher rate of cited deficiencies per home as determined by state inspectors in both the quality-of-care and quality-of-life categories.

Some have theorized that higher quality is of greater importance to the survival of not-for-profit nursing homes. Sponsoring organizations may be more concerned about the supply of quality services to their members than about the realization of profit.[5] For-profit homes, on the other hand, tend to host larger facilities that offer economies of scale with fewer staff members and services[13] and to compensate by supplying residents with more medication.[14] Therefore, reduced nonprofit market share could result in lower quality within for-profit homes by lowering the standard of quality care within a community.[5]

This chapter explores whether the demographic and policy changes of the mid-1960s not only resulted in the closure of not-for-profit facilities like the Jane Dent Home in Grand Boulevard, but also led to the unequal distribution of not-for-profit beds around the city. Given the racial segregation of nursing homes in American cities,[15] the class differences between residents of for-profit and not-for-profit homes may have a spatial dimension as well, with fewer not-for-profit homes located in poor communities than elsewhere. If so, the quality of long-term care available to the residents of such neighborhoods may be reduced.

The development of effective urban health policy[16] requires the spatial analysis of health care access because race and class affect the distribution and utilization of health care institutions in cities. The numbers of persons living in poor communities is growing all over the country.[17] Although Chicago is one of the most segregated urban areas, the patterns of unequal access found here may be the precursor of emerging, if not existing, patterns elsewhere.

Employing a combination of historical and statistical methods, the following research question was addressed: Has there been a decline in not-for-profit long-term care beds in Chicago's poorest neighborhoods compared with other neighborhoods? If so, does this uneven distribution result in unequal access to quality care for the poor? We hypothesized that an examination of all Chicago's nursing homes would reveal a shortage of not-for-profit beds in poor communities as well as differences in the quality of the homes serving the poor.

The history of the Jane Dent Home compared with another home for the aged in Grand Boulevard was examined as a case study of how the concentration of poverty in the community affected the distribution of not-for-profit beds in Chicago. We hypothesized that the increasing concentration of poverty in the community, combined with stricter regulation of care, would affect one home's decision to move and another home's decision to close. The residential segregation of the poor in communities of Chicago and elsewhere may be seen as a contributing factor in the growing trend toward for-profit long-term care for the poor and not-for-profit long-term care for the nonpoor.

Methods

For this analysis, the history of the Jane Dent Home was studied, using documents archived at the University of Illinois at Chicago Library, and the Jane Dent Home was compared to a similar home for the aged in the same community, using a previously published history. The University of Illinois at Chicago Library's Special Collection Room houses the Jane Dent Home papers, which consist of the home's board minutes and annual reports through the 1930s. The Chicago Historical Society houses the papers of the Welfare Council of Metropolitan Chicago, including annual reports in which information about the Jane Dent Home is contained. These papers led us to several living members of the board of the Jane Dent Home, whom we interviewed.

To understand the probable effect of these two histories on access to long-term care for the poor, Chicago's contemporary nursing homes were analyzed using a data set constructed from the 1990 U.S. Census of Population and the 1994 Long Term Care Facility Survey of the Illinois Department of Public Health. Facilities categorized as for profit were compared with those categorized as not for profit on the following variables: resident characteristics (age, race, gender, form of payment), facility characteristics (size, nurse staffing, violations), and community characteristics (race, poverty level). The purpose of this analysis was to determine whether for-profit homes are more likely to be located in poor, black neighborhoods than elsewhere; whether poor, black elders are more likely than wealthier white elders to reside in for-profit homes; and whether there are indications of lower quality in Chicago's for-profit homes compared with Chicago's not-for-profit homes.

The Establishment of the Jane Dent Home at the End of the Nineteenth Century

The Jane Dent Home was originally called the Home for Aged and Infirm Colored People and grew out of a decision by an African American woman, Gabriella Knighten Smith, to take several homeless elders into her residence on Chicago's 47th Street. Smith was quickly joined in her efforts by African American club-women, specifically Fannie Mason, Joanna Snowden, and Maggie Stewart, who were actively supporting the establishment and growth of a range of community endeavors. A larger home was donated to Smith and became the location of the Home for Aged and Infirm Colored People (hereafter referred to as the Jane Dent Home) in 1898, along with another piece of property as an endowment, the income from which could help support the work of the home.[18–20]

The decision to establish the Jane Dent Home may have been influenced by the exhortations of black leaders such as Harriet Tubman and W.E.B. DuBois at the end of the nineteenth century to ensure care for formerly enslaved black elderly. Nineteen similar institutions were established in African American communities around the country about the same time.[21] These homes were very much community institutions, with food, funds, clothing, and furniture provided largely by African American clubs, churches, and individuals. The Jane Dent Home appeared to cater to the very old in the black community, people in their 70s, 80s, and 90s, who were without surviving children. Records for the Jane Dent Home indicate that some were centenarians (this at a time when black life expectancy was less than 40 years).[22]

The mission of the Jane Dent Home included at various times a commitment to homeless black elderly and to serving a more economically advantaged African American clientele (especially in its early decades). The board of the Jane Dent Home, like that of other white and black private elderly facilities, began charging an entrance fee of $100 as early as 1900.[23] A *sponsor*, or a *voucher*, someone whom the resident had been employed by, could pay this fee. However, without assistance from an outside source, the entrance fee precluded the admission of the most impoverished. With such fees in place, homes like the Jane Dent Home catered to the very old of the black working- and middle-class populations.

The racial segregation of health care services, including Chicago's homes for the aged, made the establishment of the Jane Dent Home a necessity, like the establishment of other health care institutions such as Provident Hospital, which was built in response to the restriction of patients of color to care at Cook County Hospital.[15] A survey of homes in the 1930s found that only two admitted blacks (the Jane Dent Home and the African Methodist Episcopal Deaconess Home).[24] McAuley[25] argued in a study of all-black towns in Oklahoma that parallel services must be viewed as a victory of community pride rather than as merely a response to racial prejudice. His observations are supported by David McGowan, a funeral home director who served as president of the Jane Dent Home Board for 50 years and pointed to the timely payment of the mortgage when discussing the "cooperation and race consciousness as shown by this institution's progress."[23]

Maintaining the home for the next 77 years would require the determination and dedication of an entire community aspiring to ensure the care of its elders. The home's first annual report[22] included pages of names of women who had donated "1 bedspread," "5 lbs. of sugar," or "6 bars of soap." These efforts were often organized by what Knupfer describes as a webbed network of women's groups aimed at ensuring the delivery of health care to the residents.[18] For 50 years, the Amateur Minstrels performed an annual show on Easter Monday to raise money for the home. When finances were tight, a board member might host a card party to raise funds for the home.[26] Jane Dent served as house committee chairwoman for many years. When she died in 1936, she left 200 shares of Union Carbide stock to the home, which was renamed in her honor three decades later.[27] Food, funds, clothing, and furniture were provided largely by African American clubs, churches, and individuals. The Jane Dent Home, though the beneficiary of community largesse, never received the large gifts from Chicago philanthropists that were given to the white ethnic elderly homes, described below. Thus, the Jane Dent Home was a truly indigenous institution.

Like other ethnically identified homes for the aged,[28] the Jane Dent Home enjoyed the support (and perhaps the protection) of local politicians. The Jane Dent Home's first president of the board was Major John C. Buckner, an African American Republican who served as a state representative from 1894 to 1898, after which he assumed leadership of the home.[29] Oscar de Priest was the city's first African American alderman and later the country's first African American congressman from the North.[30] De Priest is credited with several contributions to the home, including the completion of "the much needed bathroom on the second floor."[23]

Maintaining the quality of the Jane Dent Home was the business of a cadre of caring individuals who frequented it and were, therefore, able to monitor relations between staff and residents, the day-to-day operations, food rations, and general upkeep. Decisions about the admission of new residents seemed to be based on how well they were known by the community. In 1925, one applicant was rejected because she listed her residence in Illinois as less than a year. On the other hand, a "good" person might be admitted even if he or she lacked the fee.

Regularly, troublesome behavior was reported to a resident's sponsor, while a worthy resident might be purchased a new pair of shoes.[23,26]

Maintaining an adequate supply of food was a continual problem for the Jane Dent Home. The minutes of the monthly board meetings reflect at least an annual discussion of the sufficiency of food supplies in the home. A report written by the Welfare Council of Metropolitan Chicago in 1935 addressed this problem and recognized that the diligence of the board was keeping the wolf from the door.

> The Home budgets its food supply as far as possible but frequently must rely upon donations. The members of the Board work very hard for the Home. Whenever there is a shortage in certain supplies, they go to the grocers in the neighborhood and solicit certain items, which are needed.[31]

Each November a Harvest Home celebration brought food donations from the community to the Jane Dent Home to see it through the winter.

One would expect that the passage of the Social Security Act in 1935 would have alleviated this problem by providing a source of income for elderly residents and, therefore, the home. In the early years after the law's enactment, Old Age Assistance (OAA, established under Title 1 of the act) was provided to the states as a block grant to provide means-tested assistance until workers' contributions to Social Security made the fund solvent enough to provide monthly assistance to all elderly regardless of means.[2] Some of the elderly in the home would have been eligible for OAA. However, there was a provision in the Social Security Act that prohibited payment to public institutions, causing some confusion within the board about the home's eligibility. Visitors from the Welfare Council were asked about this issue in 1943,[32] when the census of the home had reached a low of 12 persons due to the inability of many of the community's elders to pay the admission fee (by then, $300). How quickly this confusion was resolved is unknown, but by 1960, 9 of the Home's 17 residents were receiving OAA support.[33]

A White Ethnic Home for the Aged in Grand Boulevard Moves North

Sixteen other homes for the aged were established in Chicago during the same decade as the Jane Dent Home, all with missions to serve a particular ethnic and/or religious population of older adults. A comparison of their histories highlights the unique circumstances that the Jane Dent Home faced, which stemmed in large part from the intersection of race and class that led to the segregation and poverty the home experienced. The names of some of the other homes for the aged were the Norwegian Old People's Home, the Orthodox Jewish Home, and the Little Sisters of the Poor (Catholic).[34] Most were located, at the time of their establishment, in large houses in areas that are now considered central or near south sides of the city.[3]

Chicago's first home for the aged was established in 1861 and was called the Home for Aged and Indigent Females. Like the Jane Dent Home, it was established by a woman (named Caroline Smith) who wanted to assist homeless elderly. Influential members of her community supported Smith's project, just as Gabriella Knighten Smith's community supported hers. One such supporter was Benjamin

Raymond, a former mayor of Chicago who put together a board of interdenominational protestant ministers with ties to wealthy donors. In 1873, the board became secular when benefactors became concerned about the refusal of a Roman Catholic applicant.[35] The name of the home changed to the Old People's Home of the City of Chicago, and the doors were opened to a more diverse population, although not to blacks.[24]

The board of the Old People's Home of the City of Chicago evolved primarily into a fundraising entity that became so successful that a large facility was built in 1911 at 47th and Vincennes, just three blocks from the Jane Dent Home and 10 times its size. Just as its community supported the Jane Dent Home with bequests and cash donations, so the Old People's Home was the beneficiary of generous gifts. However, these benefactors were the likes of George Pullman and Marshall Field, who contributed up to $40,000 to the support of the Old People's Home of the City of Chicago.[35]

Until World War II, the Board of the Old People's Home of the City of Chicago had been content to reside in the elegant community of Grand Boulevard, dubbed Bronzeville. Southern black families had moved to the north in three waves between the turn of the century and the two world wars and developed a thriving economy in Grand Boulevard despite the economic hardships imposed by a segregated city.[30] However, successful families began to leave the neighborhood after World War II, causing the population of Grand Boulevard to decline from approximately 114,000 in 1950 to about 80,000 in 1960.[36] The swinging, smoky Savoy Ballroom that was in close proximity to the Old People's Home made the residents uncomfortable. When several thefts occurred, a fence was constructed around the property and other measures were taken to distance the Old People's Home from the surrounding community. In time, the board had the Old People's Home follow the first wave of residents out of Grand Boulevard, purchasing property on the city's north side in 1959 and opening a facility, renamed the Admiral, that still operates today.[35] About half of Chicago's homes for the aged established at the turn of the century were able to survive such demographic transitions.

The Old People's Home of the City of Chicago was established with a similar mission to that of the Jane Dent Home, to provide charitable care for elders without family who could provide care for them. When the rate of poverty began to increase in Grand Boulevard, the Old People's Home had the resources to relocate to another neighborhood, where many of its constituents were also moving. Because it was not serving an African American population that was still constrained by racial and economic segregation, the Old People's Home could more readily respond to neighborhood changes. In addition, the institution's ability to construct a new facility enabled it to meet the stricter standards set by the federal government in 1965.

The Jane Dent Home Faces State Regulation with Declining Resources

During the same period, state agencies were requiring changes to the structure and operation of the Jane Dent Home. Throughout that year the board felt pressure from the Illinois Department of Public Health to upgrade the building, install sprinklers, post menus, and add more citrus to the residents' diet.[34] The license of the home was temporarily suspended in 1960 for failure to comply with the state's new regulations for shelter care homes.

The passage of Medicaid in 1965 offered the Jane Dent Home an opportunity to serve more low-income residents of Grand Boulevard, but the standards of care required for a facility to be eligible for Medicaid necessitated construction. The Illinois Department of Health found many of Chicago's nursing homes "nonconforming"; in fact only 11% of the homes in the district where the Jane Dent Home was located were found to conform to national standards, in part due to the danger of fire in older buildings.[3] Smith describes the closure of smaller homes in Philadelphia during this same era and reports that half of the homes existing in 1960 were replaced with new construction.[15]

The shortage of beds for black elders in Chicago prompted the Welfare Council to recommend additional changes in the operation of the Jane Dent Home. In a 1960 Welfare Council report, the board of the Jane Dent Home (especially the president) was criticized for "carrying the staff" by handling too many of the day-to-day problems themselves. They were advised to hire an administrator, to recruit whites to the board, and to apply for federal funding so that the home could expand to meet the growing need for care.[33] The 1960 Welfare Council Report represents a turning point in the degree of board control over the operation of the home. Whereas the Old People's Home of the City of Chicago chose to leave Grand Boulevard after the postwar population shift changed the economic base of the community, the board of the Jane Dent Home fought to keep it open and in the same neighborhood, despite dwindling community resources and growing regulatory pressure.

The mission of the Jane Dent Home and its role in the Grand Boulevard community was altered again in the 1960s with the changing of its name and constitution to deemphasize the home's focus on serving African American elders. The name, Jane Dent Home for Aged Colored People, was changed to the name Jane Dent Home for the Aged to remove reference to race. Then, in 1966 (two years after the Civil Rights Act required health care institutions to prohibit discrimination explicitly), the home's constitution was revised to remove language that stated their mission to serve elders of color.[33]

All of these developments coincided with the resettlement of middle-class families from Grand Boulevard to nearby community areas farther south, a resettlement that caused a leadership crisis on the board of the home. Efforts were made to reinvigorate support as 25 young women were recruited to a junior board to carry on the tradition of fundraising and entertaining the elders.[37] Land was purchased in the 1970s and negotiations began with the federal Department of Housing and Urban Development (HUD) to develop a new facility with Section 202 funds for housing for the elderly.[38] Unhappily, sufficient funds were never acquired for expansion. The passage of Illinois' stricter licensing requirements in 1972[39] may have been the obstacle that the fledgling new board of the Jane Dent Home could not overcome. The home ceased operation in 1975. This was part of a larger decline in the fortunes of the neighborhood. By 1979, Grand Boulevard had the lowest median family income of Chicago's 77 community areas.[36]

In summary, the Home for Aged and Infirm Colored People, later the Jane Dent Home, like other homes for the aged, was established to care for the elders of the community and, as such, enjoyed the devotion of a community dedicated to ensuring its survival. Although racial segregation throughout Chicago made the establishment of parallel services necessary, the longevity of the home can only be attributed to the diligence of community leaders even after middle-class families began to leave Grand Boulevard. However, the home did not enjoy the financial resources available to other homes for the aged, which were able to comply with the new licensing requirements of the state by building, or relocating into, new facilities.

As poverty in Grand Boulevard became more concentrated, the resources available to the leadership of the Jane Dent Home dwindled. A not-for-profit association dedicated to the home's history and possible future survives today; one participant stated, "We're still holding the mortgage on the lots at 83rd and King Drive but there aren't enough younger people coming up to take the place of the older participants to make it happen."[40] Perhaps commitment to the home and its mission was eroded when the leadership of the Jane Dent Home succumbed to agency demands that they open the facility to other ethnic groups from outside the community. The surviving members of the board and other supporters who maintain the not-for-profit association harbor hope that the land that they still own will be developed for the care of the community's older adults.

The history of the Jane Dent Home demonstrates how racial and economic segregation combined with stricter regulation after the passage of Medicaid to close homes for the aged that had provided community-based care for the elderly since the end of the nineteenth century. With the support of Medicaid funds, the nursing homes that replaced them were businesses, not indigenous institutions. One former participant in the Jane Dent Home Association shared his observations on the role that government agencies now play in maintaining the quality of care for the elderly when he said of the nursing homes in his community, "They're businesses now and the government has it so tightly regulated that they're worrying about whether there's a 5-foot hall or a 6-foot hall."[40] What had begun as the fruit of the goodwill of Grand Boulevard's leaders slowly became an entity compelled to respond to state dictates, which, most importantly, meant building infrastructure but also meant meeting dietary guidelines and requirements concerning resident profiles. The history of the Jane Dent Home reflects a more widespread redistribution of homes for the aged that leaves few residents of poor, black neighborhoods with an alternative to for-profit nursing home care.

Today's Shortage of Not-for-Profit Beds in Chicago's Poorest Communities

For Chicago, the rise of for-profit and the decline of not-for-profit long-term care resulted in an increase in the number of beds overall but an unequal distribution of beds by ownership type around the city. The City of Chicago begins the twenty-first century with a healthy supply of long-term care beds in most communities of the city.[41] Half of the 20 homes for the aged established at the beginning of the twentieth century still exist, all of them on the city's north side or in suburbs. Another 6 ethnically or religiously based homes for the aged were opened in the 1920s and 5 in the 1950s, half of which remain in operation today.[42,43] In all, Chicago has 17 not-for-profit homes for the aged that provide either skilled or intermediate care. Two more not-for-profit (and three for-profit) homes offer only shelter care. By 1994, 12 skilled nursing units were operating within not-for-profit hospital systems and another 71 nursing homes in Chicago were for-profit enterprises.

Mirroring national research showing income differences between the residents of not-for-profit and for-profit homes, table 5.1 shows that the residents of not-for-profit homes in Chicago in recent years are likely to be female, over 85 years of age, white, and paying for their own care. The majority of residents of for-profit homes are also white women, as are the majority of nursing home residents nationwide, but their proportions, and those of residents over 85, are smaller than those of their counterparts in not-for-profit facilities. The proportion of Chicago's nursing home residents who are reimbursed by Medicaid is much higher among for-profit than not-for-profit establishments. Although 69% of nursing home residents in the United States are on Medicaid (64% in Illinois),[44] 85% of residents in Chicago's for-profit nursing homes are covered by the federal program, compared with only 29% in not-for-profit facilities.

Higher poverty rates also characterize the census tracts in which Chicago's for-profit nursing homes are located. In areas where poverty is concentrated, 11% of nursing homes are nonprofit, compared with 30% of all homes in the city. In a city that is still racially segregated,[45] black census tracts are more likely to host a for-profit nursing home than a not-for-profit facility, whereas predominately white census tracts have more not-for-profit beds.

Today, two nursing homes are located within the boundaries of the Grand Boulevard community area; both are for-profit facilities with about 180 beds each. The census tracts in which they are located have 70% and 44% of residents below the poverty level. Grand Boulevard residents are not restricted to nursing homes within their own community, but Chicago's nursing homes reflect the residential segregation patterns of the city, with blacks and whites residing in different nursing homes.[41] Along with the restrictive effects of segregated housing patterns, 3 of the 17 homes for the aged do not accept Medicaid at admission[46] in order to reduce administrative costs and maintain control over resident admission.

The facility characteristics reported in table 5.1 do not provide decisive evidence of differences in the quality of homes by ownership because our data do not allow for case mix controls. Chicago's not-for-profit nursing homes have higher nurse staffing levels, but these differences could be required by higher levels of functional disability among residents, as has been found in previous studies of not-for-profit homes. Nonprofit facilities were also cited less frequently for deficiencies of care and safety by Illinois Department of Public Health inspectors. Although Harrington and colleagues found a similar pattern,[7] the authors conceded the subjective nature of such evaluations and the possibility that for-profit homes are less favored by state inspectors. We also concur with Harrington and her associates in finding for-profit homes to be larger.

Table 5.1

Chicago's nursing homes: resident, facility and community characteristics, 1994 (n=101[a])

	For profit[b]	Not for profit
Resident characteristics, mean %		
Female	60	76**
Over 85 years old	20	47***
Black	38	17**
White	56	77**
Medicaid	85	29***
Facility characteristics, mean number		
Residents	163	103**
LPN/resident	0.06	0.11**
RN/resident	0.07	0.18***
Violations[c]	2.06	0.79*
Administrative warnings	27	14*
Community characteristics		
Beds in poorest tracts,[d] % (n)	90(16)	11(2)**
Black in census tract, mean %	39	20*
White in census tract, mean %	41	54*

Source: 1990 U.S. Census of Population; 1994 IDPH, Long Term Care Facility Survey.

[a]Facilities with either intermediate or skilled-care beds; shelter care, facilities for those younger than 22 years, and persons with developmental disabilities not included in this analysis. Illinois houses mentally ill in nursing homes, but removing homes with ≥85% mentally ill did not change these findings, although differences in the percentage female became insignificant. One for-profit nursing home lacks data on several variables (staffing, Medicaid, race of resident); data on violations is missing for all hospital-based not-for-profit and three for-profit homes.

[b]*For-profit homes* are those coded by IDPH as "proprietary corporation" or "proprietary partnership"; *not-for-profit homes* were coded as "non profit church related" and "non profit corporation."

[c]Only the less life-threatening violations are included; severely life-threatening violations are rare.

[d]Nursing homes located in census tracts with 40% or more residents at the poverty level. Differences significant at *p<0.05, **p<0.01, ***p<0.001.

These data support national research that finds the poor more likely to reside in for-profit nursing homes. They provide further evidence that the income differential by ownership type has a spatial dimension, with poor communities unlikely to host a not-for-profit home for the aged in the present day. Seventeen percent of Chicago's not-for-profit residents are African Americans, although 39% of the city's total population is black. Therefore, it may be concluded that poor, black residents of these communities are restricted in their long-term care options.

Conclusion

The passage of Medicaid in 1965 changed the local market for long-term care by increasing the supply of nursing home beds, particularly but not exclusively to low-income communities, while Medicare increased skilled care for the elderly.

The long-term care market became increasingly dominated by proprietary facilities anxious to invest in federally funded health care, while community-based not-for-profits found it harder to compete in a market-driven, more medical environment. The result was an increase in the availability of both housing and long-term care to elderly of all incomes, but no corresponding growth in the supply of not-for-profit nursing home care.

In the coming century, federal policymakers wanting to support not-for-profit long-term care through the development of assisted-living beds or by steering home-and community-based care funds to local voluntary associations may consider providing additional technical assistance to those communities most in need. While recognizing the importance of Medicaid and Medicare in promoting the health of low-income adults, and increasing the number of beds to address the need for care, persistent health inequality requires a commitment to target and tailor health promotion programs to meet the specific health care requirements of those communities most in need.[47] Efforts to combine federal and local funding with authentic community organizations, like the Jane Dent Home Board (based as it was on local leadership, resources, and enthusiasm), could contribute to Healthy People 2010's goal to eliminate racial/ethnic and socioeconomic disparities in health.[48] At the same time, for-profit as well as not-for-profit nursing homes can work with families and communities to utilize their insight and concern for improving the quality of long-term care. Some programs have been successful[49] in reopening the doors of nursing homes to families and encouraging their involvement in the day-to-day operation of the home without carrying the full burden of financing and operating the home.

Inequities that result from the segregation of poverty from wealth can undermine the effect of policies, such as Medicaid, specifically intended to improve health care access to the very poorest citizens. Wallace, Enriquez-Haass, and Markides[50] pointed out the importance of "race-sensitive policies" that recognize the effects of historical discrimination on access to care: "Few major health and aging policy initiatives specifically address race, even though most such initiatives are not neutral in their consequences for older persons of various racial and ethnic backgrounds." Federal policy for the twenty-first century that identifies and addresses disparities in access to quality care will help to ensure a healthy population in all communities.

Notes

1. Wilson WJ. The truly disadvantaged: the inner city, the underclass, and public policy. Chicago: University of Chicago Press, 1987.
2. Vladek BC. Unloving care: the nursing home tragedy. New York: Basic Books, 1980.
3. Hospital Planning Council for Metropolitan Chicago. Utilization and status of nursing homes and nursing care units in homes for the aged in the Chicago metropolitan area for calendar years 1964–1966. Chicago: Hospital Planning Council for Metropolitan Chicago, 1968.
4. Reed SC. The history of nursing home bed supply in Chicago: the effect of federal policy and urban settlement on utilization. Res Sociol Health Care. 2001; 19:103–30.

5.   Spector WD, Selden TM, Cohen JW. The impact of ownership type on nursing home outcomes. Health Econ. 1998 Nov;7(7):639–53.

6.   Bell R, Krivich M. Effects of type of ownership of skilled nursing facilities on residents' mortality rates in Illinois. Public Health Rep. 1990 Sep–Oct;105(5):515–8.

7.   Harrington C, Woolhandler S, Mullan J, et al. Does investor ownership of nursing homes compromise the quality of care? Am J Public Health. 2001 Sep;91(9):1452–5.

8.   Lemke S, Moos RH. Ownership and quality of care in residential facilities for the elderly. Gerontologist. 1989 Apr;29(2):209–15.

9.   Cohen JW and Dubay LC. The effects of Medicaid reimbursement method and ownership on nursing home costs, case mix, and staffing. Inquiry. 1990 Summer;27(2):183–200.

10. Aaronson WE, Zinn JS, Rosko MD. Do for-profit and not-for-profit nursing homes behave differently? Gerontologist. 1994 Dec;34(6):775–86.

11. Zinn JS, Aaronson WE, Rosko MD. Variations in the outcomes of care provided in Pennsylvania nursing homes: facility and environmental correlates. Med Care. 1993 Jun;31(6):475–87.

12. Spector WD, Takada H. Characteristics of nursing homes that affect resident outcomes. J Aging Health. 1991 Nov;3(4):427–54.

13. Weisbrod B, Schlesinger M. Public, private, nonprofit ownership and the response to asymmetric information: the case of nursing homes. In: Rose-Ackerman S, eds. The economics of nonprofit institutions: studies in structure and policy. New York: Oxford Press, 1986.

14. Weisbrod, BA. Rewarding behavior that is hard to measure: the private nonprofit sector. Science. 1989 May 5;244(4904):541–6.

15. Smith DB. Health care divided: race and healing a nation. Ann Arbor: University of Michigan Press, 1999.

16. Freudenberg N. Time for a national agenda to improve the health of urban populations. Am J Public Health. 2000 Jun;90(6):837–40.

17. Kasarda JD. Cities as places where people live and work: urban change and neighborhood distress. In: Cisneros HG, ed. Interwoven destinies: cities and the nation. New York: W.W. Norton, 1993.

18. Knupfer AM. Toward a tenderer humanity and a nobler womanhood: African American women's clubs in turn of the century Chicago. New York: New York University Press, 1996.

19. Davis EL. The story of the Illinois Federation of Colored Women's Clubs. Chicago, 1922. Reprinted by G.K. Hall, 1996.

20. Davis N, Reed S. Chicago's Home for Aged and Infirm Colored People: a paradigm for examining changes in African American institutional support. West J Black Stud. In press.

21. Pollard LJ. Complaint to the lord: historical perspectives on the African American elderly. Cranbury, NJ: Associated University Presses, 1996.

22. Home for Aged and Infirm Colored People. Board meeting minutes, 1899. Jane Dent Home for Aged Papers, box 1. Chicago: University of Illinois at Chicago Library Special Collections, 1899.

23. Home for Aged and Infirm Colored People. Board meeting minutes, 1924. Jane Dent Home for Aged Papers, box 1. Chicago: University of Illinois at Chicago Library Special Collections, 1924.

24. Glick FZ. Admissions to homes for the aged with special reference to Chicago. Dissertation for master's degree. Chicago: University of Chicago, 1930.

25. McAuley WJ. Historical and contextual correlates of parallel services for elders in African American communities. Gerontologist. 1998 Aug;38(4):445–55.

26. Home for Aged and Infirm Colored People. Board meeting minutes, 1927. Jane Dent Home for Aged Papers, box 1. Chicago: University of Illinois at Chicago Library Special Collections, 1927.

27. Home for Aged and Infirm Colored People. Annual Report, 1936. Jane Dent Home for Aged Papers, box 1. Chicago: University of Illinois at Chicago Library Special Collections, 1927.

28. Skocpol T. Protecting soldiers and mothers: the political origins of social policy in the United States. Cambridge: Belknap Press, 1992.

29. Lewis M. The Old Folk's Home of Chicago. Colored American Magazine. Mar 1901; 2:329–35.

30. Drake SC, Cayton HR. Black metropolis: a study of Negro life in a northern city. New York: Harper and Row, 1945.

31. Welfare Council of Metropolitan Chicago. Report on the Home for Aged and Infirm Colored People. Welfare Council Papers, box 327. Chicago: Chicago Historical Society, 1935.

32. Welfare Council of Metropolitan Chicago. Report on the Home for Aged and Infirm Colored People. Welfare Council Papers, box 327. Chicago: Chicago Historical Society, 1943.

33. Welfare Council of Metropolitan Chicago. Report on the Home for Aged and Infirm Colored People. Welfare Council Papers, box 327. Chicago: Chicago Historical Society, 1960.

34. Chicago Department of Public Welfare. Social service directory. Chicago Department of Public Welfare, 1915.

35. Hilliard C. Providing a home: a history of the Old People's Home of the City of Chicago. Chicago: Old People's Home of the City of Chicago, 1983.

36. Chicago Fact Book Consortium, eds. Local community fact book, Chicago metropolitan area: based on the 1970, 1980 census. Chicago: Chicago Review Press, 1984.

37. Welfare Council of Metropolitan Chicago. Report on the Home for Aged and Infirm Colored People. Welfare Council Papers, box 327. Chicago: Chicago Historical Society, 1959.

38. Landis LL. Community care key to this home. Chicago Tribune 12 Sep 1970.

39. Wittenborn EL. A history of the Illinois Department of Public Health: 1962–1977. Springfield: State of Illinois, 1983.

40. Participant interview, 31 May 2000, Chicago.

41. Reed SC, Andes S. Supply and segregation of nursing home beds in Chicago communities. Ethn Health. 2001 Feb;6(1):35–40.

42. Welfare Council of Metropolitan Chicago. Social service directory. Chicago: Welfare Council of Metropolitan Chicago, 1926.

43. Welfare Council of Metropolitan Chicago. Social service directory. Chicago: Welfare Council of Metropolitan Chicago, 1956.

44. Kane RA, Kane RL, Ladd RC. The heart of long-term care. New York: Oxford University Press, 1998.

45. Massey DS, Denton NA. American apartheid: segregation and the making of the underclass. Cambridge, MA: Harvard University Press, 1993.

46. Better Government Association. A consumer guide to long term health care facilities. Chicago: Better Government Association, 1994.

47. Geronimus AT. To mitigate, resist, or undo: addressing structural influences on the health of urban populations. Am J Public Health. 2000 Jun;90(6):867–72.

48. U.S. Department of Health and Human Services. Healthy people 2010: understanding and improving health. (DHHS Pub. no. 17-001-00543-6.) Washington, DC: U.S. Department of Health and Human Services, 2000.

49. Pillemer K, Hegeman CR, Albright B, Henderson C. Building bridges between families and nursing home staff: the Partners in Caregiving program. Gerontologist. 1998 Aug;38(4):499–503.

50. Wallace SP, Enriquez-Haass V, Markides K. Consequences of color-blind health policy for older racial and ethnic minorities. Stanford Law Pol Rev. 1998 Spring;9:329–46.

Chapter 6

Early Collaboration for Adaptation: Addressing Depression in Low-Income New Mothers

Susan G. Pfefferle
Ben Cooper
Debbie Layton
Sharon Rohrbach

Numerous studies demonstrate that, in settings for the care of the medically underserved, evidence-based depression treatments are underused.[1-4] Locating mental health services in nonspecialty settings has the potential to increase access to services for underserved populations.[5,6]

This chapter describes collaboration by a university-based researcher and a nurse home visitation agency aimed at fitting depression treatment into a setting where new mothers who reside in economically disadvantaged neighborhoods receive services. The Nurses for Newborns Foundation (NFNF) provides services to economically disadvantaged mothers with children under the age of two. For this intervention, we focused on mothers living in the St. Louis metropolitan area. The majority of families living in poverty in St. Louis are African American.

Although there are several effective treatments for depression, we chose problem-solving therapy (PST) for the intervention because it is not stigmatizing, is a brief treatment, and fits well with the mission of NFNF because it can empower women to take control over their own lives. It also has a history of use by non–mental health specialists. Originally, PST was developed from the problem-solving component of cognitive behavioral therapy.[7] It uses everyday problems that individuals encounter (such as not having enough quiet time) to teach problem-solving skills related to symptoms of depression. The therapy uses seven steps, which are reviewed in each session.[8] These steps take the client through the process of identifying problems related to depression and then breaking the problems down into manageable steps.

We describe the initial collaborative process between researcher and agency for this project; collaboration between researcher and agency is ongoing. Including

Susan G. Pfefferle, PhD, is a researcher in behavioral health at Abt Associates, Cambridge, Massachusetts. *Ben Cooper, BA, MPH,* is a statistical data analyst at Washington University, St. Louis. *Debbie Layton, RN,* is the director of nursing at the Nurses for Newborns Foundation, St. Louis. *Sharon Rohrbach, RN,* is the executive director of the Nurses for Newborns Foundation.

depressed mothers as collaborators was beyond the scope of this study. We solicited feedback through qualitative interviews about the acceptability of PST to mothers.

The description offered here is intended as a practical guide for researchers concerned with targeting work for treatment adaptation, including those for adapting the treatment to the setting, considering populations' needs and preferences, and addressing organizational influences to ensure sustainability of interventions. We strove to be principled in our collaboration.[9]

The Collaboration

In spring 2006, NFNF in St. Louis, Missouri, began screening for maternal depression, as was mandated by their Healthy Start contract.[10] The nurses, however, were soon overwhelmed by the number of women who screened positive for depression but were unable to access treatment.

Simultaneously, the research partner was looking for an agency partner with whom to conduct research about maternal depression. In August 2006, NFNF and the researcher began to design a study on the feasibility of co-locating depression treatment in nurse home visitations. In November 2006, we submitted a small grant to the Fahs-Beck Fund for Research and Experimentation. The grant was funded in January 2007.

Shared decision making

A team met on a bi-weekly basis to design and monitor progress of the work. Initial meetings were with the researcher and NFNF senior management and later progressed to a small working team at the agency. After the team identified the project's needs and interests, it chose PST[8] as the intervention with the greatest potential to address depression safely during home visitation.

The team obtained funding for the PST feasibility study and had several meetings to address operational issues. These included pay for the nurses, development of research time sheets, applying for institutional review board (IRB) approval, training and supervision in PST, and ongoing support for the nurses. For delivery of the intervention, the team explored whether to tag PST onto the end of a regular home visit or whether to provide it during separate visits (ultimately leaving the decision to the nurse and mother).

As the work progressed, a clinical team took shape, composed of the nurses providing the intervention, the director of nursing, and the researcher. The nurses were active participants in identifying obstacles as well as providing solutions. Meeting biweekly at the agency, the team reviewed and contributed to the adaptation of all study materials. Meetings were scheduled for the nurses' convenience, and the nurses were reimbursed for their work during the planning phase. We developed crisis protocols and provided back-up from a psychiatric nurse practitioner in case women needed medication or a higher level of care. We also arranged fidelity monitoring by sending audio-recorded sessions to a clinical psychologist.

In real-world research, confidentiality of data can be trickier than in controlled settings. It was important that the agency retain control over data to ensure confidentiality, yet it was equally important that the researcher receive data in a timely and consistent manner. Flexibility in adjusting our strategies to meet the needs of the agency and researcher turned out to be important.

Equal partnership

An understanding of differing agendas and motivations as well as consensus building on the core goal of the collaboration was crucial to success. The researcher has a background in community mental health and an interest in placement or co-location of mental health services in nonspecialty settings.[11,12] The NFNF, which was founded on the principles of David Olds, strives to ensure that its nurses provide the most effective services to a high-risk population.[13-15]

In our small study, funded by the Fahs-Beck Fund for Research and Experimentation, it was impossible to have the agency as a funded co-investigator, because none of the parties were receiving salary support from the grant. However, agency and researcher had equal weight in decision making.

Shortly after we received funding for the feasibility study of PST in nurse home visitation, we started working on a larger treatment adaptation study initiated by the researcher. The NFNF team contributed to the research design and participated in the school's internal peer review process. For example, the researcher provided the literature review and feedback on screening tools and outcome measures. The NFNF was already using the Center for Epidemiological Studies Depression Scale (CESD)[16] and did plan to switch to another tool in the near future; therefore, CESD was used to determine study eligibility. The Parenting Stress Index,[17] also already in use by NFNF, was used as an outcome measure for the intervention adaptation study. Management at NFNF participated in a number of university-based trainings on use of evidence-based practices in community organizations. For our second proposal to the National Institute of Mental Health (NIMH), we did include the agency team as funded co-investigators.

Expanding the agency's capacity to conduct research
and use of evidence-based practices

Washington University's institutional review board (IRB) approved the work reported here. The university's research office also provided technical support for NFNF to go through the Federal Wide Assurance (FWA) process. The FWA process prepares agencies to engage in further research. These actions increased NFNF's capacity to carry out future research projects.

Information technology is one area where agencies often need help in building capacity, but NFNF has a sophisticated, proprietary database that can track client progress. Because NFNF owns the system, it is able to integrate assessment tools into the electronic medical record and make other changes as needed. Additionally, this system can capture data from an array of assessment tools that NFNF has utilized. Numerous studies have shown that patient registries and integrated information systems are associated with improved quality of care for individuals with chronic conditions, including depression.[18]

Long-term commitment to the partnership
with the agency and its clients

The researcher was a postdoctoral scholar with a two-year appointment at the university. In order to address the long-term stability of the university-agency partnership, we engaged a senior researcher from the university as coprincipal investigator on our treatment adaptation grant for NIMH. The researcher also made a commitment to continue this relationship if working at another university. Finally, one of the agency collaborators joined the university's IRB, further strengthening the agency's relationship with the university and increasing the agency's understanding of the IRB process.

Particular challenges of adapting depression
treatment to nurse home visitation

Avoiding assumptions. The team had to account for the nurses' time in our small project budget. The researcher budgeted for the nurses' training rate assuming the nurses were on salary, but this turned out not to be the case, and the training pay was less than the nurses' hourly rate. Confusion ensued when the nurses expressed their concerns to their direct supervisor, who was not part of the management team for the project. The NFNF responded by offering to make up the difference in the nurses' pay (since the team had already submitted its budget). Learning from this experience, the team corrected the budgeted nurse salary in the treatment adaptation study submitted to NIMH.

IRB. Gaining IRB approval was another challenge. First, the IRB staff did not understand identifying agency staff as both researchers *and* subjects in the application. Confusion may have arisen because collaborating researchers are not usually research subjects. It was important, however, to gain through formal interviews staff nurse perspectives on PST implementation and adaptation and about challenges to nontherapists delivering therapy. The IRB expressed concern about coercion, raising the possibility of staff nurses feeling obliged to participate. The team revised its research plan numerous times before the IRB was satisfied.

The team intended to use language at the 3rd-or 4th-grade reading level in the client consent forms to ensure that all NFNF clients could read and understand them. While we strove not to exclude anyone from the intervention due to low literacy, the IRB required that certain specific legal phrases be included. We negotiated adjustments, resulting in materials at the 9th-grade reading level. All these negotiations, including developing a contract to have NFNF covered under the university's IRB, took over seven months, greatly affecting the feasibility study's timeline, including the nurses' ability to be formally certified in the therapy.

Power asymmetries. Information asymmetries often divide people in universities, communities, and programs. Universities have extensive library resources, including scholarly journals, and research assistants to cull through the literature. It remained important for the researcher to remember and seek the agency perspective in all intervention-related decisions. Community agencies have a wealth of knowledge about their communities, organizational cultures, and methods of service delivery. In the case reported here, NFNF was particularly savvy regarding technology and quality improvement.

Discussion

Researcher-agency collaboration forms part of an ongoing process of quality improvement, in which research is a tool to improve practice and, ultimately, outcomes. Through our collaboration, we identified several lessons that may assist others when collaboratively adapting interventions for use in their particular setting.

Lesson 1: Don't make assumptions about collaborating organizations; rather, ask questions ahead of time.

Lesson 2: Transparency, relationship building, and long-term commitment to the research partnership are key to developing trust.

Lesson 3: Collaborators must be funded co-investigators. While this is easier said than done, it is essential to adapting interventions to settings in an equal partnership.

Lesson 4: Collaborative research takes time. This includes added time for planning negotiation, and IRB approval.

Lesson 5: Adapting services for medically underserved communities is complex. It includes collecting data from direct service staff, directly observing services, and seeking feedback from clients. If we miss data from a source, we could miss something that would make the intervention more effective.

Lesson 6: Services must be perceived as relevant to the populations being served. Interventions may fail if not made relevant and convenient for client use. Access barriers must be identified and addressed in the intervention adaptation.

Conclusion

Adapting depression services for underserved populations requires meaningful and sustainable academic and community partnerships. Our experience highlights the fact that community partnerships take time, resources, and personal commitment. Intervention adaptation research is a substantial undertaking for any community organization. Such collaborations can increase the likelihood that relevant and effective services reach underserved populations and the chances for sustainability through attention to fit for populations and providers at the treatment development stage. Collaboration for mental health treatment adaptation requires a long-term commitment.

Notes

1.   Anderson CM, Robins CS, Greeno CG, et al. Why lower income mothers do not engage with the formal mental health care system: perceived barriers to care. Qual Health Res. 2006 Sep;16(7):926–43.

2.   Das AK, Olfson M, McCurtis HL, et al. Depression in African Americans: breaking barriers to detection and treatment. J Fam Pract. 2006 Jan;55(1):30–9.

3.   Miranda J, Green BL, Krupnick JL, et al. One-year outcomes of a randomized clinical trial treating depression in low-income minority women. J Consult Clin Psychol. 2006 Feb;74(1): 99–111.

4.   Ojeda V, McGuire T. Gender and racial/ethnic differences in use of outpatient mental health and substance use services by depressed adults. Psychiatr Q. 2006 Fall; 77(3):211–22.

5.   Institute of Medicine. Improving the quality of health care for mental and substance-use conditions. Washington, DC: National Academies Press, 2006.

6.   New Freedom Commission on Mental Health. Achieving the promise: transforming mental health care in America; final report. Rockville, MD: Substance Abuse and Mental Health Services Administration (SAMHSA), 2003.

7.   D'Zurilla TJ, Nezu AM. Problem solving therapies. In: Dobson KS, ed. The handbook of cognitive-behavioral therapies; 2nd edition. New York: Guilford Press, 2001.

8.   Mynors-Wallis L. Problem-solving treatment for anxiety and depression: a practical guide. Oxford: Oxford University Press, 2005.

9.   Wells KB, Staunton A, Norris KC, et al. Building an academic-community partnered network for clinical services research: the Community Health Improvement Collaborative (CHIC). Ethn Dis. 2006 Winter;16(1 Suppl 1):S3–17.

10.   The Children's Health Act of 2000. Public Law 106–310. Passed by the 106th U.S. Congress (2nd Session).

11.   Pfefferle SG. Pediatrician perspectives on children's access to mental health services: consequences and potential solutions. Adm Policy Ment Health. 2007 Sep;34(5):425–34. Epub 2007 Apr 10.

12.   Pfefferle SG, Gittell JH, Hodgkin D, et al. Pediatrician coordination of care for children with mental illnesses. Med Care. 2006 Dec;44(12):1085–91.

13.   Rohrbach S. Healthy from the start. Home care for newborns. Caring. 1993 Dec; 12(12):13–5.

14.   Olds DL, Henderson CR Jr, Chamberlin R, et al. Preventing child abuse and neglect: a randomized trial of nurse home visitation. Pediatrics. 1986 Jul;78(1):65–78.

15.   Olds DL, Henderson CR Jr, Kitzman HJ, et al. Prenatal and infancy home visitation by nurses: recent findings. Future Child. 1999 Spring–Summer;9(1):44–65.

16.   Radloff LS. The CES-D Scale: a self-report depression scale for research in the general population. Applied Psychological Measurement. 1977;1(3):385–401.

17.   Abidin RR. Parenting Stress Index clinical manual (PSI); 3rd ed. Charlottesville, VA: Pediatric Psychology Press, 1995.

18.   Katon W, Von Korff M, Lin E, et al. Collaborative management to achieve treatment guidelines. Impact on depression in primary care. JAMA. 1995 Apr 5;273(13): 1026–31.

Chapter 7
Neighborhood Clinics: An Academic Medical Center–Community Health Center Partnership

Mina Silberberg
Kimberly S. H. Yarnall
Fred Johnson
Devdutta Sangvai
Rupal Patel
Susan D. Yaggy

The number of uninsured and underinsured in the United States is growing,[1] and the challenges of their care are complex. The providers and services available to the un/underinsured are limited, and financial barriers are compounded by such obstacles as lack of transportation and language nonconcordance between providers and patients.[2–4] The result for consumers is insufficient, delayed, or fragmented care, with adverse health consequences. The result for the health care system is emergency department (ED) use for primary and non-emergent acute care needs, as well as unnecessary hospitalizations and ED visits for ambulatory-care-sensitive conditions.[5] What can academic medical centers (AMCs) do to help? This chapter describes the Lyon Park Clinic, a neighborhood clinic created and run through the partnership of a federally qualified health center (FQHC) and an AMC. Since this writing began, a second such clinic has been opened through the same partnership and is operating successfully; discussions have begun about a third clinic. Because Lyon Park Clinic has had time to develop, this chapter will focus on its history, operation, finances, services, and patient base.

Community health centers are essential to the health care safety net but are stretched thin. In the 1990s the number of individuals served by these centers

Mina Silberberg, PhD, is an assistant professor of community and family medicine at the Duke University Medical Center (DUMC) and Duke Translational Medicine Institute (DTMI). *Kimberly S. H. Yarnall, MD,* is an associate professor and the medical director of the Division of Community Health at DUMC. *Fred Johnson, MBA,* is an assistant professor and a deputy director of the Division of Community Health, DUMC. *Devdutta Sangvai, MD, MBA,* is the division chief of family medicine, medical director of the Duke Center for Eating Disorders, and vice chair of quality and safety, community and family medicine, DUMC. *Rupal Patel, MPP,* is a former research analyst at DUMC now living in the United Kingdom. *Susan D. Yaggy, MPA,* is chief of the Division of Community Health, DUMC, and associate director of the Duke Center for Community Research of the DTMI.

grew, as did the proportion who were uninsured; a 2000 report concluded that 50% of FQHCs faced operational or financial problems.[6] While the funding for community health centers has increased in recent years, overall federal spending on the safety net has not kept pace with the rise in the number of uninsured.[7]

Hill and Madara argue that urban AMCs should complement, rather than substitute for, community-based clinicians in general, and community health centers in particular.[8] As a provider of highly specialized care, an AMC serves a larger community than the one in which it is located. Conversely, when an AMC takes on a large role in providing primary care, it can hurt community providers' bottom line. "The responsibility of the urban academic medical center," the authors conclude, "is to assist in protecting the primary care capacity of urban neighborhoods, not to compete with them" (p. 2220).

The authors of this report add that the responsibilities of the AMC include developing new models of care—not only new surgical approaches and pharmaceuticals, but also new financial and organizational approaches to meeting health care needs.

There have been collaborations between FQHCs and AMCs for years,[6] but they principally provide training opportunities for AMC learners in the FQHC. Health systems have also provided funds and resources to FQHCs in return for the latter shouldering a disproportionate share of indigent care.

The partnership described here, between Duke University Medical Center and Lincoln Community Health Center, an FQHC, represents a different approach, one which we believe meets the mandates to enhance community-based primary care and develop new approaches to meeting community needs.

The service model is familiar from rural clinics, small FQHCs, and nurse-managed health centers; mid-level practitioners under off-site physician supervision provide primary, preventive, and acute services, as well as referrals and limited labwork on site. However, the administrative and financial partnership that makes the model possible is new. For example, nurse-managed health centers are often ineligible for cost-based reimbursement from Medicaid and Medicare, threatening their financial viability.[9] The neighborhood clinic described here would be ineligible as well, except for the FQHC's role in running it. As will be described, this is one of several benefits deriving from the FQHC-AMC partnership that the clinic represents.

Clinic Model

Durham, North Carolina, home of Duke and Lincoln, is a county of 237,000. In 2003, when Lyon Park opened, 19.4% of the county's nonelderly were uninsured.[10] Duke University Hospital and Durham Regional Hospital, both part of Duke, provide ED care, which is often used for non-emergent needs. Lincoln, an FQHC, provides primary care, as well as pharmacy and some specialty services, but is overwhelmed with patients; waiting times and the lead time to schedule an appointment are long. Inadequate public transportation is also a barrier, and Lincoln's four vans cannot accommodate all requests. Lincoln's increasing bilingual capacity has been outpaced by the growth in Durham's Latino immigrant population.

In response to these problems, Lyon Park Clinic was opened in April 2003 as a Lincoln satellite operated by Duke, providing basic primary, preventive, and acute care in a primarily low-income area of Durham. Lincoln and Duke recognized that, while not replicating Lincoln's range of services, a neighborhood clinic could extend Lincoln's primary care, facilitate continuity of care, and respond more easily to specific local needs (e.g., for bilingual providers).

Lyon Park Clinic is located in a community center owned and operated jointly by the city and a community-based organization. When it opened, the clinic had two examination rooms and was staffed by a .75-time bilingual physician assistant, a full-time nurse, a receptionist, and a .10-time supervising family physician (all Duke employees). The clinic has since expanded to five examination rooms and 1.75-time physician assistants, in addition to a half-time registered nurse, full-time certified medical assistance, a bilingual receptionist, and the .10-time supervising physician.

Clinicians at Lyon Park undergo standard institutional credentialing for privileges in family medicine at both Duke and Lincoln; credentialing allows clinicians to practice and the organization to bill for services. Patients at Lyon Park are enrolled as Lincoln patients, and the clinic follows joint Lincoln-Duke protocols. Lincoln's electronic medical record is the official chart. Radiology and pharmacy services are provided through Lincoln. Laboratory services, other than those performed on site through Clinical Laboratory Improvement Amendment waivers, are provided through Lincoln or Durham Regional Hospital. (For all patients, radiology and pharmacy services at Lincoln are staffed by Durham Regional, and laboratory work is processed at Duke at a discounted rate.) Billing is handled by Lincoln. Patients who would benefit from being seen by a pediatrician or internist because of complicated conditions are referred to Lincoln. Those in need of specialty care are referred to Lincoln or Duke. For the uninsured, the Lincoln referral system coordinates referrals, contacting the specialist's office for information on making an appointment, charity care, and transportation, as well as making sure, when relevant, that x-ray results get to the specialist before the visit.

Services are provided weekdays, year-round. The patient population is 75% uninsured; 18% are covered by Medicaid or Medicare. Over 60% of the patients are Latino, and the balance is primarily African American. Although the initial supposition was that patients would come primarily from Lyon Park's surrounding neighborhood, patients come from wide-ranging areas of Durham, in large part because Lincoln has begun referring patients requesting same-day appointments to Lyon Park after their own slots are filled. Lyon Park's draw may also be its accessibility, intimate atmosphere, and bilingual staff.

Duke received $216,000 from the Duke Endowment to equip the clinic space, and set up and later enlarge the clinic. The Duke Endowment funding also initially underwrote some salary and equipment costs.

As an FQHC, Lincoln receives what is called *cost-based* reimbursement from Medicaid and Medicare Part B, including for Lyon Park patients. Co-pays are required of all patients, with a sliding scale fee ($10–$50) applied to the uninsured. Lincoln averages $44 per visit for Lyon Park patients. Lincoln pays Duke $35 per visit, regardless of patient insurance status.

There were 4,983 visits to Lyon Park from July 1, 2005, to June 30, 2006, equaling 79% of capacity, based on clinic space. Expenses for the year were $356,293, an average per-visit cost of $71.50. After reimbursement from Lincoln, Duke had uncompensated per-visit costs of $36.50, falling $181,789 short of break-even. Recognizing the importance of Lyon Park Clinic, Duke Health System began subsidizing it in fiscal year 2006. Once Lyon Park reaches capacity, savings in per-visit costs will be partially offset by small additional expenses for added equipment and support staff time; overall the required subsidy will drop.

Clinic Benefits

Lyon Park Clinic represents an AMC-FQHC partnership that expands community-based primary care capacity for low-income people. While not self-sustaining, Lyon Park provides high-volume, high-quality care with low overhead and per-visit costs. The low costs result from space rental in a community-owned facility, use of mid-level providers, provision only of primary and acute care, and maximizing the resources of both Duke and Lincoln.

The clinic combines advantages of big and small settings in other ways, too. Duke and Lincoln provide much of the infrastructure needed to run the clinic, and affiliation with Lincoln allows the clinic to meet regulatory standards (e.g., volume requirements for accreditation). Yet, Lyon Park offers the familiarity, accessibility, and responsiveness of a small neighborhood clinic.

Lyon Park has taken on new roles over time. The clinic trains limited numbers of residents and a community health physician fellow, increasing the pool of new providers with experience working with indigent populations. The Division of Community Health also uses the community center for health education (e.g., health literacy, diabetes management) through service learning staffed by Duke medical, nursing, and physician assistant students. Duke Community Health's in-home care-management programs for Medicaid and uninsured patients can provide assistance to Lyon Park patients between visits, helping patients improve self-management and navigate health and social resources.

A postvisit survey of clinic patients conducted in 2004 demonstrates other benefits of the clinic model for patients, Lincoln, and the health care system. Figure 7.1 illustrates respondents' alternatives to Lyon Park. Almost half reported that, had the clinic not existed, they would have delayed getting health care for the problem that brought them there. About one-third said they would have gone to Lincoln, although many volunteered that they had tried and been unable to get a timely appointment there. Another third said they would have gone to an ED. Only 9% would have considered another health care provider; most could not identify such a provider.

Figure 7.2 confirms the importance of the clinic in preventing ED use and delayed care. Three-tenths of the patients saw the ED as the *only* alternative to Lyon

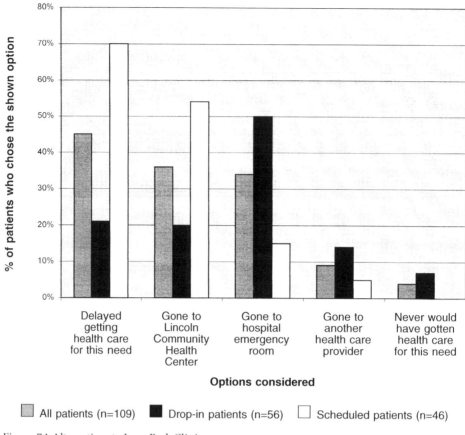

Figure 7.1 Alternatives to Lyon Park Clinic.

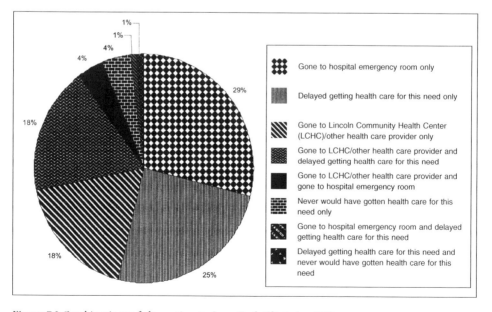

Figure 7.2 Combinations of alternatives to Lyon Park Clinic (n =109).

Park. One-fourth saw delaying care as their only option. Many who said they would have gone to Lincoln or another provider also mentioned delaying care.

Having both walk-in and scheduled appointments seems important to Lyon Park's capacity to divert patients from the ED and also address preventive health and chronic care needs. Half of walk-ins would have considered going to an ED had the clinic not been there, vs. 15% of those with scheduled visits. Among those with scheduled visits, 70% said they would have delayed getting care if the clinic had not existed, scheduled care was primarily routine checkups (86%) and chronic disease management (41%).

Lyon Park Clinic, then, is playing an important role in its clients' health, with much of the service directly preventing delays in receiving needed health care. It is also preventing non-emergent use of the ED, which is an impediment to continuity of care. In addition, many clinic patients receive care for ambulatory-care sensitive chronic conditions, which may prevent ED use.

Lowering ED use has important benefits for the health care system, reducing ED overcrowding and protecting hospitals and government from the costs of uncompensated care. The clinic also rationalizes the health care system, providing primary and acute care more cost-effectively than an ED would and freeing the AMC to provide a range of services to the community.

It was recognition of these community and system benefits that led Duke Health System to begin subsidizing Lyon Park and expanding the clinic program. Other AMCs, FQHCs, and policymakers should explore the costs and benefits of implementing and supporting this model.

Acknowledgments

The authors gratefully acknowledge the contributions to Lyon Park Clinic of Lincoln Community Health Center and its director, Evelyn Schmidt, MD; the Duke Endowment; Calvary Ministries of the West End; Duncan Yaggy, PhD, chief planning officer, Duke University Health System; J. Lloyd Michener, MD, chairman, Duke Department of Community and Family Medicine; and the staff of Lyon Park: Diane Davis, PA-C, Walter Jenkins, PA-C, Sherry Davis, LPN, Shauna Johnson, CNA, and Marquita Robertson.

Notes

1. Holahan J, Cook A. Changes in economic conditions and health insurance coverage, 2000–2004. Health Aff (Millwood). 2005 Jul–Dec;Suppl Web Exclusives: W5-498–508.
2. Mechanic D. Disadvantage, inequality, and social policy. Health Aff (Millwood). 2002 Mar–Apr;21(2):48–59.
3. Fiscella K, Franks P, Doescher MP, et al. Disparities in health care by race, ethnicity, and language among the insured: findings from a national sample. Med Care. 2002 Jan;40(1):52–9.
4. Jerant AF, von Friederichs-Fitzwater MM, Moore M. Patients' perceived barriers to active self-management of chronic conditions. Patient Educ Couns. 2005 Jun; 57(3):300–7.
5. Cunningham PJ. Medicaid/SCHIP cuts and hospital emergency department use. Health Aff (Millwood). 2006. Jan–Feb;25(1):237–47.

6. Government Accounting Office (GAO). Community health centers: adapting to changing health care environment key to continued success. (Pub. No. GAO/HEHS-00-39). Washington, DC: GAO, 2000 Mar.

7. Hadley J, Cravens M, Coughlin T, et al. Federal spending on the health care safety net from 2001–2004: has spending kept pace with the growth in the uninsured? (Report No. 7425). Washington, DC: Kaiser Commission on Medicaid and the Uninsured, 2005 Nov.

8. Hill LD, Madara JL. Role of the urban academic medical center in US health care. JAMA. 2005 Nov 2;294(17):2219–20.

9. Hansen-Turton T, Line L, O'Connell M, et al. The nursing center model of health care for the underserved. Philadelphia, PA: National Nursing Centers Consortium, 2004 Jun.

10. Holmes M. County-level estimates of the number of uninsured in North Carolina: 2003 update. Chapel Hill: Cecil G. Sheps Center for Health Services Research, 2003.

Chapter 8

Free Clinics Helping to Patch the Safety Net

Stephanie Geller
Buck M. Taylor
H. Denman Scott

Volunteer-based clinics, sometimes called free clinics, have existed in the United States for decades. These clinics, which provide free or low-cost care to uninsured and underinsured patients, depend largely on the philanthropic community for financial support and operate largely through the efforts of volunteer physicians and other health care providers. Care at many volunteer-based clinics is completely free of charge, while other clinics request a nominal fee or operate on a sliding-scale fee structure based on the patient's income. Some free clinics exist under the umbrella of churches, health departments, or hospitals, while others are independently governed nonprofit agencies.

The common thread binding free clinics together is their dependence on volunteers. A small clinic might operate with a handful of physicians who come together one evening a week to see patients in borrowed space. Some larger clinics have a volunteer base of hundreds of clinicians, including physicians, nurses, and dentists, and provide care several days and evenings a week. Most free clinics provide some care at the clinic and arrange for their patients to receive additional services, such as laboratory, radiology, and specialty care off site for free or reduced rates. A number of articles have been published describing how individual clinics operate,[1-12] but little has been published on the impact of free clinics as a group or how they contribute to the nation's safety net.

The first account of a survey of free clinics was published more than 30 years ago.[13] In 1970, the University of California Health Services Research Program conducted a survey of free clinics through a grant from what was then the National Center for Health Services Research and Development, Health Services and Mental Health Administration. This survey, designed to identify and describe all known free clinics in the United States and Canada, identified 59 clinics that had opened between 1967 and 1969. A large number of the clinics identified were in California, where the project was housed, but clinics in 19 other states,

Stephanie Geller, EdM, is a policy analyst at Rhode Island Kids Count. *Buck M. Taylor, MPH,* is the chief operating officer at Community Health Partners in Bozeman, Montana. *H. Denman Scott, MD, MPH,* is professor emeritus of medicine and heath services, policy, and practice and dean of the faculty at Brown University.

the District of Columbia, and Canada also were identified. The authors noted that by 1971, when the paper was published, there were more clinics (as many as 135) in North America.

Since that time, there have been a few articles published describing how free clinics operate or the role they play in the larger safety net,[14,15] but no published accounts of large-scale surveys. A few organizations have conducted informal surveys in order to create directories of free clinics,[16,17] and some state and regional free clinic associations produce directories of their member clinics.

This chapter describes a survey of volunteer-based clinics in seven midwestern states, conducted through a cooperative effort of Volunteers in Health Care, a national resource center funded by the Robert Wood Johnson Foundation to support programs serving the uninsured, and the Free Clinics of the Great Lakes Region (FCGLR), an association of free clinics in the Midwest. The FCGLR was started by free clinic directors from Illinois, Indiana, Iowa, Michigan, and Ohio who sought to formalize the grassroots networks of free clinics in the Midwest. Since its early development in 1996, the network has grown to include clinics in seven states: Illinois, Indiana, Iowa, Michigan, Minnesota, Ohio, and Wisconsin. The data were compiled to chronicle the efforts of these mostly private, independent clinics and to make more visible the role that free clinics play within the larger safety net. The clinics that participated in the survey represent only a small fraction of the clinics operating across the country. Nonetheless, these findings may help to focus attention on the number of uninsured being cared for by volunteer-based clinics and offer a glimpse of how these clinics operate and how they fit into the larger safety net.

Methods

In 1999, the Free Clinics of the Great Lakes Region (FCGLR), in partnership with Volunteers in Health Care, conducted a mail survey of the FCGLR member clinics. The survey was conducted to learn more about the member clinics, increase the visibility of volunteer-based clinics and the patients they serve, and facilitate information sharing and networking. The four-page survey included questions on clinic operations, the population served, the volunteers and staff providing care, and the services provided. Some of the questions were derived from other surveys of free clinics,[16,18] while others were newly developed with input from the FCGLR steering committee. All questions related to 1998, the last full year of service at the time the survey was conducted. All the clinics included in the analysis met the FCGLR definition of a free clinic: a volunteer-based clinic that provides free or low-cost health care services to medically uninsured and underinsured people.

In June 1999, the survey was mailed to 156 organizations and individuals that were on the FCGLR mailing list. Several methods were used to optimize response rates. Respondents were given the option of mailing or faxing back their completed surveys and given a stamped return envelope. In addition, two follow-up mailings containing a reminder and another copy of the questionnaire were sent to clinics that did not respond promptly. Finally, state coordinators (free clinic directors who represent their state's clinics on the FCGLR board) called clinics that did not respond to the initial or follow-up mailings and encouraged them to send back their completed surveys. While making these follow-up calls, state coordinators sometimes found that nonresponders were not eligible because the clinic had not yet opened, and these cases were excluded when calculating the response rate. In other instances, they found that the questionnaire had been misplaced, in which case another was mailed out.

By mid-November of 1999, 106 completed surveys had been returned. Of the surveys that were not returned, 38 were determined to represent ineligible entities (ineligibility being established on the basis of the organization being otherwise included in the survey, not being a health clinic, not being operational, or not being in the FCGLR region). Once ineligible surveys were removed, only 12 nonresponders remained, which may or may not have represented eligible free clinics. Overall, 106 of 118 surveys from eligible clinics were returned, translating to a response rate of 89.8%. Certain states had higher response rates than others, perhaps due to the remarkable persistence of some state coordinators, who called clinics repeatedly to encourage them to participate in the survey (table 8.1).

Results

The clinics

Of the 106 clinics that responded, half described their target area as mixed, while 25% described it as urban, 17% as rural, and 8% as suburban. Although some of the clinics had been operating for decades, the overwhelming majority (78, or 75% of those responding) had been in operation for fewer than 10 years (table 8.2). In fact, 13 clinics had opened just since 1998. The 2 oldest clinics (the Cabrini Clinic

Table 8.1

Response rate breakdown

State	Number of surveys returned	Number not responding	Number surveyed	Response rate (%)
Illinois	23	3	26	88.5
Indiana	10	0	10	100
Iowa	7[a]	1	8 (18)	94.4
Michigan	18	4	22	81.8
Minnesota	4	0	4	100
Ohio	17	4	21	81.0
Wisconsin	27	0	27	100
Total	106	12	118 (128)	89.8

[a]Although only seven surveys from Iowa were included in the analysis, these represented 17 clinics because one survey was returned that reported statistics for an 11-clinic network.

Table 8.2
Summary data on free clinics

			n	%[a]
Years in operation	under 10	78	75	
	under 2	13	13	
	2–9	65	62	
	10–19	16	15	
	20–29	8	8	
	30–39	0	0	
	40+	2	2	
	Not reporting	2	—	
Annual budget[b]		<$200,000	50	63
		$200,000–$399,999	19	24
		$400,000–$1 million	6	8
		>$1 million	4	5
		Not reporting	27	—
Insurance allowed		Medicaid	33	34
		Medicare	39	40
		Veterans' benefits	24	24
		Other public insurance	24	24
		Private insurance	35	36
		Any insurance	53	54
		Not reporting	8	—
Age groups seen		Children (age <18)	75	71
		Adults (age 18–64)	105	99
		Elderly (age ≥65)	44	42
		Not reporting	0	—
Services provided		Primary care	97	93
		Pharmaceutical services	93	89
		Specialty care	76	73
		Dental care	55	53
		Vision care	52	50
		STDs / communicable diseases	50	48
		Mental health services	49	47
		Urgent care	40	38
		Immunizations	39	38
		Other	38	36
		Not reporting	2	—
Total			106	10

[a]Percentages are based on those reporting.

[b]When considering these results, the number of clinics that did not respond should be taken into account because nonresponders' budgets may have differed from responders'. Also, some survey respondents included both dollars and donated time and goods in the budget they reported. When actual dollars and donations were reported separately, only dollars were used in the analysis. Other clinics may have included donated time and goods in their budgets and not noted this fact. Therefore, some clinics' budgets of cash may be much lower than the figures they reported.

in Detroit, Michigan, and the Pacific Garden Mission Clinic in Chicago, Illinois) have been open since the early 1950s.

The free clinics generally operate on a small budget (table 8.2). Well over half (63%) reported annual budgets for 1998 of less than $200,000, while only four clinics (5%) reported annual budgets exceeding $1 million. The mean annual budget was $235,170 (median = $157,000; range = $0–$2,147,000).

The patients

The free clinics reported varying eligibility criteria but primarily served low-income, uninsured people in their communities. The percentage of clinic clients having no health insurance ranged from 12% to 100%, with a mean of 93% (with 14 clinics not reporting). Half of those responding (46 clinics) reported that all of their patients were uninsured.

Some clinics reported that, in addition to uninsured patients, they accept patients who are underinsured. Respondents were asked if the clinic sees patients who may be underinsured "because they have public or private insurance that providers will not accept or that does not cover certain needed services" (table 8.2). Thirty-nine clinics (40%) reported accepting patients with Medicare, 35 (36%) with some type of private health insurance coverage, 33 (34%) with Medicaid, 24 (24%) with veterans' benefits, and 24 (24%) with other public insurance. These clinics do not bill public or private insurers but see all patients, irrespective of insurance status, for free or for a small fee.

While many clinics reported that insurance status was a major factor used to establish eligibility for services, 65 clinics (62% of those reporting) noted that they base eligibility for services on income. Of these clinics, 91% base their cutoffs on some percentage of the federal poverty level (FPL). Income eligibility standards varied substantially by clinic, with some using eligibility cutoffs as low as 100% of FPL ($16,450 for a family of 4 in 1998[19]) and others using cutoffs as high as 300% of FPL, the most common cutoff being 150% of FPL (mean=169% of FPL; median=150% of FPL).

Some clinics also reported using age as a factor for determining eligibility for services. Probably because low-income children and the elderly are often eligible for state or federal programs (including, for children, state-run Medicaid and State Children's Health Insurance Programs, and, for the elderly, Medicare) many clinics target nonelderly adults. In fact, all but 1 clinic (99%) serve adults ages 18 to 64, and 23 (22%) serve only this age group. Despite the existence of health insurance programs for children and the elderly, 75 clinics (71%) serve children and 44 clinics (42%) serve the elderly (table 8.2). Several clinics specifically noted that the only service they provide to the elderly is prescription assistance, since this service is not available through Medicare.

Because clinics differ widely in size, number of providers, hours of operation, and services offered, there was a wide range in the number of patient visits reported. One clinic that had just opened in 1998 reported only 32 patient visits that year, while a large clinic that had been open for more than 20 years reported 21,000 patient visits during the year. The mean and median numbers of patient visits were 2,986 and 1,686, respectively. Seventy percent of those responding to the question stated that the number of visits reported was an actual count, while 30% said it was an estimate. Twelve clinics did not report the number of patient visits. Because free clinics face no requirement to collect uniform statistics, there is no guarantee that one clinic's definition of a visit is comparable to another's, nor can we be sure that a free clinic's definition would be comparable to a visit as defined by another health care institution, such as a hospital or federally qualified health center (FQHC).

Fewer clinics were able to provide information on the number of patients served separately from visits made, presumably because some clinics do not have the capacity to count unduplicated patients. Of those responding, 47% were able to provide actual counts, while 53% provided estimates. The range of responses was again wide, with a newly opened clinic reporting only 32 clients and a large clinic reporting over 24,000. The mean and median were 2,522 and 1,173, respectively. Clinics were also asked to report the number of new clients seen in 1998, to provide a picture of growing need. The number reported ranged from 0 to 9,300, with a mean of 753 and a median of 450. Of those responding, 54% provided actual counts and 46% estimates. Ten clinics did not report the number of new clients.

As a whole, Wisconsin clinics reported the largest number of patients served and Minnesota the smallest. As a group, with 80 reporting, the clinics in the seven-state Great Lakes region provided care to over 200,000 patients in 1998 (table 8.3).

The services

The free clinics reported providing a wide variety of services to their patients, both on site and through established referral networks (table 8.2). For clinics reporting, the most commonly offered services were primary care (93%) and pharmaceutical assistance (89%). Clinics reported arranging for medications for patients through a variety of means. The most common methods were distributing physician samples (93%), applying to pharmaceutical manufacturers' patient assistance programs (79%), and purchasing medications (75%). Some clinics also reported having arrangements with pharmacies, hospitals, state and local charities, and state and local government-sponsored pharmaceutical assistance programs that allow them to obtain free or reduced-cost medications for their patients.

Some volunteer-based clinics also reported offering specialty care (73%), dental care (53%), vision care (50%), STD/communicable disease diagnosis and treatment (48%), mental health services (47%), urgent care (38%), and immunizations (38%). Other commonly reported offered services included podiatry, family planning, minor surgeries, and substance abuse recovery services.

The volunteers and staff

Forty-one percent of the clinics reported having no full-time staff, and of these, eight reported also having no part-time paid staff. Even those clinics that did employ paid staff relied on a very small number of full-(mean=2; median=1) and part-timers (mean=2; median=2).

Given their small budgets and staffs, free clinics could not operate without the contribution of a large corps of volunteer physicians, nurses, dentists, and other

Table 8.3

Number of patients served by free clinics in each state

State	Number of patients served	Number reporting	Number not reporting
Illinois	26,231	14	9
Indiana	33,097	7	3
Iowa	24,223	7	0
Michigan	19,165	16	2
Minnesota	7,013	4	0
Ohio	44,489	12	5
Wisconsin	46,527	20	7
Total	200,745	80	26

clinicians and nonclinicians. Some volunteers work at the clinic and others volunteer off site, participating in a formal network of providers and accepting patient referrals from the clinic.

Clinics reported a mean of 22 volunteer physicians providing care to patients on site, with the number of volunteer physicians ranging from 0 in a few nurse-managed and dental-only clinics to 113 at a large clinic. The number of volunteer nurses providing care at clinics was even higher, ranging from 0 to 330, with a mean of 27. Clinics reported a much smaller number of other volunteers on site, with a mean of 4 volunteer dentists, 2 volunteer pharmacists, 1 volunteer mental health professional, and 46 unspecified "other" volunteers providing medical care or other assistance to patients.

Clinics reported a mean of 56 volunteer physicians providing care to patients off site or through referrals, with the number of volunteer physicians in the clinics' referral pools ranging from 0 to 1,800. Through referrals, clinics also used a mean of 32 volunteer nurses, 5 volunteer dentists, 1 volunteer pharmacist, 2 volunteer mental health professionals, and 5 other volunteers providing medical care or other assistance to patients off site.

Eighty-two clinics provided information on the total number of hours that volunteers contributed in 1998. Of those reporting, 23 (29%) reported actual counts of the number of hours volunteers contributed; the remaining 59 clinics (71%) estimated this contribution. Clinics reported a mean of 4,342 hours contributed by volunteers in 1998. Hours contributed ranged from a low of 2 hours, reported by a clinic operating with mostly paid staff clinicians, to a high of 52,620, reported by a clinic network operating with 113 volunteer physicians and 330 volunteer nurses. Overall, the clinics surveyed reported a total of 16,425 clinicians volunteering 356,060 hours of their time during 1998.

Discussion

In 1998, the FCGLR clinics together provided care to over 200,000 patients. Since this survey was conducted, the number of clinics in the Great Lakes has grown to more than 200.[20] The most recent directory from the National Free Clinic Foundation of America now lists over 300 clinics nationwide.[16] Volunteers in Health Care's database of volunteer-based health care programs now includes over 1,000 free clinics.[17] Several state and regional free clinic associations have growing directories of their own member clinics. Unfortunately, because many clinics are small and informally operated, because clinics continually open and close, and because there is disagreement about the definition of a free clinic, it has been difficult to generate a definitive list or to determine how many free clinics exist across the country. It would be reasonable to estimate, however, that there are well over 1,000.

The U.S. Census Bureau estimates that there are 43.6 million Americans without health insurance[21] and that there are many more without real access to health care. Although this survey shows impressive numbers of patients being served by free clinics, free clinics are far from being an adequate means of addressing the health care needs of uninsured and underinsured populations in the United States. Far-reaching new policy will be required to create a program serving everyone in need.

This study has limitations. First and foremost, the survey only included clinics in the Midwest, and therefore we cannot say with confidence that the results would hold true for clinics nationwide. Also, not all clinics to which the survey was sent responded. Although we have no evidence that responders differed from non-responders, we also have no detailed information on nonresponders (other than the state they are in), so we cannot say with confidence that the responders are representative of all clinics in the region. There are similar limitations because of nonresponse to certain questions. Some questions, such as the annual budget question, were skipped by a substantial number of clinics.

Finally, the survey did not explore many questions that may have policy implications. For example, we did not ask about the clinics' patient mix (with respect to age, sex, and race/ethnicity, for example), only about the age groups that the clinic served. We asked this question in order to confirm anecdotal information we had that suggested that clinics develop very specific eligibility criteria in order to serve age groups that have the most difficulty obtaining services elsewhere (in most cases adults under the age of 65). We also did not ask questions about how free clinics interact with other safety net providers.

Future research efforts on free clinics should focus on developing a more conclusive count of the number of free clinics nationwide and determining what the patient mix is and how many uninsured and underinsured people are being cared for at these clinics. These studies should examine how volunteer-based clinics interact with other safety net providers, including federally qualified health centers, public health clinics, hospitals, and the like. It is not clear yet whether free clinics most often exist in communities that are lacking other safety net providers or whether they simply provide another access point for patients in communities that have established resources. Most importantly, future analyses of safety net providers should recognize the important role that free clinics are playing in helping to patch the health care safety net.

Acknowledgment

We thank all of the clinics who participated in the survey and the members of the Free Clinics of the Great Lakes Region steering committee who contributed to the development of the survey and helped ensure that so many surveys were returned. The Robert Wood Johnson Foundation provides funding for Volunteers in Health Care. The W. K. Kellogg Foundation and Volunteers in Health Care have provided funding for the Free Clinics of the Great Lakes Region.

Notes

1. Ahmed SM, Maurana CA. Reaching out to the underserved: a collaborative partnership to provide health care. J Health Care Poor Underserved. 1999 May;10(2):157–68.

2. Ahmed SM, Maurana CA. Reaching out to the underserved: a successful volunteer model. Am J Public Health. 2000 Mar;90(3):439–40.

3. Ahmed SM, Maurana CA, Wymyslo TE. Lessons learned: developing a volunteer health care program for the underserved. J Health Care Poor Underserved. 2002 May;13(2):164–70.

4. Bera AB. Caring for the medically indigent and uninsured. Sacramento Medicine. 2000; 30:24–25.

5. Finke M. Free clinics: the simplicity and joy of practicing medicine in free clinics has been discovered by numerous Iowa physicians. Iowa Med. 1997 Oct;87(8):314–6.

6. Hansen HC. How to open a free medical clinic. C Med J. 1997 Nov–Dec;58(6):449–51.

7. Kelleher KC. Free clinics: a solution that can work . . . now! JAMA. 1991; 266:838–40.

8. Lucey D, Parker S. The Open Door Medical Clinic: a community response to the medically indigent. NC Med J. 1987;48(9):457–8.

9. Nadkarni MM, Philbrick JT. Free clinics and the uninsured: the increasing demands of chronic illness. J Health Care Poor Underserved. 2003 May;14(2):165–74.

10. Peterson L. Free clinic's volunteers help patch the safety net. AHA News. 1996 Jul 22;32(29):2.

11. Smego RA Jr., Costante J. An academic health center—community partnership: the Morgantown Health Right Free Clinic. Acad Med. 1996 Jun;71(6):613–21.

12. Zeitlin A. Charity begins at home: there was no free clinic in his town's inner city. So Robert Zufall, M.D., started his own. Diversion. 1997 Dec;25(14)133–6.

13. Schwartz JL. First national survey of free medical clinics: 1967–69. HSMHA Health Rep 1971 Sep;86(9):775–87.

14. Doll W. Whatever happened to the '60s free clinics? New Physician. 1985 Apr;34(3):8–11.

15. Scott HD, Bell J, Geller S, Thomas M. Physicians helping the underserved: the Reach Out Program. JAMA. 2000 Jan 5;283(1):99–104.

16. Free Clinic Foundation of America. National free clinic directory. 3rd ed. Roanoke, VA: Free Clinic Foundation of America, 2000.

17. Volunteers in Health Care. Volunteers in Health Care technical assistance database. Pawtucket, RI: Volunteers in Health Care, 2004.

18. Nelson MK. Vermont Coalition of Clinics for the Uninsured: year 2 evaluation. Middlebury, VT: Middlebury College, 1999.

19. Fed Reg 1998 Feb 24;63(36):9235–8.

20. Personal communication, Jane Zwiers, convener, Free Clinics of the Great Lakes Region (December 5, 2003).

21. Mills RJ, Bhandari S. Health insurance coverage in the United States: 2002. Washington, DC: U.S. Census Bureau, 2003.

Chapter 9
Impact of Providing a Medical Home to the Uninsured: Evaluation of a Statewide Program

James M. Gill
Heather Bittner Fagan
Bryan Townsend
Arch G. Mainous, III

Previous studies have shown that having a regular source of care (RSOC) is associated with higher quality of care, increased preventive care, and decreased emergency department (ED) visits.[1-4] While the majority of people in the United States have as RSOC, many do not. Barriers to having an RSOC include lack of insurance, low income, and unreliable transportation. Since low-income uninsured people represent a vulnerable population who are likely to be without an RSOC,[5-7] many programs aim to improve access and quality for the uninsured by providing an RSOC.

The Community Health Access Program (CHAP) is a statewide program intended to improve access to care for low-income, uninsured persons in Delaware who do not qualify for Medicaid or other insurance programs. CHAP's main mechanism of improving access is to provide an RSOC for eligible persons who do not already have one. The program operates in all hospitals in the state as well as all community health centers (CHCs), both federally qualified and non-qualified. In addition, it includes a volunteer network of private physicians (both primary care and specialists) who have agreed to take uninsured patients at a reduced fee, through a program run by the Medical Society of Delaware (the Voluntary Initiative Program, or VIP). Finally, CHAP is coordinated with the state Medicaid bureau.

People are eligible for CHAP if they are Delaware residents who are uninsured (or have insurance that does not cover basic health care services), are not eligible

James M. Gill, MD, MPH, is an associate professor at Jefferson Medical College, in Philadelphia, and president of Delaware Valley Outcomes Research, in Newark, Delaware. *Heather Bittner Fagan, MD, MPH,* is director of health services research at Christiana Care, in Wilmington, Delaware, and an associate professor at Thomas Jefferson University, in Philadelphia. *Bryan Townsend, MA, JD,* was a research assistant at Christiana Care and is currently an associate attorney with Morris James, in Wilmington. *Arch G. Mainous, III, PhD,* is director of research and fellowship director in the Department of Family Medicine at the Medical University of South Carolina.

for Medicaid or the State Children's Health Insurance Program (SCHIP), and have incomes below 200% of the federal poverty level. Eligible people are identified by a variety of mechanisms: hospital staff identify people who seek care in their emergency departments (EDs) or inpatient services who are uninsured and need an RSOC; other clients are identified at community sites or through the Medicaid bureau (after being denied Medicaid); potential clients may also refer themselves to the program by calling a toll-free number.

Once a client has been identified as eligible for CHAP, he/she is referred to one of the participating agencies (including the VIP network), which becomes his/her RSOC, based on geographic proximity. The CHAP care coordinator at this agency then helps the client get an appointment. The care coordinator also assists him or her with other health care needs, including transportation and referrals to specialists or ancillary services. The care coordinator also keeps track of CHAP enrollees who are assigned to his or her site and contacts those enrollees every six months to assess continuing eligibility.

The objective of CHAP is to provide an RSOC to its target population. The goal is to improve access to care and thereby increase use of primary and preventive care, reduce hospital ED visits and hospital admissions, and improve patient satisfaction with care. The purpose of this study was to determine the extent to which CHAP was achieving these goals. Specifically, we examined the impact of CHAP on preventive services, ED visits, hospitalizations, and satisfaction with care. We compared these indicators from before to six months after enrollment in CHAP.

Methods

A retrospective cohort design was used to determine changes in preventive services, ED visits, hospitalizations, and satisfaction with care from enrollment in CHAP to six months after enrollment. Data were obtained from CHAP enrollees through interviewer-administered surveys at each point in time. The survey was modeled after the national Behavioral Risk Factor Surveillance System (BRFSS) survey[8] and included questions on demographic characteristics, health insurance, access, utilization, preventive services, awareness of medical problems, satisfaction, and health status (see chapter appendix for full survey). The surveys were administered by trained interviewers at baseline and every six months thereafter. The interviews were conducted either in person (at EDs and CHCs) or via telephone, and were conducted in either English or Spanish, as the enrollees preferred. For this study, data were used from the baseline survey and the first six-month follow-up survey for each client.

People were eligible for this study if they were enrolled in CHAP anytime since the beginning of the program (June 2001), had been enrolled at least six months, had completed their first follow-up interview by January of 2003, and were re-enrolled in CHAP after their follow-up interview. We began with 1,596 individuals who were enrolled in CHAP for at least six months as of January of 2003. Of these 1,596 people, 211 had completed their re-enrollment process but were determined to be no longer eligible for CHAP; 110 of these had acquired insurance (predominantly Medicaid); 19 were over the income limit; and 82 were ineligible for other reasons. An additional 341 were in the process of eligibility determination but had not yet completed the re-enrollment process, and 17 had insufficient data for the researchers to determine eligibility. Two hundred and thirty two people (14.5%) did not respond after multiple attempts to contact them to determine eligibility; these people were considered disenrolled from the program. The remaining 795 people were included in this analysis.

For this study, we examined preventive care services, ED visits, hospital admissions, and satisfaction with care. Eight selected variables available within the CHAP data set were used as indicators for preventive care. These variables were analyzed within appropriate age and sex subgroups defined by the U.S. Preventive Services Task Force (USPSTF).[9] The list included cholesterol tests, mammograms, breast exams, Pap tests, influenza and pneumococcal immunizations, sigmoidoscopy, colonoscopy, and fecal occult blood tests (FOBT). For each test, we used the most current USPSTF guideline that was available as of the beginning of the study period (see table 9.2 for specific applicable ages, sex, and intervals.) Since the primary intervention of CHAP was to provide a regular source of care (RSOC), we conducted an additional analysis that stratified these outcome variables within two CHAP subgroups: those reporting an RSOC and those not reporting an RSOC after six months of enrollment in CHAP.

We analyzed three additional outcome variables: ED visits, hospital admissions, and satisfaction with health care. The details on how these were measured are discussed below.

Data analysis

For the primary outcome variables (preventive services, hospital admissions and ED visits, and satisfaction), we examined the change in proportions from baseline to follow-up. All variables were analyzed as dichotomous variables. For preventive services, we compared whether or not eligible persons were up to date with the service at each time period. For ED visits and hospital admissions, we compared whether or not the person had an ED visit or admission in the previous six months. For satisfaction, we compared the proportion who rated their satisfaction as excellent with those who rated it as less than excellent. All outcomes are compared using the McNemar's test for paired samples, with $p < 0.05$ as the cutoff for statistical significance.

Results

The characteristics of the study population are shown in table 9.1. Study participants were predominantly young adults (66% ages 18–39), female (71%), noncitizens (82%), and Hispanic (79%). A small proportion (3.2%) had a diagnosis of diabetes, and another small proportion (4.1%) had a diagnosis of asthma. These rates are lower than the rates for people who were not re-enrolled in CHAP, of whom 6.8% had diabetes and 7.7% had asthma.

Table 9.1

Demographic characteristics of CHAP Population
(*n*=795)

	Number	%
Age		
Under 18	85	10.7
18–39	523	65.9
40–64	172	21.7
65+	14	1.8
1 missing		
Gender		
Male	227	28.6
Female	568	71.4
County		
New Castle	556	69.9
Kent	56	7.0
Sussex	183	23.0
Citizenship		
U.S. Citizen	144	18.1
Noncitizen	651	81.9
Race/ethnicity		
White	70	8.9
Black	75	9.5
Hispanic	620	78.9
Other	21	2.7
9 missing		
Employment		
Employed	402	52.6
Unemployed	273	35.7
Other	90	11.7
30 missing		

There were large and significant increases in all measures of cancer screening for women in the recommended age categories, as shown in table 9.2; the proportion having had the preventive service in the recommended time period increased for Pap tests (60% to 89%, $p<0.001$), breast exams (48% to 69%, $p<0.001$) and mammograms (43% to 56%, $p<0.01$). There were also large and significant increases for cholesterol testing (40% to 59%, $p<0.001$). There were smaller improvements for influenza immunizations (21% to 28%, $p<0.01$) and sigmoidoscopy (14% to 21%, $p<0.05$). The changes were not significant for pneumococcal vaccinations or FOBT.

From before to six months after CHAP enrollment, the percentage of people who reported having a regular source of care increased from 19.8% to 59.8%. The proportion with a regular doctor/provider increased from 13.7% to 29.5%.

Table 9.2

Preventive services before and after CHAP

Service/test	Baseline number	%	Follow-up number	%
Cholesterol[a] (n=225)	90	39.6	147	58.8***
Mammogram[b] (n=110)	48	42.9	67	56.3**
Breast exam[c] (n=112)	56	48.3	83	68.6***
Pap smear[d] (n=457)	284	60.0	426	89.1***
Flu shot[e] (n=132)	28	21.1	38	27.7**
Pneumonia vaccination[f] (n=41)	8	18.6	11	25.0
Sigmoidoscopy[g] (n=97)	14	14.1	22	21.2*
Blood stool[h] (n=95)	13	13.3	19	18.3

[a]Cholesterol test within past five years (age 35 years or greater)
[b]Mammogram within past two years (females age 40 years or greater)
[c]Breast exam within past two years (females age 40 years or greater)
[d]Pap smear within past three years (females age 18 or greater who have not had a hysterectomy)
[e]Flu shot in past year (age 50 years or greater or with diabetes or asthma)
[f]Pneumonia vaccination ever (age 65 years or greater or with diabetes)
[g]Sigmoidoscopy within past 5 years (age 50 years or greater)
[h]Blood stool test within past year (age 50 years or greater)
*$p<0.05$ for change from baseline to follow-up
**$p<0.01$ for change from baseline to follow-up
***$p<0.001$ for change for baseline to follow-up

Since not all individuals reported a regular source of care, we re-examined the preventive care outcomes detailed above to determine if those reporting an RSOC were the group predominantly accounting for higher rates of preventive care. As shown in table 9.3, those who reported having an RSOC at their six-month follow-up had higher rates for all preventive care measures except pneumococcal vaccine and cholesterol screening.

The proportion of people having an ED visit in the preceding six months decreased from 10% for the six-month period prior to CHAP enrollment to 4% for the six-month period after CHAP ($p<0.001$). The number hospitalized did not change (21 and 22 people in the six months before and after CHAP, respectively). Most hospitalizations were for unavoidable conditions, such as pregnancy and surgery. The percentage who rated their satisfaction with health care as *excellent* increased from 9% to 46% ($p<0.001$), while the percentage who rated their health care as *poor* or *fair* decreased from 9.5% to 3.7%.

Discussion

This study demonstrates that Delaware's Community Health Access Program (CHAP) has achieved many of its objectives. For people enrolled in the first year of the program, there were improvements in access to a regular provider, increases in

Table 9.3

Differences for individuals reporting vs. not reporting a regular source of care at the end of the study

	Patients with a regular source of care (*n*=469)	Patients without a regular source of care (*n*=326)
Age		
Under 18	11.5% (*n*=54)	9.5% (*n*=31)
18–39	62.5% (*n*=293)	70.6% (*n*=230)
40–64	25.4% (*n*=119)	16.3% (*n*=53)
65+	0.4% (*n*=2)	3.7% (*n*=12)
Sex		
Male	32.0% (*n*=150)	23.6% (*n*=77)
Female	68.0% (*n*=319)	76.4% (*n*=249)
Preventive services		
Cholesterol	55.0% (90/158)[a]	61.9% (57/92)
Mammogram	68.8% (55/80)	30.8% (12/39)
Breast exam	82.3% (65/79)	42.9% (18/42)
Pap smear	91.5% (258/282)	84.1% (191/227)
Flu shot	31.4% (27/86)	21.6% (11/51)
Pneumonia vaccination	16.7% (4/24)	35.0% (7/20)
Colonoscopy/sigmoidoscopy	27.2% (18/65)	10.3% (4/39)
Fecal occult blood testing	26.2% (17/65)	5.1% (2/39)

*Number of individuals who had the test divided by the number who should have had the test, according to guidelines in table 9.2.

most preventive services, decreases in ED use, and improvements in satisfaction with care.

These positive results are likely related to access to a regular source of care (RSOC). The CHAP population at baseline had a lower rate of having an RSOC than the general rate for the low-income uninsured in Delaware (which BRFSS data suggest is about 70–80%). Within the CHAP population, the percentage of people who reported having an RSOC and the proportion with a regular provider more than doubled six months after enrollment. Furthermore, the rates of completing most preventive services was much higher for the subgroup who reported having an RSOC after being in the program for six months. These findings are important in that the key objective of the CHAP program is improving access to care by providing an RSOC. Perhaps more importantly, CHAP participants are more likely than they were before enrolling in CHAP to have a regular doctor, which is important for continuity of care. Many patients did not report an RSOC or a regular doctor; this is because not all individuals offered an RSOC will avail themselves of it (due to a variety of barriers, including lack of perceived need and transportation). However, the increases in the rates of having an RSOC and having a regular doctor are important positive effects. Earlier research has shown that continuity is associated with fewer ED visits[10–12] and hospitalizations,[13] higher immunization rates,[14] and improved recognition of medical problems.[15–17] Furthermore, earlier research has shown that having an RSOC without such a personal provider does not have the same positive outcomes.[18] Our results show that the Delaware CHAP is fostering not only access to an RSOC but also continuity with an individual provider.

Given the improvements in access to a regular provider, it is not surprising that such improvement translated into a decrease in ED utilization, a finding that is consistent with previous studies showing continuity to be associated with fewer ED visits[10] and that providing Medicaid patients with an RSOC results in reductions in ED use.[1] The increased satisfaction with care also makes intuitive sense and is consistent with previous studies.[19,20] Finally, the improvements in cholesterol screening and breast and cervical cancer screening are consistent with previous studies on providing an RSOC.[2]

It may come as a surprise that not all preventive services increased after enrollment. For example, colorectal cancer (CRC) screening was very low at baseline, and increased only minimally. There are several possible reasons for this. First, it could be that patients are less educated about CRC screening than they are about breast and cervical cancer screening. If so, they may be less likely to request screening for CRC and may be less likely to adhere to their physicians' recommendations about it. There are also relevant differences in payment arrangements among preventive services for uninsured patients. For example, breast and cervical cancer screening were paid for at the time of this study by the Centers for Disease Control's national program,[21] while CRC screening was not.

Hospitalizations did not decrease after enrollment in CHAP and, given the young age of the CHAP population, this is not surprising. Closer analysis of the data reveals that the majority of hospitalizations were appropriate and unavoidable. When patients were asked at baseline the reason for their most recent hospitalization, 34% reported childbirth/pregnancy, 23% reported surgery, and another 13% reported trauma (data not reported). These conditions are not likely to be affected by having an RSOC. Enrollees in CHAP reported few hospitalizations for conditions that are usually considered ambulatory-care sensitive, such as asthma (4 persons) and diabetes (1 person), probably because only small percentages of the CHAP population had these illnesses (4.1% and 3.2%, respectively). Note that these rates are lower than the rates for the general population of low-income uninsured persons in Delaware. According to data from Delaware BRFSS, 18% of low-income uninsured persons have asthma, and 5% have diabetes. The lower rates for our CHAP population may signify a healthier population, or it may signify underdiagnosis due to the CHAP group not having regular sources of care.

This study has several limitations. First, since it was a retrospective cohort study with no control group, it is difficult to demonstrate causation. Improvements in preventive care or ED use could be due to selection bias (i.e., people who want to increase their preventive care use and decrease ED use are more likely to seek out a program that provides them with an RSOC). Furthermore, there is a potential Hawthorne effect, where people who are asked questions about their health care use may be prone to report outcomes that they perceive to be desired by their physician. Even if the improvements are due to the CHAP program, it is difficult to determine which components of the program are responsible for the effect. Improvements may, for example, be due to obtaining an RSOC or to the attention paid to this energetic and aggressive program.

There are also limitations to the validity of self-reported survey results. When patients reported on the last time they received a preventive service or visited the ED, they were relying on recall that might not always have been accurate; this issue was somewhat attenuated by the use of standardized questions from national surveys (i.e., BRFSS). Finally, there are limits to how the results can be generalized. Our population consisted predominantly of young women who were Hispanic noncitizens. Although their documentation status is unknown, we believe that most were undocumented; the demographic profile of CHAP enrollees is shaped in large part by the fact that low-income adults who are citizens or legal residents are generally eligible for Medicaid. Two of the CHAP health homes attracted a high proportion of Hispanic persons, and this also shaped the demographic profile of the average enrollee. These health homes are known for culturally competent care of the Hispanic population and were particularly successful in recruiting people into CHAP. While the success of CHAP in targeting this hard-to-reach population is a positive attribute, it must be borne in mind that the results of this study may not be generalized to other vulnerable populations. More recent recruitment efforts indicate that approximately 54% of CHAP enrollees are noncitizens; this reflects active recruitment of other low-income uninsured populations.

CHAP in the context of the health care safety net

It is important to note that CHAP is one part of the larger effort to improve the health care safety net in the state of Delaware. The program recruited participants through established health homes, hospitals, emergency rooms, the Delaware Medical Society, and community outreach. There are other programs that assist the low-income uninsured to get recommended medical care, although each of them differs from CHAP in its approach. For example, the Screening for Life program (which is Delaware's version of the Breast and Cervical Cancer Screening Program of the Centers for Disease Control) covers only specific preventive services (breast, cervical, and colorectal cancer screening) and SCHIP provides insurance for a specific age group (children), while other programs provide direct services at local health care sites for the uninsured in their geographic area. The Community Healthcare Access Program aims to provide a more comprehensive service through referral to health homes and through the coordination of already existing services. The extent to which these various programs interact and complement each other is unclear; however, we plan to explore this interaction in future studies.

Comparative analysis of the BRFSS data for Delaware indicates that CHAP is effectively reaching its target population. Delaware's 2002 BRFSS data show approximately 24,000 low-income people without insurance and, within that group, just under 5,000 who do not have a health home or have difficulty accessing care. Thus far, over 3,000 uninsured persons have been referred to an RSOC through CHAP, and another 500 have been successfully referred for Medicaid enrollment, which means that CHAP is reaching about 60% of its target number. Like CHAP participants, the Delaware low-income uninsured tend to be younger and are more likely to be female than the general population of adults. However, the predominance of Hispanic people in CHAP is not matched by a proportionate predominance of Hispanics among all of Delaware's low-income uninsured. The preventive care measures at baseline for the CHAP population were lower than those for the general uninsured population of Delaware, which further demonstrates the effectiveness of CHAP in reaching vulnerable populations.

Because of CHAP's demonstrated success in reaching the target population and in improving care for clients, the state of Delaware has decided to continue the program, which was originally funded by a grant from Health Resources and Services Administration of the U.S. Department of Health and Human Services and later augmented by tobacco settlement money. The state has recently decided to use state funds to continue the program, as part of its plan to improve the safety net for the uninsured in Delaware. The state has augmented the program by including mechanisms for referral to specialty care and for laboratory and imaging studies at a reduced cost. It also has developed mechanisms for CHAP to interact with other programs for the uninsured, such as SCHIP and the Breast and Cervical Cancer Early Detection Program of the Centers for Disease Control.

In summary, we found that a program providing an RSOC to low-income, uninsured adults had beneficial effects on preventive screening and rates of ED use. These findings have significant implications for improving health care for the uninsured. As the number of uninsured people steadily rises in the United States, CHAP can serve as a model that other states may use to improve health care for their uninsured populations. While several states have implemented programs to increase health care coverage on a statewide level, many such efforts have been impeded by current fiscal problems in many states. In fact, many states have attempted to limit eligibility for Medicaid and other programs in order to save money. Given these fiscal barriers, CHAP represents one way to improve care for the uninsured without requiring a new and large allocation of state funds. Rather than providing new services or new insurance coverage, CHAP focuses on coordinating services that already exist. Such a program requires only limited funding for administration and coordination and therefore is sustainable in times of budget crunch. Delaware's Community Healthcare Access Program represents a successful and financially sustainable model for states seeking to improve health care for their poor and uninsured populations.

Acknowledgments

We would like to thank Betsy Wheeler, Gina Perez, and Joy Blasier for their assistance with the study and with survey development and implementation. We would also like to thank Cheryl Mongillo and Marie Littlefield for their assistance with manuscript preparation. This study was funded by a grant from the Delaware Health Care Commission.

Appendix

CHAP Survey Instrument

This interview will only take a short time, and all the information obtained in this study will be confidential.

Name: _____
First   Last   MI

Home Address:_____

City _____ State _____ Zip Code _____

Daytime Phone Number: _____

Date of Birth: _____

Interviewer Name: _____

Location: _____

Date of Interview: _____

Section 1. Health Insurance

1.1   Do you have any kind of health care coverage, including health insurance, prepaid plans such as HMOs, or government plans such as Medicare?

      ☐ a. Yes

      ☐ b. No.. *Go to question 1.4*

      ☐ c. Don't know / Not sure...................................... *Go to question 2.1*

      ☐ d. Refused .... *Go to question 2.1*

1.2   What type of health care coverage do you use to pay for most of your medical care? Is it coverage through:

    Please read and check all that apply.

      ☐ a. Your employer

      ☐ b. Someone else's employer

      ☐ c. A plan that you or someone else buys on your own

      ☐ d. Medicare

      ☐ e. Medicaid or Medical Assistance

      ☐ f. The military, CHAMPUS, TriCare, or the VA

      ☐ g. The Indian Health Service

      ☐ h. Some other source

      ☐ i. None

    Do not read these responses.

      ☐ Don't know / Not sure

      ☐ Refused

1.3   Is there a cost factor associated with your insurance that keeps you from using it?

      ☐ a. Yes

      ☐ b. No

If it is determined at this point that this person will not be eligible for CAP (based on CAP policies and procedures), stop the interview here. Otherwise, go to question 2.1.

1.4   About how long has it been since you had health care coverage?
       Read only if necessary.
       ☐ a. Within the past 6 months (1 to 6 months ago)
       ☐ b. Within the past year (6 to 12 months ago)
       ☐ c. Within the past 2 years (1 to 2 years ago)
       ☐ d. Within the past 5 years (2 to 5 years ago)
       ☐ e. 5 or more years ago
       ☐ f. Never
       ☐ Don't know / Not sure
       ☐ Refused

1.5   What is the main reason you are without health care coverage?
       Read only if necessary.
       ☐ a. Lost job or changed employers
       ☐ b. Spouse or parent lost job or changed employers [includes any person who had been providing insurance prior to job loss or change]
       ☐ c. Became divorced or separated
       ☐ d. Spouse or parent died
       ☐ e. Became ineligible because of age or because left school
       ☐ f. Employer doesn't offer or stopped offering coverage
       ☐ g. Cut back to part time or became temporary employee
       ☐ h. Benefits from employer or former employer ran out
       ☐ i. Couldn't afford to pay the premiums
       ☐ j. Insurance company refused coverage
       ☐ k. Lost Medicaid or Medical Assistance eligibility
       ☐ l. Other
       ☐ Don't know / Not sure
       ☐ Refused

Section 2. Demographics

2.1   Are you a United States Citizen?
       ☐ Yes
       ☐ No

2.2   What is your race?
       Would you say:
       Please read.
       ☐ a. White
       ☐ b. Black
       ☐ c. Asian, Pacific Islander
       ☐ d. American Indian, Alaska Native
       ☐ e. Other: *[specify]*

Do not read these responses.
- ☐ Don't know / Not sure
- ☐ Refused

2.3. Are you of Spanish or Hispanic origin?
- ☐ a. Yes
- ☐ b. No
- ☐ Don't know / Not sure
- ☐ Refused

2.4. Are you currently:
Please read.
- ☐ a. Employed for wages
- ☐ b. Self-employed..*Go to Question 2.6*
- ☐ c. Out of work for more than 1 year............................*Go to Question 2.6*
- ☐ d. Out of work for less than 1 year.............................*Go to Question 2.6*
- ☐ e. Homemaker...*Go to Question 2.6*
- ☐ f. Student...*Go to Question 2.6*
- ☐ g. Retired...*Go to Question 2.6*
- ☐ h. Unable to work..*Go to Question 2.6*
- ☐ Refused..*Go to Question 2.6*

2.5 What is your employment status?
- ☐ Part time (Less than 20 hours per week)
- ☐ Part time (Greater than or equal to 20 hours per week)
- ☐ Full time

Are you considered:
- ☐ Permanent
- ☐ Temporary
- ☐ Seasonal

2.6 What is your household size?
Number of adults (over 18 years of age): _____
Number of children: _____

2.7 Is your annual household income from all sources:
(All sources includes income from other household members, child support, Social Security, and all public assistance.)
Read as appropriate.

If respondent refuses at any income level, code refused.
- ☐ a. Less than $25,000.................................*If "no," ask e; if "yes," ask b*
  ($20,000 to less than $25,000)
- ☐ b. Less than $20,000..............................*If "no," code a; if "yes," ask c*
  ($15,000 to less than $20,000)
- ☐ c. Less than $15,000...............................*If "no," code b; if "yes," ask d*
  ($10,000 to less than $15,000)
- ☐ d. Less than $10,000...*If "no," code c*

    ☐ e. Less than $35,000. . . . . *If "no," ask f*
        ($25,000 to less than $35,000)
    ☐ f. Less than $50,000. . . . . *If "no," ask g*
        ($35,000 to less than $50,000)
    ☐ g. Less than $75,000. . . . . *If "no," code h*
        ($50,000 to $75,000)
    ☐ h. $75,000 or more
    Do not read these responses.
    ☐ Don't know / Not sure
    ☐ Refused

Section 3. Access

3.1   Was there a time during the last 12 months when you needed to see a doctor but could not because of any of the following reasons? *(Please check all that apply.)*
    ☐ Cost
    ☐ Inconvenient hours
    ☐ Transportation
    ☐ Language barriers

3.2   Is there one particular clinic, health center, doctor's office, or other place that you usually go to if you are sick or need advice about your health?
    ☐ a. Yes
    ☐ b. No. . . . . *Go to Question 4.1*
    ☐ Don't know / Not sure. . . . . *Go to Question 4.1*
    ☐ Refused . . . . *Go to Question 4.1*

3.3   What kind of place is it?
    Would you say:
    Please read.
    ☐ a. A doctor's office or HMO
    ☐ b. A clinic or health center
    ☐ c. A hospital outpatient department
    ☐ d. A hospital emergency room.
    ☐ e. An urgent care center
    ☐ f. Some other kind of place
    Do not read these responses.
    ☐ Don't know / Not sure
    ☐ Refused

3.4   Is there one particular doctor or health professional you usually see at this place?
    ☐ a. Yes
    ☐ b. No. . . . . *Go to Question 4.1*
    ☐ Don't know / Not sure. . . . . *Go to Question 4.1*
    ☐ Refused . . . . *Go to Question 4.1*
    If it is determined at this point that this person will not be eligible for CAP (based on CAP policies and procedures), stop the interview here. Otherwise, go to question 3.5

3.5   How long have you been seeing this doctor?
    ☐ a. Less than 6 months
    ☐ b. 6 months up to 1 year
    ☐ c. 1–2 years
    ☐ d. 3–5 years
    ☐ e. 6–10 years
    ☐ f. more than 10 years

3.6   In the past 6 months when you needed medical advice or treatment, how often did you see someone other than your regular doctor?
    ☐ a. Never . . . . *Go to Question 4.1*
    ☐ b. Sometimes
    ☐ c. Usually
    ☐ d. Always
    ☐ e. Did not seek care in last 6 months . . . . *Go to Question 4.1*

3.7   Why did you see someone other than your doctor for medical advice or treatment?
    ☐ a. Couldn't pay so he/she would not see me
    ☐ b. More convenient to use someone else
    ☐ c. Couldn't pay so chose to go to another provider
    ☐ d. Other

Section 4. Utilization

4.1   When was the last time you went to a hospital Emergency Department for care?
    If interview is being conducted in an Emergency Department, do not count today's visit in the response.
    Read only if necessary.
    ☐ a. Within the past 6 months (0 to 6 months) . . . . *Go to Question 4.2*
    ☐ b. Within the past year (6 to 12 months ago) . . . . *Go to Question 4.3*
    ☐ c. Within the past 2 years (1 to 2 years ago) . . . . *Go to Question 4.3*
    ☐ d. Within the past 5 years (2 to 5 years ago) . . . . *Go to Question 4.3*
    ☐ e. 5 or more years ago . . . . *Go to Question 4.3*
    ☐ Don't know / Not sure. . . . . *Go to Question 4.3*
    ☐ Never . . . . *Go to Question 4.4*
    ☐ Refused . . . . *Go to Question 4.4*

4.2   How many times have you been seen in a hospital Emergency Department in the past 6 months?
    If interview is being conducted in an Emergency Department, do not count today's visit in the response.
    Number_____

4.3   What was the reason for your last visit to the Emergency Department?
    If interview is being conducted in an Emergency Department, do not count today's visit in the response.

4.4   When was the last time you were admitted to the hospital?
      Read only if necessary.
    ☐ a. Within the past 6 months (0 to 6 months ago)..................*Go to Question 4.5*
    ☐ b. Within the past year (6 to 12 months ago) ....*Go to Question 4.6*
    ☐ c. Within the past 2 years (1 to 2 years ago) ....*Go to Question 4.6*
    ☐ d. Within the past 5 years (2 to 5 years ago) ....*Go to Question 4.6*
    ☐ e. 5 or more years ago ....*Go to Question 4.6*
    ☐ Don't know / Not sure.......................................*Go to Question 4.6*
    ☐ Never ....*Go to Question 4.7*
    ☐ Refused ....*Go to Question 4.7*

4.5   How many times have you been hospitalized in the last 6 months?
    Number ——————————

4.6   What was the reason for your last hospitalization?

4.7   About how long has it been since you last visited a doctor for a routine checkup?
    (*A routine checkup is a general physical exam, not an exam for a specific injury, illness, or condition.*)
    If interview is being conducted in a health care facility, do not count today's visit.
    Read only if necessary.
    ☐ a. Within the past year (1 to 12 months ago)
    ☐ b. Within the past 2 years (1 to 2 years ago)
    ☐ c. Within the past 5 years (2 to 5 years ago)
    ☐ d. 5 or more years ago
    ☐ Don't know / Not sure
    ☐ Never
    ☐ Refused

Section 5. Health Problems

5.1   Would you say that in general your health is:
    Please read.
    ☐ a. Excellent
    ☐ b. Very good
    ☐ c. Good
    ☐ d. Fair
    or
    ☐ e. Poor
    Do not read these responses.
    ☐ Don't know / Not Sure
    ☐ Refused

5.2   Have you ever been told by a doctor that you have diabetes?
    If "Yes" and female, ask "Was this only when you were pregnant?"
    ☐ a. Yes, but today was the first time
    ☐ b. Yes, prior to today's visit

☐ c. Yes, but told only during pregnancy
☐ d. No
☐ Don't know / Not sure
☐ Refused

5.3   Did a doctor ever tell you that you had asthma?
☐ a. Yes, but today was the first time . . . . *Go to Question 5.5*
☐ b. Yes, prior to today's visit
☐ c. No . . . . *Go to Question 5.5*
☐ Don't know / Not sure . . . . *Go to Question 5.5*
☐ Refused . . . . *Go to Question 5.5*

5.4   Do you still have asthma?
☐ a. Yes
☐ b. No
☐ Don't know / Not sure
☐ Refused

5.5   Have you ever been told by a doctor, nurse, or other health professional that you have high blood pressure?
☐ a. Yes, but today was the first time
☐ b. Yes, prior to today's visit
☐ c. No
☐ Don't know / Not sure
☐ Refused

5.6   Blood cholesterol is a fatty substance found in the blood. Have you ever had your blood cholesterol checked?
☐ a. Yes, but today was the first time . . . . *Go to Question 5.8*
☐ b. Yes, prior to today's visit
☐ c. No . . . . *Go to Question 5.9*
☐ Don't know / Not sure . . . . *Go to Question 5.9*
☐ Refused . . . . *Go to Question 5.9*

5.7   About how long has it been since you last had your blood cholesterol checked?
If interview is being conducted in a health care facility, do not count today's visit.
Read only if necessary.
☐ a. Within the past year (1 to 12 months ago)
☐ b. Within the past 2 years (1 to 2 years ago)
☐ c. Within the past 5 years (2 to 5 years ago)
☐ d. 5 or more years ago
☐ Don't know / Not sure
☐ Refused

5.8   Have you ever been told by a doctor or other health professional that your blood cholesterol is high?
☐ a. Yes, but today was the first time
☐ b. Yes, prior to today's visit
☐ c. No

☐ Don't know / Not sure
☐ Refused

If male, skip to Question 5.16

5.9   A mammogram is an x-ray of each breast to look for breast cancer. Have you ever had a mammogram?
☐ a. Yes, but today was the first time . . . . *Go to Question 5.11*
☐ b. Yes, prior to today's visit
☐ c. No. . . . . *Go to Question 5.11*
☐ Don't know / Not sure. . . . . *Go to Question 5.11*
☐ Refused . . . . *Go to Question 5.11*

5.10   How long has it been since you had your last mammogram?
If interview is being conducted in a health care facility, do not count today's visit.
Read only if necessary.
☐ a. Within the past year (1 to 12 months ago)
☐ b. Within the past 2 years (1 to 2 years ago)
☐ c. Within the past 3 years (2 to 3 years ago)
☐ d. Within the past 5 years (3 to 5 years ago)
☐ e. 5 or more years ago
☐ Don't know / Not sure
☐ Refused

5.11   A clinical breast exam is when a doctor, nurse, or other health professional feels the breast for lumps. Have you ever had a clinical breast exam?
☐ a. Yes, but today was the first time . . . . *Go to Question 5.13*
☐ b. Yes, prior to today's visit
☐ c. No. . . . . *Go to Question 5.13*
☐ Don't know / Not sure . . . . *Go to Question 5.13*
☐ Refused . . . . *Go to Question 5.13*

5.12   How long has it been since your last breast exam?
If interview is being conducted in a health care facility, do not count today's visit.
Read only if necessary.
☐ a. Within the past year (1 to 12 months ago)
☐ b. Within the past 2 years (1 to 2 years ago)
☐ c. Within the past 3 years (2 to 3 years ago)
☐ d. Within the past 5 years (3 to 5 years ago)
☐ e. 5 or more years ago
☐ Don't know / Not sure
☐ Refused

5.13   A Pap smear is a test for cancer of the cervix. Have you ever had a Pap smear?
☐ a. Yes, but today was the first time . . . . *Go to Question 5.15*
☐ b. Yes, prior to today's visit
☐ c. No. . . . . *Go to Question 5.15*
☐ Don't know / Not sure . . . . *Go to Question 5.15*
☐ Refused . . . . *Go to Question 5.15*

5.14   How long has it been since you had your last Pap smear?

If interview is being conducted in a health care facility, do not count today's visit.
Read only if necessary.

- ☐ a. Within the past year (1 to 12 months ago)
- ☐ b. Within the past 2 years (1 to 2 years ago)
- ☐ c. Within the past 3 years (2 to 3 years ago)
- ☐ d. Within the past 5 years (3 to 5 years ago)
- ☐ e. 5 or more years ago
- ☐ Don't know / Not sure
- ☐ Refused

5.15   Have you had a hysterectomy?

A hysterectomy is an operation to remove the uterus (womb).

- ☐ a. Yes
- ☐ b. No
- ☐ Don't know / Not sure
- ☐ Refused

5.16   During the past 12 months, have you had a flu shot?

- ☐ a. Yes, but today was the first time
- ☐ b. Yes, prior to today's visit
- ☐ c. No
- ☐ Don't know / Not sure
- ☐ Refused

5.17   Have you ever had a pneumonia vaccination?

- ☐ a. Yes, but today was the first time
- ☐ b. Yes, prior to today's visit
- ☐ c. No
- ☐ Don't know / Not sure
- ☐ Refused

5.18   A sigmoidoscopy, or colonoscopy, is when a tube is inserted in the rectum to view the bowel for signs of cancer and other health problems. Have you ever had this exam?

- ☐ a. Yes, but today was the first time .... *Go to Question 5.20*
- ☐ b. Yes, prior to today's visit
- ☐ c. No... *Go to Question 5.20*
- ☐ Don't know / Not sure...................................... *Go to Question 5.20*
- ☐ Refused .... *Go to Question 5.20*

5.19   When did you have your last sigmoidoscopy, or colonoscopy?

If interview is being conducted in a health care facility, do not count today's visit.
Read only if necessary.

- ☐ a. Within the past year (1 to 12 months ago)
- ☐ b. Within the past 2 years (1 to 2 years ago)
- ☐ c. Within the past 5 years (2 to 5 years ago)
- ☐ d. 5 or more years ago
- ☐ Don't know / Not sure
- ☐ Refused

5.20   A blood stool test is when the stool is examined to determine if it contains blood. This can be done by a doctor or other health professional as part of a rectal exam, or it can be done at home using a special home kit. Have you ever had a blood stool test done?

☐ a. Yes, but today was the first time . . . . *Go to Question 6.1*

☐ b. Yes, prior to today's visit

☐ c. No. . . . . *Go to Question 6.1*

☐ Don't know / Not sure. . . . . *Go to Question 6.1*

☐ Refused . . . . *Go to Question 6.1*

5.21   When was the last time you had a blood stool test?
If interview is being conducted in a health care facility, do not count today's visit.
Read only if necessary.

☐ a. Within the past year (1 to 12 months ago)

☐ b. Within the past 2 years (1 to 2 years ago)

☐ c. Within the past 5 years (2 to 5 years ago)

☐ d. 5 or more years ago

☐ Don't know / Not sure

☐ Refused

Section 6. Satisfaction

6.1   How would you rate your satisfaction with your overall health care?
Would you say:
Please read.

☐ a. Excellent

☐ b. Very good

☐ c. Good

☐ d. Fair

☐ e. Poor

Do not read these responses.

☐ Not applicable / don't use any health services

☐ Don't know / Not sure

☐ Refused

Notes

1.   Gill JM, Diamond JJ. Effect of primary care referral on emergency department use: evaluation of a statewide Medicaid program. Fam Med. 1996;28(3):178–82.

2.   Gill JM, McClellan SA. The impact of referral to a primary physician on cervical cancer screening. Am J Public Health. 2001;91(3):451–4.

3.   Xu KT. Usual source of care in preventive service use: a regular doctor versus a regular site. Health Serv Res. 2002;37(6):1509–29.

4.   Koopman RJ, Mainous AG 3rd, Baker R, et al. Continuity of care and recognition of diabetes, hypertension, and hypercholesterolemia. Arch Intern Med. 2003;163(11): 1357–61.

5.   Rask KJ, Williams MV, Parker RM, et al. Obstacles predicting lack of a regular provider and delays in seeking care for patients at an urban public hospital. JAMA. 1994;271(24):1931–3.

6.   Kogan MD, Alexander GR, Teitelbaum MA, et al. The effect of gaps in health insurance on continuity of a regular source of care among preschool-aged children in the United States. JAMA. 1995;274(18):1429–35.

7. Lave JR, Keane CR, Lin CJ, et al. Impact of a children's health insurance program on newly enrolled children. JAMA. 1998;279(22):1820–5.

8. Centers for Disease Control and Prevention. 2003 Behavioral Risk Factor Surveillance System State Questionnaire, Vol. 1.5. United States Department of Health and Human Services, 2002.

9. U.S. Preventive Services Task Force. Guide to clinical preventive services: report of the U.S. Preventive Services Task Force, 2nd ed. Baltimore, MD: Williams & Wilkins, 1996.

10. Gill JM, Mainous AG 3rd, Nsereko M. The effect of continuity of care on emergency department use. Arch Fam Med. 2000;9(4):333–8.

11. Sweeney KG, Gray DP. Patients who do not receive continuity of care from their general practitioner—are they a vulnerable group? Br J Gen Pract. 1995;45(392):133–5.

12. Cristakis DA, Wright JA, Koepsell TD, et al. Is greater continuity of care associated with less emergency department utilization? Pediatrics. 1999;103(4, pt. 1):738–42.

13. Gill JM, Mainous AG 3rd. The role of provider continuity in preventing hospitalizations. Arch Fam Med. 1998;7(4):352–7.

14. Christakis DA, Mell L, Wright J, et al. The association between greater continuity of care and timely measles-mumps-rubella vaccination. Am J Public Health. 2000;90(6):962–5.

15. Becker MH, Drachman RH, Kirscht JP. Continuity of pediatrician: new support for an old shibboleth. J Pediatr. 1974;84(4):599–605.

16. Steinwachs DM, Yaffe R. Assessing the timeliness of ambulatory medical care. Am J Public Health. 1978;68(6):547–56.

17. Blankfield RP, Kelly RB, Alemagno SA, et al. Continuity of care in a family practice residency program. Impact on physician satisfaction. J Fam Pract. 1990;31(1):69–73.

18. Mainous AG 3rd, Gill JM. The importance of continuity of care in the likelihood of future hospitalizations: is site of care equal to a primary clinician? Am J Public Health. 1998;88(10):1539–41.

19. Becker MH, Drachman RH, Kirscht JP. A field experiment to evaluate various outcomes of continuity of physician care. Am J Public Health. 1974;64(11):1062–70.

20. Wasson JH, Sauvigne AE, Mogielnicki RP, et al. Continuity of outpatient medical care in elderly men. A randomized trial. JAMA. 1984;252(17):2413–7.

21. Anonymous. From the Centers for Disease Control and Prevention. Strategies for providing follow-up and treatment services in the National Breast and Cervical Cancer Early Detection Program—United States, 1997. JAMA. 1998;279(24):1941–2.

Chapter 10

Characteristics of Patients at Three Free Clinics

Rachel Mott-Keis
Linda Gifford DeGeus
Suzanne Cashman
Judith Savageau

First seen in the 1960s,[1,2] free clinics were established to provide medical care for individuals, particularly those who were underinsured or uninsured, and were unable to obtain needed care elsewhere. Free clinics are part of an extensive patchwork safety net system that attempts to care for financially disenfranchised people. According to the Free Clinic Foundation of America, a *free clinic*, which by definition does not charge for its services, is a private, community-based health care clinic for families of the working poor and the retired.[3] In 2000, the Free Clinic Foundation of America listed over 300 registered free clinics nationwide; the actual number is far higher because many free clinics are not registered. According to Volunteers in Health Care, a national resource center supporting programs that serve the uninsured, in 2004, more than 1,000 free clinics were functioning in the United States.[4] Because there is no organized body tracking or monitoring free clinics, it is difficult to determine the precise number of free clinics operating in any particular state or region.

As more free clinics are developed and an increasing number of patients rely on these sites for care,[4,5] the need to understand who uses the clinics, why they are used, and whether patients view them as an addition to another usual source of care or as their only source of care, becomes more compelling. Answers to questions such as these can help community, state, and national planning bodies make informed decisions about resource allocation and ensure that safety net providers are able to cope with demands placed on their resources. This assumes deeper importance as increasing strains are placed on health care safety net facilities. Although articles on free clinics appear in the literature,[1-13] many of the issues related to who uses them and why have not been addressed. This chapter helps to fill

Rachel Mott-Keis, MD, is a clinical instructor of family medicine at Boston University School of Medicine. *Linda Gifford DeGeus, MD,* is a pediatrician at Thundermist Health Center, in Woonsocket, Rhode Island. *Suzanne Cashman, ScD,* is a professor and the director of community health in the Department of Family Medicine and Community Health at University of Massachusetts Medical School (UMMS), Worcester. *Judith Savageau, MPH,* is an associate professor in the Department of Family Medicine and Community Health, UMMS.

that gap by reporting on a comprehensive patient survey conducted at three free clinics in central Massachusetts.

Methods

During a seven-week interval, between January 24 and March 12, 2001, a descriptive study of patients using any of the then three free clinics in Worcester, Massachusetts, for medical or dental care was conducted. For almost a decade, students from the University of Massachusetts Medical School, also located in Worcester, had been working in each of these clinics. The clinics were chosen as study sites because of the authors' (RMK and LGD) work there. Additionally, given that this city of 175,000 people is also the site of a major tertiary care teaching hospital and two federally funded community health centers, there was significant administrative and provider interest in learning more about the free clinic patient population. We were interested particularly in why people felt the need to use free clinics when what should be accessible forms of medical care for individuals, regardless of insurance or socioeconomic status, exist in the city.

The free clinics in this study do not turn away any patients, nor do they request information related to a patient's immigration status. The presence of the other safety net providers has not affected the clinics' view of whom they should serve. Based on the beliefs of their founders, patients with and without insurance, as well as patients known to have care elsewhere, were seen at each of the clinics. The clinics are not formally connected but do share the philosophy that all patients desiring care should receive it. The clinics share a friendly, cooperative relationship with one another as well as with the other major local safety net providers. Many of the free clinic physician volunteers are on staff at the Worcester hospital and teach at the medical school. In addition, free clinic staff members routinely refer patients to the community health centers for care that will be comprehensive and continuous.

A detailed profile of each of the participating clinics appears in this chapter's appendix. Patients who were able and willing to complete a four-page survey written at a fifth-grade level in English, Portuguese, or Albanian were included. Attempts were made to approach every patient who entered the clinics during the study weeks.

Using the Anderson-Newman model for health services utilization as a reference for survey content,[14–16] a survey instrument that consisted of issues related to access, reasons for use, health insurance status and source, self-rated health status, medical diagnoses and comorbidities, and basic demographic information was developed. Where appropriate, questions for the survey were taken from previous instruments that had been tested and validated, including selected national surveys such as the Medical Outcomes Study 36-Item Short-Form Health Survey and the National Health Interview Survey.[17–21] Several original questions that reflected specific areas of interest for the investigators, personnel at the free clinics, and medical leaders in the community were also developed. In particular, these questions related to patients' reasons for using the free clinics, frequency of use, and patients' ability to access the health care system. The questionnaire was translated into Portuguese and Albanian, the two languages most frequently spoken at these clinics. The instrument was approved through the University of Massachusetts Medical School's Human Subjects Committee and then pilot tested. Two of the authors, fourth-year medical students (RMK, LGD) who were participating in a senior scholars research project at the time of the study, attended each clinic in order to approach patients, explain the study, invite them to complete the study instrument, and answer questions. The self-administered questionnaire took an average of 10 minutes to complete.

Data for this convenience sample were collected during four 2-hour blocks of survey time per week, coincident with the hours of operation for each clinic. Each clinic had first-time as well as repeat patients. Patients registered for medical care with administrative volunteers. After the registration process was complete, patients were approached and invited to complete the survey if they had not done so in a prior week. All persons were informed of the voluntary nature of the study. If the patient was under 18 years of age, the parent responded on behalf of the child. Because of time constraints at the clinic, patients generally were not approached if a physician saw them immediately upon their arrival. This tended to occur only at the very beginning of a clinic session. During the first two weeks of the seven-week data collection period, patients who spoke only Albanian or Portuguese were not invited to participate, because the questionnaire had not yet been translated into those two languages.

Data analyses were performed using the Statistical Package for the Social Sciences.[22] Frequency distributions were used to describe the study sample, especially respondents' perceived reasons for using free clinics, type of health insurance coverage, access to health care, and health status. Bivariate analyses were conducted to examine the association between health insurance status and selected sociodemographic characteristics, as well as several health care access variables. Additionally, characteristics of long-term (>1 year) and short-term (<1 year) clinic users were compared. For analysis purposes, the study sample was viewed as a cohort of free clinic patients; no attempt was made to draw distinctions among patients at the three study sites. Depending on the categorical or continuous nature of the variables, chi square or t-tests were applied. A p value of 0.05 was used to define statistical significance.

Results

During the survey weeks, a total of 402 patient visits were made to the study clinics. Fifty-nine encounters were repeat visits. Among the 343 persons who presented for nonrepeat care during the survey time period, 36 patients were unable to complete the instrument because of language difficulties. An additional 39 were not asked to do so for logistical reasons (e.g., patients were seen immediately after their arrival at the clinic or patients arrived within 15 minutes of clinic closing time and could not delay the visit start to complete the questionnaire). Consequently, the total number of persons who were able to complete a questionnaire and who were invited to participate was 268. Nine patients refused. Reasons for not partici-pating included difficulty reading, not having eyeglasses, not feeling well, and lack of interest. Eleven surveys were less than 50% completed and were subsequently omitted from the analyses. With 248 completed surveys, the resulting completion rate was 93%. Of the total number of patients who visited the clinic during the survey period, the response rate of this study was 72%.

Sociodemographic characteristics

The majority of patients were women (55%). Adults between the ages of 20 and 44 accounted for 45% of patients (table 10.1). Almost three-fourths of patients (71%) were in a household with children under the age of 18. Among those in families with members under 18 years of age, 57% reported that the children did not have health insurance. One-half of the respondents over 18 years of age were employed. The majority of patients at the clinics were white. Twenty-two percent were of His-panic origin. Twenty-five percent of patients reported being unable to converse with health care providers in English. Portuguese and Albanian were the most frequently spoken non-English languages (14% and 6%, respectively). Many re-spondents viewed the clinics as a safe source of health care; slightly more than three-quarters (79%) of patients who noted that Immigration Services played an important role in their lives indicated that one of the reasons for using the free clinics was because they felt safe there. Eighteen percent of respondents met criteria for homeless/unstable housing. A large majority (90%) reported annual household incomes below $30,000; 58% made less than $15,000 per year. Twenty-four percent of free clinic users reported their health status as fair or poor.

Health insurance

A large majority of patients (81%) seen at the free clinics were uninsured (table 10.2). Among uninsured patients, most (41%) had been uninsured for 2 or more years; only about one-quarter (24%) had been uninsured less than 6 months. Among the insured patients, 34% reported that their insurance did not cover prescription drugs. Patients who had insurance were significantly more likely than their unin-sured counterparts to use the free clinic for prescriptions (53% vs. 35%; chi square=5.41, p=0.02), because the time to wait for an appointment elsewhere was too long (30% vs. 10%; chi square=12.32, p<0.001), or because of a physician's refer-ral (19% vs. 6%; chi square=8.30, p=0.004). Insured patients were also more likely than uninsured patients to report having used the clinic for more than 1 year (30% vs. 16%; chi square=5.18, p=0.02; data not shown).

As shown in table 10.3, free clinic patients who were uninsured were more likely to be female than male (chi square = 6.35, p = 0.03); to be under age 65 (chi square=13.59, p<0.01) and, when over age 18, to be employed (chi square = 6.92, p<0.01). Thirteen percent of employed patients who used the free clinics had health insurance. Differences between insured and uninsured patients relative to race, ethnicity, education, and income were not statistically significant.

Patients without insurance were less likely than insured patients to have a usual source of care other than a free clinic or emergency room (chi square = 13.74,

Table 10.1

Demographic characteristics of free
clinic patients (n=248[a])

Variable	%	Variable	%
Gender		If children at home, have insurance	
Female	55	No	57
Male	45	Housing status	
Age ranges (y)		Rent	69
0–19	13	Staying with friend/family	17
20–44	45	Own	14
45–64	27	Shelter/street	1
≥65	16	Employed, >18 years old	
Primary language		Yes	50
English	59	Race	
Portuguese	14	White	77
Albanian	6	Black	14
Spanish	5	Multiracial	7
Other (20 different languages)	15	Asian / Pacific Rim Islander	2
Able to communicate in English		American Indian / Alaskan	<1
No	25	Native	
Immigrated within 5 years		Ethnicity	
Yes	36	Hispanic	22
Immigration services important		Non-Hispanic	78
Yes	31	Highest grade completed (years,	
If yes, feel safer at clinic	79	adults only)	
Marital status		≤12 (high school or less)	50
Married	39	13–15 (some college)	33
Single	39	≥16 (college degree)	18
Divorced	13	Income (combined family, $)	
Living with partner	4	<15,000	58
Widowed	4	15,000–<30,000	32
Separated	3	≥30,000	10
Children at home (≤18 years old)			
Yes	71		

[a]The n varies slightly per question due to
sporadic missing responses.

p<0.001). Similarly, they were significantly less likely to have a consistent provider
(chi square = 24.27, p<0.001), to know where to go when the clinic was not open
(chi square = 23.44, p<0.001), and to know where to go or whom to call for urgent
medical advice (chi square=28.47, p<0.001). In addition, uninsured respondents
were more likely to delay seeking medical care and to fail to take medicine as prescribed (65% vs. 42%; chi square=7.88, p<0.001 and 40% vs. 18%; chi square=4.40,
p=0.036, respectively; data not shown).

Table 10.2

Health insurance status of free clinic patients ($n=248^a$)

Variable	n	%
Health insurance		
No	198	81
Yes	48	19
Time uninsured		
<6 months	40	24
6 months to <1 year	32	19
1 year to <2 years	27	16
≥2 years	68	41
If insured, what type[b]		
Medicaid	16	35
Medicare	19	41
Private	19	41
Veteran	1	<1

[a]The *n* varies slightly per question due to sporadic missing responses.

[b]Subjects could indicate more than one response; therefore, totals do not add up to 100%.

Why patients use the free clinic

The most frequent response to the question asking why patients used the clinic was lack of insurance (table 10.4). When combined with patients who reported having inadequate insurance, a total of 93% of respondents reported an insurance/ financial reason for using the free clinics for medical care. About one-third (34%) stated that they used the free clinic because they did not know where else to go to receive care. Logistical reasons, such as transportation, inability to take time off from work and/or find child care in daytime hours, and too long to wait for a scheduled appointment combined to account for another 36% of reasons patients gave for using these sites for care.

Health care utilization and access

A majority (53%) of patients at the free clinics were first-time users. Seventy-two percent reported that the visit during which they were surveyed was their first or second visit to the clinic. Only 18% of respondents fit the definition of a long-term user (>1 year). Thirty-eight percent reported having a usual source of care. Among these patients, 43% identified one of the free clinics or the emergency room as that source. Notably, when free clinics and the emergency room were excluded, 74% of patients were unable to identify a usual source of care. Sixty percent of respondents reported that they delay seeking medical care. Slightly more than one-quarter (29%) reported delaying care because they did not have sufficient funds.

Table 10.3

Health insurance status and selected demographic characteristics ($n=248$[a])

	Insured (%)	Uninsured (%)	Chi square	p value
Gender			6.35	0.03
Female	13	87		
Male	26	74		
Age (y)			13.59	<0.01
0–19	20	81		
20–44	12	88		
45–64	17	83		
≥65	39	62		
Employment status (over age 18)			6.92	<0.01
Employed	13	87		
Unemployed	28	72		
Race			9.28	0.06
White	23	77		
Black	9	91		
Asian / Pacific Rim Islander	25	75		
American Indian	100	0		
Other/Multiracial	6	94		
Ethnicity			0.26	0.61
Hispanic	18	82		
Non-Hispanic	21	79		
Education			0.02	0.88
High school or less (age ≥18 years)	19	81		
Some college (age ≥18 years)	20	80		
Income ($)			0.90	0.64
≤15,000	18	82		
15,001–30,000	23	77		
≥30,001	16	84		

[a]The n varies slightly per question due to sporadic missing responses.

Delaying medical care did not appear to be associated with health status, having a usual source of care, or gender (data not shown).

Interestingly, long-term free clinic users (defined as those who have used the clinic for ≥1 year) were significantly more likely than other patients to have a usual source of care that is not the free clinic or emergency department (43% vs. 22%; chi square=7.11, $p<0.01$) and to have a regular provider elsewhere (43% vs. 25%; chi square=10.02, $p<0.01$). This group was also more likely to rank their health as fair or poor (38% vs. 21%; chi square=5.81, $p<0.01$). Additionally, patients who had been coming to the free clinics for more than 1 year were close to two times more likely to have insurance than short-term users (32% vs. 16%; chi square=5.18, $p=0.02$); they were also more likely than patients who used the clinic for less time to

Table 10.4

Patients' reasons for using the free clinics (*n*=247)

Reason[a]	*n*	%
No health insurance	202	82
Told by friends/family	146	59
Prescriptions	94	38
Do not know where else to go	83	34
Speak native language	47	19
Privacy	45	18
Too long to get an appointment	34	14
Safe from immigration services	33	13
Cannot take off work	30	12
Inadequate insurance	27	11
Transportation	30	8
Do not know how to make an appointment	15	6
Told by doctor	21	9
Children in school	10	4
Safe from violent partner	9	4
Staff rude elsewhere	7	3
Child care	6	2

[a]Subjects could indicate more than one response; therefore, totals do not add up to 100%.

cite inadequate insurance as a reason (24% vs. 8%; chi square=9.94, *p*<0.01) and to use the clinic as a way to obtain prescription drugs (67% vs. 31%; chi square=19.48, *p*<0.001; data not shown).

An examination of self-reported diagnoses showed that almost one-quarter of respondents (22%) noted emotional/nervous problems. Approximately one-fifth indicated that they had dental problems or high blood pressure (21% and 19%, respectively). Although 50% of the patients surveyed had health problems for which they required medicine on a regular basis, 66% of these patients reported that they were unable to take the medicine as prescribed. Cost was the main reason reported for not taking medicine as recommended. Patients who were uninsured were more likely than their insured counterparts to report being unable to take medicine as prescribed (40% vs. 18%; chi square=4.40, *p*=0.04; data not shown).

Discussion

The purpose of this study was to obtain information that would contribute to understanding who uses free clinics for medical care and why. The results are consistent with the literature describing the origins of free clinics[1-2]; the study sites serve a population in need. Patients who use the free clinics in the Worcester, Massachusetts, area are disproportionately low income, uninsured, and more likely than the general population to report their health status as fair or poor, an indicator of increased risk for morbidity and mortality.[23]

The large majority of respondents were without health insurance. National studies have shown that uninsured individuals have less access overall to medical care.[24-26] Individuals without insurance are less likely to have a regular source of care,[27] to have seen a physician recently, or to use preventive services.[28] They are more likely to delay care and to report not receiving care because of cost.[27-29] This study's results were largely consistent with these findings. The free clinic patients were not likely to have a medical home or to be knowledgeable navigators of the medical care system. Eighty percent of the uninsured respondents did not have a usual source of care. Similarly, these patients were less likely to have a consistent provider or to know where to go or whom to call for medical advice when the clinic was not open. In addition, they were more likely to delay medical care and to not take medicine as prescribed.

The issues presented by the long-term user of the free clinics indicate that the need for free prescription drugs may be driving this use. Although only a small portion of the total number of respondents, the long-term users tended to have a usual source of care other than the free clinic; possibly the inadequacy of their insurance coverage, combined with their poor health, prompted this subset of the patient population to turn to the free clinics as a way to obtain needed prescription drugs. If using these sites primarily for pharmaceutical purposes, in conjunction with regular, comprehensive primary care from an established health provider, then these patients, while experiencing some duplication of service, may feel they are getting the best of both worlds (i.e., regular primary care and free prescription drugs). Having multiple primary care providers who are not in contact with each other, however, is not viewed as high-quality care.

Alarmingly, recent local discussions regarding the Worcester free clinics' medication despite dispensing policies indicate that, patients' on-going reliance on the clinics for medications, the clinics are electing to limit prescription drugs to an initial, one-time-only basis or to cease dispensing medications altogether.[30] Although the stated rationale, namely that (1) patients "swamp the clinics," causing supplies to become too limited, and (2) patients come to rely on the clinics for medication, thereby bypassing more regular, comprehensive care altogether, may be reasonable, the implications for health and health care are but worrisome. This study showed that the majority of patients who have insurance but still need to use the free clinics do so because of the need for prescriptions. Free clinics and comprehensive primary care centers, such as the federally funded community health centers, must work together closely to ensure that barriers patients see to using these centers are reduced or eliminated entirely. Additionally, this circumstance speaks to the importance of community health centers having on-site pharmacy services. (At the time of this study, only one of the city's community health centers had such a service.)

The importance of the safety factor relative to immigration-related services that many respondents expressed indicates that, even before the events of September 11, 2001, foreign-born individuals in this country without proper documentation were wary of the possibility of being identified through obtaining health care services.[31] The clinics in this study followed a "don't ask" policy related to immigrants' status and documentation. Post-9/11, the country's state of hypervigilance relative to foreign-born individuals is likely to reinforce immigrants' concerns, thereby placing additional strain on the health care system's free clinic safety net. The type of surveillance and monitoring represented by this one study warrants regular replication to document the degree to which a potentially greater burden begins to be placed on the safety net's free clinic component.

Although free clinics play an important role in serving a segment of the population that needs care, it is important to emphasize that they are only Band-aids on the system; they do not represent a solution to the lack of access to health care. Frequently held in church basements or local community centers rather than in fully equipped medical buildings, free clinics address neither hospital nor long-term care needs. Moreover, they cannot provide continuity, and they raise the question of a two-tiered system, with low-income and uninsured patients potentially receiving lower-quality care.[1] Furthermore, most free clinics are not comprehensive health centers. Because they are open for limited hours, patients who use the free clinics as their sole means of health care may wait several weeks for medical care. Patients at free clinics are not able to choose a medical provider, nor can they expect consistency of provider. Although free clinics have become an important means of providing some heath care to low-income populations, they are a last resort, making amends for a system that is failing a significant proportion of its citizens.[32–34]

Despite these shortcomings, however, free clinics offer several advantages to the indigent population they serve. First and foremost, they provide needed medical care. They are inexpensive if not free, provide prescription medications, are easily accessible, frequently have evening hours, attempt to coordinate with other services in the medical community, and promote community volunteerism and social commitment.[1,6] In addition, through decreasing inappropriate use of the emergency room and institutions' bad debt,[1,24] free clinics have been shown to be cost effective. Furthermore, it has been suggested that these clinics are well poised to promote health education and involve patients in health promotion programs.[8]

As welfare reform, a slowing economy, and reductions in employer-sponsored health insurance threaten to increase the number of uninsured people in this country, more and more patients may feel forced to turn to free clinics for care. A dramatic increase in volume could put excessive strain on clinics that depend on volunteers and function with very modest budgets.[35] At a time when policymakers are concerned about the strain being placed on the health care safety net facilities in general, this type of increased demand could pose serious challenges.

The present study had a very high response rate, and a large sample of patients using the free clinics was obtained. Nevertheless, it has several limitations. An important one is that, because of the student-researchers' academic schedule, the seasonal variations in patient numbers and diagnoses that are common in free clinics could not be captured and documented. Results reflect patient use during the winter season only and as a consequence, may represent a higher or lower use than would have been documented in more temperate months. That the questionnaire was available in the three most prevalent languages spoken at the clinics means that, although the majority of patients could be accommodated, patients speaking another language exclusively were omitted from the respondent pool. Finally, in attempting to provide a sketch of patients who use the three free clinics in one urban area, we did not develop a sampling plan that would permit analysis of comparisons among the patient populations at the three sites. We elected to view them as an aggregate pool of patients and, for analytic purposes, to disaggregate along sociodemographic and health-related characteristics, rather then exploring potential differences among patients according to the clinic they visited.

Access to comprehensive primary health care services continues to be a challenge for many people in this country. As the number of individuals uninsured and underinsured continue to rise,[32-34] we can expect additional stress to be placed on free clinics. With health care financing and other related access issues manifesting a renewed sense of urgency,[26,36-41] studies continue to document the increased risk for adverse health outcomes that uninsured individuals experience.[24] [29,36,37,42] [44] Recent studies also note that simply attempting to increase access through philanthropic endeavors will not address the growing problem of access to health care.[4,5,45]

While federal and state governments debated the issue of insuring all citizens, local communities have developed free clinics as one means of providing health care to community members who are uninsured or underinsured.[5,7,46] Across the country, free clinic sites are serving patients who need health care; for many, a free clinic is a last resort. Despite the growing number of free clinics in the United States, however, limited information exists on the patients who use them. This study begins to fill that gap; defining and characterizing the free clinic patient population is the first step in designing a health care system that is responsive to all who need it. Additional studies should determine the extent to which free clinics can provide patients entry into a more comprehensive primary care system. In the meantime, however, health care policymakers must renew their determination to ensure that all residents have the access to health care services that insurance provides.

Acknowledgments

We thank the staff of the three free clinics, particularly the medical directors, Paul Hart, MD, Harvey Clermont, MD, Morris Spierer, MD, and Frank Joyce. In addition, we thank Jerry Gurwitz, MD, and Michael Huppert, MPH, for their consultation, assistance, and encouragement.

Notes

1. Kelleher KC. Free clinics: a solution that can work . . . now! JAMA. 1991 Aug 14;266(6):838–40.

2. Smith DE. The 1995 distinguished lecturer in substance abuse. J Subst Abuse Treat. 1996 Jul–Aug;13(4):289–94.

3. Nicholls AE. Manual: how to start a free clinic. Roanoke, VA: Free Clinic Foundation of America, 1992.

4. Geller S, Taylor BM, Scott HD. Free clinics helping to patch the safety net. J Health Care Poor Underserved. 2004 Feb;15(1):42–51.

5. Scott HD, Bell J, Geller S, et al. Physicians helping the underserved: the Reach Out Program. JAMA. 2000 Jan 5;283(1):99–104.

6. Smego RA Jr, Costante J. An academic health center–community partnership: the Morgan-town Health Right Free Clinic. Acad Med. 1996 Jun;71(6):613–21.

7. Bibeau DL, Howell KA, Rife JC, et al. The role of a community coalition in the development of health services for the poor and uninsured. Int J Health Serv. 1996;26(1):93–110.

8. Bibeau DL, Taylor ML, Rife JC, et al. Reaching the poor with health promotion through community free clinics. Am J Health Promot. 1997 Nov–Dec;12(20):87–9.

9. Scott L. Minnesota free clinic off to solid start. Mod Healthc. 1996 Jun 24;26(26):58.

10. Adams CJ, Flynn BC. Establishing an indigent health care clinic in an Indiana "Healthy City." Am J Public Health. 1996 Dec;86(12):1818–9.

11. Terry K. He heals on wheels. Med Econ. 1998 Oct 19;75(20):102–3.

12. Wood FG. The free clinic as a service learning opportunity. Nurse Educ. 2001 Jan–Feb; 26(1):4.

13. Lenehan GP. Free clinics and parish nursing offer unique rewards. J Emerg Nurs. 1998 Feb; 24(1):3–4.

14. Andersen R. Revisiting the behavioral model and access to medical care: does it matter? J Health Soc Behav. 1995 Mar;36(1):1–10.

15. Aday LA, Andersen RM. Equity of access to medical care: a conceptual and empirical over-view. Med Care. 1981 Dec;19(12):4–27.

16. Andersen R, Newman JF. Societal and individual determinants of medical care utilization in the United States. Milbank Mem Fund Q Health Soc. 1973 Winter;51(1):95–124.

17. Winkleby MA. Health-related risk factors of homeless families and single adults. J Commu-nity Health. 1994 Feb;19(1):7–23.

18. Liberatos P, Elinson J, Schaffzin T, et al. Developing a measure of unmet health care needs for a pediatric population. Medical Care. 2000 Jan;38(1):19–34.

19. Moss A. UCSF Reach Project Screening Instrument. San Francisco: University of California, Department of Epidemiology, 2000.

20. SF-36 Health Survey. Boston: Medical Outcomes Trust, 1992.

21. Aday LA. Designing and conducting health surveys. San Francisco: Jossey-Bass, 1989.

22. SPSS Version 10. Chicago: SPSS, 2000.

23. Idler EL, Benyamini Y. Self-rated health and mortality: a review of twenty-seven community studies. J Health Soc Behav. 1997 Mar;38(1):21–37.

24. Smith-Campbell B. Access to health care: effects of public funding on the uninsured. J Nurs Scholarsh. 2000;32(3):295–300.

25. American College of Physicians–American Society of Internal Medicine. No health insur-ance? It's enough to make you sick—scientific research linking the lack of health coverage to poor health. Philadelphia: American College of Physicians–American Society of Internal Medicine, 1999.

26. Baker DW, Shapiro MF, Schur CL. Health insurance and access to care for symptomatic conditions. Arch Intern Med. 2000 May 8;160(9):1269–74.

27.   Schoen C, Lyons B, Rowland C, et al. Insurance matters for low-income adults: results from a five-state survey. Health Aff (Millwood). 1997 Sep–Oct;16(5):163–71.

28.   Ayanian JZ, Weissman JS, Schneider EC, et al. Unmet health needs of uninsured adults in the United States. JAMA. 2000 Oct 25;284(16):2061–9.

29.   Berk ML, Schur CL, Cantor JC. Ability to obtain health care: recent estimates from the Robert Wood Johnson Foundation National Access to Care survey. Health Aff (Millwood). 1995 Fall;14(3):139–46.

30.   Health Access Network Meeting. Boylston, MA, Nov 22, 2002. Unpublished conference presentation.

31.   Clemetson L. A neighborhood clinic helps fill the gap for Latinos without health care. New York Times, 7 Oct 2002.

32.   Mills RM. Current population reports: health insurance coverage: 2001 (P60-220). Washington, DC: Bureau of Census, 2002. Available at http://www.census.gov/hhes/www/hlthin01.html.

33.   Mills RM. Current population reports: health insurance coverage: 1999 (P60-211). Washington, DC: Bureau of Census, 2002. Available at http://www.census.gov/hhes/www/hlthin99.html.

34.   Mills RM. Current population reports: health insurance coverage: 2000 (P60-215). Washington, DC: Bureau of Census, 2002. Available at http://www.census.gov/hhes/www/hlthin00.html.

35.   O'Toole TP, Gibbon JL, Hanusa BH, et al. Preferences for sites of care among urban homeless and housed poor adults. J Gen Intern Med. 1999 Oct;14(10):599–605.

36.   Mainous AG III, Hueston WJ, Love MM, et al. Access to care for the uninsured: is access to a physician enough? Am J Public Health. 1999 Jun;89(6):910–2.

37.   Andrulis DP. Access to care is the centerpiece in the elimination of socioeconomic disparities in health. Ann Intern Med. 1998 Sep 1;129(5):412–6.

38.   Holahan J, Pohl MB. Changes in insurance coverage: 1994–2000 and beyond. Health Aff (Millwood). 2002;Supp Web Exclusives:W162-71.

39.   Health Foundation of Greater Cincinnati. Access to health care: the uninsured and underserved. Cincinnati: Health Foundation of Greater Cincinnati, 2000.

40.   Bear R. A million parents lost Medicaid, study says. New York Times 19 Jun 2000.

41.   Friedrich MJ. Medically underserved children need more than insurance card. JAMA. 2000 Jun 21;283(23):3056–7.

42.   Billings J, Anderson BM, Newman LS. Recent findings on preventable hospitalizations. Health Aff (Millwood). 1996 Fall;15(3):239–49.

43.   Newacheck PW, Hughes DC, Stoddard JJ. Children's access to primary care: differences by race, income and insurance status. Pediatrics. 1996 Jan;97(1):26–32.

44.   Alliance for Health Reform. Health coverage: how much does insurance matter? Washington, DC: Alliance for Health Reform, 2000.

45.   Kemble S. Charity care programs: part of the solution or part of the problem? Public Health Rep. 2000 Sep–Oct;115(5):419–29.

46.   McDonough JE. Healthcare policy: the basics. Boston: Access Project, 1999.

Appendix:
Characteristics of the three free medical care program study sites

Free clinic	Hours of operation	Year of initiation	Patients visits per session	Paid staff	Volunteer staff	Services provided
Worcester Evening Free Medical Service Program (church basement)	Monday 6–8 p.m.	1994	40–50	Social worker Physician	Administrators Physicians Nurses Medical students	Adult/child physicals Immunizations Acute/chronic treatment Glucose monitoring Blood pressure check HIV testing Social services Chiropractic therapy
Green Island Neighborhood Center (community center)	Tuesday 9:30–11:30 a.m.	1997	10	Manager of center	Physicians	Adult/child physicals
	Wednesday 6–8 p.m.	1999	5	Case manager	Medical students	Immunizations
	Thursday 9–11 a.m., pediatrics	clinic added		Interpreter		Acute/chronic treatment Glucose monitoring Blood pressure check Dental exams Social services Albanian interpreter
St. Anne's Catholic Church (church annex)	Tuesday 6–8 p.m.	1996	50–60	Interpreter Social worker	Administrators Pharmacist Physicians Nurses Medical students Dentists	Adult/child physicals Immunizations Acute/chronic treatment Glucose monitoring Blood pressure check Free meals Social services Portuguese interpreter

Chapter 11

Donated Care Programs: A Stopgap Measure or a Long-Run Alternative to Health Insurance?

Jeffrey T. Kullgren
Erin Fries Taylor
Catherine G. McLaughlin

In the wake of the failure to enact broad federal health care reform in 1994, interest in local solutions to the problem of providing health care to the uninsured has grown.[1-3] Volunteer-based clinics, sometimes referred to as free clinics, have long been an important source of free or highly subsidized health care for the uninsured, and their numbers have grown substantially in recent years.[4] Other community-based approaches have emerged as outgrowths of the free clinic movement. Project Access, a model that originated in Buncombe County, North Carolina in 1996, is one such approach.[5]

Project Access initiatives seek to coordinate and formalize the provision of charity care by local physicians and health care organizations. Although specific details vary by community, these projects are generally structured around primary care and specialist clinicians agreeing to provide free services to a specific number of patients annually. Enrolled patients receive access to primary and specialty care and sometimes access to free or subsidized prescription drugs and other services. Such arrangements allow communities to provide more coordinated care (and often more comprehensive services) than free clinics while still avoiding the state regulation associated with insurance programs. Participation is attractive to clinicians because it enables them to limit their provision of free care to a well-defined number of patients. Further, participating clinicians can provide care to enrollees within their own offices, instead of in a separate free clinic. As of April 2003, 20 communities had implemented projects patterned after Project Access, and over 300,000 uninsured people throughout the United States

Jeffrey T. Kullgren, MPH, is an assistant professor of internal medicine in the Division of General Medicine at the University of Michigan Medical School and a research scientist in the VA Center for Clinical Management Research at the VA Ann Arbor Healthcare System. *Erin Fries Taylor, PhD, MPP,* is an associate director of health research and a senior researcher at Mathematica Policy Research, in Washington, DC. *Catherine G. McLaughlin, PhD,* is a senior fellow at Mathematica Policy Research as well as a professor of health management and policy at the University of Michigan School of Public Health.

had received care from donated care programs.[6] In 2002, another 40 communities were planning or contemplating similar initiatives.[7]

Project Access programs vary somewhat in their intended purpose. Some are explicitly designed to serve as stopgap measures for temporarily uninsured people on their way to securing health insurance through another source. Others have a longer-term focus, specifically targeting those who foresee few if any affordable health insurance options in the near future (e.g., low-income, self-employed workers).

In this chapter, we examine the early experience of a program in southern Maine called CarePartners, which utilizes a model similar to Project Access. Using data from a telephone survey, we provide information on the baseline characteristics of individuals who enrolled in CarePartners and then examine what happened to participants' health care coverage in the six months after joining the program.

CarePartners, which began in June 2001, offers access to health care services for low-income adults in Kennebec, Lincoln, and Cumberland Counties in southern Maine. CarePartners differs from other Project Access programs, which tend to be organized around local medical societies, in that (1) MaineHealth, a local health system, initiated the program and provides substantial program funding (including staff salaries) and (2) hospitals in the MaineHealth system have worked with their medical staffs to secure physician involvement. CarePartners' services are provided by seven hospitals (representing all hospitals in the three-county area, including those outside of the MaineHealth system) and approximately 950 local physicians who have volunteered to provide free health care to low-income uninsured adults. Primary care physicians (PCPs) who participate are each asked to take on 10 patients; specialists are each asked to accept 10 referrals annually.

CarePartners was created as a more systematic alternative to local hospitals' existing charity care programs, which provide free but uncoordinated care to recipients. CarePartners also seeks to provide more comprehensive and coordinated services through a care management component and pharmacy benefits. The program sets its income eligibility levels to match the charity care guidelines of local hospitals in order to discourage unfavorable selection into either CarePartners or charity care programs.

At the time of our survey, eligibility criteria for CarePartners required that an individual be an adult aged 18 to 64 with an annual household income under 150% of the federal poverty level (FPL) and ineligible for either government or employer-sponsored health care coverage. In addition, in order to be eligible an individual had to have resided within the program's service area for at least six months and not had assets exceeding $10,000 for an individual or $12,000 for a family.

New CarePartners enrollees are assigned a PCP and given a membership card. With this card, they may visit their assigned PCP for both acute and routine preventive care. For specialty care, enrollees must get an initial referral from their PCP. Unlike an insurance product, CarePartners does not provide a list of covered services but generally offers access to physician visits, hospital services, inpatient or outpatient surgery, and home care. Co-payments are required for certain services (e.g., $10 per physician visit). There are no co-payments for emergency department care, inpatient or outpatient surgeries, or other hospital services.

CarePartners recertifies eligibility every six months, at which point enrollees must document their current income and employment status. If all eligibility criteria are still met, the individual remains enrolled in the program for the next six months. The program originally expected to provide care to enrollees for a year or more (in contrast to many Project Access initiatives, which only intend to enroll individuals for periods of three to six months), but staff found that enrollees cycled through the program more quickly than expected. As of November 2004, CarePartners had about 950 enrollees.

Methods

Data come from a multiwave telephone survey of CarePartners participants. Wave 1 occurred between November 2001 and June 2002. The sample frame consisted of all new enrollees during that time period who agreed to release their contact information for possible inclusion in the survey (approximately 82% of new enrollees over that period).

Enrollees were interviewed within 6 to 8 weeks of enrollment. The Wave 1 interview collected baseline data on enrollees' health care utilization, access, satisfaction; and health insurance status in the 12 months prior to joining CarePartners, as well as socioeconomic characteristics and current health status. Of the 346 new enrollees between November 2001 and May 2002 (who constituted the sample frame) 300 (87%) participated in Wave 1 of the survey. These 300 individuals served as the sample frame for Wave 2 of the survey, regardless of their enrollment status at that time.

The Wave 2 interview occurred approximately six months later, between May and December 2002. The Wave 2 instrument included many of the same questions as Wave 1 but also incorporated additional satisfaction questions and questions on the reasons for disenrollment among those who were no longer enrolled in the program. Two hundred sixty-six (89%) participated in the Wave 2 interview.

Results

Baseline characteristics of CarePartners enrollees

The profile of an average enrollee is a single white female with a high-school education, in her early 40s, living in a two-person household with a mean annual household income of $16,500 (table 11.1). Approximately half of the participants were employed upon entering the program. Among participants who were working, most were employed part-time by a small (fewer than 25 employees) private employer and had been with the same firm for over a year. Nearly one-third of workers were self-employed.

Almost half of all enrollees had health insurance in the year prior to enrolling in CarePartners, and most had had some form of coverage at some point in the

Table 11.1

Baseline characteristics of CarePartners enrollees (*n*=266)

Demographic characteristics (%)	
Female	67
Married	23
Own home	45
Employed	49
Demographic averages	
Age (years)	42.1
Education (years)	12.5
Household size	2.2
Annual household income ($)	16,520
Worker characteristics[a]	
Mean months with current employer	45
Percentage with current employer for longer than 1 year	60
Percentage working full time (over 34 hrs a week)	42
Percentage self-employed	32
Percentage working for firm with more than 25 people	28
Percentage with employer-sponsored insurance in previous year	26
Percentage whose current employer offers insurance	25
Percentage eligible to participate in employer's plan	8
Other insurance coverage before CarePartners (%)	
Any coverage in previous year	47
Medicaid coverage in last year	9
Never insured before CarePartners	16
Current health status (%)	
Fair or poor general health	30
Limiting or chronic nonlimiting condition	53
Mean number of days of poor health in last month	10.4
Access to health care (%)	
Usual source of care or personal doctor	87
Unmet need in previous year	58
Medical care utilization in previous year (%)	
Any hospital stays	17
Any ED visits	49
Any doctor visits	80

Source: Communities in Charge Survey of CarePartners Enrollees, Wave 1, 2002.

[a]Among the 130 people employed at the time of the Wave 1 survey.

past (84%). Only one-quarter of those employed worked for a firm that offered health insurance to any of its employees. Among those who did, fewer than one-third reported being eligible for their employer's plan (n=20). Eligibility was self-reported and therefore subject to reporting error.

Thirty percent of enrollees reported being in fair or poor health, and a majority (53%) reported having a limiting or chronic nonlimiting health condition. Most enrollees (87%) had a usual source of care or personal doctor prior to enrollment, and most (89%) had utilized health care in the last year. Eighty percent had made a physician visit and roughly half had made at least one emergency department visit. Over half of enrollees reported having had an unmet medical or prescription drug need in the previous year. Since CarePartners enrolled many individuals who formerly received care through local hospitals' charity care programs, CarePartners' staff anticipated that enrollees would have characteristics like these.

Coverage status six months after enrollment

Characteristics of participants by six months after enrolling in CarePartners are reported in tables 11.2 and 11.3. Over two-thirds of CarePartners enrollees were still enrolled in the program at the six-month mark. Many individuals who remained enrolled resembled the average enrollee described above. Half were employed, most in a part-time job with a small firm for which they had worked, on average, for over six years. Less than one-quarter of these workers' firms offered health insurance to at least some employees. Among those who worked for a firm that offered coverage, only a few reported being eligible. Few continuous enrollees had experienced a change in employment status in the six months since enrolling in the program; in both interviews, most reported either working for the same employer or not working.

Twelve enrollees (5%) left CarePartners within six months of enrolling and acquired employer-sponsored insurance (ESI) through their own employer. These individuals had been in their jobs for 16 months on average, had a significantly higher average annual household income ($32,200) than other respondents, and were most likely to work full-time for a large firm (over 25 employees). Most reported having employer coverage in the year before enrolling in CarePartners. None were in fair or poor health, and all had a usual source of care and health care utilization in the previous six months.

Fourteen individuals (5%) left CarePartners within six months of enrolling and obtained Medicaid coverage. These individuals had an average annual household income of $13,000 and were significantly more likely than other respondents to report having a limiting or chronic nonlimiting health condition. Eleven of the 14 had been to a hospital emergency room at least once during the six months since enrollment. Nearly one-quarter had one or more hospital stays during this time. Five individuals had been covered through Medicaid at some point during the year before enrolling in CarePartners.

About 20% of enrollees (n=54) left CarePartners and were without health insurance at six months after enrollment. The average uninsured disenrollee was an employed female in her late thirties with an annual household income of $19,000. Most of those employed worked full-time for a large firm. Approximately half reported disenrolling from CarePartners because of problems meeting eligibility criteria. Twenty-seven percent disenrolled because their income was too high to remain eligible, and 13% disenrolled because of a failure to complete recertification paperwork. Another 24% reported that an employer offer of coverage made them ineligible for the program.

Similarities and differences across groups

Each group primarily comprised single white females living in two-person households. Over 90% of each group reported having a usual source of care or personal doctor in the first six months after enrollment, and approximately the same percentage reported any health care utilization over the same period. The majority of people in all groups had been insured previously, and at least 40% of each group had had health coverage in the year before enrolling in CarePartners.

Despite small sample sizes, the four groups differed significantly in notable ways. Continuous enrollees tended to be older than those who left the program. Workers still enrolled after six months were most likely to be self-employed or working for a small firm and had, on average, been with the same employer longer than those who left the program. Disenrolled workers were more likely than workers still enrolled to work for a firm that offers health insurance to some or all of its employees and were more likely to report being eligible for that coverage.

Compared with all others, disenrollees with ESI had higher incomes and more years of education and were the most likely to be working. Among all workers, they were most likely to be employed full-time and to be working for large firms and were least likely to be self-employed. They were also most likely to have had ESI in the year before joining CarePartners. Many reported a change in employment since enrolling; they were more likely than others to have changed jobs or to have gone from not working to working.

Disenrollees with Medicaid had the lowest average household income of any group and were the least likely to be working. According to CarePartners staff, many of the 14 individuals in this category likely are disabled adults whose income exceeded Maine's Medicaid eligibility limit for this group (i.e., 100% FPL) at the time of enrollment into CarePartners. These disabled adults eventually may have qualified for Medicaid through its spend-down provision.

Uninsured disenrollees fall somewhere in between the other groups of disenrollees. Half were employed, and most worked full time for a large firm that offered health insurance for which they were eligible, thereby making them ineligible to re-enroll in CarePartners. The question, of course, is why do they not take up ESI? Results from the survey suggest that the answer may be affordability. While these individuals were from households with average incomes higher than the incomes of continuous enrollees, they still earned significantly less than disenrollees with ESI.

Discussion

Our survey data suggest that CarePartners functions differently for different groups of low-income uninsured adults. It appears to be very useful, for example, for those needing a temporary source of care before gaining health insurance, and for those without affordable insurance options who are able to maintain eligibility requirements. For the many who are unable to meet eligibility requirements continuously

Table 11.2

Demographic and employment characteristics of survey participants at six months after enrollment (n=262)

	Enrolled at both interviews (n=182)	Disenrolled at six months			Significant differences groups
		ESI Coverage (n=12)	Medicaid Coverage (n=14)	Uninsured (n=54)	
Percentage of total participants	68	5	5	20	
Demographic characteristics[a] (%)					
Female	69	75	57	63	
Married	25	8	36	25	
Employed	50	100	21	57	***
Demographic averages[b]					
Household income ($)	14,980	32,210	13,000	19,090	***
Household size	2.0	2.2	2.2	2.4	**
Education (years)	12.3	13.2	12.4	13.2	*
Age (years)	43.4	40.2	38.7	38.5	
Worker characteristics[c]	(n=91)	(n=12)	(n=3)	(n=31)	
Mean months with firm[b]	78.1	15.5	6.0	17.0	**
Full time (%)[a]	36	75	33	68	***
Self-employed (%)[a]	32	0	0	10	*
In firms with more than 25 workers (%)[a]	26	67	100	68	***
Employer offers ESI (%)[a]	22	100	100	68	***
Eligible for ESI (%)[a]	7	100	67	48	***

Changes since enrolling (%)[a]				
Same employer	34	42	7	20 **
Employer change	5	25	7	17 **
Not working to working	10	33	7	24 **
Working to not working	9	0	21	11
Not working both waves	41	0	57	31 ***

Source: Communities in Charge Survey of CarePartners Enrollees, Wave 2, 2002.

[a]Chi-square test used for comparison between groups.

[b]ANOVA test used for comparison between groups.

[c]Among participants employed at Wave 2 survey.

*Significant difference between all groups at $p<0.1$.

**Significant difference between all groups at $p<0.05$.

***Significant difference between all groups at $p<0.01$.

Note: Four additional Wave 2 respondents had disenrolled and were insured at the time of the Wave 2 interview; two had obtained private nongroup coverage, and two reported having some other unspecified type of coverage. These individuals are omitted from our analysis because of the impossibility of developing meaningful summary statistics and making statistical inferences for this extremely small group.

Table 11.3

Health, utilization, and previous insurance characteristics of CarePartners enrollees six months after enrollment (n=262)

	Enrolled at both interviews (n=182)	Disenrolled at six months			Significant differences groups
		ESI Coverage (n=12)	*Medicaid Coverage* (n=14)	*Uninsured* (n=54)	
Percentage of total participants	68	5	5	20	
Health status (%)[a]					
Fair or poor health	33	0	21	22	**
Health condition[b]	49	42	79	37	**
Mean days of poor health[c,d]	7.3	2.2	9.9	7.1	
Access to care (%)[a]					
Usual source / personal doctor	97	100	93	91	
Unmet need	26	33	21	30	
Utilization (%)[a]					
Any utilization	97	100	93	96	
Any physician visits	93	100	93	91	
Any hospital visits	15	8	23	14	
Any ER visits	37	25	79	33	**
Utilization means among users[d,e]					
Physician visits	6.7	5.1	11.5	5.2	
Hospital stays	1.7	1.0	1.3	4.6	
ED visits	2.1	2.3	2.5	2.5	

Coverage before enrolling (%)[a,f]				
Any coverage	45	75	57	43
Never insured	18	0	0	17
ESI	24	75	21	24	***
Medicaid	10	0	36	4	***
Mean months covered[d,g]	7.4	8.1	6.5	7.7

Source: Communities in Charge Survey of CarePartners Enrollees, Wave 1 and Wave 2, 2002.

[a]Chi-square test used for comparison between groups.

[b]Limiting or chronic nonlimiting health condition.

[c]Mean number of days of poor health in last month.

[d]ANOVA test used for comparison between groups.

[e]Among those reporting use of the respective service.

[f]Wave 1 data on coverage in 12 months prior to enrolling in CarePartners.

[g]Among those with coverage in the year before Wave 1.

*Significant difference between groups at $p<0.1$

**Significant difference between groups at $p<0.05$

***Significant difference between groups at $p<0.01$

Note: Four additional Wave 2 respondents had disenrolled and were insured at the time of the Wave 2 interview; two had obtained private nongroup coverage, and two reported having some other unspecified type of coverage. These individuals are omitted from our analysis because of the impossibility of developing meaningful summary statistics and making statistical inferences for this extremely small group.

or to complete re-enrollment procedures successfully, however, the utility of the program is limited to a short-term period of access to affordable care.

Most respondents to our survey stayed in the program for more than six months. Workers in this group had been working for the same firm for longer than disenrollees, and the prevailing trends in this group's employment status (relatively high levels of part-time work, self-employment, and working for small firms that do not offer coverage to any employees) correlate with having more lim ited access to ESI than other workers.[8-10]

Unemployed individuals enrolled in CarePartners for more than six months appear similar to enrollees who left CarePartners for Medicaid with respect to household income and health status measures. Despite these similarities, they may lack some of the other characteristics needed to qualify for public coverage (e.g., household income under 100% of the FPL for disabled adults). It is this group for whom MaineCare (Maine's Medicaid program) expansions to low-income adults may be particularly beneficial; starting in October 2003, MaineCare raised its income threshold for covering childless adults to 125% FPL.

For two relatively small groups of individuals (10% of all enrollees surveyed), the program appears to have served as an effective stopgap measure during a short-term spell of being uninsured. Disenrollees with ESI were more likely than others to have had employer coverage in the year before enrolling in CarePartners. Similarly, disenrollees who obtained Medicaid coverage were most likely to have had Medicaid sometime in the year before enrolling in CarePartners. For these two groups, CarePartners seems to have helped bridge a gap in coverage.

The bulk of CarePartners' disenrollees, however, were uninsured six months after enrollment, suggesting that this and other donated care programs may not be a viable solution for all the uninsured. Most disenrollees left not because of the advent of another coverage alternative, but because they became ineligible for the program, either because of a change in income, an employer offer of coverage (that was not taken up), or failure to complete recertification paperwork. Notably, of the people who became disenrolled, significantly more were working full-time, employed by large firms, working for an employer that offers insurance, and eligible for ESI at the time of disenrollment than had been at the time of enrollment. However, household incomes of working, uninsured disenrollees averaged only two-thirds the household incomes of workers who disenrolled and obtained ESI. Possibly, ESI is unaffordable even when it is offered, and CarePartners may be one of their few viable options for accessing health services.

CarePartners has taken important steps to address affordability concerns in this population. Previously, applicants were not eligible for CarePartners if they had an employer offer of coverage, regardless of the size of the premium. CarePartners modified this eligibility criterion in September 2003 so that individuals are now eligible if their employer offer of insurance has a premium exceeding 5% of their gross income (provided they meet the remaining criteria). Furthermore, the income eligibility threshold was raised to 175% of the FPL in December 2002 in response to the MaineCare expansion.

This research represents a small case study analysis of a donated care program in one community and may not be generalizable. The data are subject to the limitations of self-reported information (e.g., misreporting and recall bias). Small sample sizes limit our ability to perform subgroup analyses and make statistical inferences.

Acknowledgments

This research was funded by the Robert Wood Johnson Foundation. We thank Deborah Deatrick of MaineHealth as well as Carol Zechman and especially Phebe King (deceased) of CarePartners (which was funded in part by the Robert Wood Johnson Foundation's Communities in Charge project) for their cooperation in this study. We also thank Cathy Huang for helpful research assistance. Any errors in this research are attributable solely to the authors.

Notes

1. Isaacs SL, Knickman JR, eds. To improve health and health care, 1997: the Robert Wood Johnson Foundation anthology. Princeton, NJ: Robert Wood Johnson Foundation, 1997.

2. Wielawski I. Congress' inaction cannot hold back health-care reform. Columbian (Vancouver, WA). 1994 Oct 5:A11.

3. Barnhill KE, Beitsch LM, Brooks RG. Improving access to care for the underserved: state-supported volunteerism as a successful component. Arch Internal Med. 2001;161(18):2177–81.

4. Geller S, Taylor BM, and Scott HD. Free clinics helping to patch the safety net. J Health Care Poor Underserved. 2004;15(1):42–51.

5. Landis SE. Buncombe County Medical Society Project Access: expanding access to care at the local level. N C Med J. 2002;63(1):23–9.

6. Siegel R. North Carolina's program for people without medical insurance. All Things Considered, National Public Radio. 2003 April 10.

7. Carrns A. Doctors treat uninsured free of charge in Project Access. Wall Street Journal. 2002 December 24:B1.

8. Collins SR, Schoen C, Colasanto D, et al. On the edge: low-wage workers and their health insurance coverage. New York: Commonwealth Fund, 2003.

9. Garrett B, Nichols LM, and Greenman EK. Workers without health insurance: who are they and how can policy reach them? Washington, DC: Urban Institute, 2001.

10. Hoffman C, Wang M. Health insurance coverage in America: 2001 data update. Washington, DC: Kaiser Commission on Medicaid and the Uninsured, 2003.

Chapter 12

Missed Appointment Rates in Primary Care: The Importance of Site of Care

Karen E. Lasser
Ira L. Mintzer
Astrid Lambert
Howard Cabral
David H. Bor

When patients miss primary care appointments, practices function less efficiently and patient access to care decreases. Valuable provider and clerical staff time may be wasted, and compensatory double-booking may disrupt patient flow. These problems are of particular concern to financially strained publicly funded neighborhood health centers, whose role is to provide continuity and access for disadvantaged patients. Prior studies have found that patients of lower socioeconomic status, lower educational level, and younger age are more likely to miss appointments,[1-4] as are patients in Medicaid managed care[5] and new patients.[6] Patients also miss appointments according to the hour of the appointment, the source of referral, and delays in the appointment date.[6]

While patient race and gender are not independent predictors of missed appointments, no previous study has simultaneously examined whether concordance between patient and primary care provider (PCP) with respect to race, language, or gender affects missed appointment rates in primary care settings. If such concordance proved to be an important factor explaining missed appointment rates, greater efforts could be made to match patients to PCPs of the same race, language, and gender. While one study of 96 Spanish-speaking patients with asthma found that patients whose physicians did not speak Spanish were more likely to miss office appointments,[7] this study was limited by inclusion of patients from only one practice. Prior studies also have not analyzed whether individual site of care is an inde-

---

Karen E. Lasser, MD, MPH, is an associate professor of medicine and public health at the Boston University School of Medicine and Public Health. *Ira L. Mintzer, MD,* is an assistant professor of medicine at Harvard Medical School (HMS) and the Cambridge Health Alliance (CHA). *Astrid Lambert, MA,* is manager of data analysis and reporting in the CHA Department of Clinical Informatics. *Howard Cabral, PhD, MPH,* is a professor of biostatistics in the Department of Biostatistics at the Boston University School of Public Health. *David H. Bor, MD,* is a Charles S. Davidson associate professor of medicine at HMS and CHA.

pendent predictor of missed appointments. Such an association would suggest that systems of care at individual health centers and practices may affect missed appointment rates.

Notably, other studies have found clear benefits to such concordance.[7-13] Cooper and colleagues[9] observed more favorable ratings of care, positive patient affect, and longer visits in settings of racial and ethnic concordance. Perez-Stable and colleagues[11] reported that non-English-speaking patients with diabetes and hypertension reported greater well being and better functioning when their PCP spoke their native language. Similarly, Manson[7] found that Spanish-speaking asthmatic patients whose physician spoke Spanish had improved adherence to treatment and less emergency department use compared with those who did not have a Spanish-speaking doctor.

For the present study, we analyzed patients in four language groups (English, Portuguese, Spanish and Haitian Creole) visiting a large local network of neighborhood health centers. We hypothesized that patients would be less likely to miss appointments when their PCP was of the same race, was proficient in the same language, and/or was of the same gender. We postulated that patients and providers from similar cultural and ethnic backgrounds with shared social experiences would form a stronger connection and have enhanced communication that might increase the chances of the patient returning for subsequent visits. We also hypothesized that site of care might be an important determinant of missed appointment rates.

Methods

Study setting and sample

Cambridge Health Alliance (CHA) is a Primary Care Practice–Based Research Network (PBRN) consisting of 25 primary care centers. The health centers predominantly serve a multicultural, low-income population in Cambridge, Somerville, and Everett, Massachusetts. Detailed demographic and attendance data for the year 2002 were available on patient visits to 16 of the health centers. We surveyed all 58 primary care providers (PCPs) at these 16 health centers on whom open access data (see below) were available, including internists, family practitioners, and adult nurse practitioners. We inquired about their self-identified race, language abilities, years in practice, and number of clinical sessions per week. All 58 PCPs (100%) responded to the survey after receiving three e-mails and a follow-up phone call. We then analyzed data on 74,120 adult primary care patient visits in the four most prevalent languages (English, Portuguese, Spanish, and Haitian Creole) to these 58 PCPs during the year 2002. We analyzed both kept appointments and appointments that the patient did not keep; we excluded cancelled appointments since such appointments are generally rescheduled. The CHA institutional review board approved the study.

Definitions of patient, provider, and visit characteristics

We examined the following patient-level characteristics: age, race, insurance status, and patient language used during the visit. On the first visit, health center staff routinely identify patients as white, black, Hispanic, or other race, on the basis of physical appearance. At each visit, staff inquire about the language in which the patient wishes to conduct the visit. We defined new patients as those who had not seen a given PCP since December 31, 1997 (i.e., four to five years prior to the date of the most recent visit). Assuming that most new patients did not know the race, gender, or language abilities of their PCP until their first visit, we excluded new patients from analyses of race, language, and gender concordance.

We sent an e-mail survey to PCPs, asking them to identify their race (white, black or African American, American Indian or Alaska native, Asian, native Hawaiian or other Pacific Islander, or other race) and ethnicity (Hispanic or Latino or other). In doing so, we followed the U.S. census categories. We also surveyed providers about their language abilities in Spanish, Portuguese, and Haitian Creole. For each language, PCPs were asked to choose the statement that best represented his or her language ability with patients if X is the patient's primary language: *I always use an interpreter; I speak X (Portuguese/Spanish/Haitian Creole) with patients, but sometimes I need an interpreter*; or *I am a native speaker [learned X in infancy]*. In some cases, PCPs reported that they spoke a foreign language so fluently that an interpreter was never needed, though they were not native speakers.

Primary care providers also provided data about the number of sessions they practiced per week, and the number of years they had been at their current practice site. We also obtained data on each PCP's average open access (see below) over the year 2002. We used open access as a proxy measure for the time elapsed between the date the appointment was scheduled and the actual date of the appointment. We defined a PCP as having open access if, on average, four or fewer days would elapse until their third next available appointment. (The number of days until third next available appointment is a standard measure of open access).[14]

In analyses restricted to follow-up visits, we defined a visit to be race concordant if the patient and PCP were of the same race, and to be gender concordant if the patient and PCP were of the same gender. If a PCP was a native speaker of Portuguese, Spanish, or Haitian Creole, and thus never used an interpreter in one of those languages due to being fluent, we classified visits with patients who spoke that language as language concordant. If a PCP agreed with one of the following statements: *I always use an interpreter*, or *I speak Portuguese/Spanish/Haitian Creole with patients, but sometimes I need an interpreter*, we classified visits with patients who spoke that language as language discordant.

Statistical methods

We performed all statistical analyses using SAS for Windows, version 8.2 (SAS Institute, Cary, NC). We used the chi-square test to compare differences in groups in the proportion of missed appointments (initial and follow-up) by patient and provider characteristics. We restricted bivariate analyses of race, language, and gender concordance to follow-up visits by established patients, since new patients who missed an initial visit with a provider may not have been aware of the provider's gender, race, or language ability. We then performed multiple logistic regression analyses, restricted to follow-up visits in the four most common languages (English, Portuguese, Spanish, and Haitian Creole), of the dichotomous outcome (missed versus kept appointment), applying the generalized estimating equation (GEE) approach in SAS PROC GENMOD[15] to adjust for the correlation that exists between different visits by the same patient.[16] We included in the model only those variables that achieved bivariate significance at $p<0.2$. We computed adjusted odds ratios (ORs) and 95% confidence intervals (CIs) based on the multiple logistic model.

In order to detect differences between white-white and non-white–non-white concordant pairs and English-English and non-English–non-English pairs, we included interaction terms between patient race and race concordance and patient language and language concordance. Since these terms were not statistically significant, we present data as race concordant and discordant, and language concordant and discordant.

Results

Table 12.1 shows the demographic characteristics of the 58 PCPs (self-identified race, gender, and language abilities). Most ($n=37$ [64%]) PCPs worked six or more half-day sessions per week. Only 48% ($n=28$) of PCPs had open access during 2002. Forty-one percent of PCPs ($n=24$) had been in practice for more than seven years at their current primary care site.

The demographic characteristics of 28,745 patients, as recorded during their initial (first) visit in 2002, are shown in table 12.2. The majority of patients were young and female and had no private insurance. Nearly half of all patients were non-white and primarily spoke a language other than English. Approximately 16% of patients did not make their initial visit in 2002. In univariate analyses, patients who were new to the PCP, young, black, Hispanic, non-English speaking and had Medicaid or Free Care insurance were more likely to miss appointments than were other patients (x^2 $p<0.001$ for all comparisons). Patients seen by PCPs who were not at open access, practiced fewer than six sessions per week, or who practiced at community health centers #2, #6, #9, or hospital-based clinic #2 were also more likely than their respective counterparts to miss appointments.

Table 12.3 presents missed appointment rates for established patients' first visits in 2002. Patients who were race (x^2 $p<0.0001$) or language (x^2 $p<0.01$) concordant with their PCP were less likely to miss appointments than were race or language discordant patients.

Due to problems with collinearity, we were unable to include patient language and race in the same multivariate model. Table 12.4 shows the results of the multivariate analysis, including patient age, insurance, and language; provider open

Table 12.1

Demographic characteristics of primary care providers

Characteristic	n (%)[a]
Female	33 (56.9)
Race or ethnicity	
White	50 (86.2)
Black	3 (5.2)
Hispanic	0 (0)
Asian	3 (5.2)
Other race	2 (3.4)
Foreign Language skills[b]	
Portuguese	
Always need interpreter; no language ability	32
Sometimes use interpreter; some language ability	21
Never use interpreter; fluent	5
Spanish	
Always need interpreter; no language ability	24
Sometimes use interpreter; some language ability	23
Never use interpreter; fluent	11
Haitian Creole	
Always need interpreter; no language ability	55
Sometimes use interpreter; some language ability	1
Never use interpreter; fluent	2

[a]Percentages may not add to 100% due to rounding.

[b]For each language, PCPs were asked to choose the statement that best represents their language ability: *I always use an interpreter; I speak Portuguese / Spanish / Haitian Creole with patients, but sometimes I need an interpreter;* or *I am a native speaker.* In some cases, PCPs reported that they spoke a foreign language fluently such that an interpreter was never needed, yet they were not native speakers.

access status and number of sessions per week; presence of language, gender, and race concordance between patient and PCP; and health center. This analysis corresponds to 74,120 visits made by 13,882 patients. In this model, young, publicly insured, and Haitian Creole–speaking patients were significantly more likely to miss appointments than were older, privately insured, English-speaking patients. Patients of PCPs at open access and patients who were proficient in the same language or were the same race as their PCP were less likely to miss primary care appointments. Patients seen at community health centers #2, #3, and #6 and at hospital-based clinic #2 were two to three times as likely to miss appointments as were patients seen at community health center #1.

Discussion

Patients who were race or language concordant with their PCPs and patients whose PCP was at open access were slightly less likely to miss primary care appointments

Table 12.2

Missed appointment rates during initial visits in 2002, according to patient, provider, and visit characteristics

Characteristic (% of sample)[a] n=28,745 patients	Did not keep appointment (%)
Total (100)	16.3
Patient characteristics	
Age (y)	
18–40 (57.4)	17.9
41–64 (33.0)	15.4
≥65 (9.6)	10.0
Female (61.3)	16.2
Male (38.7)	16.5
Race or ethnicity	
White (54.4)	14.5
Black (16.8)	19.1
Hispanic (19.3)	18.3
Asian (1.2)	12.7
Other race (8.4)	17.1
Language	
English (54.3)	15.1
Portuguese (25.5)	17.6
Spanish (12.7)	17.8
Haitian Creole (7.4)	18.2
Insurance	
Freecare (34.1)	15.2
Medicaid (9.8)	21.3
Medicare (12.1)	12.3
Private (39.2)	8.4
Other[b] (4.8)	3.8
New[c] (51.7)	18.8
Not new (48.3)	13.6
Provider characteristics	
Visit with open access PCP[d] (48.9)	15.4
Visit with non–open access PCP (51.1)	17.2
Visit with PCP practicing >5 sessions per week (66.2)	16.1
Visit with PCP practicing ≤5 sessions per week (33.8)	16.7
Visit characteristics	
Visit with PCP in practice >7 years (41.2)	16.6
Visit with PCP in practice ≤7 years (58.8)	16.1
Practice site	
Community health center #1 (11.2)	6.0
Community health center #2 (7.9)	21.4

(*continued*)

Table 12.2 (*continued*)

Characteristic (% of sample)[a] *n*=28,745 patients	Did not keep appointment (%)
Community health center #3 (4.9)	18.4
Community health center #4 (6.5)	15.6
Community health center #5 (6.5)	15.6
Community health center #6 (14.1)	21.5
Community health center #7 (3.1)	13.4
Community health center #8 (11.0)	10.0
Community health center #9 (10.9)	20.0
Hospital-based clinic #1 (13.5)	17.1
Hospital-based clinic #2 (5.8)	18.7
Other health centers[e] (4.6)	19.4

[a]Percentages may not add to 100% due to rounding.

[b]This category includes the following insurance types: industrial accident, champus, and elder service plan.

[c]New patients are defined as those who had not seen a given PCP since December 31, 1997.

[d]We defined a PCP to be open access if, on average, four days or less would elapse until their third next available appointment.

[e]This category is composed of 5 smaller primary care sites: 3 community health centers and 2 hospital-based clinics.

Table 12.3

Missed appointment rates during initial visits in 2002, according to language and race concordance; new patients excluded

Characteristic (% of sample)[a] *n*=13,882 patients	Did not keep appointment (%)
Language concordance	
English-English (57.2)	12.6
Spanish-Spanish (6.5)	15.4
Portuguese-Portuguese (5.4)	12.2
Haitian Creole–Haitian Creole (1.8)	22.2
Discordant (29.0)	15.0
Race concordance	
White-white (53.3)	11.8
Black-black (3.7)	17.3
Other-other and Asian-Asian (<1)	26.7
Discordant (42.8)	15.5
Gender concordance	
Female-female (44.2)	14.5
Male-male (25.1)	13.1
Discordant (30.7)	12.9

[a]Percentages may not add to 100% due to rounding.

Table 12.4

Multivariate analysis of patient, provider, and visit characteristics associated with missed follow-up appointments to primary care

Characteristic n=74,120 visits (by 13,882 patients)	Odds ratio (95% CI)	p value
Patient characteristics		
Age, y		
18–40	2.12 (1.91–2.35)	$p<0.0001$
41–64	1.66 (1.51–1.83)	$p<0.0001$
≥65	1.00 (reference)	
Insurance		
Private	1.00 (reference)	
Medicaid	1.76 (1.61–1.93)	$p<0.0001$
Free care	1.36 (1.26–1.46)	$p<0.0001$
Medicare	1.59 (1.44–1.75)	$p<0.0001$
Other insurance[a]	0.17 (0.13–0.23)	$p<0.0001$
Language		
English	1.00 (reference)	
Haitian Creole	1.18 (1.04–1.33)	$p<0.05$
Portuguese	0.98 (0.87–1.09)	NS
Spanish	0.91 (0.82–1.01)	NS
Provider characteristics		
Open access	0.80 (0.74–0.86)	$p<0.0001$
Visit with PCP practicing >5 sessions per week	1.05 (0.97–1.14)	NS
Visit characteristics		
Language concordance	0.90 (0.81–0.99)	$p<0.05$
Gender concordance	1.01 (0.95–1.07)	NS
Race concordance	0.84 (0.79–0.90)	$p<0.0001$
Health center		
Community health center #1	1.00 (reference)	
Community health center #2	2.30 (1.99–2.65)	$p<0.0001$
Community health center #3	2.47 (2.13–2.86)	$p<0.0001$
Community health center #4	1.85 (1.58–2.17)	$p<0.0001$
Community health center #5	1.93 (1.67–2.23)	$p<0.0001$
Community health center #6	2.75 (2.44–3.11)	$p<0.0001$
Community health center #7	1.65 (1.38–1.98)	$p<0.0001$
Community health center #8	1.32 (1.16–1.52)	$p<0.0001$
Community health center #9	1.92 (1.68–2.19)	$p<0.0001$
Hospital-based clinic #1	1.71 (1.52–1.93)	$p<0.0001$
Hospital-based clinic #2	2.03 (1.73–2.38)	$p<0.0001$
Other heath centers[b]	1.19 (1.02–1.39)	$p<0.05$

[a]This category includes the following insurance types: industrial accident, champus, and elder service plan.

[b]This category comprises 5 smaller primary care sites: 3 community health centers and 2 hospital based clinics.

than were other patients. Site of care was a more powerful predictor of missed appointments. Patients seen at community health centers #2, #3, and #6 and at hospital-based clinic #2 were more than twice as likely to miss appointments as patients seen at community health center #1 were, even with control for age, insurance status, and other risk factors for missing appointments.

Our finding that young and publicly insured patients are more likely than their counterparts to miss primary care appointments is consistent with previous studies.[1-5] While Vikander and colleagues[6] found an improved attendance rate among patients scheduled with little delay, our study found that decreasing delays until the time of the appointment had only a modest effect on missed appointment rates. Our finding that patients of PCPs working fewer clinical sessions were no more likely to miss appointments than were patients of PCPs working more clinical sessions is a novel one and suggests that part-time PCPs may not decrease practice efficiency. Our finding that gender concordance does not affect missed appointment rates adds to prior literature about the effect of gender concordance on processes of care.[8,17-19]

Although we found that race and language concordance between patients and PCPs had only modest effects on missed appointment rates, other studies have found clear benefits of such concordance, as we noted at the beginning of this chapter.[7-13]

Our study is limited by the fact that we used different methods to collect data on patients and providers. Health center staff identified the race and language abilities of patients, while providers identified their own race and language abilities. Misclassification of patient race (and less likely of patient language) may have attenuated our findings. It is also possible that the wide availability of trained medical interpreters in our health centers may diminish differences between care delivered in language-concordant and discordant visits. At the same time, we may have overestimated the effect of language concordance on missed appointment rates, given that we did not control for the clustering that occurs between patient visits to the same provider.

Another limitation of our study is that we had low numbers of minority and Haitian Creole–speaking providers. However, our study findings are not limited to concordance between white PCP-patient dyads and English-speaking PCP-patient dyads. The fact that interaction terms between patient race and race concordance and patient language and language concordance were not statistically significant suggests that our findings also hold true for non-white PCP-patient dyads and non-English-speaking PCP-patient dyads.

Why is site of care among a local network of community health centers such a strong determinant of missed appointments? In many respects, the sites of care included here were similar to one another. All of them have similar financial resources and operate in an open-access system. All use telephone reminder calls one to three days prior to the scheduled appointment[20] to decrease the number of missed appointments, and all sites follow a standardized protocol to notify patients of missed follow-up appointments.[21] Most of the health centers (community health centers #2, #3, #4, #5, #6, #9, 5 and both hospital-based clinics) included in this study have on-site interpreters in the languages most prevalent at the site.*

Other systems, however, may vary from one health center to another in ways that affect missed appointment rates. For example, organizational culture and leadership at each health center are other potential determinants of variability.[22,23] Community health center #1, the site with the lowest missed appointment rate, was previously a private practice. The culture of a private practice, with its greater incentive for efficiency and customer service, still exists at this health center. For example, this site is open on weekends and has excellent staff retention. This site also sends out an introductory registration and medical history package to all new patients. This mailing may make patients feel welcome at the center and also serve as an appointment reminder. Finally, this site sends out a strongly worded letter to patients who miss their appointments and provides a designated telephone number for them to call and cancel appointments in the future.

In contrast, community health center #6, the site with the highest missed appointment rate, has had considerable staff turnover. At the time of this study, this site sent letters to patients who missed appointments asking the patients to reschedule; the letter did not encourage patients to cancel appointments, nor did it include a designated cancellation line. Community health center #6 is not open on weekends and does not send out an introductory registration and medical history package to new patients, factors that may contribute to the high missed appointment rate at this site.

Other conceivable causes of variation are unestablished. For example, while all sites use telephone reminder calls prior to scheduled appointments, there may be variability in the time of day during which such calls are made, the number of times a patient is called, and whether calls are made in all non-English languages. Telephone access varies among health centers, with long telephone wait times at some health centers, discouraging patients from calling to cancel an appointment.

It is also possible that unmeasured cultural and socioeconomic differences between patients at different health centers could explain the high variability in missed appointment rates. For example, community health center #6 is located in the same building as the CHA Outpatient Addiction Services program. This health center, which had the highest missed appointment rate, provides a disproportionate amount of primary care services to patients with substance use disorders, a group at risk for missing appointments.[24]

Our study, based on administrative data collected in the routine course of clinical care, is limited by a lack of data on occupation, education level, income, and reason for visit, all potential confounders. Lacking data on country of origin, we

---

*For example, community health center #2 has an on-site Portuguese interpreter, while community health center #3 has an on-site Haitian Creole interpreter. Since community health center #1 has bilingual PCPs and bilingual staff, it does not utilize on-site interpreters. The remaining health centers (community health centers #7 and #8, as well as the smaller health centers listed under "other health centers") are sent interpreters from a central office on an as-needed basis or use telephone interpreting.

were unable to distinguish Brazilian Portuguese-speaking patients from Portuguese speakers whose country of origin is Portugal, the Azores, or Madeira. The latter group is an established immigrant community while the former are largely economic refugees with greater transience and family instability. Based on our PCPs' clinical experience, we know that the Brazilian Portuguese tend to use community health center #6, while Portuguese speakers whose country of origin is Portugal, the Azores, or Madeira tend to use community health center #1. We also had no data on individual PCP's culturally specific interpersonal styles. It is possible that culturally competent PCPs, regardless of their language ability, might form stronger bonds with their patients (and thus that these patients might be less likely to miss appointments).

Though limited by its dependence on administrative data, our study is unprecedented in its size and provides valuable information about why patients may miss primary care appointments. Our findings suggest a need to scrutinize differences in systems of care among practice sites. Our study also provides evidence to support the continued use of open access systems to decrease missed appointments. Race and language concordance between patient and provider does not have a large effect on missed appointment rates. Nevertheless, the other positive effects that such concordance has on processes of care should encourage continued efforts to recruit minority PCPs and those with non-English language fluency to practice in community health centers.

Acknowledgments

We would like to acknowledge Danny McCormick, MD, MPH, and David U. Himmelstein, MD, for their help with study design; Melbeth G. Marlang, BA, for her help with manuscript preparation; and Steffie J. Woolhandler, MD, MPH, and Maxim D. Shrayer, PhD, for their constructive comments on earlier drafts of this chapter. We would also like to thank the PCPs who participated in the survey.

This study was supported by grant R21 HS 13559-01 from the Agency for Health Care Quality and Research (Dr. Lasser and Ms. Lambert).

Notes

1. Deyo RA, Inui TS. Dropouts and broken appointments. A literature review and agenda for future research. Med Care. 1980;18(11):1146–57.

2. Neal RD, Lawlor DA, Allgar V, et al. Missed appointments in general practice: retrospective data analysis from four practices. Br J Gen Pract. 2001;51(471):830–2.

3. Barron WM. Failed appointments. who misses them, why are they missed, and what can be done. Prim Care. 1980;7(4):563–74.

4. Waller J, Hodgkin P. Defaulters in general practice: who are they and what can be done about them? Fam Pract. 2000;17(3):252–3.

5. Majeroni BA, Cowan T, Osborne J, et al. Missed appointments and Medicaid managed care. Arch Fam Med. 1996;5(9):507–11.

6. Vikander T, Parnicky K, Demers R, et al. New-patient no-shows in an urban family practice center: analysis and intervention. J Fam Pract. 1986;22(3):263–8.

7.   Manson A. Language concordance as a determinant of patient compliance and emergency room use in patients with asthma. Med Care. 1988;26(12):1119–28.

8.   Cooper-Patrick L, Gallo JJ, Gonzales JJ, et al. Race, gender, and partnership in the patient-physician relationship. JAMA. 1999;282(6):583–9.

9.   Cooper LA, Roter DL, Johnson RL, et al. Patient-centered communication, ratings of care, and concordance of patient and physician race. Ann Intern Med. 2003;139(11):907–15.

10. Seijo R, Gomez H, Freidenberg J. Language as a communication barrier in medical care for Hispanic patients. Hisp J Behav Sci. 1991;13(4):363–76.

11. Perez-Stable EJ, Napoles-Springer A, Miramontes JM. The effects of ethnicity and language on medical outcomes of patients with hypertension or diabetes. Med Care. 1997;35(12): 1212–9.

12. Saha S, Komaromy M, Koepsell TD, et al. Patient-physician racial concordance and the perceived quality and use of health care. Arch Intern Med. 1999;159(9):997–1004.

13. Rosenheck R, Fontana A, Cottrol C. Effect of clinician-veteran racial pairing in the treatment of posttraumatic stress disorder. Am J Psychiatry. 1995;152(4):555–63.

14. Murray M, Berwick DM. Advanced access: reducing waiting and delays in primary care. JAMA. 2003;289(8):1035–40.

15. SAS Institute. SAS/STAT® user's guide, version 8, Cary, NC: SAS Institute, 1999:1363–464.

16. Zeger SL, Liang KY. Longitudinal data analysis for discrete and continuous outcomes. Biometrics. 1986;42(1):121–30.

17. Schmittdiel J, Grumbach K, Selby JV, et al. Effect of physician and patient gender concordance on patient satisfaction and preventive care practices. J Gen Intern Med. 2000;15(11):761–9.

18. Garcia JA, Paterniti DA, Romano PS, et al. Patient preferences for physician characteristics in university-based primary care clinics. Ethn Dis. 2003;13(2):259–67.

19. Franks P, Bertakis KD. Physician gender, patient gender, and primary care. J Womens Health (Larchmt). 2003;12(1):73–80.

20. Cambridge Health Alliance. Follow-up appointments in ambulatory sites. (Policy C-PFH-0011) Cambridge Health Alliance, 1999.

21. Cambridge Health Alliance. Failure to keep appointment protocol. (Policy C-PFH-0012) Cambridge Health Alliance, 1999.

22. Clancy C. Quality improvment: getting to how. Health Serv Res. 2003;38(2):509–13.

23. Jackson S. Does organizational culture affect out-patient DNA (did not attend) rates? Health Manpow Manage. 1997;23(6):233–6.

24. Backeland F, Lundwall L. Dropping out of treatment: a critical review. Psychol Bull. 1975;82(5): 738–83.

Chapter 13

Free Clinics and The Uninsured: The Increasing Demands of Chronic Illness

Mohan M. Nadkarni
John T. Philbrick

Despite the economic prosperity of the 1990s, the number of uninsured individuals and families in the United States has continued to increase. In 1998, approximately 44 million Americans younger than 65 lacked health insurance.[1] The traditional safety net providers for the uninsured have been community health centers, public hospitals, academic health centers, and private practitioners willing to treat patients for reduced or no fees. Volunteer free clinics emerged in the 1960s as an alternative health care delivery model for this population. Free clinics are private, nonprofit corporations with tax-exempt status. They are designed to provide primary and specialty care, access to laboratory services, and prescription medications. Services are provided at little or no charge and delivered primarily or exclusively by volunteer licensed health care professionals.[2] In recent years, particularly after the 1994 failure of health care reform, free clinics have taken a prominent place on the list of safety net providers proposed as nongovernmental solutions to the problems of the uninsured. President Bush and others in the federal government stressed policies that called for an even bigger role for nongovernmental, charitable organizations to fill gaps in medical care for the nation's uninsured.[3] There were 345 free clinics registered in the United States in 2000.[2] Despite their long history, there is surprisingly little published about them. Several reports have addressed the challenges of starting free clinics.[2,4–10] Some of these reports provide brief summaries of patient demographics and categories of clinical problems seen.[5,11] At the time of this chapters original publication, there were no publications providing detailed descriptions of demographic and clinical characteristics of free clinic patients. This information is vital for clinic management as well as broader public policy concerns. To begin to fill the gap, we describe in this chapter the experience from the first five years of operation (1992–97) of the Charlottesville Free Clinic in Charlottesville, Virginia.

Mohan M. Nadkarni, MD, FACP, is a professor of medicine at the University of Virginia School of Medicine and chief of the Section of General Internal Medicine, University of Virginia Health System. *John T. Philbrick, MD,* is a professor of internal medicine at the University of Virginia School of Medicine.

The Charlottesville Free Clinic is a nonprofit organization staffed by volunteer health care providers.[4] It is 1 of 32 clinics in Virginia. Since 1992, it has provided free primary care medical services, including x-ray and pharmacy services, to uninsured patients from the city of Charlottesville and the surrounding counties. The clinic is open three evenings a week and provides internal medicine, pediatric, basic gynecology, and limited psychiatric and dental services. Patients are eligible for care if they have no private insurance, are not covered under Medicaid or Medicare, and do not qualify for free care at the local university medical center. It has four full-time administrative staff members and a panel of approximately 200 volunteer health professionals, including physicians, nurses, nurse practitioners, physician assistants, dentists, and pharmacists. Since its inception in 1992, the Charlottesville Free Clinic has maintained a computerized database that includes patient demographic information along with clinical information about each encounter. In this report, we describe patient demographics, the most common primary diagnoses, trends in acute and chronic illness visits, and information on sources of care for patients served at the clinic during its first five years of operation.

Methods

All patients provided demographic and survey data at the time of their first visit to the clinic. Patients were asked several questions about their usual source of care and emergency room usage and where they would have sought care if the free clinic had not existed. Primary visit diagnoses were coded by the treating physicians using ICD-9-CM criteria. These diagnoses were compared with National Ambulatory Medical Care Survey data, a national survey of diagnoses and demographics of patients presenting to physician offices and outpatient departments.[12] Statistical analysis included use of the chi-square test for comparison of categorical variables and the Cochran-Armitage trend test to assess trends in categorical variables. Statistical analysis was performed using SAS version 8.1 (SAS Institute, Cary, NC).

Results

From 1992 through 1997, 4,680 patients made 13,373 visits to the Charlottesville Free Clinic. Table 13.1 shows the demographic information according to numbers of patients and visits. The patients were primarily uninsured, nonindigent, younger than 65 years, and employed. Table 13.1 also provides information on self-reported use of other health care services by Charlottesville Free Clinic patients at the time of their first visit. Emergency rooms were named most frequently as the patient's usual source of health care. For the index visit, approximately one-third reported they would have visited an emergency room if they had not gone to the Charlottesville Free Clinic. One-quarter would not have sought care in the absence of the Charlottesville Free Clinic.

Table 13.1

Demographic characteristics of free clinic patients

	Patients[a]		Visits[b]		
	n	**%**	**n**	**%**	**p[c]**
Sex					
Female	2,631	57.2	8,622	63.8	<0.0001
Male	1,966	42.8	4,885	36.2	
Race					
White	3,269	71.0	10,259	76.5	<0.0001
Black	1,068	23.2	2,540	19.0	
Other	268	5.8	607	4.5	
Age (years)					
<15	895	19.5	1,929	14.4	<0.0001
15–24	908	19.7	1,951	14.5	
25–44	2,134	46.5	6,206	46.2	
45–64	631	13.7	3,272	24.4	
65–74	28	0.6	61	0.4	
Marital status (age 15 and older)					
Single	1,793	48.9			
Married	1,114	30.4			
Divorced	499	13.6			
Widow(er)	83	2.3			
Other	181	4.9			
Employment (age 15 and older)					
Full time	2,395	64.7			
Part time	998	27.0			
Not employed	308	8.3			
Living situation					
Owner	884	19.5			
Renter	2,387	52.6			
Shelter/homeless	357	7.9			
Family member	664	14.6			
Other	244	5.3			
Annual family income					
<$5,000	756	17.2			
$5,000–10,000	1,040	23.7			
$10,000–15,000	1,177	26.8			
$15,000–20,000	648	14.7			
$20,000–25,000	397	9.1			
>$25,000	370	8.4			
Insurance status					
Private insurance	110	2.5			
Medicare	51	1.1			
Medicaid	125	2.8			
Veterans' benefits	45	1.0			
Uninsured	4,134	92.6			

Table 13.1 (*continued*)

	Patients[a]		Visits[b]		
	n	%	*n*	%	*p*[c]
Usual source of health care (self-reported)					
Emergency room	1,263	28.0			
Private physician	954	21.2			
No usual source	800	17.7			
University clinic	474	10.5			
City/county health department	164	3.6			
Other	855	19.0			
Emergency room visits in past year (self-reported)					
0	2,699	60.0			
1	943	21.0			
2–5	726	16.1			
>5	133	3.0			
Alternative to free clinic[d]					
No provider	1,121	24.9			
Emergency room	1,554	34.5			
Other provider	1,820	40.2			

[a]Total number of patients is 4,680. Due to missing values, subgroup numbers may be less.

[b]Age was calculated from date of each visit. Since all demographic information was obtained only at the time of the first visit, visit distributions were not provided for items that could have changed at subsequent visits.

[c]Patients versus visits, χ^2 test

[d]Answer to the question: "Where would you have gone if the Charlottesville Free Clinic did not exist?"

Table 13.2 presents the most common principal diagnosis categories and table 13.3 the most common diagnoses coded for the 13,373 office visits, along with corresponding information from the 1995 National Ambulatory Medical Care Survey.[12] Patient diagnoses were similar in distribution to other ambulatory office settings, although acute respiratory infection, essential hypertension, and depressive disorder not elsewhere classified appeared to be more common at the Charlottesville Free Clinic. Table 13.4 shows the most common principal diagnoses according to visit year. The total number of visits per year fluctuated, but the proportion of patients seen for essential hypertension, depressive disorder not elsewhere classified, and diabetes mellitus steadily increased during the five years of clinic operation.

Discussion

Demographic characteristics of free clinic patients show considerable variation according to their settings. Charlottesville Free Clinic patients are uninsured but represent the working near-poor population. All age groups are represented except those age 65 and older. The racial mix is similar to that of Charlottesville and

Table 13.2

Free clinic visits (1992–97) by principal diagnosis category compared with National Ambulatory Medical Care Survey (1995)

Major disease category	ICD-9-CM code range[a]	Free clinic		NAMCS[b] (%)		
		Number of visits	%	physician offices	outpatient departments	emergency departments
All visits		13,373	100.0	100.0	100.0	100.0
Infectious and parasitic diseases	001–139	745	5.6	3.0	3.0	3.5
Neoplasms	140–239	61	0.5	2.9	5.0	0.3
Endocrine, nutritional, and metabolic diseases and immunity disorders	240–279	713	5.3	3.9	5.3	1.3
Mental disorders	290–319	823	6.2	4.5	7.2	2.9
Diseases of nervous system and sense organs	320–389	866	6.5	10.4	7.2	5.9
Diseases of the circulatory system	390–459	1,118	8.4	7.4	6.6	4.4
Diseases of the respiratory system	460–519	2,505	18.7	14.1	10.3	13.2
Diseases of the digestive system	520–579	683	5.1	3.8	3.3	5.8
Diseases of the genitourinary system	580–629	917	6.9	5.5	4.5	4.3
Diseases of the skin and subcutaneous tissue	680–709	592	4.4	4.9	3.7	2.7
Diseases of the musculoskeletal system and connective tissue	710–739	727	5.4	7.8	6.4	4.0
Symptoms, signs, and ill-defined conditions	780–799	1,016	7.6	4.9	5.1	13.0
Injury and poisoning	800–999	396	3.0	7.1	6.1	31.6
Supplementary classification	V01–V82	2,132	15.9	15.8	20.3	3.5
All other diagnoses		140	1.0	4.0	6.0	3.6

[a]Based on the *International Classification of Diseases: 9th Revision: Clinical Modification* (Los Angeles: Practice Management Information, 1997).
[b]National Ambulatory Medical Care Survey.

Table 13.3

Free clinic visits (1992–97) by most common principal diagnosis compared with National Ambulatory Medical Care Survey (1995)

Principal diagnosis group	ICS-9-CM code range[a]	Free clinic		NAMCS[b] (%)		
		Number of visits	%	physician offices	outpatient departments	emergency departments
All visits		13,373	100.0	100.0	100.0	100.0
Acute upper respiratory infections (excluding pharyngitis)	460–461,463–466	1,248	9.3	4.6	2.9	4.0
Essential hypertension	401	990	7.4	3.2	3.4	0.5
Depressive disorder, not elsewhere classified	311	465	3.5	0.6	1.0	0.3
Diabetes mellitus	250	420	3.1	1.9	2.8	0.4
General medical examination	V70	418	3.1	3.0	2.4	0.3
Acute pharyngitis	462	357	2.6	1.4	1.1	1.9
Rheumatism, excluding back	725–729	353	2.6	2.2	1.4	1.4
Otitis media and eustachian tube disorders	381–382	333	2.5	2.9	2.2	3.1
Contact dermatitis and other eczema	692	247	1.8	1.0	0.8	0.6
Asthma	493	229	1.7	1.3	1.9	1.9
Chronic and unspecified bronchitis	490–491	201	1.5	1.6	0.8	1.8
Chronic sinusitis	473	198	1.5	1.7	1.4	0.7
Dorsopathies	720–724	191	1.4	2.2	1.6	1.4
Urinary tract infection, site not specified	599	183	1.4	0.3	0.2	0.2
All other diagnoses		7,540	56.6	72.1	76.1	81.5

[a]Based on the *International Classification of Diseases: 9th Revision: Clinical Modification* (Los Angeles: Practice Management Information., 1997).
[b]National Ambulatory Medical Care Survey.

Table 13.4

Free clinic visits (1992–97) by most common principal diagnosis and visit year (in percentages)

Principal diagnosis group	ICD-9-CM code range[a]	Year					total visits (n)	p[b]
		1	2	3	4	5		
All visits (n)		2,924	2,564	3,104	2,484	2,297	13,373	
Acute upper respiratory infections (excluding pharyngitis)	460–461, 463–466	5.4	7.6	13.4	10.7	9.1	1,248	<0.0001
Essential hypertension	401	5.6	6.0	7.1	9.0	9.7	990	<0.0001
Depressive disorder, not elsewhere classified	311	0.4	0.8	3.7	5.1	8.0	465	<0.0001
Diabetes mellitus	250	2.2	1.8	2.0	4.0	6.1	420	<0.0001
General medical examination	V70	3.2	5.3	1.8	2.2	3.0	418	0.001
Acute pharyngitis	462	4.0	2.8	2.5	2.0	1.6	357	<0.0001
Rheumatism, excluding back	725–729	3.6	3.2	2.5	2.2	1.3	353	<0.0001
Otitis media and eustachian tube disorders	381–382	2.5	3.7	2.8	1.6	1.5	333	<0.0001
Contact dermatitis and other eczema	692	1.9	1.6	2.0	1.8	1.6	247	ns
Asthma	493	2.0	1.7	1.2	1.5	2.0	229	ns
Chronic and unspecified bronchitis	490–491	3.7	2.4	0.5	0.3	0.1	201	<0.0001
Chronic sinusitis	473	3.4	2.8	0.2	0.2	0.3	198	<0.0001
Dorsopathies	720–724	1.4	1.0	1.9	1.3	1.2	191	ns
Urinary tract infection, site not specified	599	1.7	1.7	1.1	1.0	1.1	183	0.01
All other diagnoses		58.3	57.0	56.6	56.4	52.7	7,540	

Note: ns = not significant.

[a]Based on the *International Classification of Diseases: 9th Revision: Clinical Modification* (Los Angeles: Practice Management Information, 1997).

[b]Cochran-Armitage trend test.

the surrounding counties. Whereas the Charlottesville Free Clinic had only 8.3% of its over-15 patients unemployed and 19.5% of its patients were younger than 15, a clinic targeted to the needs of the homeless in an urban setting in Georgia reported 67 percent unemployed and 73 percent male patients,[7] and a rural clinic in West Virginia had only 6 percent of patients younger than 21 years.[5]

Tables 13.2 and 13.3 show striking similarities in the frequencies of the major disease categories and principal diagnosis groups for Charlottesville Free Clinic patient visits, compared with physician office and outpatient department data from the National Ambulatory Medical Care Survey. As one would expect for this younger-than-65 population, fewer Charlottesville Free Clinic patients were seen for malignancy and more for acute infectious illnesses, including upper respiratory infections, acute pharyngitis, and urinary tract infections. However, when taking into account the absence of patients age 65 and older in the Charlottesville Free Clinic population, there appears to be a disproportionate number of Charlottesville Free Clinic visits for hypertension and diabetes. Table 13.4 shows that the percentage of patients seen for these two diagnosis groups steadily increased during the first five years of clinic operation. In year 5, almost 16% of visits were for the two diagnoses, three times the total percentage for these diagnosis groups from the National Ambulatory Medical Care Survey. These data support the conclusion that the Charlottesville Free Clinic, while providing urgent care for episodic illnesses, is becoming a primary care delivery site dealing with chronic medical problems. Our findings are supported by those from the West Virginia clinic, which reported that 70% of their visits were for "chronic illness," including 10% for "diabetes/endocrine" and 25% for "cardiac/hypertension" diagnoses.[5]

Although this study describes the patients of only one free clinic, it has a number of methodological strengths. These include its prospective collection of data, the relatively large number of patients and visits, ICD-9-CM diagnosis coding, and the paucity of missing data. Due to differences in how the data are collected, we acknowledge that Charlottesville Free Clinic and the National Ambulatory Medical Clinic Survey data should be only roughly compared.

Our observations raise important questions concerning the future direction of free clinics as part of the safety net for the uninsured. It is clear that those with chronic disease who lack health insurance have unmet health needs, including care for hypertension, diabetes, elevated cholesterol, and obesity.[13] Just as important, the uninsured are less likely to receive preventive services, including those focused on cancer screening, cardiovascular risk reduction, substance abuse, and HIV risk.[13] There are important adverse clinical consequences to being uninsured, including avoidable hospitalization,[14] increased severity of illness on hospitalization,[15] increased risk of death (particularly when hospitalized),[16,17] more advanced stage of cancer at diagnosis,[18,19] lower cancer survival rates,[18] lower infant birth weight,[20] and higher infant mortality.[19]

Free clinics face a number of challenges if they are to play an important role in meeting these needs. First, they should be able to provide comprehensive primary care, including preventive services, to all patients rather than a patch-work mix of acute care and preventive services determined by the resources that happen to be available. Appropriate care for the more common chronic diseases of adults, such as hypertension, diabetes, and hyperlipidemia, includes regular office visits, chronic medications, periodic laboratory testing, and occasional subspecialty visits. Preventive services involve office visits for counseling as well as for screening mammography, Pap smears, fecal occult blood testing, sigmoidoscopy, colonoscopy, cholesterol testing, and immunizations. To meet the mission of providing comprehensive care, free clinics will have to find additional resources. An even greater challenge facing free clinics is the need to expand their services to more of the uninsured patients they currently do not reach. In Virginia in 1999, there were approximately 900,000 uninsured persons. However, for that year, Virginia's 32 free clinics served only 37,715 patients, with 82,521 primary care visits.[21] Thus, Virginia, which has more free clinics than any other state, served less than 5 percent of the uninsured via the free-clinic system.

Conclusion

Charlottesville Free Clinic provides care to uninsured patients who have illnesses similar to those reported in a national survey of all patients using physician offices and outpatient departments. Many free clinic patients reported they would either use an emergency room or would not seek care if the free clinic had not existed, behaviors leading to inappropriate care and poor health outcomes. While many patients are seen for urgent care of episodic illnesses, during the first five years of the Charlottesville Free Clinic, the proportion of patients seen for chronic illness steadily increased. This shift away from urgent care toward the care of chronic illnesses carries the obligation to provide comprehensive care of these illnesses as well as appropriate preventive services. Free clinics will have to find significant additional resources to meet the mission of providing comprehensive primary care to a patient population with chronic illnesses.

Notes

1. Fronstin P. Sources of health insurance and characteristics of the uninsured: analysis of the March 1999 current population survey. Washington, DC: Employee Benefit Research Institute, 2000.

2. Scott HD, Bell J, Geller S, et al. Physicians helping the underserved: the Reach Out program. JAMA. 2000 Jan 5;283(1):99–104.

3. Drazen JM, Bush GW, Gore A. The Republican and Democratic candidates speak on health care. N Engl J Med. 2000 Oct 19;343(16):1184–9.

4. DeMarco PV, Nadkarni M. The Charlottesville Free Clinic: residents breaking barriers to care. JAMA. 1993 May 19;269(19):2496.

5. Smego RA Jr, Costante J. An academic health center-community partnership: the Morgantown Health Right free clinic. Acad Med. 1996 Jun;71(6):613–21.

6. Yap OW, Thornton DJ. The Arbor Free Clinic at Stanford: a multidisciplinary effort. JAMA. 1995 Feb 1;273(5):431.

7. Carter KF, Green RD, Dufour L. Health needs of homeless clients accessing nursing care at a free clinic. J Community Health Nurs. 1994;11(3):139–47.

8. Morris GS. Memphis's medical Graceland: traditional health care neglects the working poor; a church-based clinic steps in. Pol Rev. 1998 May–June;(89):45–8.

9. Bibeau DL, Howell KA, Rife JC, et al. The role of a community coalition in the development of health services for the poor and uninsured. Int J Health Serv. 1996;26(1):93–110.

10. Fordham H. Burton Free Clinic. A point of light for Flint's indigent population. Mich Med. 1993 Oct;92(10):51–2.

11. Stein JA, Gelberg L. Comparability and representativeness of clinical homeless, community homeless, and domiciled clinic samples: physical and mental health, substance use, and health services utilization. Health Psychol. 1997 Mar;16(2):155–62.

12. Schappert SM. Ambulatory care visits of physician offices, hospital outpatient departments, and emergency departments: United States, 1995. Vital Health Stat [13]. 1997 Jun;(129):1–38.

13. Ayanian JZ, Weissman JS, Schneider EC, et al. Unmet health needs of uninsured adults in the United States. JAMA. 2000 Oct 25;284(16):2061–9.

14. Weissman JS, Gatsonis C, Epstein AM. Rates of avoidable hospitalization by insurance status in Massachusetts and Maryland. JAMA. 1992 Nov 4;268(17):2388–94.

15. Franks P, Clancy CM, Gold MR. Health insurance and mortality: evidence from a national cohort. JAMA. 1993 Aug 11;270(6):737–41.

16. Hadley J, Steinberg EP, Feder J. Comparison of uninsured and privately insured hospital patients: condition on admission, resource use, and outcome. JAMA. 1991 Jan 16;265(3):374–9.

17. Ayanian JZ, Kohler BA, Abe T, et al. The relation between health insurance coverage and clinical outcomes among women with breast cancer. N Engl J Med. 1993 Jul 29;329(5):326–31.

18. Roetzheim RG, Pal N, Tennant C, et al. Effects of health insurance and race on early detection of cancer. J Natl Cancer Inst. 1999 Aug 18;91(16):1409–15.

19. Schriver M. No health insurance? It's enough to make you sick. Scientific research linking the lack of health coverage to poor health. ACP-ASIM report October 1999. Retrieved from http://www.acponline.org/ininsured/index.html.

20. Does health insurance make a difference? OTA background paper. Washington, DC: Congress of the United States, Office of Technology Assessment, 1992.

21. Nadkarni MN, Cruise M, Philbrick JT. Virginia's free clinics: valuable asset for uninsured care. J Gen Intern Med. 2001 Apr; 6 Suppl 1:210.

Chapter 14

Missed Opportunities for Patient Education and Social Worker Consultation at the Arbor Free Clinic

Marie Soller
Lars Osterberg

A staggering 43.6 million Americans were uninsured in 2002, according to the United States Census Bureau.[1] Uninsured patients frequently rely on free clinics for health care because they are often unable to use other clinics in their communities. Physician contact, patient education materials, and social worker consultation are among the important health care opportunities that free clinics offer. The limited availability of volunteer staff and donated medical supplies often restricts the range of health care services that free clinics are able to provide to their patients. Free clinics must strive to make the most out of available resources by making them accessible to their target clientele and ensuring that patient satisfaction is high.

Missed opportunities are instances in which patients do not receive care that they desired and/or had an apparent need for. The occurrence of missed opportunities is often high in underserved patient populations; those documented in the literature include health screening,[2] vaccination,[3,4] STD and pregnancy counseling,[5,6] and breast-feeding education.[7] Low-income, minority, and uninsured patients who do not receive health education materials and social worker consultation may be missing essential services that free medical clinics are able to provide. Providing printed health education materials is a relatively inexpensive and feasible service that may strengthen physician–patient communication and promote self-care.[8,9] Social worker consultation provides low-income patients the opportunity to apply for public insurance programs and other services.

Previous research suggests not only that missed opportunities might exist for receiving patient education materials and social worker consultation but that clinics are more likely to miss opportunities to provide these services for certain groups of patients than for others.[10] Hispanics typically use fewer general health services than whites, perhaps because many Hispanics face cultural or language barriers to receiving health care that whites do not face.[11] Blacks, Hispanics, and

Marie Soller, MD, is a psychiatrist at the Wildwood Psychiatric Resource Center, in Beaverton, Oregon. *Lars Osterberg, MD, MPH,* is director of Educators 4 CARE and a clinical associate professor of medicine at Stanford University School of Medicine.

Asians have been shown to have more difficulty than whites in communicating with providers and understanding health information.[12] Language differences between provider and patient constitute an important barrier to health care efficacy.[13] Therefore, clinics may more frequently miss opportunities to serve patients who need an interpreter during the medical visit or who are from a culture different from that of their health care provider.

In addition to making health care services accessible, free clinics, like all other medical care facilities, must attempt to promote the satisfaction of patients. Patient satisfaction has been studied in detail in the settings of Medicaid programs in general[14] and Medicaid-managed care programs specifically.[15-17] No less important is the satisfaction of patients in free and volunteer clinics, although satisfaction has not been sufficiently studied in this health care setting.

The objectives of our study were to (1) measure overall levels of patient satisfaction, (2) investigate whether the free clinic missed the opportunity to provide desired or needed patient education materials or social worker consultation, and (3) determine if certain groups of patients were more susceptible to missed opportunities than others.

Methods

A cross-sectional survey was conducted among 210 patients who presented over an eight-month period at the Arbor Free Clinic in San Mateo County, California. Arbor is managed by Stanford University medical students and staffed entirely by student and physician volunteers.[18] The clinic was created to address the immediate health care needs of the underserved in the south San Francisco Bay area, who have few other options for accessing health care. Arbor provides medical services, gateway access to county social services, and health education materials in several languages. The Arbor Free Clinic has operated for more than 10 years with the goal of providing quality health care to its underserved community. Until recently, Arbor had yet to conduct a substantial evaluation of its patient care.

A two-part survey was designed to meet the specific aims of the study. The survey was approved by the Stanford University Human Subjects Review Board, and administered over an eight-month period. Research volunteers, who were not regular clinic staff, offered participation in the study to all patients as they entered the clinic. Patients were assured that their responses would be anonymous and would not influence their care. The written survey was available in English and Spanish, and volunteers were available to read the survey in both languages and record responses for any patient who could not or preferred not to read and write on their own. Patients who agreed to participate completed a consent form and were given the survey. The sample size was determined by the number of patients who agreed to participate during the eight-month period during which staff was available to administer the survey.

The first part of the survey contained questions regarding sociodemographic characteristics, including gender, age, ethnicity, primary language, interpreter status for the visit and survey, current and past housing situation, educational background, and health insurance status. This section was given to patients after they had checked in with the front desk but before the medical examination. The second part of the survey asked questions relating to the patients' experience at Arbor that day and was given to patients after the completed medical examination. These questions addressed topics such as patient satisfaction, receipt of patient education materials, and use of the social worker.

Patient satisfaction was measured by asking patients to rate the overall services that they received during their visit on a scale of 1–5 (1=inadequate and 5=great). Three types of missed opportunities were defined in the following way: as instances in which patients (1) desired to receive patient education materials but did not, (2) desired to visit the social worker but did not, (3) or could have benefited from visiting the social worker (because they were homeless, temporarily housed, or uninsured) but did not.

Statistical analyses, including chi square, t-test, and ANOVA analyses, were conducted using the statistical program SAS.[19]

Results

In all, 210 patients were surveyed, representing approximately 25% of patients who visited the clinic during the study period. The remaining 75% included patients who were not interested in participating, those who did not have time because they were taken directly into an examining room, and those who were missed by the research volunteer as they entered the clinic. The patient population consisted of 45.7% women (n=92); 42.6% English speakers (n=97), 32.2% Spanish speakers (n=74), and 25.2% other language speakers (n=39); and 81.9% uninsured patients (n=168). Table 14.1 summarizes the sociodemographic characteristics of the patient sample. These characteristics are not statistically different from those of the Arbor Clinic population as a whole.

Of the 210 respondents, 168 (80.0%) completed both parts of the survey (including the second part, which had questions related to patient satisfaction, receipt of patient education, and social worker consultation). The remaining 20% of patients were given the second part of the survey but did not return it. No significant differences by sociodemographic characteristics (including gender, age, ethnicity, primary language, interpreter status for the visit and survey, current and past housing situation, educational background, or health insurance status) were found between those who completed both parts of the survey and those who completed only the first part.

Patient satisfaction

The mean level of satisfaction with overall services was extremely high (4.6±0.9).

Missed opportunities

Table 14.2 summarizes the missed opportunities. Only 27.7% (n=44) of respondents received patient education materials, and 31.7% (n=53) of patients visited the social worker. Instances in which patients did not receive desired or clearly needed

Table 14.1

Sociodemographic characteristics of the survey population

Variable	Respondents (%)
Gender (data available on 202)	
Men	52.5
Women	47.5
Primary language (data available on 210)	
English	46.2
Spanish	35.2
Other	18.6
Health insurance (data available on 205)	
Insured	81.9
Uninsured	18.1
Ethnic identity (data available on 210)	
African American	18.1
Caucasian	15.2
Hispanic	40.0
Pacific Islander	15.2
Other	11.4
Interpreter required (data available on 207)	
No	63.8
Yes	36.2
Housing status (data available on 190)	
Permanent	70.5
Temporary	22.1
Homeless	7.4
Ever been homeless	27.0
Education completed (data available on 198)	
9th grade or less	26.7
High school	40.9
Vocational	5.1
College or more	27.3
Employment status (data available on 203)	
Full-time	13.8
Part-time	22.2
Unemployed	64.0

Note: The total sample consisted of 210 respondents, whose mean age ($\pm$ SD) was 39.7 $\pm$ 16.8 years.

care were significant at Arbor. More than one-quarter (28 of 99) of patients who did not receive patient education materials desired to receive them. One-third (35 of 104) of all patients who did not visit the social worker desired to do so. Patients were not routinely asked why they did not receive education materials or visit the social worker, even though these services were available at Arbor; therefore, this information is not available.

Table 14.2

Missed opportunities

	%	Number[a]
Patients who received patient education materials	27.7	44/159
Patients who did not receive patient education materials but desired to	28.3	28/99
Patients who visited the social worker	31.7	53/167
Patients who did not visit the social worker but desired to	33.7	35/104
Patients who did not visit the social worker but could have benefited from doing so because they were homeless, temporarily housed, or uninsured		
Homeless	90.9	10/11
Homeless who did not visit the social worker but desired to	40.0	4/10
Temporarily housed	72.4	21/29
Temporarily housed who did not visit the social worker but desired to	31.6	6/21
Uninsured	67.4	93/138
Uninsured who did not visit the social worker but desired to	30.6	26/93

[a]Denominator represents data available for each response.

Missed opportunities for social worker consultation were particularly high among patients who clearly could have benefited from such consultation (as indicated by their housing or insurance status). For example, the majority of homeless (90.9% [n=10]), temporarily housed (72.4% [n=21]), and uninsured (67.4% [n=93]) patients did not visit the social worker. A large proportion of these patients indicated that they would have liked to visit the social worker. Four of 10 homeless patients (40%), 6 of 19 temporarily housed (31.6%), and 26 of 85 uninsured patients (30.6%) who did not visit the social worker would have liked to do so.

Susceptibility to missed opportunities

All respondents were equally likely to receive patient education materials, whether or not they used an interpreter for the survey. Half of respondents who used an interpreter for the survey visited the social worker, while a significantly smaller 28.7% of those who did not use an interpreter for the survey did so (chi square=4.02; p<0.05 [<n=165]). No other sociodemographic characteristic correlated with significant differences in the rates of receiving patient education materials or visiting the social worker (all p>0.05).

Contrary to the initial hypotheses, neither Hispanics, Spanish speakers, nor those who required interpreters were more likely than other groups to experience any type of missed opportunity. In fact, no sociodemographic characteristic correlated with significant differences in the rates of missed opportunities (all p>0.05).

Discussion

This study measured overall levels of patient satisfaction, investigated whether Arbor patients who either desired or could have benefited from receiving patient education materials or visiting the social worker missed the opportunity to do so, and determined if certain groups of patients were more susceptible to missed opportunities than others. Patient satisfaction is high at the Arbor Free Clinic, a finding that reflects well upon the student-run clinic. Nonetheless, missed opportunities for patient education and social worker consultation appear to be a significant problem for Arbor.

One-quarter of patients received patient education materials, a service that is inexpensive, often easy to provide, and could be given to many more patients. Clinic staff at Arbor missed the opportunity to provide patient education materials to a significant percentage (27%) of patients who would have liked to receive such materials. This missed opportunity is significant because the staff could easily improve this outcome with its current resources. There are a number of possible explanations for the low percentage of patients receiving educational material. The diversity of patients from many different cultures makes it difficult to keep health education materials for the many different languages (and diseases) that are encountered. Reliable Internet access and printing capabilities are also required to provide quality health education materials consistently and this can be a challenge, particularly when these services are donated to the free clinic. This is a simple method for promoting patient self-care, however, and should be a priority for improving care at the clinic.

Only one-third of patients visited the social worker, a deficiency that may be the result of many clinic- and patient-specific factors. Even though most of Arbor's underserved patients seemingly would benefit from the social worker consultation, many patients may not have desired to meet with the social worker or may have had other opportunities to consult a social worker outside of the clinic. However, it is troubling that 28% of those who did not consult the social worker indicated that they would have liked to do so. Perhaps most worrisome is the finding that the majority of homeless patients, those in temporary housing, and those without health insurance did not consult with the social worker. A large proportion of these patients indicated on the survey that they would have liked to see the social worker. These results strongly suggest that missed opportunities for social worker consultation should be a target area for improvement at the Arbor Free Clinic. A deficiency of this study is that patients were not asked why they did not see the social worker. Such data might have suggested alternative methods to improve this missed opportunity.

Many competing pressures discourage these patients from seeing a social worker, including their priority to get their acute care needs met and the limited time they are willing to spend at the clinic. Although it is not necessary that a patient have an appointment or referral to visit the in-house social worker, patients may not be aware that a social worker is available or may not know where to locate these services. Patients who used interpreters throughout the visit were more likely to visit the social worker, suggesting that staff members working closely with patients may effectively direct patients to needed services that they might not be able to find on their own.

The hypotheses that we proposed based on the literature (that Hispanics, Spanish-speaking patients, and patients requiring interpreters would be more susceptible to missed opportunities than other groups) were not supported by the findings of this study. This is a favorable result for Arbor; it demonstrates that the current level of cultural and language competency of the clinic is not differentially preventing certain ethnic groups and non-English speakers from receiving the same type of care as other groups. Further study with an adequately powered and randomized sample is warranted because these negative results may be the result of a statistical error and not of a true lack of correlation.

Interpretation of the results must be tempered by the fact that 20% of respondents did not complete both parts of the survey and that some respondents left other questions blank. These deficiencies were possibly related to time constraints, lack of interest or lack of understanding of the survey instrument. Such gaps are drawbacks of using a written survey as the method for collecting patient information and opinions. The rate of incomplete surveys did not significantly correlate with any measured patient characteristic, and thus we assume that these occurrences were random and should not influence or bias this analysis.

Possible strategies for reducing the frequency of missed opportunities include the following:

1. If volunteer resources are available, designate patient advocates to check in with each patient at established times during the clinic visit (e.g., in the waiting room, before check-out) to encourage patients to receive patient education materials and visit the social worker.
2. In a setting of more limited volunteer resources, create and provide each patient with a handout that clearly explains the benefits and availability of patient education materials and visits to the social worker. Intake volunteers should give this handout to every patient to ensure that every patient is aware of these opportunities and has the chance to ask for them.
3. In any setting, train all volunteers more effectively to encourage every patient to take home patient education materials and to visit the social worker.
4. Patient education materials should be in multiple languages and easily read and understood.

Other free clinics are likely to face the same challenges as the Arbor Free Clinic in providing care to underserved patients from many cultural backgrounds. The results of this study and the proposed strategies for improving the level of missed opportunities indicate useful approaches for Arbor and other free and volunteer clinics.

Acknowledgment

This research was funded by grant support from the Stanford University School of Medicine Community Partners Medical Scholars Program.

Notes

1.   Mills R, Bhandari S. Health insurance coverage in the United States: 2002. Washington, DC: US Census Bureau, 2003.

2. Mitchell JB, Haber SG, Khatutsky G, et al. Impact of the Oregon Health Plan on access and satisfaction of adults with low income. Health Serv Res. 2002 Feb;37(1):11–31.

3. Hellinger FJ. The effect of managed care on quality: a review of recent evidence. Arch Intern Med. 1998 Apr 27;158(8):833–41.

4. Fields TT, Gomez PS. Utilizing patient satisfaction surveys to prepare for Medicaid managed care. J Health Care Poor Underserved. 2001 Feb;12(1):59–76.

5. Landon BE, Huskamp HA, Tobias C, et al. The evolution of quality management in state Medicaid agencies: a national survey of states with comprehensive managed care programs. Jt Comm J Qual Improv. 2002 Feb;28(2):72–82.

6. Cousineau M, Whitttenberg E, Pollatsec J. A study of the Health Care for the Homeless Program: final report. Washington, DC: Bureau of Primary Health Care, 1995.

7. Vryheid RE. A survey of vaccinations of immigrants and refugees in San Diego County, California. Asian Am Pac Isl J Health. 2001 Summer–Fall;9(2):221–30.

8. Harper PG, Murray DM. An organizational strategy to improve adolescent measles-mumps-rubella vaccination in a low socioeconomic population. A method to reduce missed opportunities. Arch Fam Med. 1994 Mar;3(3):257–62.

9. Gelberg L, Leake BD, Lu MC, et al. Use of contraceptive methods among homeless women for protection against unwanted pregnancies and sexually transmitted diseases: prior use and willingness to use in the future. Contraception. 2001 May;63(5):277–81.

10. Pourat N, Brown ER, Razack N, et al. Medicaid managed care and STDs: missed opportunities to control the epidemic. Health Aff (Millwood). 2002 May–Jun;21(3):228–39.

11. Raisler J. Against the odds: breastfeeding experiences of low income mothers. J Midwifery Womens Health. 2000 May–Jun;45(3):253–63.

12. Sullivan SD, Weiss KB, Lynn H, et al. The cost-effectiveness of an inner-city asthma intervention for children. J Allergy Clin Immunol. 2002 Oct;110(4):576–81.

13. Gallefoss F, Bakke PS. Cost-benefit and cost-effectiveness analysis of self-management in patients with COPD—a 1-year follow-up randomized, controlled trial. Respir Med. 2002 Jun;96(6):424–31.

14. Giles WH, Anda RF, Jones DH, et al. Recent trends in the identification and treatment of high blood cholesterol by physicians. Progress and missed opportunities. JAMA. 1993 Mar 3;269(9):1133–8.

15. Rogler LH. Research on mental health services for Hispanics: targets of convergence. Cult Divers Ment Health. 1996;2(3):145–56.

16. Collins KS, Hughes DL, Doty MM. Diverse communities, common concerns: assessing health care quality for minority Americans. Findings from the Commonwealth Fund 2001 Health Care Quality Survey. New York: Commonwealth Fund, 2002.

17. Kirkman-Liff B, Mondragon D. Language of interview: relevance for research of southwest Hispanics. Am J Public Health. 1991 Nov;81(11):1399–404.

18. Yap OW, Thornton DJ. The Arbor Free Clinic at Stanford: a multidisciplinary effort. JAMA. 1995 Feb 1;273(5):431.

19. SAS, version 8. Cary, NC: SAS Institute, 1999.

Chapter 15

Adapting the Chronic Care Model to Treat Chronic Illness at a Free Medical Clinic

Robert J. Stroebel
Bonnie Gloor
Sue Freytag
Douglas Riegert-Johnson
Steven A. Smith
Todd Huschka
Jim Naessens
Thomas E. Kottke

In 2000, an estimated 38 million nonelderly adults in the United States were without health insurance.[1] The literature suggests a high chronic disease burden among uninsured and minority populations and a greater degree of morbidity and mortality compared with their insured counterparts.[2-4] Increasingly, in response, free clinics have developed across the United States to provide health care to the uninsured.[5,6] Effective models of care delivery must be explored to ensure that the medically uninsured are not underserved in such settings.

In 1995, the Salvation Army Free Clinic (SAFC) was founded by a group of physicians in Rochester, Minnesota, to provide medical care to a low-income, uninsured, culturally diverse population in our community. Since its inception, SAFC clinicians have recognized the need to provide chronic illness care to SAFC patients. A number of conditions characteristic of free clinics, however, interfere with the delivery of effective chronic illness care. Typically, providers are rotating volunteers, a circumstance that interrupts continuity of care, and specialty con-

Robert J. Stroebel, MD, is an assistant professor of medicine in the Division of Primary Care Internal Medicine at the Mayo Clinic College of Medicine (MCCM), in Rochester, Minnesota. *Bonnie Gloor, RN,* is a nurse study coordinator at MCCM. *Sue Freytag, RN,* is a staff nurse at Golden Living Centers in Rochester, Minnesota. *Douglas Riegert-Johnson, MD,* is an assistant professor of medicine at Mayo Clinic, Jacksonville, Florida. *Steven A. Smith, MD,* is a professor of medicine in the Division of Endocrinology at the MCCM. *Todd Huschka, BS,* is a master health systems analyst at MCCM. *Jim Naessens, MPH, ScD,* is an associate professor of health services research and an assistant professor of biostatistics in the Division of Health Care Policy and Research and the Center for Science and Delivery at MCCM. *Thomas E. Kottke, MD, MSPH,* is a professor of medicine in the Cardiology Division at the University of Minnesota, Twin Cities.

sultation is often limited and inconsistent. Finally, the frequent transience of the uninsured patient population impedes appropriate follow-up. Many of our patients were migrant workers, spending anywhere from four to six months in the area before moving on to other work locales. Many other patients were also in transition, both geographically and economically. As a result of these obstacles, the SAFC had no capacity to provide effective ongoing care to patients with chronic illnesses such as diabetes or hypertension.

A retrospective chart review of patients with hypertension seen at our clinic in the two years prior to this study supports this assertion. We reviewed the charts of 48 patients with at least two recorded blood pressures who were receiving usual care for hypertension at our clinic. No change was seen in the average mean arterial pressure between their first (111.18 mm Hg) and last (111.06 mm Hg) blood pressure readings during this period, and only 13% of these patients had blood pressure values considered to be under control.

The chronic care model is a comprehensive approach to the management of chronic illness that enables the health care team to achieve a planned, productive interaction with an informed, activated patient. The focus of the model is the transformation of chronic care delivery from a reactive, acute illness model to a proactive, planned care approach. Six elements of the model contribute to the delivery of high-quality chronic illness care: community involvement, health system leadership buy-in, self-management support, delivery system redesign, decision support, and clinical information systems.[7]

The effectiveness of the chronic care model has been demonstrated in many primary care settings.[8] Several adaptations of the model described in the literature seemed potentially useful in the delivery of chronic disease care at the SAFC. For example, nurse managers guided by evidence-based treatment protocols might provide improved continuity of care in a system relying wholly on volunteer physicians.[9,10] Innovative primary care–specialist interaction might allow a volunteer endocrinologist to provide specialty expertise to a large group of patients.[11,12] Entry of patients into a chronic disease registry might facilitate effective tracking and disease management of a relatively transient population of patients.[13,14] Finally, language-sensitive and culturally competent adaptations could better serve the ethnically diverse population cared for at the SAFC.[15,16]

Given these potential benefits, the leadership of the SAFC endorsed a proposal to proceed with a trial implementation of an adaptation of the chronic care model in an effort to improve the quality of chronic illness care we were providing to our medically uninsured patients. This chapter presents a description of that pilot project and a summary of our results.

Methods

Setting

The SAFC operates two nights per week in the Rochester Salvation Army building. A staff nurse is available on a limited basis during the day. The Salvation

Army building is centrally located in the downtown area. A satellite office was established in the Rochester Red Cross building, staffed by a second nurse, with flexible office hours to accommodate patients' working schedules. The Red Cross building is located near a canning factory employing large numbers of migrant workers. The two staff nurses devoted a total of 0.75 full-time equivalent nurse time to this project. Both offices were supported by a roster of volunteer physicians, nurses, diabetes educators, dietitians, social workers, and lay personnel. A core group of two internists, one endocrinologist, one dietitian, and two diabetes educators provided the majority of volunteer support. The study was approved by both the Mayo Clinic Institutional Review Board and the governing board of the SAFC. All participating patients provided informed consent.

Population

The population of Rochester, Minnesota, and surrounding Olmsted County is approximately 120,000. The study population consisted of uninsured patients who lived or worked in the Rochester area. A small number of patients in the study had some form of health insurance coverage (e.g., catastrophic care) but were unable to afford ongoing care for their chronic disease. Patients with hypertension and/or diabetes mellitus visiting the SAFC from March 2001 through September 2002 were invited to join the study. These patients were then screened for hyperlipidemia.

Of the 149 enrolled patients, 117 had hypertension, 91 had diabetes, and 51 had hyperlipidemia. Ninety-two patients had multiple diagnoses. There were 76 female patients; the mean age was 51.9 years. The racial/ethnic background of the sample was as follows: 71 Hispanic, 57 white, 11 African American, 4 Asian, and 6 other. English was the primary language of 59 patients; Spanish of 58; English learned as a second language of 23; and 9 spoke other languages.

Intervention

Key components of the chronic care model were integrated and utilized in our intervention strategy (figure 15.1). We employed several strategies that had previously been demonstrated to be effective in other care settings. The community component was relatively limited in scope.

Information system. At enrollment, patients were entered into a chronic disease registry. The registry was a Microsoft Excel spreadsheet adapted for use in this project to record pertinent demographic and clinical information. Evidence-based, disease-specific guidelines were integrated into the registry to organize data collection, stratify outcomes, and trigger appropriate management. Conditional formatting was used to highlight needed testing or values and test results not meeting the target goal. The registry resided on a single computer with password protection and restricted user access to ensure patient confidentiality. One of the staff registered nurses assumed primary responsibility for registry maintenance. She entered the majority of data and used the registry data to guide proactive visit planning for enrolled patients.

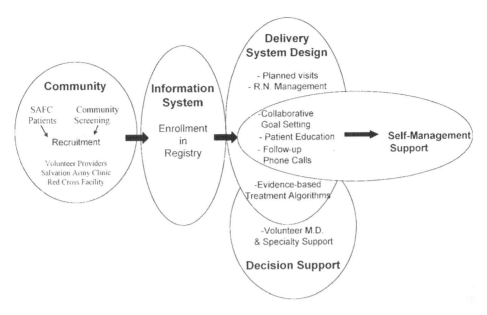

Figure 15.1 Intervention strategy.

Delivery system design. The delivery system was designed to maximize continuity and optimize resource utilization. The two staff nurses provided primary patient management using evidence-based algorithms derived from the Institute for Clinical System Integration (ICSI) Clinical Guidelines for Hypertension, Diabetes, and Hyperlipidemia.[17-19] ICSI is a nonprofit quality improvement organization that supports the development and implementation of evidence-based clinical guidelines for use within member medical groups.[20] Patients were seen at enrollment by one of the two staff RNs and within four weeks by a volunteer physician. Timing of subsequent visits was determined by the care team, according to guideline recommendations and based on disease status. The majority of contacts were with the staff nurses, but volunteer physician and limited specialty consultation was available.

Algorithm-driven medication changes were made by the nurses and reviewed by a volunteer physician. Telephone and e-mail consultation were used extensively to maximize efficient use of physician resources.[21] Management decisions not requiring direct physician assessment, such as medication adjustment or timing of follow-up, were handled by phone, chart review, or e-mail whenever possible. Physician visits were arranged for patients with acute problems, difficult medication management issues, or specific questions for the doctor. A volunteer endocrinologist saw particularly challenging diabetes cases in consultation.

Patients completing the study had an average of 9.5 encounters with a staff nurse, either in person or by telephone follow-up. There was an average of 1.8 encounters with a primary care physician. Among the patients with diabetes, nine had one clinic visit with an endocrinologist and one patient saw the endocrinologist twice.

Medications were provided at no cost to patients, in keeping with clinic policy. Generic medications were used whenever possible and were purchased by the clinic. Brand name medications were used when indicated or necessary. Brand name medications historically had been donated to the free clinic by area pharmaceutical representatives, and this practice continued during the course of the study.

Decision support. Decision support was facilitated by the integration of the ICSI clinical guidelines into the registry design and the treatment algorithms. In addition, the core physicians supporting the project were proponents of guideline-based management. As mentioned, specialty expertise was consistently available by phone or e-mail with a volunteer endocrinologist. A certified diabetes educator met at least once with 24 of the diabetic patients.

Patient self-management. Patient self-management was encouraged through the use of collaborative goal setting. Goal options addressed self-monitoring and lifestyle modification and were displayed visually using a self-management wheel (figure 15.2). All patients were asked to establish a self-management goal. Nurse follow-up phone calls or visits were used to monitor progress toward the goal.

A menu of educational topics, based on the American Diabetes Association self-management education program content areas, was offered to patients in support of their collaborative goals.[22] Education was offered by the staff nurses and diabetes educators, one of whom was fluent in Spanish. All educational materials were available in English and Spanish.

Community involvement. The SAFC itself is a product of community partnership and collaboration. Both project sites were community resources. The volun-

Figure 15.2 Self-management wheel.

teer staff of the free clinic was drawn widely from both the lay and professional local community.

Health system and leadership. The health system, as represented by the governing board of the SAFC, was (crucially) fully supportive of the project. Our efforts were facilitated through allocation of space and resources.

Study design and measures

The primary research design was a prospective cohort study. Individuals were assessed on enrollment and reassessed after a minimum intervention of 100 days. We felt this was the minimum time necessary to assess meaningful change in a chronic disease parameter. Individuals were then followed as long as possible, up to the 22-month study duration.

Patients were considered lost to follow-up if they did not complete 100 days of management or did not complete postintervention assessment. Enrolled patients who acquired insurance during the course of the study were considered lost to follow-up if they had not completed 100 days of intervention. If they had completed a minimum of 100 days in the study, we included for analysis the exit labs obtained by us or the patient's entry labs with his or her new provider.

Patients with chronic disease were recruited and enrolled from March 1, 2001, through September 30, 2002, at both the SAFC and at the satellite clinic. Screening and informed consent occurred at the time of initial visit with one of the two staff nurses. Patients choosing to not participate in the pilot program were invited to continue receiving usual care through the SAFC.

The primary efficacy endpoint was the proportion of patients with clinically significant improvement in at least one chronic disease. Disease-specific endpoints were a minimum one-stage reduction in blood pressure for hypertensive patients, a decrease of at least 1% of HbA1c for diabetic patients, and a reduction of risk group in low-density lipoprotein (LDL) cholesterol for patients with hyperlipidemia.[4,23,24] Additional measures included change in mean arterial pressure (MAP), change in HbA1c, and change in LDL cholesterol for patients completing the study. Enrollment rates, dropout rates, and length of participation were also measured.

Statistical analysis

The primary efficacy endpoint was assessed by developing a 95% confidence interval around the overall proportion of patients who attained clinically significant improvement in at least one of their chronic diseases. This endpoint was assessed both for all patients completing the study and for all patients enrolled (intent to treat). We assumed that under normal circumstances, if this cohort were to remain untreated, no more than 10% of patients would experience a one-class drop in chronic disease status. Based on our clinical experience with the SAFC, this is an optimistic estimate for unmanaged patients. Although any clinical improvement for patients in the study would be beneficial, we established a goal of 50% of the patients experiencing an improvement in one disease outcome to demonstrate the effectiveness of the program.

Further assessment included analysis of the disease-specific changes for those patients completing the study. Paired *t*-tests were used to determine degree of change for the physiologic measurements underlying each disease entity. We also compared disease-specific control rates to published national control targets.[25]

Results

We enrolled 149 patients into the study. There were 40 patients lost to follow-up within 100 days of enrollment. Of those patients lost to follow-up, 17 acquired insurance, 13 moved from the area, and 10 were unaccounted for. Over the 22 months of the study 109 patients were managed for a mean of 361 days (SD143.3). The success of our colleagues in maintaining these patients in the program is demonstrated in figure 15.3.

A clinically significant improvement was obtained in at least one chronic disease for 79 patients. Of the patients completing the study, 72.5% improved. Of all enrolled patients (intent to treat), 53% improved. For the 89 patients with the diagnosis of hypertension who completed the study, 57 (64%) improved at least one stage. For the 60 patients with diabetes completing the study, 32 (53%) reduced

100 days needed for statistical analysis.

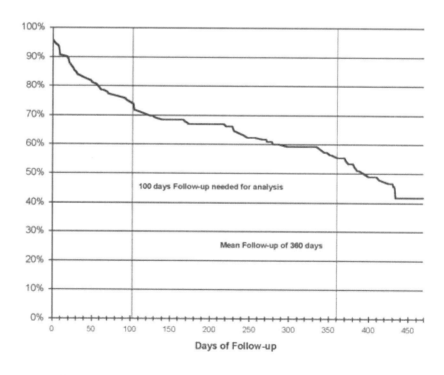

Figure 15.3 Follow-up of enrolled patients. 100 days needed for statistical analysis

their HgbA1c values at least 1%. For the 19 patients with elevated LDL cholesterol completing the study, 11 (58%) dropped one risk group. Several patients with hyperlipidemia did not complete postintervention lipid testing but were able to complete postintervention assessment of blood pressure or HgbA1c testing.

The degree of change in MAP, HgbA1c, and LDL using paired t-tests is displayed in table 15.1. Pre- and postintervention control rates for hypertension, diabetes, and hyperlipidemia are displayed in figure 15.4 and compared with the NCQA/ADA Diabetes Physician Recognition Program targets at the time of the study.[25]

Table 15.1

Changes in disease-specific parameters

Measure	Initial	Final	Change	p-value*	n
Mean arterial pressure** (SD)	110.1 (15.8)	97.4 (10.6)	−12.7 (15.4)	<0.001	89
Mean HgbA1c (SD)	9.68 (2.12)	8.44 (1.92)	−1.24 (2.05)	<0.001	60
Mean LDL (SD)	174.2 (33.3)	130.6 (43.2)	−43.5 (33.1)	<0.001	19

*A paired t-test was used to calculate significance.

**Mean arterial pressure calculated as (diastolic + [systolic −diastolic] / 3)

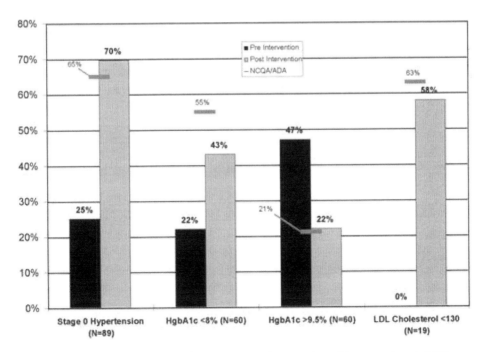

Figure 15.4 Change in key measure from pre- to postintervention with comparison to 2002 NCQA/ADA targets.

Discussion

The chronic care model was successfully used as a template for the delivery of chronic disease care to an uninsured population using the relatively limited resources of a free medical clinic staffed primarily by volunteers. Several elements of the chronic care model were adapted for use in the project and contributed to the success of the project.

The chronic disease registry enabled effective tracking and management of a diverse, uninsured patient population. Dropout rates of over 40% are documented in the delivery of chronic disease care to similar populations.[26] In our study, 27% of patients were lost to follow-up. If we exclude from analysis those who acquired health insurance during the study, only 17% of patients were lost to follow-up.

The nurse-managed delivery system, evidence-based disease management guidelines, volunteer specialty support, and promotion of patient self-management together proved to be a viable format for the sustained delivery of quality chronic disease care. This approach to chronic disease management enabled a group of uninsured patients to achieve clinically significant improvement in the control of their chronic illnesses. With the exception of a case study describing implementation of the chronic care model in a community health center, we are unaware of published data chronicling the use of the model for the medically uninsured.[8]

There are a number of limitations in this study. A randomized, controlled trial would have more clearly demonstrated the effectiveness of this model. The experience of our hypertension patients in the two years prior to the study (as described in the beginning of this chapter) offers some basis for comparison. Unfortunately, a similar analysis of prior diabetes care is not feasible due to a paucity of laboratory data. We felt it was important to demonstrate the feasibility of applying the chronic care model to the free clinic despite the lack of a control group.

The length of intervention varied greatly among our patients, confounding data analysis and raising questions about sustainability of the results. In large part, the variation was inherent in our highly transient patient population.

Finally, beyond extensive volunteer involvement, the community component of our adaptation of the chronic care model was quite limited. A more coordinated effort with community agencies and resources may have resulted in more significant improvements in care.

We faced a number of significant challenges frequently encountered in providing care to underserved populations. No systematic approach to chronic disease care existed at the SAFC prior to this project. Our patients were racially and culturally diverse. Transportation difficulties, childcare concerns, extended work hours, and language barriers were all obstacles to care delivery. Finally, space and financial constraints interfered with optimal management. The improvements our patients achieved attest to the strength of both the chronic care model elements and the patients. Clinics and organizations facing similar challenges are likely to find the chronic care model similarly useful. Potential sites for additional trials include other free care clinics and community-based health organizations.

Randomized, controlled trials could further strengthen the case for widespread implementation of the model.

Acknowledgments

This research was supported by grant #041860 from the Robert Wood Johnson Foundation's Improving Chronic Illness Care national program.

Notes

1. Holahan J, Pohl M. Changes in insurance coverage: 1994–2000 and beyond. Health Aff (Millwood). 2002 Jul–Dec;Suppl Web Exclusive:W162–71 Available at http://content .healthaffairs.org/cgi/reprint/hlthaff.w2.162v1.

2. American College of Physicians (ACP)–American Society of Internal Medicine (ASIM). No health insurance? It's enough to make you sick—scientific research linking the lack of health coverage to poor health. Philadelphia, PA: ACP-ASIM 2000. Available at http://www.acpon line.org/uninsured/lack-contents.htm.

3. Ayanian JZ, Weissman JS, Schneider EC, et al. Unmet health needs of uninsured adults in the United States. JAMA. 2000;284(16):2061–9.

4. The sixth report of the Joint National Committee on Prevention, Detection, Evaluation, and Treatment of High Blood Pressure. Arch Intern Med. 1997;157(21):2413–46.

5. Scott HD, Bell J, Geller S, et al. Physicians helping the underserved: the Reach Out program. JAMA. 2000;283(1):99–104.

6. Geller SL, Taylor B, Scott D. Free clinics helping to patch the safety net. J Health Care Poor Underserved. 2004 Feb;15(1):42–51.

7. Wagner EH. Chronic disease management: what will it take to improve care for chronic illness? Eff Clinc Prac. 1998 Aug–Sep;1(1):2–4.

8. Bodenheimer T, Wagner EH, Grumbach K. Improving primary care for patients with chronic illness. JAMA. 2002;288(14):1775–9.

9. Aubert RE, Herman WH, Waters J, et al. Nurse case management to improve glycemic control in diabetic patients in a health maintenance organization. A randomized, controlled trial. Ann Intern Med. 1998;129(8):605–12.

10. Rich MW, Beckham V, Wittenberg C, et al. A multidisciplinary intervention to prevent readmission of elderly patients with congestive heart failure. N Engl J Med. 1995;333(18):1190–5.

11. McCulloch DK, Price MJ, Hindermarsh M, et al. A population-based approach to diabetes management in a primary care setting: early results and lessons learned. Eff Clin Pract. 1998;1(1):12–22.

12. Dinneen SF, Bjornsen SS, Bryant SC, et al. Towards an optimal model for community-based diabetes care: design and baseline data from the Mayo Health System Diabetes Translation Project. J Eval Clin Pract. 2000;6(4):421–9.

13. Sperl-Hillen J, O'Connor PJ, Carlson RR, et al. Improving diabetes care in a large health care system: an enhanced primary care approach. Jt Comm J Qual Improv. 2000; 26:615–22.

14. Renders CM, Valk GD, Griffin SJ, et al. Interventions to improve the management of diabetes mellitus in primary care, outpatient and community settings (review). Cochrane Database Syst Rev. 2000; 1:CD001481.

15. Piette JD, McPhee SJ, Weinberger M, et al. Use of automated telephone disease management calls in an ethnically diverse sample of low-income patients with diabetes. Diabetes Care. 1999;22(8):1302–9.

16. Brown SA, Hanis CL. Culturally competent diabetes education for Mexican Americans: the Starr County study. Diabetes Educ. 1999;25(2):226–36.

17. Institute for Clinical Systems Improvement (ICSI). Health care guideline: hypertension diagnosis and treatment. Bloomington MN: ICSI, Apr 1998. Available at http://www.icsi.org/knowledge/detail.asp?catID=29&itemID=173.

18. Institute for Clinical Systems Improvement (ICSI). Health care guideline: treatment of lipid disorders in adults. Bloomington MN: ICSI; Sep 1998.

19. Institute for Clinical Systems Improvement (ICSI). Health care guideline: management of type 2 diabetes mellitus. Bloomington MN: ICSI, Apr 1999. Available at http://www.icsi.org/knowledge/detail.asp?catID=29&itemID=182.

20. Mosser G. Clinical process improvement: engage first, measure later. Qual Manag Health Care. 1996;4(4):11–20.

21. Montori VM, Smith SA. Information systems in diabetes: in search of the holy grail in the era of evidence-based diabetes care. Exp Clin Endocrinol Diabetes. 2001;109(Suppl. 2): S358–72.

22. Mensing, C, Boucher J, Cypress M, et al. National standards for diabetes self-management education programs and American Diabetes Association review criteria. Diabetes Care. 2000 May;23(5):682–9.

23. UK Prospective Diabetes Study (UKPDS) Group. Intensive blood-glucose control with sulphonylureas or insulin compared with conventional treatment and risk of complications in patients with type 2 diabetes (UKPDS 33). Lancet. 1998;352(9131):837–53.

24. National Cholesterol Education Program. Second report of the Expert Panel on Detection, Evaluation, and Treatment of High Blood Cholesterol in Adults (ATP II). Circulation. 1994;89(3):1333–445.

25. National Committee for Quality Assurance (NCQA). Diabetes physician recognition program. Washington, DC: NCQA, 2002. Available at http://www.ncqa.org/dprp/.

26. Finnerty FA Jr, Mattie EC, Finnerty FA III. Hypertension in the inner city. I. Analysis of clinic dropouts. Circulation. 1973;47(1):73–5.

Chapter 16

Medical Respite Care for Homeless People: A Growing National Phenomenon

Suzanne Zerger
Bruce Doblin
Lisa Thompson

Homeless people experience health problems, especially chronic medical illness, with much greater prevalence than those who are housed, and they suffer mortality rates three to four times higher than those of the general population.[1,2] Lack of housing also creates major obstacles to obtaining necessary medical services and adhering to treatment. Studies have consistently shown that homeless people rely heavily upon hospitals and emergency departments to address their needs, though these are often the medically least appropriate and most costly solutions.[3] Current trends in the health care marketplace are exacerbating this problem. Uninsured rosters are at an all-time high, and health costs are rising; entitlement programs such as Medicaid remain inaccessible to most homeless people.[4,5] Hospitals are discharging patients "quicker and sicker" as more procedures are provided on an outpatient basis, and community hospital beds are disappearing.[6,7] These trends shift responsibility for aftercare to families and communities. This causes a dilemma for hospital personnel preparing to discharge homeless patients who are no longer sick enough to justify a bed but have nowhere to go to recuperate safely and sufficiently. Even simple directives for aftercare, such as bed rest, wound care, use of a wheelchair, or nutritional requirements, cannot be followed by someone living on the streets or in shelters and relying on emergency food programs for meals. As a result, emergency homeless shelters already over capacity are seeing steady increases in the number of individuals entering directly from hospitals with aftercare needs they are unable or ill-equipped to provide.

Suzanne Zerger, PhD, is the senior associate in research for the Center for Social Innovation, and former coordinator of the National Respite Care Providers' Network. *Bruce Doblin, MD,* is an associate professor at Northwestern University Medical School, an instructor at the School of the Art Institute of Chicago, and founding medical director of Interfaith House, and has a private practice in internal medicine and palliative and hospice medicine. *Lisa Thompson, DNP, APRN-BC,* is a psychiatric nurse practitioner and the former respite care coordinator for the Colorado Coalition for the Homeless Respite Care Program.

This phenomenon received media attention in 2007 when the *Los Angeles Times* reported that a hospital van dropped off an acutely ill paraplegic homeless man on Skid Row in downtown Los Angeles, leaving him crawling on the street wearing a soiled hospital gown and a leaking colostomy bag.[8] A follow-up story on the CBS news program *60 Minutes* brought the Los Angeles story to national attention, but comparable dilemmas confront many towns and cities across the country.[9–12] Far less attention has been paid to an escalating community response to this hospitals-to-streets gap in health care for homeless people: the development of medical respite care services, occasionally termed *infirmary* or *recuperative care.*[13,14]

The first known medical respite care services for homeless people cropped up in the mid-1980s, but the trends in health systems and services described above have led to rapid proliferation of such services across the country in the past decade. The existence of homeless medical respite care was recognized by a limited federal pilot initiative, which funded 10 emerging respite programs beginning in 2000, but the services remain ineligible for either Medicare or Medicaid reimbursement. In 1999, a group of respite care providers convened in Chicago and subsequently formalized their collaboration by creating the national Respite Care Providers' Network (RCPN) to support nascent respite programs and advocate for sustained funding. Although their services differed, RCPN members reached consensus that medical *respite* refers to acute and postacute medical care for homeless people too ill or frail to recover from illness or injury on the street but not ill enough to be in a hospital.* This report summarizes findings developed by a task force of the RCPN from a survey of respite programs.

Medical respite programs and facilities differ from one another in availability of funding and community resources. Models of care range from collaborative arrangements with local shelters or motels and visiting clinical teams to stand-alone facilities with 24-hour medical care. The limited body of research suggests not only that these respite options provide a viable and humane option for hospitals and other institutions seeking to discharge their homeless patients but also that they are cost effective, reduce hospital readmissions, and have important social support and service-networking benefits for clients.[15–18] Because respite care is typically provided by programs experienced in and committed to serving homeless people, it can provide a window of opportunity for homeless clients, resting in a clean bed, free from the dangers of life on the streets, to ponder help and services they might not otherwise be open to or able to access. Preliminary evidence suggests such interventions may be critical links in the continuum of care local communities provide homeless people, to stabilize their health and end their homelessness. This chapter offers the first attempt to draw a national picture of the wide variety of medical respite programs that have only recently emerged throughout the United States.

---

*The Respite Care Providers' Network (RCPN) is affiliated with the National Health Care for the Homeless Council. More information about the RCPN, its definition of medical respite, and the respite programs described here can be found at http://www.nhchc.org/respitecareprovidersnetwork.html.

Survey of Medical Respite Programs

In 2006, the steering committee of the national RCPN appointed a task force to collect basic descriptive information about all known respite programs and the clients they serve. This chapter summarizes this study and its findings.

In 2006, a total of 32 programs were known to be actively providing respite services to homeless people in the United States; this represents all of those known to the RCPN and its host organization, the National Health Care for the Homeless Council. Task force members enlisted RCPN steering committee members to help recruit medical respite coordinators from these programs to take part in a one-month data collection effort and to serve as mentors throughout the data collection process. This grassroots approach, with all aspects of the study overseen by medical respite providers actively working in the field, served several important purposes: it introduced respite providers to the RCPN as a resource for the development and enhancement of their services, provided them with support from others in the field doing similar work, and ensured the overall relevance and importance of this study to the field.

Data collection tools were designed to maximize the information obtained from these programs while acknowledging the time burden the process would add to programs already short of resources. A brief survey requested basic descriptive information about the program, including sites of care and number of beds, clinical and support staffing services provided, and common patient diagnoses. Additional data forms captured information over a one-month period on the number of clients served, referral sources, and outcomes. Participating respite coordinators also assessed their capacity to respond to five different patient scenarios, which helped us to achieve a better understanding of the complexity of needs that these programs address.

Twenty-nine of the respite programs were successfully contacted; most (25) agreed to participate. Respite coordinators or staff completed the survey and data forms for the period February 1–March 3, 2006, and returned them via e-mail or mail to the RCPN coordinator.

Program descriptions

Participating respite programs were geographically dispersed across 24 cities in 21 states, primarily in large urban centers. As expected, a large majority (20 of 25 respondents) had been created in the past decade. A key feature of these programs is their innovation in finding existing beds and resources within their communities; they are providing medical services in beds located in (in order of frequency) homeless shelters, stand-alone facilities, transitional housing, nursing homes/assisted living facilities, hotels/motels, treatment programs, apartments, health centers, and hospice units. Several respite programs are providing care in multiple locations. The location of beds largely determines the admission criteria for respite programs and the level of acuity the program can address. On average, these programs are small, with a median of 13 beds. In most cases (20 of 25 respondents), the clients served are male; just two programs have the capacity to serve children and/or families.* The programs surveyed are designed to provide acute medical care, so the median length of stay for clients is just over two weeks (17.5 days).

All of the programs surveyed provide comprehensive clinical and social support services to their clients, either directly or by referral, during the respite stay. A majority provide physician (18 of the 25 respondents) and/or nursing (20 of the 25 respondents) services. All of the programs provide case management services to respite clients, and most also provide meals (24 of the 25 respondents) and transportation (23 of the 25 respondents). A majority also assist clients with medications (dispensing and storage), substance use and/or mental health services, housing referrals, and job training or placement. Other ancillary services include laundry, spiritual support, physical therapy, and educational services. Because respite services are not eligible for reimbursement, the programs tend to patch together a variety of funding sources.

Referrals

These programs served 595 patients during the one-month period covered by the survey and reported that they did *not* admit an additional 384 clients who were referred to them during this time period. That is, these programs were able to serve approximately six out of every ten patients referred to them. The referral source was known for 552 of these patients; of these, just over half (291 of 552) came to the respite program from hospitals, and one-quarter (131 of 552) from community-based Health Care for the Homeless clinics or programs. In many cases, the programs provided reasons for the nonadmission (339 patients): two out of five of the nonadmissions (138) were due to lack of beds; in just over one-quarter of the nonadmission cases (98), the respite care program reported that the referral was inappropriate (e.g., needs did not match program criteria), and 41 were cases where the client chose not to be admitted.

Client needs

Respite programs addressed varied and complex health problems. The most common diagnoses included (in order of frequency) fractures/injuries, diabetes, cellulitis/infections, respiratory problems, heart disease, hypertension, surgical recovery, and cancer.

Task force members developed five case scenarios based on representative referrals to respite programs; these were used to further define the capacity of respite programs to address multiple, complex, medical and psychosocial needs. For example, nearly all (95%) would accept Juan (names are fictional, and cases are based on a range of typical referral scenarios), an illegal immigrant with uncontrolled diabetes, and John, a man with a broken leg and an uncontrolled seizure disorder.

---

*Though these respite programs offer their services to women, the reality that women are underrepresented among homeless populations generally and that most of these programs cannot accommodate children makes this percentage unsurprising.[19] It is comparable to the finding from an evaluation of ten respite programs that 78% of those clients served were male.[18]

Four-fifths said they could care for Maria, who had breast cancer and needed eight weeks of chemotherapy, and two-thirds would admit Philip, a 45-year-old with advanced AIDS, who had no family or friends and was likely to die within a few months. Nearly two-fifths (38%) could admit Susan, an intravenous drug user with an infection of the heart. Her need for four to six weeks of IV antibiotics was a barrier for those programs unable to admit her, but many said they would attempt to arrange a visiting nurse to come to their facility if no other options were available.

Conclusions

This descriptive study includes only programs that self-identified as respite programs and therefore probably under-represents the true number of programs and agencies in the country attempting to address the need for medical respite care for homeless people. For example, the absence of rural areas represented in the study may suggest differences in defining and responding to the need for respite care, as opposed to the absence of the need in those locations. Furthermore, much remains to be learned about these respite programs, including their funding sources, their relationships and arrangements with hospitals and other referral sources, and where patients go when they are discharged from respite programs. Additionally, while it is clear from this preliminary study that there is a dearth of respite beds relative to need, more information is needed. The survey reported here represents the first attempt to characterize respite care nationally.

Respite programs represent a creative response to the rapidly growing need to address the gap in the continuum of homeless health care, a gap with dire consequences for homeless people who are often shuttled between hospitals and the streets. Though small, the respite care programs surveyed are serving large numbers of clients with complex physical and psycho-social needs. They are maximizing existing beds and services in their communities and providing comprehensive medical and social supports to address both immediate and long-term needs. The survey results reported here indicate that respite programs across the country are a critical component of the continuum of homeless health care. These programs remain under-resourced, however, and must obtain more adequate and sustainable funding if they are to continue to meet the growing need for them.

Notes

1. McMurray-Avila M, Gelberg L, Breakey WR. Balancing act: clinical practices that respond to the needs of homeless people. In: Fosburg LB, Dennis DL, eds. Practical lessons: the 1998 national symposium on homelessness research. Washington, DC: U.S. Department of Housing and Urban Development and U.S. Department of Health and Human Services, 1999.

2. O'Connell J. Premature mortality in homeless populations: a review of the literature. Nashville, TN: National Health Care for the Homeless Council, 2005. Available at http://www.nhchc.org/PrematureMortalityFinal.pdf.

3. Salit SA, Kuhn EM, Hartz AJ, et al. Hospitalization costs associated with homelessness in New York City. N Engl J Med. 1998 Jun 11;338(24):1734–40.

4.   U.S. Department of Health and Human Services. 2005–2006 health care for the homeless: grantee profiles. Washington, DC: Health Resources and Services Administration, 2006.

5.   Post P. Casualties of complexity: why eligible homeless people are not enrolled in Medicaid. Nashville, TN: National Health Care for the Homeless Council, 2001. Available at http://www.nhchc.org/Publications/CasualtiesofComplexity.pdf.

6.   Kaiser Family Foundation. Trends and indicators in the changing health care marketplace. Washington, DC: Kaiser Family Foundation, 2005.

7.   Bazzoli GJ, Lindrooth RC, Kang R, et al. The influence of health policy and market factors on the hospital safety net. Health Serv Res. 2006 Aug;41(4, pt. 1):1159–80.

8.   Blankstein A. Winton R. Paraplegic allegedly 'dumped' on skid row. L.A. Times. 2007 February 9. Available at http://articles.latimes.com/2007/feb/09/local/medumping9.

9.   ABC 7 News. Witnesses: hospital employees dump homeless woman. Denver Colorado Channel 7 news 2006 October 5. Available at http://www.thedenverchannel.com/7newsinvestigates/10011494/detail.html.

10. Suchetka D. A safety net full of holes: ill homeless dumped on shelters. Cleveland Plain Dealer. 2007 May 6. Available at http://www.nhchc.org/ ClevelandPlainDealer050607.pdf

11. KGBT 4–TV news. Hospital's struggle to care for the homeless. Brownsville, KGBT 4–TV news. 2007 Nov 27.

12. Jackson MP. Nowhere to go. State hospital moving patients into area's homeless shelters. Winston Salem Journal. 2006 Feb 5.

13. Kelly F. Where do they go after the hospital? Healing sought for homeless, visiting federal official cites recuperative care as pricey gap in services. Charlotte Observer. 2008 Jan 11.

14. Korn P. The $471,000 man: hospitals find paying for housing helps keep homeless out of ER. Portland Tribune. 2008 March 28.

15. Buchanan D, Doblin B, Garcia P. Respite care for homeless people reduces future hospitalizations. J Gen Intern Med. Apr 2003;18(S1):203.

16. Podymow T, Turnbull J, Tadic V, et al. Shelter-based convalescence for homeless adults. Can J Public Health. 2006 Sep–Oct;97(5):379–83.

17. Buchanan D, Doblin B, Sai T, et al. The effects of respite care for homeless patients: a cohort study. Am J Public Health. 2006 Jul;96(7):1278–81. Epub 2006 May 30.

18. Zerger, S. An evaluation of the respite pilot initiative: final report. Washington, DC: Health Resources and Services Association, 2006. Available at http://www.nhchc.org/ Research /RespiteRpt0306.pdf.

19. Daiski I. Perspectives of homeless people on their health and health needs priorities. J Adv Nurs. 2007 May;58(3):273–81.

Part II **Student-Run Clinics**

Chapter 17
Balancing Service and Education:
Ethical Management of Student-Run Clinics

David Buchanan
Renee Witlen

In a cramped hallway of a cash-strapped student-run clinic at a homeless shelter, six medical students interview patients with minimal provisions for privacy. Senior students tutor first-year students on how to present to the faculty preceptor and write a progress note. The volunteer faculty member supervises the care of 20 patients during the three-hour session. The patients feel comforted by the students' enthusiastic and attentive care.

This evening, there are 5 patients with severe persistent asthma, all treated with only short-acting beta-agonists. (Short-acting beta-agonists without concurrent inhaled steroids have been linked with increased mortality.)[1] Three have been treated previously in the clinic. After teaching the students about the assessment and treatment of asthma, the preceptor gives each patient another beta-agonist inhaler (no other inhalers are available) and tells them they can obtain better medicines free of charge at the public hospital one mile away.

Student-run free medical clinics have been established in homeless shelters and other locations by students of many United States medical schools.[2] Often, these clinics begin as small student-initiated grassroots efforts.[3] Some have grown into extensive enterprises that provide clinical services for low-income patients and educational opportunities for students.[4] As these clinics grow in size and number, it is important to evaluate their clinical and educational impact and to reflect on the relationships that support their operation.

The central groups involved in student-run clinics (SRCs) are patients, students, faculty or community preceptors, and medical school administrators. We will examine student-run clinics from each of these perspectives, emphasizing the essential role of faculty and administration support for their clinical and educational activities.

David Buchanan, MD, MS, is chief clinical officer at Erie Family Health Center and an associate professor at Northwestern University. *Renee Witlen, MD,* is a clinical fellow in psychiatry at Cambridge Health Alliance.

The Patients

Patients who seek care from SRCs typically lack insurance or face other barriers to accessing more traditional points of entry to the health care system.[5] Student-run clinics providing quality medical services confer advantages to patients, including the physical benefits of health care and the psychological benefits of having time and attention spent on their needs.[6] However, depending on the resources available, patients may receive diagnostic evaluations or treatments that would be considered unacceptable within the traditional medical system, as in the vignette above.[3,7] Appropriate medications and supplies may be unavailable.[8] Because clinics are often set up in facilities not designed for patient care (e.g., homeless shelters, churches), a clinic's limited space and its arrangement may deprive patients of privacy as they discuss intimate health situations.[9] In the worst case, SRCs with limited resources could unintentionally divert patients from more established and better supported safety net institutions. Although the quality of care provided in SRCs has been questioned in at least one instance,[10] we were not able to identify any published health outcomes of patients served by an SRC.

Clinic patients and community members can play an important advisory role in SRCs. By engaging community-based advisers, students can help ensure that the clinic addresses the community's most urgent health needs.

The Students

Although students establish clinics for the benefit of indigent patients, students also benefit professionally from gaining clinical experience with diverse patients and personally by experiencing feelings of self-worth and personal satisfaction.[11] First-and second-year students particularly benefit from hands-on clinical experience during a time when their training is largely classroom based. Two published descriptions of student-run clinic programs have documented a preponderance of preclinical students among their volunteers.[3,9] Another noted that, "Many medical students have their earliest clinical experiences at student-run clinics" (p. 430).[10] At our institution, two preclinical students are scheduled for each student who is in the third or fourth year; even this ratio can be difficult to achieve at times due to the enthusiasm of the preclinical students. While this imbalance likely results from the time pressures faced by students in their clinical years, it also may reflect the relative importance of the educational benefits that first-and second-year students receive.[12]

In addition to the educational benefits of providing direct patient care, students volunteering in SRCs can also benefit from the opportunity to improve their cross-cultural communication skills through interactions with patients from socioeconomic, racial, and ethnic backgrounds different from their own. However, if students do not have the opportunity to reflect upon and interpret their experiences with the help of faculty, this exposure could also reinforce harmful stereotypes.

Training prior to volunteering at a student-run clinic varies widely. Some clinics require students to complete an elective prior to volunteering.[9] Other clinics restrict first-and second-year students to administrative duties, leaving patient care to junior and senior students. Still others require on-site training, which can vary in duration from a few hours to six months.[13] The extent and quality of preparation that students receive prior to working with patients at SRCs likely affects the quality of care they provide and the educational messages they retain.

The Faculty

Students are required to work with licensed physicians to provide medical care. Medical school faculty members typically supervise and/or directly provide the clinic's patient care. Faculty members also educate students and patients about the medical conditions encountered.

Faculty members may also provide other services to SRCs. They may implement service-learning curricula to contextualize students' clinical work, act as liaisons to the school administration and pharmaceutical companies to acquire resources, organize clinic space to maximize patient privacy, and facilitate patients' follow-up care. Students will have difficulty fulfilling these responsibilities due to their inexperience with clinical care, the health care system, and the administrative structure of medical schools. While students are legally bound not to practice medicine without the direct oversight of licensed physicians, their roles in organizational and administrative tasks that affect patient care are often not well defined. Committed but inexperienced students may in some instances be operating without sufficient faculty involvement in clinic administration.

The Medical School Administration

Medical school administrators manage their curricula to ensure that graduating students are prepared to become practicing physicians. In 1998, the Association of American Medical Colleges (AAMC) released the first report of the Medical School Objectives Project (MSOP). The MSOP's goal was to establish learning objectives for the medical school curriculum derived from "a consensus within the medical education community on the attributes that medical students should possess at the time of graduation" (p. 1). Medical educators determined that graduating physicians must demonstrate *altruism* to "meet society's expectations of them in the practice of medicine" (p. 4) and must be *dutiful*, which includes demonstrating a commitment to care for the poor and to advocate for health care access for the underserved.[14] Experiences in student-run clinics can play a significant role in helping students to meet these educational objectives.

Student-run clinics, like other settings in which students observe and participate in patient care, contribute to the values imparted by the "structure of medical work and the learning environment" (p. 865).[15] As the size and scope of student-run free clinics continue to expand, their role in helping to craft the values imbued by medical education increases proportionally. The structure and organization of SRCs, as elements of a medical education, contribute to and in some cases detract from medical students' acquisition of altruism and duty.

Depending on the organization and operation of a particular SRC, unintended, counter-productive lessons that might be conveyed verbally or nonverbally include:

- It is acceptable to provide less privacy to patients living in poverty.
- It is acceptable to provide lower quality care to patients living in poverty (e.g., using expired medications, practicing with few opportunities for specialty referrals).
- Doctors should focus on medical issues and avoid talking explicitly about nonmedical issues affecting their patients' health.
- It is preferable for students to learn by practicing their skills on people living in poverty.

Ideally, both the implicit and explicit curricula of student-run clinics could be sources of desirable ethics and professionalism education. Positive lessons include:

- Care of patients living in poverty should be provided with the same compassion that is afforded all other patients, regardless of the setting where the care is provided.
- Altruism and commitment to service are integral to good medical practice.

The appropriateness of the lessons learned by medical students in any clinic depends on numerous factors, including the preceptor's attitudes and beliefs, the physical environment, and the clinic's resources. Preceptors' engagement of students in critical reflection is crucial and may determine whether students become discouraged, inspired, complacent, or actively engaged in addressing the social conditions they observe.

If someone with experience developing service-learning curricula takes responsibility for ensuring that positive lessons are communicated, a resource-poor clinical environment can provide positive educational experiences. For example, a preceptor can help students reflect on the clinic's limitations rather than having his or her silence convey that the environment is acceptable. Ultimately, an engaged faculty preceptor can shape positive educational messages in nearly any context by personally modeling ethical professional conduct and by urging students to consider the broader context of their work.

Discussion

Student-run clinics can be an important part of the safety net for low-income uninsured patients. Students, faculty, and administrators who participate in initiating and sustaining these efforts should be commended for their important work. Many SRCs provide care of the highest quality. As SRCs grow in number and scope, it is important for each institution to reflect upon the state of the SRCs that they support and to assess how these clinics meet the dual goals of patient care and clinical education.

Student-run clinics confer benefits upon patients, students, and medical school administrations. However, given the vulnerabilities of both patients and medical students, clinic organizers must ensure that an appropriate balance of benefits accrues to each group. The patients served by a clinic should be the first population considered, and it is essential that their benefits not be compromised by the needs or interests of the other involved parties. Patients who can afford to pay for health care can reject care they perceive as inadequate and seek medical attention elsewhere. Those who receive care free of charge at SRCs often do not have this freedom. The heightened vulnerability of such patients implies a greater responsibility on the part of those who care for them. Having patients or community members actively involved in the clinic's organization helps to ensure that patient perspectives are not overlooked. This involvement may take the form, for example, of a community advisory board or periodic audits by community members.[16,17] Detailed resources for establishing and maintaining effective community partnerships exist through the nonprofit organization Community-Campus Partnerships for Health.[18]

Additionally, when medical students participate in health care delivery, the responsibility for patient care implies a need for greater oversight by faculty and administrators to ensure that adequate care is provided. Appropriate medical care depends on students "using skills commensurate with [their] level of education and training" (p. 211) and operating with sufficient oversight from faculty in individual clinical encounters.[19] The legal requirements for student-provided care dictate this oversight, but, as in any student-service setting, tension may arise between students' need to practice and patients' need to receive quality care.[20] That tension must be monitored both by students themselves and by the faculty overseeing their work.

Even when faculty oversight and student skills are exemplary, reaching an adequate level of patient care depends upon the availability of adequate facilities, medical supplies, and pharmaceuticals. Students early in their training are generally unqualified to judge a clinic's resource needs independently. Therefore, responsibility for this function must be entrusted to a faculty supervisor. Faculty members are also best positioned to oversee the use of the clinic's physical space. This does not imply that faculty must perform these tasks alone; after plans for clinical resources are established, students and medical school administrators can assist in soliciting medications from pharmaceutical companies, applying for grants, or engaging in other fundraising efforts.

Faculty and community preceptors also have a crucial role to play in overseeing the ethical and professional lessons conveyed in the SRC setting. These educational benefits are central to the SRC experience, and they benefit not only the students but also the students' future patients. Faculty must clearly communicate the meaning of what students observe in the SRC setting in order to ensure that the experience inculcates values central to the medical curriculum.[14] The extreme poverty and need students are likely to encounter in this setting and the opportunity for meaningful interaction with the community make the SRC an ideal place to role-model ethical behavior and professionalism, including altruism and respect for all patients.[21] Beyond role-modeling, preceptors should initiate frank discussions with students about the nonmedical determinants of health that affect the patients they encounter. Ideally, students will acquire a broad conception of the role of medical professionals in society and of their own responsibilities to work toward ameliorating the social conditions that harm their patients.

Faculty time is one of the central resources of the student-run clinic, and like all resources, it must be allocated with careful attention to the needs of each participating group. Given the competing needs for education and patient care, it is essential that a faculty preceptor put the needs of patients first. Students may miss opportunities to learn about diagnosis and disease management as a result, but they will benefit from witnessing the values of altruism and duty embodied and reinforced.

Faculty participation in clinical resource management and oversight of the explicit and hidden curricula in SRCs ultimately depend on the commitment of the

Table 17.1
Role-specific recommendations for student-run clinic participants

---

Students
- Request designated supervision from at least one clinical faculty member, community representative, and medical school administrator.
- Review plans for the clinic's organization and design with these supervisors.
- Review clinic charts to determine the most common chief complaints and diagnoses.
- Collaborate with faculty to establish systems to ensure access to key medications and equipment needed to adequately address these conditions.

Clinic preceptors
- Know which faculty and administrators have been appointed to supervise the clinic.
- Bring questions, concerns, and ideas to the attention of supervisors and student organizers.
- Explain to patients and students when care the clinic provides deviates from that provided in other faculty-staffed clinics and discuss the clinical significance of this difference.
- Use such opportunities to educate students about health disparities and health issues faced by vulnerable populations.

Faculty supervisors
- Facilitate communication between clinic preceptors, students, and administrators.
- Make clear to student volunteers that service takes priority over practicing skills, and work with student leaders to ensure that all volunteers understand and share the clinic's mission.
- Organize chart reviews to determine common chief complaints and diagnoses.
- Review preceptor and patient feedback with students and collaborate with students and community representatives on plans for clinic improvement.
- Ensure that effective referral mechanisms are in place to address patients' medical problems that fall beyond the clinic's scope.

Administrators
- Designate a faculty member to supervise the clinic, with input from student organizers.
- Consider reviewing the educational content of the clinic or making the clinic a part of the school's curriculum.
- Assist students and faculty members in identifying resources to support the clinic.

---

medical school's administration. Administrators are the final arbiters on issues of institutional resource distribution, including financial resources necessary for SRC function and faculty time. Administrators are responsible for ensuring that students fulfill the MSOP objectives, and SRCs are ideal environments for teaching the challenging domains of altruism and duty. By valuing faculty time dedicated to this work, administrators help ensure the quality of this educational and service opportunity. Our recommendations for role-specific responsibilities are summarized in table 17.1.

Conclusion

Student-run clinics have the potential to provide substantial benefits for patients, students, and medical educators. Students provide the enthusiasm and energy necessary to make these health care endeavors a success, but they need assistance from more experienced clinicians to monitor the quality of each clinic's educational climate and medical care. By providing oversight, medical school faculty, administrators, and community members can assure that care meets the community's standards and that the educational messages conveyed are consistent with their curricular goals. Oversight is especially important in SRCs given the vulnerability of the populations served. An SRC can reach its full potential when students enlist needed assistance, faculty and community members provide effective oversight, and administrators furnish institutional support.

Acknowledgments

The authors are grateful to Faith Lagay, PhD, and Steven K. Rothschild, MD, for their thoughtful comments. David Buchanan was supported in part by a Physician Advocacy Fellowship from the Open Society Institute during the writing of this chapter.

Disclaimer

The opinions in this chapter are those of the authors and should in no way be construed as official policy positions of, nor should they be attributed to, the American Medical Association.

Notes

1. Lanes SF, Garcia Rodriquez LA, Huerta C. Respiratory medications and risk of asthma death. Thorax. 2002 Aug;57(8):683–6.
2. Nordling MK. Starting a student-run homeless clinic: a guidebook for health professions students on the process of establishing a clinic. Reston, VA: American Medical Student Association, 2004. Available at http://www.amsa.org/programs/homelessclinic.cfm.
3. Pi R. The Asian Clinic at UC Davis: serving a minority population for two decades. JAMA. 1995 Feb1;273(5):432.
4. Fournier AM, Perez-Stable A, Green PJ Jr. Lessons from a clinic for the homeless. The Camillus Health Concern. JAMA. 1993 Dec 8;270(22):2721–4.

5.   Keis RM, DeGeus LG, Cashman S, et al. Characteristics of patients at three free clinics. J Health Care Poor Underserved. 2004 Nov;15(4):603–17.

6.   Salinsky E. Necessary but not sufficient? Physician volunteerism and the health care safety net. Washington DC: George Washington University, National Health Policy Forum, 2004 Mar 10. Availableathttp://www.nhpf.org/pdfs_bp/BP%5FPhysicianVolunteerism%5F3%2D04%2Epdf.

7.   Yap OW, Thornton DJ. The Arbor Free Clinic at Stanford: a multidisciplinary effort. JAMA. 1995 Feb1;273(5):431.

8.   Sorensen TD, Song J, Westberg SM. The limitation of good intentions: prescribing medications for the uninsured. J Health Care Poor Underserved. 2004 May;15(2): 152–60.

9.   Beck E. The UCSD Student-Run Free Clinic Project: transdisciplinary health professional education. J Health Care Poor Underserved. 2005 May;16(2):207–19.

10. Poulsen EJ. Student-run clinics: a double opportunity. JAMA. 1995 Feb 1;273(5):430.

11. Eckenfels EJ. Contemporary medical students' quest for self-fulfillment through community service. Acad Med. 1997 Dec;72(12):1043–50.

12. Fournier AM. Service learning in a homeless clinic. J Gen Int Med. 1999 April;14(4):258–9.

13. Steinbach A, Swartzberg J, Carbone V. The Berkeley Suitcase Clinic: homeless services by undergraduate and medical student teams. Acad Med. 2001 May;76(5): 524.

14. The Medical School Objectives Project Report Writing Group. Report I Learning objectives for medical student education—guidelines for medical schools. Washington, DC: Association of American Medical Colleges, 1998 Jan. Available at http://www.aamc.org/meded /msop/msop1.pdf.

15. Hafferty FW, Franks R. The hidden curriculum, ethics teaching, and the structure of medical education. Acad Med. 1994 Nov;69(11):861–71.

16. Phillips L. A seat at the table. Community advisory boards help consumers direct their own health care. Trustee. 1995 Apr;48(4):10–3.

17. Conway T, Hu TC, Harrington T. Setting health priorities: community boards accurately reflect the preferences of the community's residents. J Community Health. 1997 Feb;22(1): 57–68.

18. National Health Care for the Homeless Council (NHCHC), Community-Campus Partnerships for Health. A guide to community-campus partnerships for the health of people experiencing homelessness. Nashville, TN: Community-Campus Partnerships for Health and NHCHC, 2004 Jun. Available at http://depts.washington.edu/ccph/ pdf_files/HCHCampus Studyf.pdf.

19. O'Toole TP, Hanusa BH, Gibbon JL, et al. Experiences and attitudes of residents and students influence voluntary service with homeless populations. J Gen Intern Med. 1999 April; 14(4):211–6.

20. Christakis DA, Feudtner C. Ethics in a short white coat: the ethical dilemmas that medical students confront. Acad Med. 1993 April;68(4):249–54.

21. Kenny NP, Mann KV, MacLeod H. Role modeling in physicians' professional formation: reconsidering an essential but untapped educational strategy. Acad Med. 2003 Dec;78(12): 1203–10.

Chapter 18

Quality of Diabetes Care at a Student-Run Free Clinic

Kira L. Ryskina
Yasmin S. Meah
David C. Thomas

Approximately 17% of the 8.5 million Americans with diabetes lack health insurance, and many suffer the consequences of poor access to health care.[1] A significant proportion of these uninsured patients receive care at free clinics supported by various community organizations; these include a growing number of student-run free clinics emerging from medical schools across the nation over the past decade.[2] While improved glycemic control, reduced blood pressure and cholesterol levels, and regular preventive screening can greatly reduce the morbidity and mortality associated with diabetes,[3-10] achieving them is particularly challenging for free clinics that care for highly vulnerable populations.[11]

Studies evaluating clinical outcomes and quality of care for patients with diabetes suggest that uninsured patients are less likely than the insured to receive recommended care,[12-14] including foot or eye examinations and cholesterol monitoring.[15] A 2005 study within a low-income, predominantly Hispanic population found that uninsured individuals had a 5.2% higher glycosylated hemoglobin (HbA1c) level than the insured, after adjusting for other factors such as demographics, disease duration, and health status.[12] An analysis of national cross-sectional population surveys determined that patients with insurance were more likely than those without insurance to receive a dilated eye examination and to have an HbA1c level less than 9.5%.[13] Another survey study conducted in 2000 found that patients without insurance were less likely to receive annual eye examinations, foot exams, or HbA1c testing.[14] Despite these findings, however, several studies failed to establish an association between glycemic control and insurance or socioeconomic status.[16-19]

Over the past decade, the United States has experienced a substantial proliferation of student-run clinics for the underserved, supplementing an existing potent yet overburdened safety net of privately, publicly, and volunteer-operated health

Kira L. Ryskina, MD, is a resident in internal medicine at New York–Presbyterian, Weill Cornell Medical College. *Yasmin S. Meah, MD,* is an assistant professor of medical education and of medicine at Mount Sinai School of Medicine. *David C. Thomas, MD, MS,* is a professor of general internal medicine, an associate professor of medical education, and an associate professor of rehabilitation medicine.

clinics.[2,20,21] Today, over 49 medical schools across the country operate more than 110 student-run outreach clinics that provide primary care services to the poor and uninsured.[2] Although the models for these student-run clinics vary widely, the stand-out theme is nonetheless a health care delivery program predominantly for uninsured persons in which undergraduate and medical students manage, with supervision, the administrative aspects of all components of care.[20] Despite this rise in student-run clinics, to date there exist no published data on the quality of care being delivered to patients in such student-led endeavors. This is particularly problematic since student-run clinics are vulnerable to the criticism of providing sub standard care to patients.[22]

The East Harlem Health Outreach Partnership (EHHOP) is a student-run attending-supervised free clinic providing primary care to uninsured residents of East Harlem, a neighborhood of 117,000 residents located in the northeast corner of Manhattan. East Harlem has one of the highest poverty rates in New York City (37%) and an unemployment rate of 17%.[23] Forty-six percent of East Harlem residents receive public assistance.[24] The population of East Harlem is 52% Hispanic, 36% black, and 7% white, with one in five residents born outside of the United States.[24] Over a quarter of East Harlem residents are uninsured, and 22% go to the emergency room when sick or in need of medical advice. Recent New York City (NYC) Department of Health findings determined that this neighborhood has the highest avoidable hospitalization rate in the city.[25] Diabetes is rampant in East Harlem, which has the city's highest prevalence rate (13%). Furthermore, overweight or obesity characterizes two-thirds of the population.[25]

The EHHOP clinic was founded in 2004 by medical students of Mount Sinai School of Medicine, with the goal of addressing the acute and chronic health needs of the uninsured in their community. Medical students manage all clinic operations under the supervision of faculty and attendings. The clinic is open every Saturday by appointment and is staffed by medical student and physician volunteers as well as a paid social worker. In addition to providing medical care, the clinic works to ensure access to prescription medications and medical supplies via pharmaceutical company charity programs, private donations, and a discount program with the Mount Sinai Hospital pharmacy. Basic laboratory tests, such as urine microalbumin and glycosylated hemoglobin, are processed through the hospital's laboratory services. The clinic makes referrals to specialists within Mount Sinai Hospital; radiologic services are supplied at no cost by the hospital. The clinic pays for all initial specialty care visits, while future visits are paid for out of pocket based on a sliding-scale assessment made by the Mount Sinai Resource Entitlement and Advocacy Program.

This study was designed to fill the gap in the literature on diabetes care quality in student-run free clinics. The objective of this study was to evaluate diabetes management at the EHHOP clinic by comparing the clinic's performance with previously reported diabetes quality-of-care rates for uninsured populations, as well as with state and national diabetes quality-of-care averages for patients with public and private health insurance coverage.

Methods

Data

Charts of adult patients at least 22 years old diagnosed with type 1 or type 2 diabetes were reviewed. A diagnosis of diabetes was established based on the following criteria: (1) a diagnosis of diabetes documented in the chart or (2) prescription of diabetes medication (e.g., sulfonylurea, meglitinide, biguanide, thiazolidinedione, alpha-glycosidase inhibitors, combination agents, or insulin). Patients with no follow-up visits to the clinic were excluded. A standardized chart abstraction form developed for this study was used to obtain information on patient demographics, comorbid conditions, relevant laboratory test results, health maintenance screenings, vaccinations, medications, emergency department visits, and hospitalizations. Chart abstraction was conducted by four reviewers over a period of three weeks; the majority of reviews (84%) were performed by a single reviewer. The study period was individualized for each patient based on the most recent 12-month interval of available data. For example, for a patient who was last seen at the clinic in April 2007, 12 data months from April 2006 through April 2007 were analyzed in this study.

Quality-of-care measures

Diabetes management was assessed using common quality-of-care indicators based on accepted practice guidelines and support by scientific evidence.[3,26–28] Indicators commonly used to evaluate Medicaid and commercial health plans were used for comparative purposes (Healthcare Effectiveness Data and Information Set, or HEDIS).[26] Fifteen indicators assessing intermediate outcomes as well as processes of care were measured. Intermediate outcomes measured included HbA1c level (poor >9.0 and good <7.0), low-density lipoprotein cholesterol (LDL-C) level (<100 and <130), and blood pressure (<140/90 and <130/80). Processes of care measured included glycosylated hemoglobin (HbA1c) monitoring, lipid panel monitoring, nephropathy screening, retinopathy screening, foot exams, aspirin prophylaxis, and smoking cessation counseling. Last, health maintenance measures included annual influenza vaccination and pneumonia vaccination within the past five years.

Commonly accepted indicator definitions[26–28] were employed (see table 18.1 for a summary of indicator definitions). The proportion of patients who received recommended care out of the total number of patients eligible to receive recommended care was calculated in each indicator category. For example, clinic performance in the HbA1c measure was calculated as the number of patients who received at least one HbA1c test during the most recent available 12-month period divided by the number of patients with diabetes. For outcome measures, a mean of test values was calculated if testing was conducted more than once during the study period. Comparative data for state and national Medicaid and privately insured populations, as well as for patients without insurance, were obtained from previously published sources.

Table 18.1

Quality-of-care indicator summary

Indicator	Definition
HbA1c testing	The percentage of patients with diabetes who received glycosylated hemoglobin A1c test within the last year.
Poor HbA1c control	The percentage of patients with diabetes whose most recent glycosylated hemoglobin A1c level indicated poor control (>9.0%). Lower percentage represents better performance for this measure.
Good HbA1c control	The percentage of patients with diabetes whose most recent glycosylated hemoglobin A1c level indicated good control (<7.0%).
Lipid panel monitoring	The percentage of patients with diabetes who had a cholesterol test within the last two years.
Lipids controlled at LDL-C <130 mg/dL	The percentage of patients with diabetes who had a cholesterol test over the past two years and whose most recent level of LDL-C was <130 mg/dL.
Lipids controlled at LDL-C <100 mg/dL	The percentage of patients with diabetes who had a cholesterol test over the past two years and whose most recent level of LDL-C was <100 mg/dL.
Nephropathy monitoring	The percentage of patients with diabetes who had at least one test for microalbumin in the last year or who had evidence of existing nephropathy.
Blood pressure controlled <140/90	The percentage of patients with most recent blood pressure <140/90 Hg.
Blood pressure controlled <130/80	The percentage of patients with most recent blood pressure <130/80 Hg.
Retinopathy screen	The percentage of patients with diabetes who had a dilated eye exam or referral to an ophthalmologist over the past two years.
Foot exams	The percentage of patients with diabetes who received at least one foot exam, defined in any manner, in the last year.
Aspirin prophylaxis	The percentage of patients with diabetes prescribed daily aspirin for prophylaxis of cardiovascular complications in the last year.
Influenza vaccine	The percentage of patients with diabetes who received influenza vaccine in the last year.
Pneumonia vaccine	The percentage of patients with diabetes who received pneumonia vaccine in the last five years.
Smoking cessation counseling	The percentage of patients who smoke and received smoking cessation counseling in the last year.

Sources:

National Committee for Quality Assurance. HEDIS 2006: health plan employer data and information set, vol. 2, technical specifications. Washington, DC: National Committee for Quality Assurance (NCQA), 2005.

National Diabetes Quality Improvement Alliance. Performance measurement set for adult diabetes. Chicago, IL: National Diabetes Quality Improvement Alliance, 2003.

HealthPartners. 2005 Clinical Indicators Report: 2004/2005 results. Bloomington, MN: HealthPartners, 2005.

American Diabetes Association. Standards of medical care in diabetes—2006. Diabetes Care. 2006 Jan;29:S4–42.

Data were analyzed using Microsoft Excel 2003 software. Means and proportions were compared between patients seen in the EHHOP clinic and values reported in the literature using two sample t-tests and Pearson's chi-square test. Z-tests were used where sample size of comparison sample was considered large enough to represent the entire population (i.e., Medicaid and privately insured populations).

This study was approved by the Mount Sinai School of Medicine Institutional Review Board.

Results

Demographic characteristics

Out of 334 patients with at least one visit to the EHHOP clinic, 40 (12%) had diabetes; 25 of those had one or more follow-up visits and were included in the study. The average age was 49±12 years (range: 30–79). Although approximately 80% of the EHHOP patient population is female, women constituted only 40% of patients in the study sample. Reflecting East Harlem demographics and overall clinic patient population, the study sample was 80% Hispanic, 12% black, 4% Asian, and 4% white. Four out of five patients were born outside the United States, predominantly in Latin America. The large majority of the Latino population emigrated from Mexico (50%), reflecting the large influx of Mexicans into the East Harlem neighborhood which was once predominantly home to African Americans and Puerto Ricans. Sixty-four percent of the study sample spoke a language other than English as their first language.

Disease burden

The majority of study patients suffered from type 2 diabetes (n=23); 8% (n=2) of study patients had type 1 diabetes. Average length of time since initial diagnosis of diabetes was 6.4 years (range: 0–33 years). Over a third of study patients (36%) had at least one emergency department visit or hospitalization for treatment of diabetes complications prior to their first EHHOP visit. Many study patients had multiple comorbid conditions, including hypertension (48%), hypercholesterolemia (48%), drug abuse (16%), and depression (12%). Sixteen percent of patients had other serious comorbid conditions, including obesity, arthritis, coronary artery disease, and peripheral vascular disease. Based on body mass index (BMI) calculations of the patients' most recent height and weight, 37% of patients were overweight (BMI: 25–29.9), 32% were obese (BMI: 30–39.9), and 16% were morbidly obese (BMI≥40). Study patients had an average of seven visits to the clinic (range: 2–18). All study patients were uninsured, and 72% had not had health insurance for five or more years prior to their first visit to EHHOP.

Diabetes care quality

Diabetes care quality measure rates for the EHHOP clinic together with comparative data from the literature are presented in table 18.2. In general, a higher

Table 18.2

Diabetes care at EHHOP clinic vs. comparative data

Indicator of care quality	EHHOP clinic (%)	Uninsured (%)	New York Medicaid(%)	National Medicaid (%)	New York commercial managed care plans(%)	National commercial health plans(%)
HbA1c monitoring	96	16.8*–88	85	78.0*	88	87.5
HbA1c level: poor >9.0	38[a]	26.9a–37.3a	37	48.7	28	29.6
HbA1c level: good <7.0	32	—	—	30.2	—	41.8
Lipid panel monitoring	76	68.3–80.7	92*	71.1	94*	83.4
LDL-C <130mg/dL	60	22.5*–40.1*	63	—	71	—
LDL-C <100mg/dL	36	—	38	30.6	44	43.0
Nephropathy monitoring	80	62*	56*	74.6	59*	79.7
Blood pressure <140/90	76	51.4*–60.8*	—	57.3*	—	61.4*
Blood pressure <130/80	56	—	—	30.4*	—	29.9*
Retinopathy screen	92	20.4*–56.4*	56*	51.4*	55*	54.7*
Foot exams	88	36.1*–80.3	73[b]*	—	73[b]*	—
Aspirin prophylaxis	56	—	48[b]	—	48[b]	—
Influenza vaccine	44	27.0*	60[b]	—	60[b]	—
Pneumonia vaccine	12	16.1	53[b]*	—	53[b]*	—

Sources: Ayanian JZ, Weissman JS, Schneider EC, et al. Unmet health needs of uninsured adults in the United States. JAMA. 2000 Oct 25;284(16):2061–9.

Porterfield DS, Kinsinger L. Quality of care for uninsured patients with diabetes in a rural area. Diabetes Care. 2002 Feb;25:319–23.

Saaddine JB, Engelgau MM, Beckles GL, et al. A diabetes report card for the United States: quality of care in the 1990s. Ann Intern Med. 2002 Apr 16;136(8): 565–74.

New York State Department of Health. 2006 New York State managed care plan performance: a report on quality, access to care, and consumer satisfaction. Albany, NY: New York State Department of Health, 2006. Available at www.health.state.ny.us/health_care/managed_care/qarrfull/qarr_2006/qarr_2006.pdf.

National Committee for Quality Assurance. The state of health care quality. Washington, DC: National Committee for Quality Assurance, 2007. Available at http://web.ncqa.org/Portals/0/Publications/Resource%20Library/SOHC/SOHC_07.pdf.

New York State Department of Health. The state of diabetes in New York State: a surveillance report. Albany, NY: New York State Department of Health, 2005. Available at www.health.state.ny.us/statistics/diseases/conditions/diabetes/docs/1997-2004_surveillance_report.pdf.

New York State Department of Health. New York State strategic plan for the prevention and control of diabetes. Albany, NY: New York State Department of Health, 2006. Available at www.health.state.ny.us/diseases/conditions/diabetes/strategicplan.htm.

*Significant at *p*<0.05 level.

[a]HbA1c >9.5% was used in these studies. Half of EHHOP clinic patients had poor glycemic control at HbA1c >9.0% level.

[b]Survey of patients with diabetes in New York State regardless of insurance.

proportion of study patients than of other uninsured patients with diabetes received recommended care at EHHOP (comparison based on previously published data).[13,15,29] Notable exceptions include poor glycemic control and lipid panel monitoring. Two studies reported between 26.9%[13] to 37.3%[29] of uninsured patients with HbA1c level >9.5%, compared with 38% of patients at EHHOP. Mean HbA1c level at EHHOP (8.9±2.4%) was higher than the mean HbA1c previously reported among uninsured patients with diabetes (8.1%)[12] (p=0.12). While two studies reported lower rates of lipid panel monitoring among the uninsured (68.3%[29] and 69.8%[15]) compared with EHHOP (76%), Saaddine and colleagues reported a slightly higher rate of lipid panel monitoring among patients with diabetes without insurance (80.7%).[13] These differences did not reach statistical significance.

Compared with previous reports of diabetes care quality among patients without insurance,[13–15,29] the EHHOP clinic had higher rates of the following processes of care: HbA1c monitoring, nephropathy monitoring, eye and foot exams, and aspirin prophylaxis ($p < 05$). In terms of clinical outcome measures, the EHHOP clinic had a significantly higher proportion of patients with LDL-C less than 130 mg/dL and blood pressure less than 140/90. Over 40% of patients at EHHOP received influenza vaccination, compared with 27% of uninsured persons reported in the literature.[15] Pneumococcal vaccination rates at EHHOP were similar to those previously reported for patients without insurance.

Compared with patients with public or private insurance, patients seen at the EHHOP clinic generally had higher rates of HbA1c monitoring, nephropathy screening, eye and foot exams, and aspirin prophylaxis. A significantly larger proportion of EHHOP patients had good blood pressure control compared with national Medicaid and even commercial health plan rates; 76% of EHHOP patients had blood pressure <140/90 vs. 57.3% of Medicaid and 61% of privately insured patients (p<0.05). Fifty-six percent of patients at EHHOP had blood pressure controlled at less than 130/80 compared with 30.4% of Medicaid and 29.9% of patients with private health insurance. However, the EHHOP clinic had significantly lower vaccination rates for influenza and pneumonia than New York State Medicaid and commercial managed care plans. Lipid panel monitoring rates were worse at EHHOP compared with patients with private or public insurance. This is especially problematic since among those EHHOP patients who received lipid panel monitoring, a larger proportion had LDL-C >130 mg/dL, although the difference was not statistically significant. The proportion of patients with poor or good HbA1c levels at EHHOP were similar to national Medicaid rates, but worse than New York State Medicaid or commercial health plan rates.

Over half (56%) of EHHOP patients reported checking blood glucose daily, a rate comparable to a New York state survey of diabetics regardless of insurance[30] and significantly higher than the proportion of patients without insurance who reported daily blood glucose monitoring (31%).[14] A quarter of patients who smoked received smoking cessation counseling at EHHOP. Data on smoking cessation counseling for other uninsured or insured populations were not available for the purposes of comparison.

Discussion

In the United States, a considerable number of patients with serious chronic conditions such as diabetes are uninsured,[1] and many receive care at free clinics. A growing number of providers staffing this important safety net are medical students under the supervision of medical school faculty.[2] Although multiple studies have been published evaluating the quality of diabetes care in the United States, most were conducted among patients with insurance. While several reports of care quality at community health centers exist,[29,31] to our knowledge this is the first report of diabetes care quality at a student-run free clinic. Despite challenges inherent in providing optimal care to the uninsured, diabetes care at this free health clinic was better in many areas than diabetes care and intermediate outcomes for patients without insurance previously reported based on Behavioral Risk Factor Surveillance System (BRFSS)[15] and U.S. National Health and Nutrition Examination Survey (NHANES)[13] data. Furthermore, according to several quality-of-care indicators, patients at the EHHOP clinic received recommended care at rates comparable to or better than state and national averages for Medicaid and even privately insured populations, as reported by the New York State Department of Health[30,42,43] and the National Committee for Quality Assurance.[34]

The EHHOP clinic performed especially well in blood pressure control, HbA1c testing, nephropathy monitoring, retinopathy screening, and foot examinations. However, EHHOP data showed worse glycemic control and lower rates of lipid panel monitoring than the NHANES III and BRFSS data.[13] These findings reflect the high disease burden of patients with diabetes seen at EHHOP, most of whom are long-term uninsured and many of whom are recent immigrants. Inadequate rates of lipid panel monitoring are especially concerning, since a large proportion of patients at EHHOP are obese and require more stringent cholesterol control. In addition to suggesting that good quality of care can be achieved in the setting of a student-run free clinic, our findings highlight significant opportunities for improvement in diabetes management that persist in all care settings.

Optimizing diabetes management in accordance with evidence-based recommendations and practice guidelines has the potential to reduce diabetes morbidity and mortality. In addition, recommended preventive screenings and tight glycemic, blood pressure, and cholesterol control have been shown to reduce the incidence of costly complications of diabetes.[5] Avoided hospitalizations and emergency department visits for costly diabetes complications translate into significant cost savings to health payers and society.[6,32] Timely diagnosis and treatment of early complications of diabetes are associated with lower costs than treatment of the more serious late complications. In one study, the cost of late-onset diabetes complications such as coronary heart disease and end-stage renal disease accounted for 38% of diabetes-related health care spending.[33]

Glycemic control is one of the foremost goals of diabetes management. According to the National Committee for Quality Assurance, inadequate glycemic control was associated with an estimated 7,100–15,900 avoidable deaths and $1.3–1.7 billion in medical costs in 2006.[34] In a study of a diabetes intervention program in community health centers that provided care to the uninsured and patients with Medicaid, increased rates of HbA1c testing, lipid testing, microalbumin testing, eye exams, ACE inhibitor and aspirin use, as well as a reduction in mean HbA1c and cholesterol levels, were significantly associated with a reduction in lifetime risk of retinopathy, blindness, end-stage renal disease, and coronary artery disease.[31]

The EHHOP clinic can significantly reduce the risk of diabetes complications by concentrating efforts on better glycemic control.[4,7-9,35] Recent evidence suggests that intensive glucose control produces significant reductions in microvascular and macrovascular complications years after the intervention and regardless of whether the initial improvement in HbA1c levels was maintained.[9] This finding is especially relevant in free clinics, in view of the difficulties of providing continuity of care to uninsured patients. While reducing HbA1c levels to American Diabetes Association target goals will be difficult since many patients at EHHOP present with very high HbA1c levels, research found that the reduction in the risk of diabetes complications is even more dramatic for patients presenting with higher HbA1c levels.[10]

Blood pressure control is associated with reduced risk of microvascular disease, diabetes-related death, or stroke,[5] but the reduction in risk disappears with loss of tight blood pressure control in long-term follow-up studies.[36] Specifically, a 10 mmHg reduction in blood pressure leads to a 35% lower risk of macrovascular and microvascular complications, including a 24% decrease in diabetes-related events, 32% decrease in diabetes-related deaths, and 21% decrease in acute myocardial infarction.[5] These findings are consistent with the results of another study that found a 34% decrease in cardiovascular events in a cohort of older adults with diabetes associated with 9.8 mmHg lower systolic and 2.2 mmHg lower diastolic blood pressure.[37] Good blood pressure control has been shown to be the most cost-effective intervention for diabetes, even compared with intensive glycemic control.[38-40]

Considering inherent challenges in providing optimal care to the uninsured, quality of care at student-run health clinics is an important concern for faculty and student volunteers, potential donors, and supporting community organizations. As different types of interventions to address the growing needs of the uninsured compete for limited funding to cover operating expenses, potential donors seek quantitative information about quality of care and patient outcomes attained by each intervention model. An objective assessment of care quality provided at free clinics is necessary to support fundraising efforts to ensure that limited health care funds are directed to effective programs that benefit the uninsured.

This study highlights several opportunities for improvement of diabetes management at the EHHOP clinic. Implementation of a targeted intervention to increase cholesterol monitoring and improve glycemic control among patients with diabetes at EHHOP has the potential to significantly improve patient outcomes. Our findings also underscore the importance of ensuring access to medications for chronic conditions at free clinics. Research shows that patients with diabetes who lack access to medications have significantly increased health care resource utilization.[41] Pharmacy expenses account for well over half of the EHHOP clinic budget (55%), and 32% of the pharmacy budget is spent on diabetes medications. Unfortunately, charity programs and grant funding available to support long-term medication use are extremely limited, with most donor organizations focusing on one-time interventions or start-up grants.

Limitations

The results of this study should be interpreted in light of several limitations. First, accurate calculation of the process of care measures depends on thorough chart documentation. For instance, some patients are offered but refuse vaccinations, and smoking cessation counseling is not always documented in the chart, possibly resulting in an underestimation of quality-of-care indicator rates. Second, our findings were based on a small sample of uninsured patients with diabetes and might not be generalizable to other patient populations. A significant proportion of patients were excluded from the study because they had only one visit to the clinic. About a third (27%) of the excluded patients were seen at EHHOP for urgent medication refills and were receiving their regular care from another provider. Other reasons for having only one visit included having Medicaid, transferring care to another clinic, and receiving palliative care for terminal cancer. Exclusion of patients with no follow-up visits from analysis creates potential bias toward better compliance among study sample and is a limitation of this study. Third, men were over-represented in the study sample compared with the overall EHHOP population. The significance of gender distribution of the study sample is unclear and constitutes a limitation of this study. Fourth, comparative quality of care measure rates were derived from previously published data derived from analyses of other patient populations with different demographic and other characteristics from the EHHOP population.

In conclusion, our findings suggest that student-run free clinics can attain intermediate clinical outcomes for patients with diabetes that are better in many areas than outcomes in the general uninsured population and comparable to those of patients with insurance. Nevertheless, significant opportunities for improvement exist in all care settings. The EHHOP clinic plans to address these concerns by disseminating guidelines among medical student volunteers for optimal diabetic management and by implementing practice improvements that facilitate a chronic care model for diabetes management. Future research should focus on identifying specific interventions aimed at improving the quality of diabetes care that can be implemented successfully in the free clinic setting.

Acknowledgments

We would like to acknowledge Melissa Wong, Clair McClung, Andrew Chow, Eric Smith, Peter Vasquez, and Jarone Lee for research assistance.

Notes

1. Wilper AP, Woodhandler S, Lasser KE, et al. A national study of chronic disease prevalence and access to care in uninsured U.S. adults. Ann Intern Med. 2008 Aug 5;149(3):170–6.

2. Simpson SA, Long JA. Medical student-run health clinics: important contributors to patient care and medical education. J Gen Intern Med. 2007 March;22(3):352–6.

3. American Diabetes Association. Standards of medical care in diabetes. Diabetes Care. 2006 Jan;29(Suppl 1):S4–42.

4. United Kingdom Prospective Diabetes Study (UKPDS) Group. Intensive blood-glucose control with sulphonylureas or insulin compared with conventional treatment and risk of complications in patients with type 2 diabetes (UKDPS 33). Lancet. 1998 Sep 12;352(9131): 837–53.

5. United Kingdom Prospective Diabetes Study (UKPDS) Group. Tight blood pressure control and risk of microvascular and macrovascular complications in type 2 diabetes: UKPDS 38. BMJ. 1998 Sep;317(7160):703–13.

6. Irons BK, Flemming B, Seifert CF, et al. Evaluation of diabetes primary care and effects on health care charges in elderly patients with diabetes. Am J Med Sci. 2008 Jun;335(6):426–30.

7. The Diabetes Control and Complications Trial Research Group. The effect of intensive treatment of diabetes on the development and progression of long-term complications in insulin-dependent diabetes mellitus. N Engl J Med. 1993 Sep 30;329(14):977–86.

8. ADVANCE Collaborative Group, Patel A, MacMahon S, et al. Intensive blood glucose control and vascular outcomes in patients with type 2 diabetes. N Engl J Med. 2008 Jun 12;358(24):2560–72.

9. Holman RR, Paul SK, Bethel MA, et al. 10-year follow-up of intensive glucose control in type 2 diabetes. N Engl J Med. 2008 Oct 9;359(15):1577–89.

10. Vijan S, Hofer TP, Hayward RA. Estimated benefits of glycemic control in microvascular complications in type 2 diabetes. Ann Intern Med. 1997 Nov 1;127(9):788–95.

11. Stroebel RJ, Gloor B, Freytag S, et al. Adapting the chronic care model to treat chronic illness at a free medical clinic. J Health Care Poor Underserved. 2005 May; 16(2):286–96.

12. Benoit SR, Fleming R, Philis-Tsimikas A, et al. Predictors of glycemic control among patients with type 2 diabetes: a longitudinal study. BMC Public Health. 2005 Apr 17: 5–36.

13. Saaddine JB, Engelgau MM, Beckles GL, et al. A diabetes report card for the United States: quality of care in the 1990s. Ann Intern Med. 2002 Apr 16;136(8):565–74.

14. Nelson KM, Chapko MK, Reiber G, et al. The association between health insurance coverage and diabetes care; data from the 2000 behavioral risk factor surveillance system. Health Serv Res. 2005 Apr;40(2):361–72.

15. Ayanian JZ, Weissman JS, Schneider EC, et al. Unmet health needs of uninsured adults in the United States. JAMA. 2000 Oct 25;284(16):2061–9.

16. Haffner SM, Hazuda HP, Stern MP, et al. Effects of socioeconomic status on hyperglycemia and retinopathy levels in Mexican Americans with NIDDM. Diabetes Care. 1989 Feb; 12(2):128–34.

17. Eberhardt MS, Lackland DT, Wheeler FC, et al. Is race related to glycemic control? An assessment of glycosylated hemoglobin in two South Carolina communities. J Clin Epidemiol. 1994 Oct;47(10):1181–9.

18. Blaum CS, Velez L, Hiss RG, et al. Characteristics related to poor glycemic control in NIDDM patients in community practice. Diabetes Care. 1997 Jan;20(1):7–11.

19. Harris MI, Eastman RC, Cowie CC, et al. Racial and ethnic differences in glycemic control of adults with type 2 diabetes. Diabetes Care. 1999 Mar;22(3):403–8.

20. Poulsen EJ. Student-run clinics: a double opportunity. JAMA. 1995;273:430.

21. Geller S, Taylor FM, Scott HD. Free clinics helping to patch the safety net. J Health Care Poor Underserved. 2004;15(1):42–51.

22. Buchanan D, Witlen R. Balancing service and education: ethical management of student-run clinics. J Health Care Poor Underserved. 2006; 17:477–85.

23. New York City Department of City Planning. 2000 census profiles for New York City. New York: New York City Department of City Planning, 2002. Available at http:// gis.nyc.gov /dcp/html/census/census.shtml/

24. New York City Department of City Planning. Community district profile for East Harlem. New York: New York City Department of City Planning, 2007. Available at: http://www.nyc .gov/html/dcp/pdf/lucds/mn11profile.pdf.

25. Olson EC, Van Wye G, Kerker B, et al. Take care, East Harlem. NYC community health profiles, 2nd ed. New York: New York City Department of Health and Mental Hygiene. 2006;21(42):1–16. Available at: http://www.nyc.gov/html/doh/ downloads/ pdf/data/2006chp-303.pdf.

26. National Committee for Quality Assurance. HEDIS 2006: health plan employer data and information set, vol. 2, technical specifications. Washington, DC: National Committee for Quality Assurance (NCQA), 2005.

27. National Diabetes Quality Improvement Alliance. National Diabetes Quality Improvement Alliance performance measurement set for adult diabetes. Chicago, IL: National Diabetes Quality Improvement Alliance, 2003.

28. HealthPartners. 2005 clinical indicators report: 2004/2005 results. Bloomington, MN: HealthPartners, 2005. Available at http://www.healthpartners.com/files/28455.pdf.

29. Porterfield DS, Kinsinger L. Quality of care for uninsured patients with diabetes in a rural area. Diabetes Care. 2002 Feb;25:319–23.

30. New York State Department of Health. New York State strategic plan for the prevention and control of diabetes. Albany, NY: New York State Department of Health, 2006. Available at www.health.state.ny.us/diseases/conditions/diabetes/strategicplan.htm.

31. Huang ES, Zhang Q, Brown SE, et al. The cost-effectiveness of improving diabetes care in US federally qualified community health centers. Health Serv Res. 2007 Dec; 42(6, pt. 1):2174–323.

32. Shetty S, Secnik K, Oglesby AK. Relationship of glycemic control to total diabetes-related costs for managed care health plan members with type 2 diabetes. J Manag Care Pharm. 2005 Sep;11(7):559–64.

33. Selby JV, Ray GT, Zhang D, et al. Excess costs of medical care for patients with diabetes in a managed care population. Diabetes Care. 1997 Sep;20(9):1396–402.

34. National Committee for Quality Assurance. The state of health care quality. Washington, DC: National Committee for Quality Assurance, 2007. Available at http:// web.ncqa.org /Portals/0/Publications/Resource%20Library/SOHC/SOHC_07.pdf.

35. Stratton IM, Adler AI, Neil HA, et al. Association of glycaemia with macrovascular and microvascular complications of type 2 diabetes (UKPDS 35): prospective observational study. BMJ. 2000 Aug; 321:405–12.

36. Holman RR, Paul SK, Bethel MA, et al. Long-term follow-up after tight control of blood pressure in type 2 diabetes. N Engl J Med. 2008 Oct; 359:1565–76.

37. Curb JD, Pressel SL, Cutler IA, et al. Effect of diuretic-based antihypertensive treatment on cardiovascular disease risk in older diabetic patients with isolated systolic hypertension. Systolic hypertention in the elderly program cooperative research group. JAMA. 1996 Dec 18; 276:1886–92.

38. United Kingdom prospective diabetes study group. Cost effectiveness analysis of improved blood pressure control in hypertensive patients with type 2 diabetes: UKPDS 40. BMJ. 1998 Sep 12; 317:720–6.

39. CDC Diabetes Cost-effectiveness Group. Cost-effectiveness of intensive glycemic control, intensified hypertension control, and serum cholesterol level reduction for type 2 diabetes. JAMA. 2002 May 15;287(19):2542–51.

40.   Vijan S, Hayward RA. Treatment of hypertension in type 2 diabetes mellitus: blood pressure goals, choice of agents, and setting priorities in diabetes care. Ann of Internal Med. 2003 Apr 1; 138:593–602.

41.   Stephens JM, Botteman MF, Hay JW. Economic impact of antidiabetic medications and glycemic control on managed care organizations: a review of literature. J Manag Care Pharm. 2006 Mar;12(2):130–42. Available at http://www.amcp.org/data/jmcp/subj_review _130-142.pdf.

42.   New York State Department of Health. 2006 New York State managed care plan performance: a report on quality, access to care, and consumer satisfaction. Albany, NY: New York State Department of Health, 2006. Available at http://www.health.state.ny.us/health_care /managed_care/qarrfull/qarr_2006/qarr2006.pdf.

43.   New York State Department of Health. The state of diabetes in New York State: a surveillance report. Albany, NY: New York State Department of Health, 2005. Available at http:// www.health.state.ny.us/statistics/diseases/conditions/diabetes/docs/1997-2004_surveillance _report.pdf.

Chapter 19

Students Who Participate in a Student-Run Free Health Clinic Need Education about Access to Care Issues

B. Brent Simmons

Daniel DeJoseph

James Diamond

Lara Weinstein

Student-run clinics contribute to the health care safety net and provide care for a significant, although small, portion of the uninsured, seeing more than 36,000 visits annually.[1,2] However, student-run clinics often have important limitations, such as difficulty with continuity, labwork, radiological studies, and free medications. Patients at student-run clinics appear to be sicker than the general population, with higher rates of diabetes, asthma, hypertension, and psychiatric disorders.[3] Clearly, this is a population in great need of care, and medical schools nationwide in increasing numbers strive to contribute such care. In a recent survey, 52% of responding medical schools report having at least one student-run clinic.[1] In all, 111 clinics were identified, and more were planned.[1] These clinics are disproportionately staffed by preclinical medical students, with twice as many first-year students as fourth-year students participating.[1] For many student-run clinics with limited resources and continuity, an important intervention is to help identify patients with chronic conditions, assess if they qualify for Medicaid benefits, or refer them to local sites that accept uninsured patients. The students staffing these clinics are highly motivated and committed to the mission, but virtually nothing is known about the knowledge and perceptions they bring to their service. The objective of this study was to evaluate preclinical medical students who have already participated in student-run clinics and determine how prepared they are to confront social problems and barriers to care that are commonly encountered at free clinics. To the best of our knowledge, there have been no studies that have surveyed medical students about their attitudes and beliefs pertaining to student-run clinics. The survey reported on here was designed to determine what

B. Brent Simmons, MD, is an assistant professor of family medicine at Drexel University College of Medicine, in Philadelphia. *Daniel DeJoseph, MD,* practices family medicine at the Greater Lawrence Family Health Center, in Lawrence, Massachusetts. *James Diamond, PhD,* is a research professor of family medicine at Thomas Jefferson University in Philadelphia. *Lara Weinstein, MD,* is an assistant professor of family medicine at Thomas Jefferson University.

information the students would have liked to have had prior to beginning their participation at student-run free clinics and whether preparation should focus on access to care, operational matters, or social issues.

Background

JeffHope

Jefferson Medical College is a large medical school located in urban Philadelphia, with 966 total students (approximately 250 per class). It has a student-run organization named JeffHope, which coordinates and runs five student-run health clinics in Philadelphia. Four of the five JeffHope sites are located at homeless shelters, and the fifth is located at a needle exchange center. JeffHope was founded in 1992 and currently receives over 2,000 patient visits per year.

Each of the JeffHope sites is open one night per week (each on a different night) and offer ambulatory care for all ages, including infants and children at two shelters that house women with their children. Given the transience of the shelter populations, these clinics do not usually experience much long-term patient continuity, but the clinics often see patients follow up during their stays at the shelter. The students are always supervised by a volunteer physician, although the experience of the supervising physician varies greatly (anyone from an intern to a veteran attending physician might fill the role). Some medications are kept on site at the clinics, but only a limited number. There are no social workers and no capacity to refer patients who do not have insurance elsewhere for ongoing care. Students receive a short orientation, which covers simple logistics of the clinics, prior to participation. Social issues and local safety net resources are not covered.

Philadelphia Health Centers

The Philadelphia Health Center system is run by the Philadelphia Department of Public Health and comprises 11 clinics throughout the city.[4] The health centers are able to provide many services to the uninsured, including medications, radiological testing, specialist services, and lab testing.

Survey

A 14-item survey was handed out to the entire first-year medical school class prior to a quiz two weeks before the end of the academic year. Students were first asked how many times they had worked at a JeffHope clinic; if the answer was greater than zero, they completed the remainder of the survey. The survey contained 10 questions inquiring about preparedness for addressing access to care issues, social issues, and operational issues. Answers were scored on a five-point Likert *agree*-to-*disagree* scale (appendix). In addition, there were three open-ended questions relating to the same topics. The responses were analyzed using descriptive statistics following data entry using an Excel spreadsheet. The International Review Board at Thomas Jefferson University approved the survey prior to distribution.

Participants

Of the 266 students in the first-year class, 209 completed surveys for a response rate of 80%. Over 70% of the first-year class had participated in the JeffHope clinics at least once. About 64% of students had participated at JeffHope once or twice, 24% three to five times, and 12% more than five times.

Access to care

The lowest scores throughout the survey dealt with access to care issues. Only 10% of students agreed (responding either *agree* or *somewhat agree*) that they felt comfortable getting an uninsured patient referred into the health care system, and specifically only 8% agreed that they understood how the Philadelphia Health Center system works and the services it provides. Finally, only 11% of students agreed that they could help an uninsured patient to get life-sustaining medications.

Preparedness and operational considerations

Only 27% of students agreed they were prepared for JeffHope the first time they participated. However, 87% of students agreed that they felt comfortable working with the patients, and 64% knew whom to ask for help with challenging situations were encountered at the clinic. A large majority of respondents (88%) agreed that an orientation prior to beginning JeffHope activities that addresses the issues covered in this survey would be beneficial.

Social context

In general, students were confident about their awareness of the social context of homelessness. Seventy-seven percent of students agreed they understood common reasons for homelessness, and 63% could name common barriers to care for the homeless. Fifty-three percent of students agreed they felt comfortable with the harm reduction model employed by needle exchange centers.

Stratification

Not surprisingly, when the sample was stratified by the number of times the student had participated in JeffHope, those who had been there more often were more comfortable with access to care issues. In addition, they became increasingly comfortable working with JeffHope patients and knowing whom to ask for help. Students were comfortable with the social topics regardless of level of participation.

Discussion

Student-run clinics are becoming an increasingly common adjunct to the health care safety net. Preclinical medical students often have their first hands-on patient encounters in this setting, which can become an enriching experience for the medical student and address important needs for the patient.[1] However, medical students (especially preclinical students) often do not have the knowl-edge or experience necessary to get these patients transferred into the health care system for medical problems beyond the scope of student-run clinics. Clin-ics at each institution have their own limitations. Students should be aware of the specific limitations of their clinic and be familiar with local resources avail-able, such as city-run health centers that are able to provide adequate care for patients without insurance. Additionally, a subset of patients will qualify for med-ical assistance and can be referred to many university or community-based health systems.

Continuity of care is better in community health centers (CHCs) than in other safety net delivery sites, and established CHC patients are more likely to present with new health problems than patients at other safety net sites.[5] Having a regular source of care, such as CHC, has been shown to lead to better health outcomes for the homeless.[6] In addition, homeless patients are usually more willing to obtain care if they perceive that care to be important.[6] Therefore, identifying a patient with a chronic condition and coordinating follow-up care might be the most im-portant contribution the medical student can make. Our survey shows that most students lack the information needed to accomplish this goal, but also that, over-whelmingly, they would welcome an orientation to these issues prior to working in the clinics. As might be expected, the students gained experience and over time figured out how to patch patients into the health centers, and in that way became more comfortable. We feel that the initial knowledge gap can be filled at the student-clinic orientation, making the students ready to render such help from the beginning. A simple one-hour lecture on the logistics involved in getting unin-sured patients referred into local health centers with an accompanying handout would suffice for most medical students. Further work can be added later to edu-cate students and faculty preceptors about streamlining the process of obtaining medical assistance and allowing patients access to primary and specialty care. At our institution, this project led to the initiation of an optional student-organized lecture series, including guest speakers from the Philadelphia Health Centers and the needle exchange site. Teaching medical students the logistics of accessing care for the uninsured is vital to managing care properly at student-run health clinics.

JeffHope Survey

This is an anonymous survey for a study by the Department of Family and Com-munity Medicine to evaluate first-year students' comfort level with various Jeff-Hope issues.

Thank you.

Appendix

			Somewhat		Somewhat	
1.	How many times have you been to JeffHope?	0	1–2		3–5	>5

		Disagree	Somewhat Disagree	Neutral	Somewhat Agree	Agree
2.	I am comfortable working with the patients at JeffHope.	1	2	3	4	5
3.	I felt prepared for JeffHope when I first started going.	1	2	3	4	5
4.	I know how to get a patient without insurance patched into the health care system.	1	2	3	4	5
5.	I know what to do for a patient who has no prescription coverage and needs a life-sustaining medicine (e.g., insulin).	1	2	3	4	5
6.	I know whom to ask for help with challenging situations unique to JeffHope.	1	2	3	4	5
7.	I understand how the Philadelphia Health Center system works.	1	2	3	4	5
8.	I can name common reasons for homelessness.	1	2	3	4	5
9.	I can name the most common barriers to care for the homeless.	1	2	3	4	5
10.	I am comfortable with the harm reduction model employed by needle exchanges.	1	2	3	4	5
11.	I feel that orientation to the above issues prior to starting JeffHope would be beneficial.	1	2	3	4	5

12. What medical problems encountered at JeffHope do you feel you need to know more about?

13. What social problems encountered at JeffHope do you feel you need to know more about?

Notes

1. Simpson SA, Long JA. Medical student-run health clinics: important contributors to patient care and medical education. J Gen Intern Med. 2007 Mar;22(3):352–6.
2. Geller S, Taylor BM, Scott HD. Free clinics helping to patch the safety net. J Health Care Poor Underserved. 2004 Feb;15(1):42–51.

3. Cadzow RB, Servoss TJ, Fox CH. The health status of patients of a student-run free medical clinic in inner-city Buffalo, NY. J Am Board Fam Med. 2007 Nov–Dec;20(6):572–80.

4. Philadelphia Department of Public Health. Department of Public Health. Philadelphia, PA: City of Philadelphia, 2008. Available at http://www.phila.gov/health/index.html.

5. Forrest CB, Whelan EM. Primary care safety-net delivery sites in the United States. JAMA. 2000 Oct 25;284(16):2077–83.

6. Gelberg L, Andersen RM, Leake BD. The behavioral model for vulnerable populations: application to medical care use and outcomes for homeless people. Health Serv Res. 2000 Feb; 34(6):1303–5.

Chapter 20

The UCSD Student-Run Free Clinic Project: Transdisciplinary Health Professional Education

Ellen Beck

The UCSD Student-Run Free Clinic Project resulted from the dreams of a group of medical students at UCSD School of Medicine. In 1996, a small group of medical students and faculty approached a community partner doing excellent work with street homeless, in a part of the city with few resources for homeless people, and offered to strengthen the community program's effort by offering some clinical services on a weekly basis. The street homeless program, based at a local Methodist church, welcomed the project and offered space one evening a week after a community meal. An affiliation agreement was signed between the university and the church, some supplies and medications were donated, appropriate arrangements were made for such things as records, charting, confidentiality, and safety, and in January 1997 the program began.

The first Wednesday night there were 10 patients, and the project grew from then on. Eventually, more students were involved than one site could handle. Less than a year later, a pastor in a downtown Lutheran church, known for its work in social justice, approached the clinic director and invited the students and faculty to start a second site in the downtown area. The second site opened on Monday nights in October 1997, and it flourished as well.

The first two sites were primarily serving adults, working poor and street homeless. The students wanted to work with women, children, and families as well, especially from underserved minority communities. A free clinic project outreach team approached a revered local African American community pastor and suggested a third site at his church. He indicated that although his church was located in the inner city, his congregation was primarily middle class. However, he went on to point out, his wife was the Montessori consultant at Baker Elementary School in the inner city. By October 1998, the third site had opened on Tuesday afternoons at Baker Elementary. The school site, where 100% of the children receive subsidized lunches, offers services to the families and commu-

Ellen Beck, MD, is a clinical professor in the Department of Family and Preventive Medicine, University of California, School of Medicine, and director of medical student education, Division of Family Medicine, the UCSD Student-Run Free Clinic Project, and the Fellowship in Underserved Healthcare.

nity of Mountain View, an inner-city neighborhood in Southeast San Diego, which is 67% Hispanic and 30% African American. If the time this chapter was written, clinical services offered every Monday night at the downtown site, every Wednesday night at the beach location, and every Tuesday afternoon and Thursday morning at the school site. Each of the three community partner sites provides at least two rooms of dedicated space for the clinic project and more during clinic sessions. In addition, a street homeless outreach team (consisting of a formerly homeless streetwise guide, a physician, a social worker, and students or residents) goes out on the streets several times a month and encounters street homeless, provides basic advice, and encourages follow-up at one of the three clinic sites.

Mission

The students and faculty developed a mission statement that focuses on the core values of respect and empowerment. *Empowerment* in this setting is defined as creating an environment in which the other (individual, family, and community) can take charge of his or her life and achieve well-being. Student leaders are expected to model these values and reinforce them among their fellow students. The mission statement that was finally adopted is the following:

> We are committed to providing free high quality health care to underserved communities of San Diego. The UCSD Student-Run Free Clinic Project, in partnership with the community, provides accessible, quality healthcare for the underserved in a respectful environment in which students, health professionals, patients and community members learn from one another. We seek to sustain health through . . .
> - free medical and preventive care
> - health education
> - access to social services

Figure 20.1 represents the clinic's mission in another form.

The faculty-student group also identified the list that follows as core values of the clinic project.
- Respect
- Trust
- Learning
- Excellence
- Respect for diversity
- Communication
- Empowerment
- Integration
- Community

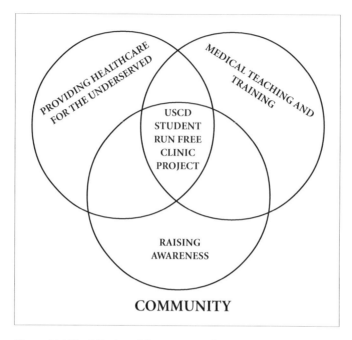

Figure 20.1 The Mission of the UCSD Student-Run Clinic Project.

Professional Partners

From the beginning, the Pacific College of Oriental Medicine has provided acupuncture faculty and students at two of the sites on a weekly basis. Patients sign up for medical or acupuncture clinic or both. Patients are also referred from one team to the other. Students and faculty consult and collaborate in the care of the patient.

The UCSD School of Pharmacy and the UCSD–UCSF Combined Pharmacy program provide faculty and students for all three sites on a weekly basis. Students and faculty from pharmacy and medicine collaborate in seeing patients and providing care and education.

Nurse practitioners function as attendings alongside physicians and supervise nurse practitioner students from the University of San Diego Nurse Practitioner Program as well as medical students. For five years, the core associate director for the clinic project was a nurse practitioner. Thus, medical students have the experience of a core mentor being a nurse practitioner early in their clinical training.

Social work and mental health staff and faculty supervise medical students and social work interns from the San Diego State University School of Social Work in the provision of care.

In many American communities, the school of dentistry is an important setting for the provision of care to the underserved. Although there is a school of dental hygiene, San Diego does not have a school of dentistry. Predental students and voluntary faculty who are dentists and orthodontists in the community collaborate in the care of the patients.

Legal Components and Organizational Structure

The clinic's legal status is that of an outreach program of UCSD School of Medicine. An affiliation agreement is established between each site and UCSD School of Medicine and the other health professional schools. All supervisory faculty are either salaried faculty or appointed as voluntary faculty in the School of Medicine or in one of the other professional schools in the partnership, which addresses the liability of supervisor and student. The clinic is organized nonhierarchically as much as possible, with students managing different administrative aspects of the clinic project. All student managers are expected to work on site at the clinic project so that there is not one tier of managers and another of workers, but all clinic leaders function as both.

Clinical Components

Epidemiology and demographics

San Diego County does not have a county hospital. Outpatient county medical services for single adults are limited to those earning less than $802 per month, which is the federal poverty level for a single adult. This amount is not a "livable wage" given the high cost of living in San Diego. Thus the "working poor"—those who earn too much to qualify for county health services, are not eligible for Medicaid, and who are self-employed or whose employers do not provide health benefits—make up a large percentage of the free clinic project's patients. Insufficient shelter space and warm weather result in a large street homeless population. In addition, San Diego's location, 15 miles from the border with Mexico, ensures that there is a large undocumented population. Thus, the need for access to care for the uninsured is great.

In 2004, 767 patients were seen in the medical clinic for 2,699 visits. (This does not include dental or acupuncture visits.) Table 20.1 summarizes demographic data from January 1, 1997, to December 31, 2004, for 2,074 individual free clinic patients at all three clinic sites. (More specifically, it includes patients at the following sites for the time periods shown here. Site 1: January 1997 through December 2004; site 2: October 1997 through December 2004; site 3: October 1999 through December 2004.)

The age data appear to reflect which groups have the least access at the state and national level. Access exists for children, through programs such as Medi-Cal Healthy Families, and for the elderly, through Medicare, but not for single adults between 18 and 65.

Personnel

Students at the free clinic project include medical students, pharmacy students, nurse practitioner students, predental students, acupuncture students, public health students, social work interns, and other pre–health profession students. We hope to involve other students as well, including nursing students, dental hygiene

Table 20.1

Demographic and background characteristics of free clinic patients, 1997–2004

Gender	Employed	Age	Ethnicity	Top 5 chronic diagnoses	Educational level	History of domestic violence	Homelessness
51.4% female 48.6% male	24.8%	<20: 4.4% 20–40: 34.3% 41–60: 47.8% >60: 13.5%	African American 8.8%, Asian 2.3%, Caucasian 28.2%, Hispanic 52.7%, other 4.4%, not specified 3.6%	Hypertension Diabetes Hyperlipidemia Depression Asthma	Completed high school 33%, some to completion of college 24%	9.2% reported a past experience of domestic violence	Not homeless 56.9%, homeless (from 1 week to >6 months) 36.2%, did not answer 6.9%

students, family therapy and psychology interns, and residents from various training programs. Medical student involvement varies according to year in medical school. This year, the breakdown is as follows: 105 of 122 first-year students; 35–45 second-year students; and 72 fourth-year students, who rotate through as part of the family medicine clerkship. An additional 12 fourth-year students devote their time as year-long clinic managers or clinical coaches. Family medicine, psychiatry, and neurology residents participate as well.

Twenty-five first-year pharmacy students rotate through, several third-year pharmacy students participate in the free clinic elective class, and 12 fourth-year pharmacy students participate during 6-week blocks in the course of the year. Eight senior acupuncture students participate for 10 weeks each quarter, supervised by acupuncture faculty funded by Pacific College of Oriental Medicine.

Community health professionals appointed as voluntary faculty and faculty health professionals who volunteer their time are known in the program as volunteer health professionals. These include 60 primary care physicians, 15 specialty physicians, 12 pharmacists, 35 dentists, and 3 nurse practitioners.

The funded members of the team provide infrastructure and supervision, as well as contributing to day-to-day management, continuity, and fundraising. These positions, most of which are part time, include the clinic project director, the fellow in underserved medicine, some clinic attending support, community health promoters from the community, psychosocial program coordinators at two of the sites, a dental program coordinator, and administrative assistance.

Primary care and continuity

Pre–health professional volunteers check patients in, prepare charts, and administer consents. All patients are initially seen by a team of a first- or second-year student and a senior student or intern. The first- or second-year student establishes the relationship and takes the history, while the senior student acts as coach and assists with the initial examination. The students present to an attending, and then the attending must see all patients with the students. Together, they write a note, consult with pharmacy staff, and consider management options, including social resources. Most patients at the clinic sites are followed for ongoing care of chronic problems. Approximately 20 patients are seen per site per week per half-day clinic, with established patients getting top priority, and new patients being seen on a space-available basis.

At the end of the evening or half day, when time permits, a learning circle is held in which all members of the health care team stand in a circle and share something they have learned that day, no matter what part of their experience it involved. This process of reflection helps to build community and reinforces the humanistic model practiced at the clinic sites.

Case management

One of the principles of the clinic is to present no barriers at entry. Thus, initially, there is no financial screening. However, if a person meets eligibility requirements for government-sponsored insurance or other programs giving them access to care at other facilities, every effort is made to help them to enroll in these other programs, so that, at the free clinic project, ongoing services are only provided to those without any eligibility for access. The only exception to this is for street homeless patients who might officially be eligible for a program such as County Medical Services but whose lives are too chaotic for them to take advantage of the opportunity.[1] At each site, students supervised by a social worker, a family therapist, or physicians provide case management services to help patients with shelter, access, legal advocacy, and other needs. In addition, each site has a limited case management budget so that if there is a specific need that prevents access, or a specific barrier to achieving health or well-being (e.g., transportation, a low-cost procedure, a special medication, a specific form of therapy, tuition at a community college for a person reentering the work force, a suit for a job interview, or shelter for two nights so that a wound can be cared for), these may be purchased based on a joint decision between the case manager and the clinic director.

Lab testing

The free clinic project is part of a San Diego purchasing cooperative, Council Connections, sponsored by the Council of Community Clinics, which makes it possible for the clinic project to purchase lab services so inexpensively that it can offer free lab tests to clients. Licensed volunteer phlebotomists and health professional students draw blood for blood tests. Through a waiver, certain tests may be performed on site. Results are delivered daily to the university administrative offices of the free clinic project, where they are reviewed for abnormalities. Routine labs are only drawn from a patient at his or her second visit to the clinic to ensure that the patient has established his or her commitment to continuity. Students are taught that they must be able to identify a way to follow up with a patient during the week, if needed, and thus make efforts to learn and record a phone number, the street corner where a person sells newspapers, the cell phone of a close friend, or the location where a homeless person tends to sleep.

Specialty services

Over time, a variety of specialty services have been developed based on the needs of the clinic and the interests of the students. These services include a monthly hepatitis clinic (supervised by a hepatitis specialist and a nurse practitioner and managed by the students), which provides patient education and helps patients with hepatitis C to access treatment, as well as monthly clinics in dermatology (pathology services for biopsies being provided as a donation by the UCSD Department of Pathology), diabetes care, neurology, and cardiology. These specialty clinics are each offered at one of the sites once a month; students refer patients and establish follow-up mechanisms. Volunteer attending practitioners supervise students at these specialty clinics. A local ophthalmologist donates retina exams and, if needed, laser retinopathy treatment for diabetics at his office once every six weeks. Students organize the clinic, and a van picks up patients at each of the three sites to go to the ophthalmologist's office.

Dental clinic

The greatest unmet health care need in the country is for dental care. The Surgeon General's *Report on Oral Health* from 2000 noted that although 44 million Americans lacked medical insurance, about 108 million lacked dental insurance.[2] Five years ago, student leaders at the clinic project estimated that 4 out of 10 free clinic patients had expressed unmet dental needs. A student, Eric Goldlust, offered to start a dental clinic project. At this point, dental services are offered once or twice a week at all three sites. At the school site, orthodontic services, using retainers and other temporary devices, are offered free of charge as well. The steering committee of the dental clinic project includes the executive director of the local dental society. The dental directors of the clinic are dedicated volunteer health professionals, including Irv Silverstein, DDS, and Melanie Parker, DDS. As part of a community advocacy elective, Dr. Parker teaches a session to the medical students on oral health and disease, a topic often overlooked in medical school curricula, bringing to bear such home truths as "toothlessness can lead to joblessness," among other things. Dr. Silverstein has become the adviser to the predental students, aiding them with the application process and encouraging their future involvement in underserved communities.

Mental health care

Another important area of unmet health needs is mental health; many of the free clinic patients have both mental and physical health needs, as well as problems with addiction. At the school site, a mental health team has formed that includes a family therapist/case manager who grew up in the Mountain View area, a community health promoter, and a family physician/psychiatrist. The mental health program supports a broad definition of mental health, in harmony with the definition of health provided by the World Health Organization: "Health is a state of complete physical, mental and social well-being and not merely the absence of disease or infirmity" (p. 100).[3]

The mental health program includes a weekly women's support group, a monthly stress management lunch program, and ongoing individual and family counseling for children and families without access to care. Care is ongoing and may include medication and psychiatric consultation. An art health program is being developed that will include creating a community mural at Baker Elementary. People from the free clinic project and children having problems at Baker Elementary and lacking access to care are referred to the Baker mental health program. The approach is to address the child's difficulties in a broad context, by attempting to work with both the family and the child to address often complex situations. At the other two sites, psychiatry residents, psychiatrists, a social worker, and family physicians provide mental health services. At the church sites, many of the clients are homeless. The free clinic project provides a safe, trusted setting that allows for the possibility of addressing the mental health as well as the physical health needs of this population. Students are taught to address the presenting concern of the patient (e.g., a skin rash or respiratory infection), letting trust develop over time.

As trust develops, they can begin to address some of the more fundamental problems (such as mental illness or alcoholism) that may contribute to the patient's homelessness.

Medications

Medications are provided free of charge to patients through three sources. One is a purchased formulary of primarily generic medications (one medication in each major category). The second source is a wish list formulary constructed to ensure that samples provided by physicians and pharmaceutical companies are those that are needed by the clinic project and to ensure consistency of medications for individual patients. The final source is patient assistance programs, through which medications are provided free of charge by the pharmaceutical companies to patients unable to purchase them, one patient at a time. It is made clear to the community that no habituating medications, such as narcotics or benzodiazepines, are dispensed by the free clinic project. This precludes patients recurrently attempting to seek commonly abused drugs from the free clinic project. An ongoing dilemma is the cost of diabetes test strips, which are not usually covered by patient assistance programs and which patients need in order to truly take charge of their diabetes.

Curricular Components

All students who work at the free clinic project are required to take an elective entitled Community Advocacy. This class comprises a weekly reflective component, a series of didactic and experiential sessions, and the students' first five sessions at clinic. These five sessions include a session at each of the three sites as a clinical trainee and two sessions as an administrative trainee. Classroom sessions include a presentation by community members and health promoters, entitled The Community as Teacher; an experiential session providing teaching skills, called Becoming a Teacher; a session by an orthodontist on oral health and disease; a participatory introduction to acupuncture; the practical use of social and legal resources; mental health and addiction care; women's health; issues of domestic violence; border health; pharmacy principles, including access to pharmaceuticals and safe practice; a community and clinical approach to diabetes; and an experiential approach to health professional well-being. Themes such as empowerment, respect, trust-building, confidentiality, safety, quality, "cultural humility,"[4] working with interpreters, the concept of vulnerable populations, and always learning from and involving the community[5] are emphasized. Students are also expected to present a health education session at one of the sites, and to complete a reflective paper synthesizing what they have learned. Students who choose to take a second elective, entitled Free Clinic II, then choose one of the clinic sites, and an administrative trainee role, and are expected to divide their time between administration and clinical work at the site. During this elective there are three group meetings, during which the students continue to reflect, share their experiences, and learn practical clinical skills (e.g., electrocardiograms or joint exams).

Students may repeat this elective and continue to receive credit throughout their first and second years. Between the first and second year of medical school, students have the opportunity to work at the free clinic project during the summer to help build its infrastructure, troubleshoot and solve problems, and ensure quality in all aspects of care. Six to 10 students work through the summer. These students often indicate that creating this type of program is a career goal for them.

In their third year, students drop in as clinical coaches. Two third-year students may also choose the Baker Elementary clinic site as their half-day weekly clinical setting for their required longitudinal primary care core clerkship. In their fourth year, students may be clinical coaches (paired with first- or second-year students), modeling a humanistic approach in the care of patients,[6] or they become clinic managers, as a team with second-year students, supervising the clinical services at one of the three sites. A humanistic approach embodies person-centered and relationship-centered care and is based on core principles, developed by Carl Rogers in the mid-twentieth century, of empathy, congruence, and unconditional positive regard.[6,7] Consistent with the free clinic project mission statement, it employs an empowerment approach and attempts to address the needs of the person's mind, body, and spirit and to create an environment in which they can take charge of their life and achieve well-being. Students at UCSD School of Medicine are expected to complete an independent study project during their four years of medical school. Students may choose to do a research project and/or a community service project. Many of the students choose to do theirs at the Free Clinic Project. This has led to the improvement of the clinic through addition of specialty clinics, development of outcome measures, creation of a clinical database, and implementation of a folic acid preconception education project as well as other programs.

Acupuncture students work at the clinic as part of a one-semester third-year option, attending once a week for 10 weeks. Pharmacy students participate in the first year as part of a required pharmacy practice class and as part of a fourth-year six-week elective. Social work interns may participate in a one-year internship. Two students from City College, a local community college, are placed at the Baker Elementary site for a year as their community service commitment, part of the Price Scholarship Program sponsored by Price Charities.

Funding: An Adventure in "Altrepeneurship" (Altruistic Entrepreneurship)

When the clinic project began, the effort was largely volunteer in nature and supported by in-kind donations. The university provided liability insurance, a key element of support; the partners provided space, telephone, utilities, and security; small donations supported supplies and basic equipment; and the students ran bake sales when the clinic was running out of medications. To this day, the project seeks no reimbursement for patient services. Some federal funding was obtained through the Health Resources and Services Administration (HRSA) primary care training funds to provide for some supervisory faculty and staff support. For the first few years, the students and faculty wrote small grants to help support the program, from foundations such as the County Employees Charitable Organization and the Harold S. Mindlin Foundation. A seminal event occurred four years after the start of the project, when the interim dean of the medical school decided to provide core infrastructure funding. This funding, which has continued for the last four years, has allowed the project to seek and receive funding from larger foundations (including the Alliance Healthcare Foundation, the California Endowment, the March of Dimes, and the Guenther Foundation). Sometimes one of the community partners is the lead agency on a proposal grant, sometimes the university. The quality of collaboration toward shared goals between the free clinic project and community partners has engendered the trust necessary for such a mutually beneficial partnership.

Replicability

In 1999, with the grant support of HRSA Title VII Primary Care Training funds, I created a three-week national faculty development program entitled Addressing the Health Needs of the Underserved; over 70 faculty from 25 states have attended this program over the last seven years. As a result, seven new student-run free clinic projects have been created, in settings as diverse as the Baylor School of Medicine in Houston, the University of Kentucky at Lexington, the University of Missouri at Kansas City, and the University of Mississippi at Jackson.[8]

In 2001, with the assistance of HRSA funding, I created a one-year fellowship in underserved medicine at UCSD for physicians, postprimary care residency, who have an interest in working with underserved communities. The fellow assists in the direction of the free clinic project, functions as an attending physician at the free clinic, and completes studies and a project in a relevant area. Fellows also have the option to earn a master's degree in public health. Of the four full-time fellows since 2001, two have previously been free clinic student leaders who did their residency elsewhere and returned to work with the clinic.

Outcomes

Clinical outcomes are measured by the Quality of Well-Being Scale (QWB-SA),[9] a well-validated and reliable measure that is administered regularly over time to free clinic patients.[10] A clinical database is maintained that allows the students to measure changes in clinical endpoints, such as blood pressure and hemoglobin A1c.

A preliminary study comparing students in the free clinic electives with those who had not taken the elective indicated that the free clinic students were more likely to have acquired more positive attitudes to working with the underserved and homeless than students who had not taken the elective.[14] A study currently being developed will look at long-term attitudes, career choices, future decisions to work with underserved individuals, and collaboration with other health professionals on the part of students involved with the free clinic project. Although the fact that the free clinic students are self-selected limits the implications of such comparisons, we still hope that they will prove useful.

Elements of Success

Medical students arrive at medical school with passion, compassion, and a desire to serve and make a difference. They are often leaders and have demonstrated this leadership prior to entering medical school. Once entering medical school, especially during the first two years, they often feel inadequate. Data indicate that cynicism often rises through medical school; some medical school environments have even been deemed abusive.[11,12] Projects such as the one described herein provide a setting in which the student's passions, compassion, and potential for leadership can thrive and be reinforced and in which the student can keep his or her values and dreams alive.

Student sense of ownership

Students strongly feel a sense of ownership in relation to the clinic project. Student leaders train and identify others who will lead after them; these new student leaders emerge as they demonstrate their commitment over time and their willingness to work hard and take on tasks as needed. Thus, the project nurtures humility, teamwork, ownership, and leadership. The students are expected to monitor and police the mission statement; if students or attending physicians behave arrogantly or rudely, they are taken aside, privately, and asked not to do so at the free clinic project. In lectures and by role modeling, teachers encourage students to leave competitiveness, academic arrogance, and prejudice at the door.

Community as teacher

Community members are seen as important, trusted partners and a key source of learning for the student. Several community members, who were initially patients and then volunteers, have become health promoters, educators, and community liaisons, essential members of the health care team at each site. These community members/leaders are invited to teach, in both the Community Advocacy elective and in the faculty development program, about advocacy and community and health issues.

Trust

The students are taught to show respect to all and to build trust. They learn that only after they and the patient establish a "trust bridge" can they begin to help the patient take charge of his or her life.

Partnerships

Both the community and the professional partnerships are the foundation of the free clinic project. Respecting and maintaining these partnerships is of prime importance. The philosophy of the free clinic project as expressed in the mission statement is actively taught and maintained and is the essence of all activities at the clinic project.

The future

There is no plan to increase the number of sites of the project because there is a risk it might then no longer be student run. Rather, the goal is to continually increase the quality, depth, and capacity of the clinics. In addition, it is important to keep the project in the community and to keep overhead low; thus, there is no desire to have a separate building, with its attendant costly overhead and distancing from the community. The almost 1,000 regular patients of the free clinic project get top priority, which means that prospective new patients often must be turned away. The need for access in the city as well as the country is vast, and the free clinic project can only address an infinitesimal bit. The current greatest unmet needs at the free clinic project are for specialty services that require a procedure or brief hospitalization. The San Diego community is attempting to address this problem by developing an Underserved Services Network to work with hospitals in the community to donate needed services on a rotating basis.

The Free Clinic Project and Transdisciplinary Health Professional Education

If health professional students from different fields work and train side by side in underserved settings with an empowerment philosophy, perhaps they will practice differently, consult each other more often, and perceive each other in a less hierarchical fashion. If health professional students are trained in environments where the students are expected to do all the tasks, whether large or small, and work together and learn from the community or with the community to achieve the goal of quality humanistic care of the patient,[13] perhaps system change is possible. The roles of health professionals as healers and teachers are at risk of being lost or mislaid during their training and subsequent practice.[13] Programs such as the UCSD Student-Run Free Clinic Project may sustain students' passion, compassion, and desire to make a difference as well as provide the needed skills to help the student make his or her dreams of practice with the underserved a reality.

Acknowledgment

Tony Jolly, a fourth-year medical student at UCSD, created the database on which the information in table 20.1 is based. Carol Bloom-Whitener provided administrative support in the writing of this article.

Notes

1.   Drury LJ. Community care for people who are homeless and mentally ill. J Health Care Poor Underserved. 2003 May;14(2):194–207.
2.   U.S. Department of Health and Human Services. Oral health in America: a report of the Surgeon General—executive summary. Rockville, MD: U.S. Department of Health and Human Services, National Institute of Dental and Craniofacial Research, National Institutes of Health, 2000.

3. Preamble to the Constitution of the World Health Organization as adopted by the International Health Conference, New York, 19–22 June, 1946; signed on 22 July 1946 by the representatives of 61 States (Official Records of the World Health Organization, no. 2, p. 100) and entered into force on 7 April 1948.

4. Tervalon, M, Murray-Garcia J. Cultural humility versus cultural competence: a critical distinction in defining physician training outcomes in multicultural education. J Health Care Poor Underserved. 1998;9(2).

5. Rhyne R, Bogue R, Kukulka G, Fulmer H. Community-oriented primary care: health care for the 21st century. American Public Health Association, 1998.

6. Rogers CR. Client-centered therapy: its current practice, implications, and theory. Boston: Houghton Mifflin, 1951.

7. Rogers CR. On becoming a person: a therapist's view of psychotherapy. Boston: Houghton Mifflin, 1961. Republished in 1965 with a new introduction by Peter Kramer.

8. Beck E. Addressing the health needs of the underserved. Bioethics Forum. 1999 Summer; 15(2):31–5.

9. Kaplan RM, Anderson JP, Ganiats TG. The quality of well-being scale: rationale for a single quality of life index. In: Walker SR, Rosser RM, eds. Quality of life assessment: key issues in the 1990s. London: Kluwer Academic Publishers, 1993.

10. O'Connor S, Ganiats TG, Beck E, Kaplan RM. Quality of life in a free clinic. Presented as a poster at the 10th Annual Conference of the International Society for Quality of Life Research, Prague, Czech Republic, November 2003. [Abstract: Qual Life Res. 2003;12(7):839].

11. Testerman JK, Morton KR, Loo LK, et al. The natural history of cynicism in physicians. Academic Medicine. 1996 Oct; 71(10 Suppl):S43–5.

12. Rosenberg DA, Silver HK. Medical student abuse. JAMA. 1984 Feb 10;251(6):739–42.

13. Beck E. Integrating the art and science of medicine—a humanistic approach. California Family Physician. 2004 Fall: 22–4.

14. Hoffman, D. Unpublished data. Independent study project, 1999.

Chapter 21
Charlottesville Health Access: A Locality-Based Model of Health Care Navigation for the Homeless

Steven E. Bishop
James M. Edwards
Mohan M. Nadkarni

Homelessness in Charlottesville, Virginia, presents a significant public health crisis. This homeless population faces uncommon challenges in both the urban Charlottesville area and the rural surrounding counties. In the city of 41,000, 27.3% of residents live below the poverty line—twice the national average.[1] The population density of Charlottesville proper is 4,048 people per square mile, making it more densely populated than Richmond (3,377 people/sq. mi.), the state's capital. In comparison, the surrounding counties range from 33 to 131 people per square mile.[2] Thus, urban/suburban Charlottesville differs sharply from its largely rural neighboring counties, with a homeless population that has trouble getting health care.

Since 2003, homelessness has been on the rise in the Charlottesville area, with more than 250 adults being reported homeless in 2007.[3] Local school systems indicate that at least 300 children and their families live in shelters or in other substandard conditions. The same report revealed that 44% of those surveyed had medical, dental, or substance abuse problems. Nearly one-half of those surveyed had difficulty obtaining a needed service from the health care system (such as a prescription drug, counseling, or dental care).[3]

This indicates a pervasive lack of access to various health care modalities for many of Charlottesville's homeless citizens. Social inequality has practical consequences for the homeless, including death rates at least four times those of the general U.S. population.[4] Whether one views these facts from a social justice standpoint or from the practicalities of lost economic productivity, they represent a significant public health problem. This problem must be addressed with new models of access.

The Charlottesville statistics predate the financial crisis that began in the early fall of 2008 and therefore likely underestimate both the current need for and the difficulty of obtaining health care. Additionally, these statistics do not expound on

Stephen E. Bishop, MD, is a resident physician at Virginia Commonwealth University. **James M. Edwards, MD,** is a resident physician at Duke University. **Mohan M. Nadkarni, MD, FACP,** is a professor of medicine at the University of Virginia School of Medicine and chief of the Section of General Internal Medicine, University of Virginia Health System.

particular challenges presented by the region's geography (mainly, that much of greater Charlottesville is rural). Thus, health care for the homeless in this area must be fashioned in order to meet the needs of both the urban homeless within the city and the rural homeless, who live in temporary camps in the surrounding counties. Specifically, transportation and coordination of care must be flexible and affordable enough to account for these different populations. Taken together, the situation demonstrates a pressing need for a new model of health care access for the homeless of Charlottesville.

A Solution

Charlottesville Health Access (CHA) began in February 2007, when a private, nonprofit community homeless shelter, PACEM (People and Congregations Engaged in Ministry) joined with medical and nursing students and physicians from University of Virginia schools of medicine and nursing (UVA SOM and SON) to organize a health fair for shelter guests. Afterward, medical students began studying existing needs assessment data from the Thomas Jefferson Area Coalition for the Homeless and PACEM regarding the medical needs of the area's homeless. These discussions led to the formation of a coalition of service providers and recently homeless people that investigated ways of providing a more permanent solution to the health care needs of the homeless in Charlottesville.

After the coalition developed a workable plan to enhance access to care for the homeless, CHA was created with the following goals:

- Provide a one-stop access point for health care resources for homeless in the Charlottesville region.
- Study the care provided, including the number of patients assisted, changes in the number of emergency room visits per homeless patient, and the number of days spent in the hospital per patient, among other variables.
- Advocate for easing health care access.
- Create opportunities for health profession students: provide a venue to teach about barriers to health care among the homeless, available community resources, and the importance of humanism in medicine.

The realization of these goals rests on the shoulders of navigator volunteers, people who have completed a short training course on caring for the homeless, written by Grete vanHorst, RN; Adriana Nicholson of PACEM; Warren Grupe, MD; and Esther Thatcher, RN, all individuals with extensive experience working with the homeless and underserved. A navigator (who may be any health profession student, undergraduate student, or community member) is charged with the following tasks:

- Engage a homeless person by building a relationship of trust.
- Assess the patient's needs.
- Guide the person to those who can provide for those needs and translate confusing information into understandable terms.

- Coordinate follow-up with health care providers.
- Empower homeless people to understand the health care system and their important role in caring for themselves.

This service is unique in our area, and perhaps anywhere. Student-run clinics have been successful in serving disadvantaged populations in many regions, but these clinics have mostly focused on providing care and treatment rather than assistance with navigating the health care system.[5] Navigation, in the form of case management, has been demonstrated to improve biologic outcomes in a homeless HIV-infected population.[6] As a general model, navigation has been studied most extensively in association with cancer treatment programs, particularly for underserved populations. In one study of such a program, navigation was associated with earlier stage of breast cancer diagnosis.[7] A review of cancer navigation initiatives showed that some programs were associated with improved cancer screening and compliance with follow-up visits.[8] One concern raised in the literature regarding these programs is their cost-effectiveness. The CHA model requires no permanent office space and utilizes only one paid part-time staff person to provide its services. This results in the program's overhead being extremely low. Therefore, any benefits reaped by CHA clients and the local health system are provided at very low overall cost.

The CHA model is student centered in many ways. Specifically, a number of the leadership opportunities are available to medical and nursing students within CHA. First, several medical students sit on the CHA board and serve as executive officers. Second, medical and nursing student leadership and staffing is central to the operation of the CHA program. All health fairs are organized through the clinic executive committee, a subcommittee of the CHA board, consisting of student leaders from both the SOM and the SON, and a faculty advisor from UVA SOM. Student leadership responsibilities are as follows:*

- The director of facilities is charged with communicating with representatives from the health fair sites.
- The director of volunteer coordination oversees the recruitment and scheduling of navigators.
- The director of logistics procures and provides for the storage of both medical and administrative items.
- The director of public relations introduces the navigator system to local health care providers not already affiliated with CHA.
- The director of finance administers funds allotted to the clinic executive committee in conjunction with the CHA board treasurer.
- The director of information and research maintains patient records in a secure location. He or she also integrates our data with the Homeless Management Information System (HMIS) used by many local groups to improve care for the homeless.

---

*Many are adapted from UVA Medical Reserve Corps.: E. Kantor, unpublished data.

- The director of training works to develop and implement an appropriate training curriculum for CHA navigators.

Each of these positions contributes to the smooth operation of a biweekly health fair. These fairs are scheduled on a day-evening rotating schedule: a biweekly fair at a PACEM shelter site in the evening and a biweekly fair at a daytime community soup kitchen. The population at PACEM shelter is a mix of the urban homeless from Charlottesville proper and the rural homeless who take refuge at PACEM during the winter months. The soup kitchen tends to attract homeless and near-homeless individuals from both Charlottesville and the surrounding counties who come into the city to work. Conducting our health fairs in association with PACEM and the soup kitchens allows us to reach a broad population base, including both the urban and rural homeless.

During each health fair, student navigators provide a basic health screening for patients, including a medical history, vital sign and blood glucose measurement, and a body mass index (BMI) assessment. Additionally, the navigator asks many other questions from our intake form, with topics ranging from housing to work and finances. This is done in order to determine the type of services with which the navigator should assist the patient.

Following this, navigators escort each patient to a resident physician and/or attending physician for further evaluation. Navigators connect patients with needed services, including a permanent health care provider, and assist in filling out financial screening forms (aided by the physician and the *Navigator Resource Manual*, a tool CHA developed). For example, a navigator might not only make an appointment at University Medical Associates (UMA, UVA Health System's general internal medicine clinic) but also assist a patient with filling out UVA Health System's financial screening form, enabling them to receive up to a 100% discount on all their care provided at UVA. Afterward, the patient and navigator set up a meeting (if necessary) for follow-up on any issues that arose the first day (such as finishing financial screening paperwork or agreeing to meet at a health care appointment).

Following this first interaction, the navigator assists the permanent health care provider in providing patient education and follow-up, employing an individual-ized scale-back navigation protocol. Each navigation protocol provides for a series of interactions between navigator and patient, encouraging patients to become self-sufficient over time once they have a permanent health care provider.

Since the navigator contingent is the backbone of CHA, the recruitment and training of these volunteers is central to the clinical executive committee's work. Since the navigators are at different levels (from first-year undergraduates to senior medical students), CHA developed two ways to train volunteers: an orientation seminar, to introduce homeless health care and interactions with vulnerable people, and the *Navigator Resource Manual*, with up-to-date information about community services.

The director of training presents the 60–90 minute orientation seminar, required for all new navigators. Members of the clinic executive committee, advisors from PACEM shelter, social workers and nurses from the UVA Health System, and others experienced working with the homeless in Charlottesville jointly developed this training program for CHA. The seminar focuses on these objectives:

- Understanding homelessness in Charlottesville
- Explaining the role of a CHA navigator in improving health care access
- Increasing awareness of barriers to health care faced by the homeless
- Teaching navigators about patient confidentiality
- Explaining safety procedures and the importance of communicating all interactions with patients to the program director or another responsible person

After completing this program, the navigators are given the *Navigator Resource Manual* to study and use at CHA health fairs. This manual includes information on many services with which a navigator may need to connect a patient, such as

- contact information for organizations such as the Salvation Army, AIDS Services Group, Alcoholics Anonymous, Virginia Department of Health, and many others;
- examples of forms for UVA financial screening; and
- local public transportation, for getting to appointments.

After their introductory training, navigators may volunteer at a health fair. Upper-level medical and nursing students and the program director mentor navigators during their first several fairs, until they are comfortable working alone. Thus, the navigators "learn while doing" and gain experience from interacting both with homeless patients and with a program director who has spent many years learning about the resources available to the homeless in the area.

Summary and Future Directions

In the future, CHA hopes to be included in the UVA SOM's Social Issues in Medicine course as a community service site and to create a senior medical student elective that focuses on in-depth scholarship about the local homeless population. Currently, none of the students involved in CHA receive course credit for their participation, but this too may be a future possibility as the program expands.

Additionally, we hope to reach more of the region's population now that CHA occupies a dedicated space inside the Haven building. The Aspire Project renovated a local church to create a community-wide resource center for the homeless and underserved. Organizations dedicated to housing, mental health, substance abuse, and other areas are housed in this building. Our relationship with this project will not only increase our population base but will also allow our navigators to more readily connect patients with providers who can address housing and other nonmedical needs.

At bottom, CHA serves its clients and volunteers by bringing them together to learn from one another. It will serve the region as a whole with the wealth of knowledge generated by studying the project's effects on the utilization of health care by the homeless.

Notes

1. U.S. Census Bureau. American Community Survey; 2005–2007. Washington, DC: U.S. Census Bureau, 2009. Available at http://www.census.gov/acs/www/.

2. U.S. Census Bureau. Population estimates program, 2008. Washington, DC: U.S. Census Bureau, 2009. Available at http://www.census.gov/popest/counties/.

3. Thomas Jefferson Area Coalition for the Homeless. Fifth annual homeless census and point in time count. Charlottesville, VA: Thomas Jefferson Area Coalition for the Homeless, 2007. Available at http://www.tjpdc.org/pdf/rep_hous_homelessCensus07.pdf.

4. Barrow SM, Herman DB, Cordova P, et al. Mortality among homeless shelter residents in New York City. Am J Public Health. 1999 Apr;89(4):529–34.

5. Simpson SA, Long JA. Medical student-run health clinics: important contributors to patient care and medical education. J Gen Intern Med. 2007 Mar;22(3):352–6.

6. Kushel MB, Colfax G, Ragland K, et al. Case management is associated with improved antiretroviral adherence and CD4+ cell counts in homeless and marginally housed individuals with HIV infection. Clin Infect Dis. 2006 Jul 15;43(2):234–42. Epub 2006 Jun 8.

7. Gabram SG, Lund MJ, Gardner J, et al. Effects of an outreach and internal navigation program on breast cancer diagnosis in an urban cancer center with a large African-American population. Cancer. 2008 Aug 1;113(3):602–7.

8. Wells KJ, Battaglia TA, Dudley DJ, et al. Patient navigation: state of the art or it is science? Cancer. 2008 Oct 15;113(8):1999–2010.

Chapter 22
UCLA Mobile Clinic Project

Joseph Hastings
Donna Zulman
Soma Wali

Case Presentation

H. E. was a 51-year-old homeless male who presented to the UCLA Mobile Clinic. He complained of chronic nosebleeds and had a history of schizophrenia. Physical examination was remarkable only for hypertension. He was referred to a local permanent free clinic for further care but did not follow up.

Two years later, the patient presented with hemoptysis, nosebleeds, gingival bleeding, and difficulty swallowing. Physical examination was remarkable for elevated blood pressure and a palpable neck mass. He refused transportation to a local hospital.

One month later, the patient returned with worsening hemoptysis and enlargement of the neck mass. One of the authors of this paper, a medical student at the time, persuaded the patient to travel by taxi to a UCLA-affiliated county hospital. The student followed, assisted with paperwork, and ensured the patient's rapid evaluation and admission.

Fine needle aspiration of the neck mass revealed potentially malignant cells. Open biopsy was recommended. The patient refused, demonstrating delusional thinking in his reasoning. The psychiatry service evaluated the patient and recommended antipsychotic medications.

Chest CT showed mediastinal lymph nodes and a large left lower lobe lung mass. FDG-PET demonstrated areas of increased activity in the left lung base and multiple regional lymph nodes. Open biopsy of the neck mass showed metastatic mucinous adenocarcinoma. The patient was not a candidate for palliative chemotherapy. He was offered comfort care and transferred to a nursing home.

Joseph Hastings, MPH, MD, is a radiation oncologist at Santa Clara Medical Center, part of the Permanente Medical Group, Santa Clara, California. *Donna Zulman, MD,* is an instructor in the Division of General Medical Disciplines, Department of Internal Medicine, Stanford University, core faculty of the Clinical Excellence Research Center, and an investigator for the Center for Health Care Evaluation, VA Palo Alto Health Care System. *Soma Wali, MD,* is an assistant professor of medicine at the David Geffen School of Medicine, UCLA.

The UCLA Mobile Clinic

Founded in 2001 in cooperation with the Greater West Hollywood Food Coalition, the UCLA Mobile Clinic provides weekly free medical services on a street corner in West Hollywood. The mobile clinic is entirely student run, with volunteers drawn from undergraduate, public health, dental, medical, and law schools. All volunteers undergo training prior to working at the site. The mobile clinic is the basis for both an undergraduate class and a medical school elective.

During a typical patient visit, an undergraduate student serves as a caseworker, obtaining a thorough social history. He or she then discusses the case with a medical student, who in turn performs a history and physical examination to present to a volunteer attending physician. The attending physician sees the patient with the students, explaining relevant teaching points while modeling a respectful and professional attitude.

Oral medications can be dispensed, but no needles are kept at the clinic. Patients are often referred to other permanent free clinics for follow-up care. Complicated or emergency cases are referred to local hospitals. Bus tokens and taxi vouchers are provided to cover transportation costs.

Student-run homeless clinics provide a critical service to the community and offer a primary care experience for medical students that can foster social awareness.

Homelessness, Mental Illness, and Health

There are an estimated 13.5 million homeless people in the United States.[1] A recent count showed 82,291 homeless individuals per night in Los Angeles County alone.[2]

Due to the transient nature of the patient population, most evidence on homeless health comes from street surveys and clinics for the underserved. Reports on experiences at a large free clinic in Los Angeles attest that homeless patients have particular health concerns and characteristics,[3] including more problems per visit, more functional limitations, and a greater prevalence of chronic disease with later presentation.[4] In comparison with housed patients, homeless patients also require a greater number of medical visits, more time per visit, more referrals, and significant nonmedical assistance, such as advocacy, food, showers, and transportation vouchers.[5]

In addition, homeless populations have a high prevalence of substance abuse and mental illness.[6-7] In Los Angeles County, approximately one-third of homeless adults suffer from mental illness, and most do not receive suitable care.[6,8-9] The prevalence of schizophrenia among homeless adults in Los Angeles is estimated to be 14%.[8] The national prevalence of schizophrenia among people who are homeless is approximately 11%, with less than half of that number receiving treatment.[10]

Mental illness decreases the likelihood of receiving proper care. Compared with matched controls having depression, homeless schizophrenic adults have fewer medical visits and fewer documented medical problems, and they are less likely to receive preventive care.[11] These data suggest the presence of undiagnosed and untreated chronic conditions. Supporting this claim, homeless schizophrenics are traditionally reported to have lower rates of so-called silent diseases, such as hypertension or diabetes, but more often present later with more advanced disease.[12]

Homeless adults have an increased risk of mortality, especially those with mental illness.[13-15] For example, homeless adults with schizophrenia have a mortality rate double that of comparable housed patients[16-17] and four times that of the general population.[13,18]

To counter lack of access to care and increased mortality among homeless populations, clinicians must often invest in a "period of courting" to establish trust.[19] The clinician's role can then expand to include increased availability outside of the clinic or travel with the patient to other health care appointments.[19]

There is evidence that clinics designed to address social issues in this fashion allow homeless patients to seek and receive suitable care successfully.[4] Free clinics have been documented as an important patch in the medical safety net.[20] Since most homeless adults have no regular source of care,[9] student-run free clinics offer a vital service.

Free Clinics, Medical Education, and Ethics

Student-run homeless clinics use a multidisciplinary team approach, incorporating social and mental health services with medical care.[21-24] Graduate students from programs such as business and law can contribute their skills to expand clinic services.[24] A student-run transdisciplinary clinic like the one at UCLA has been successful at the University of California at San Diego (UCSD).[25]

Medical students benefit from their experiences in clinics for the underserved. First- and second-year Wisconsin medical students working in a clinic for the poor and homeless rated their experiences very highly.[22] In one Texas program, students reported a positive contribution to their professional education and understanding of biopsychosocial issues. The students cited four themes: social awareness, compassion and empathy, teamwork, and confidence building.[21] At the Berkeley Suitcase Clinic, the benefits cited by students included the opportunity to learn new skills, experience with patients, discussion with physicians, and exposure to the issues of underserved populations.[24]

Free clinics may counteract problematic changes in medical student attitudes. A survey of students at one institution found that attitudes toward people who are homeless became more negative during medical school.[26] Other work has shown that a lack of specific training and negative attitudes among health care professionals can create significant barriers to health care for the homeless.[27] It is possible that student-run clinics address these problems by providing meaningful exposure to homeless patients and their needs.[28]

Similarly, the education of health professionals is fraught with ethical dilemmas, especially concerning socioeconomic status and access to care.[29] Prior work has rightly called for a balance of service and education, with an emphasis on adequate training, appropriate health care, and altruism.[30]

Conclusions

The case of H. E. demonstrates the particular challenges of caring for people who are homeless and mentally ill. After a lengthy "period of courting" to form a trusting relationship, the patient agreed to enter a hospital with the assistance of a medical student. Although the patient was ultimately diagnosed with terminal disease, he was able to find stable shelter in a nursing home as he received hospice care. Perhaps most importantly, the patient did not die anonymously on the streets.

On a more positive note, student-run free clinics also identify and treat many reversible conditions among underserved populations, including cardiovascular disease, malnutrition, and infectious illnesses.

We believe that the challenges of caring for people who are homeless can be addressed at a student-run free clinic. In addition, such clinics are a valuable educational experience, affect student attitudes positively, and can serve as a model of respectful and compassionate care. Further research is needed on a national scale to evaluate how well student-run free clinics are meeting the needs of homeless populations in order to better provide appropriate services and increase access for the underserved.

Notes

1. Link BG, Susser E, Stueve A, et al. Lifetime and five-year prevalence of homelessness in the United States. Am J Pub Health. 1994 Dec;84(12):1907–12.
2. Los Angeles Homeless Services Authority. 2005 Greater Los Angeles Homeless Count. Los Angeles: Los Angeles Homeless Services Authority, 2006 Jan 12. Available at http://www.lahsa.org/pdfs/Current/LAHSA%20Report%20-%20Final%20Version6-4.pdf.
3. Usatine RP, Gelberg L, Smith MH, et al. Health care for the homeless: a family medicine perspective. Am Fam Physician. 1994 Jan;49(1):139–46.
4. Gelberg L, Linn LS, Usatine RP, et al. Health, homelessness, and poverty. A study of clinic users. Arch Intern Med. 1990 Nov;150(11):2325–30.
5. Gelberg L, Doblin BH, Leake BD. Ambulatory health services provided to low-income and homeless adult patients in a major community health center. J Gen Intern Med. 1996 Mar;11(3):156–62.
6. Gelberg L, Linn LS, Leake BD. Mental health, alcohol and drug use, and criminal history among homeless adults. Am J Psychiatry. 1988 Feb;145(2):191–6.
7. Fischer PJ, Shapiro S, Breakey WR, et al. Mental health and social characteristics of the homeless: a survey of mission users. Am J Pub Health. 1986 May;76(5):519–24.
8. Koegel P, Burnam MA, Farr RK. The prevalence of specific psychiatric disorders among homeless individuals in the inner city of Los Angeles. Arch Gen Psychiatry. 1988 Dec;45(12):1085–92.
9. Gallagher TC, Andersen RM, Koegel P, et al. Determinants of regular source of care among homeless adults in Los Angeles. Med Care. 1997 Aug;35(8):814–30.
10. Folsom D, Jeste DV. Schizophrenia in homeless persons: a systematic review of the literature. Acta Psychiatr Scand. 2002 Jun;105(6):404–13.
11. Folsom DP, McCahill M, Bartels SJ, et al. Medical comorbidity and receipt of medical care by older homeless people with schizophrenia or depression. Psychiatr Serv. 2002 Nov;53(11):1456–60.
12. Muck-Jorgensen P, Mors O, Mortensen PB, et al. The schizophrenic patient in the somatic hospital. Acta Psychiatr Scand Suppl. 2000; 407:96–9.

13. Hibbs JR, Benner L, Klugman L, et al. Mortality in a cohort of homeless adults in Philadelphia. N Engl J Med. 1994 Aug 4;331(5):304–9.

14. Hwang SW, Orav EJ, O'Connell JJ, et al. Causes of death in homeless adults in Boston. Ann Intern Med. 1997 Apr 15;126(8):625–8.

15. Barrow SM, Herman DB, Córdova P, et al. Mortality among homeless shelter residents in New York City. Am J Pub Health. 1999 Apr;89(4):529–34.

16. Mortensen PB, Juel K. Mortality and causes of death in schizophrenic patients in Denmark. Acta Psychiatr Scand. 1990 Apr;81(4):372–7.

17. Tsuang MT, Woolson RF, Fleming JA. Premature deaths in schizophrenia and affective disorders. An analysis of survival curves and variables affecting the shortened survival. Arch Gen Psychiatry. 1980 Sep;37(9):979–83.

18. Babidge NC, Buhrich N, Butler T. Mortality among homeless people with schizophrenia in Sydney, Australia: a 10-year follow-up. Acta Psychiatr Scand. 2001 Feb; 103(2):105–10.

19. Levy BD, O'Connell JJ. Health care for homeless persons. N Engl J Med. 2004 Jun 3; 350(23):2329–32.

20. Geller S, Taylor BM, Scott HD. Free clinics helping to patch the safety net. J Health Care Poor Underserved. 2004 Feb;15(1):42–51.

21. Clark DL, Melillo A, Wallace D, et al. A multidisciplinary, learner-centered, student-run clinic for the homeless. Fam Med. 2003 Jun;35(6):394–7.

22. Haq CL, Cleeland L, Gjerde CL, et al. Student and faculty collaboration in a clinic for the medically underserved. Fam Med. 1996 Sep;28(8):570–4.

23. Fournier AM, Perez-Stable A, Greer PJ Jr. Lessons from a clinic for the homeless. The Camillus Health Concern. JAMA. 1993 Dec 8;270(22):2721–4.

24. Steinbach A, Swartzberg J, Carbone V. The Berkeley Suitcase Clinic: homeless services by undergraduate and medical student teams. Acad Med. 2001 May;76(5):524.

25. Beck E. The UCSD Student-Run Free Clinic Project: transdisciplinary health professional education. J Health Care Poor Underserved. 2005 May;16(2):207–19.

26. Masson N, Lester H. The attitudes of medical students towards homeless people: does medical school make a difference? Med Educ. 2003 Oct; 37(10):869–72.

27. Lester H, Bradley C. Barriers to primary healthcare for the homeless: the general practitioner's perspective. Eur J Gen Practice 2001;7(1):6–12.

28. Jain S, Buchanan D. A curriculum in homeless health care was effective in increasing students' knowledge. Med Educ. 2003 Nov;37(11):1032–3.

29. Christiakis DA, Feudtner C. Ethics in a short white coat: the ethical dilemmas that medical students confront. Acad Med. 1993 Apr;68(4);249–54.

30. Buchanan D, Witlin R. Balancing service and education: ethical management of student-run clinics. J Health Care Poor Underserved. 2006 Aug;17(3):477–85.

Chapter 23

The Promise Clinic: A Service-Learning Approach to Increasing Access to Health Care

Manuel Jimenez
Jennifer Tan
John Babineau
Jennifer Jimenez
Todd Billet
Charlene Flash
Steven J. Levin
Bernadette West
Alfred F. Tallia

The Homeless and Indigent Population Health Outreach Project (HIPHOP) was founded in 1995 by medical students at the University of Medicine and Dentistry of New Jersey–Robert Wood Johnson Medical School (UMDNJ-RWJMS) to add a community-based service-learning component to their curriculum. The project offered medical students the opportunity to interact with the community through health education workshops, shadowing opportunities at local community health centers, and diverse outreach projects.

Members of the HIPHOP leadership committee were disappointed that the 2003 medical school curriculum offered no opportunities for medical students to use their clinical skills directly to serve the community, few opportunities to learn

Manuel Jimenez, MD, MS, is a fellow in developmental behavioral pediatrics at the Children's Hospital of Philadelphia. *Jennifer Tan, MD,* is an associate physician and instructor in dermatology at Brigham and Women's Hospital, Harvard Medical School. *John Babineau, MD,* is a fellow in pediatric emergency medicine at New York Presbyterian Hospital, Columbia University Medical Center. *Jennifer Jimenez, MD,* is a fellow in pediatric gastroenterology at Alfred I. duPont Hospital for Children, in Wilmington, Delaware. *Todd Billet, MPH,* is a clinical science specialist with the renal division at Sanofi. *Charlene Flash, MD,* is a clinical fellow in medicine at Beth Israel Deaconess Medical Center, Harvard Medical School. *Steven J. Levin, MD,* is an associate professor of family medicine and community health at the Robert Wood Johnson Medical School and medical director of the Eric B. Chandler Health Center. *Bernadette West, PhD, MA,* is an associate professor in the School of Public Health at the University of Medicine and Dentistry of New Jersey. *Alfred F. Tallia, MD, MPH,* is a professor and chair of the Department of Family Medicine and Community Health, RWJMS.

as a team, and little opportunity for a continuity experience with patients. Additionally, students recognized that, while physicians are called upon to be altruistic, knowledgeable, skillful, and dutiful,[1] they needed more guidance in professionalism,[2] and that community-based experiences can serve as the basis for such guidance.[3] These students believed a partnership could be formed with the community to address existing health issues that would also enable them to learn from the community. Recognizing that health care is only one aspect of health, a group of first-year medical students set out to understand better the diverse set of problems facing the New Brunswick, New Jersey, community, especially those involving health care.

Seventeen percent of families and 27% of individuals in New Brunswick live below the federal poverty level.[4] Two of New Brunswick's three largest employers are university hospitals,[5] yet citizens still have difficulty getting health care. New Brunswick is filled with organizations and coalitions dedicated to identifying needs and mobilizing and providing social services. Elijah's Promise, one of these community organizations, helps people with low incomes by providing nutritious meals, a broad range of social services, culinary arts training, and health screenings integrated with other services.

Medical students became active in Elijah's Promise and held several meetings with its administration to learn more about the problems faced by clients. Access to primary health care by clients at the soup kitchen was identified as a major problem. So, in 2004, students initiated an institutional review board–approved survey to investigate health care access problems among clients of the Elijah's Promise Soup Kitchen. The survey instrument included questions adapted from the Medical Expenditure Panel Survey.[6] The most critical finding was that approximately one-third of the respondents did not have a regular source of care.

To address this problem, medical students worked with the administration of Elijah's Promise, the medical director and administrative staff of St. John's Family Health Center (a clinic operated by Catholic Charities), the RWJMS senior associate dean of community health, and more than 15 faculty members from the departments of family medicine and internal medicine to develop the Promise Clinic, the RWJMS student-run continuity clinic.

Intervention

The Promise Clinic directly combines the efforts of academic medicine with those of a community social service organization to provide continuity health care. The clinic is led by a group of student volunteers from each class (figure 23.1). This ensures continuity despite students graduating each year. The student leaders are responsible for recruiting patients, student doctors, and faculty to staff the clinic. They are also responsible for grant writing and budgeting as well as managing day-to-day operations of the Promise Clinic. The student leaders are supervised by two physician faculty members who serve as chief faculty advisers. The chief faculty advisers help the students with budget allocation, grant writing, and decision making regarding day to day operations. The leadership of the Promise Clinic

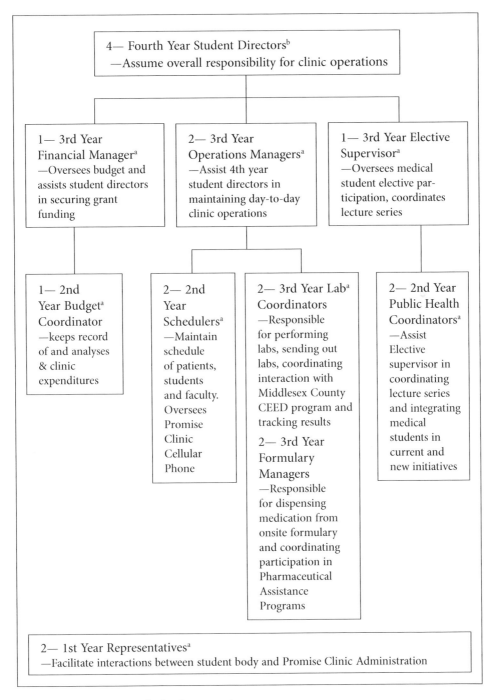

Figure 23.1 Promise Clinic leadership committee.

[a]It is expected that first-, second-, and third-year members of the leadership committee will assume the upperclass positions, except under special circumstances, to maintain continuity among the leadership.

[b]Student directors must have participated on the steering committee in other capacities for at least two years prior to assuming the role of student director.

is directed by a board of overseers, which meets at least quarterly each year. The board of overseers includes the fourth-year student directors, the chief faculty advisers, deans from the medical school and school of public health, the executive director and director of social services for Elijah's Promise, and the program coordinator of HIPHOP. The board of overseers is responsible for maintaining the mission of the Promise Clinic and ensuring that its goals are being met.

Under the direct supervision of volunteer licensed physicians, teams of medical students serve as primary care providers for clients from Elijah's Promise. Together, medical students and a social worker from Elijah's Promise work to identify clients who do not have a current source of primary care and are eligible for Charity Care (the New Jersey hospital care payment assistance program that provides free or reduced-charge care for eligible patients who receive care at an acute care hospital in New Jersey). At weekly blood pressure screenings by medical students during lunchtime at the soup kitchen, eligible clients are identified. The social worker may also directly schedule an appointment for a client. Identified clients are subsequently matched with a team of students consisting of a member of each medical school class.

On the evening of clinic, patients are greeted by a scheduler who keeps track of appointments and schedules student teams and attending physicians. The patient is then introduced to his or her student-doctor team. The first-and second-year students elicit a chief complaint and obtain the patient's vital signs. The third- or fourth-year student then joins the team and completes the history and physical. Together, team members develop an assessment and a plan, then present their findings to the attending physician. The attending physician reviews the history, examines the patient, and amends the plan as necessary. The final plan is explained to the patient and a follow-up visit is scheduled with the same student-doctor team.

Through grant funding, the clinic provides prescription medications, basic laboratory studies, and vaccinations at no cost to the patient. One of two student formulary coordinators, who provide prescription medications as needed, manage an on-site formulary for prescription drugs. Oversight is provided by the medical director of the clinic, a licensed physician who also serves as the chief faculty adviser of the Promise Clinic. The formulary has evolved over time and depends on the availability of low-cost generic medications. It consists of common classes of medication (such as but not limited to antibiotics, beta blockers, calcium channel blockers, ace inhibitors, and nonsteroidal anti-inflammatory drugs [NSAIDs]). The formulary does not include controlled medications. If necessary medications are not available in the formulary, we often request them through pharmaceutical assistance programs, programs run by the pharmaceutical companies that provide free medications to individuals who cannot afford them. If the need for such medications is urgent, we use grant money to subsidize the cost at a local commercial pharmacy. Many labs and diagnostic studies are completed through the on-site laboratory at the time of the visit. If the necessary lab facilities are not available at the clinic or further work-up is required, patients are sent to Robert Wood Johnson University Hospital, where they may benefit from Charity Care. The student-doctor team and social worker at Elijah's Promise, help the patient enroll in Charity Care.

Following his or her initial visit, a client is considered to be the patient of his or her student-doctor team. Follow-up visits are scheduled with the patient's original student-doctor team at the close of the initial visit. Patients can also schedule follow-up appointments through the Promise Clinic phone line, a cellular phone maintained by the student leaders. Messages are checked twice daily so that patients can communicate with their student doctors and schedule appointments.

The Promise Clinic is open Thursday evenings from 6 to 9 p.m., excluding holidays. The clinic uses the facilities of St. John's Family Health Center, a clinic operated by Catholic Charities of the Diocese of Metuchen, New Jersey, which is located across the street from Elijah's Promise. Volunteer licensed physicians (who commit to precept at the clinic four times annually for at least three years) supervise the students' work on a rotating basis. In the event that a patient needs inpatient care, he or she is admitted to Robert Wood Johnson University Hospital under the family medicine service. Inpatient costs are covered in part by Charity Care. Physician inpatient services are donated by the physicians. The Promise Clinic is funded through the Pfizer / Association of American Medical Colleges (AAMC) Caring for the Community award, the J. Seward Johnson Charitable Trust, as well as generous private donations.

The team approach to patient care serves three purposes. First, it ensures continuity for the patient. Although one member of each team graduates each year, three students remain, and a first-year medical student is added. Second, the team approach provides students with valuable continuity, since the patient schedules all follow-up with his or her team. Under this system it is possible for a student to follow a patient throughout the student's four years of medical school. Finally, the program provides underclassmen with clinical exposure while upperclassmen gain valuable teaching experience. The continuity model implemented in the design of the student-doctor teams has also been applied to the leadership structure of the Promise Clinic and is summarized in figure 23.1.

In addition to its valuable clinical care, the Promise Clinic also represents an opportunity for community-based participatory research. While there is a wealth of information regarding the impact of student-run clinics on students,[7-11] there is very little data on the health outcomes and satisfaction levels of the patients served in these settings. To address this deficit, we have worked with students and faculty at the UMDNJ–School of Public Health to design a program evaluation that determines impact, outcomes, and process measures of this intervention.

First Year of Operations

From January 20 to December 15, 2005, a total of 129 medical students participated in the Promise Clinic. Sixty-six were first- or second-year students, and 63 were third- or fourth-year students. In that time, a total of 42 clients from Elijah's Promise enrolled as patients. At the conclusion of 2005, 30 of these patients were considered active. Demographic data for the Promise Clinic patient population is

Table 23.1

The Promise Clinic patient population demographic data (n=42)

Variables	%
Age (in years)	
<18	2.4
18–29	7.1
30–39	21.4
40–49	47.6
50–59	16.7
60 and older	4.8
Gender	
Male	64.3
Female	35.7
City of residence	
New Brunswick	69
Other	30
Permanent place to stay	
Yes	52.4
No	47.6
Employment	
Employed	26.2
Unemployed	73.8
Race/ethincity	
White/Caucasian	38.1
African American	28.6
Hispanic/Latino	19
Other	14.3

summarized in table 23.1. Approximately 71% of the forty-two patients we encountered had no form of insurance, whereas 12% had Medicaid, 7% had Medicare, 2% had private insurance, and 8% were missing insurance data.

In 2005, there were 113 patient encounters. Forty-two of these visits were considered new patient visits, while 66 were scheduled follow-up appointments with established patients. Five of these encounters were unscheduled follow-up appointments with established patients. A total of 218 appointments were scheduled, and 108 scheduled patients attended their visit, accounting for a show rate of approximately 50%. Common chief complaints and diagnoses are summarized in table 23.2.

During its first year of operation, the Promise Clinic struggled in some of its efforts. Perhaps most prominent was difficulty obtaining specialty care for patients. Despite the outstanding support of some faculty specialists, we have yet to establish a systematic method to obtain other specialty care services; we are currently exploring methods to provide these services. Initially, the Promise Clinic

Table 23.2

Summary of Promise Clinic patient encounters

5 most common chief complaints	5 most common diagnoses
High blood pressure	Hypertension
Back pain	Depression
Desire for well visit	Tobacco dependence
Difficulty obtaining medication	Eczema
Headache	Psoriasis

intended to accept only patients without health insurance. However, as time progressed, we found that Elijah's Promise clients with Medicaid, Medicare, and even private health insurance sought our services. The reasons consisted mostly of difficulty obtaining an appointment at the other local clinics for the underserved and difficulty affording medication. Although our intention is to link these patients with other local clinics or to a private practitioner's office, our clinic has served as a temporary site for them.

With 15 rotating preceptors, there was concern that different management styles might lead to fragmented care. In order to avoid this unwanted consequence of volunteerism, all charts are periodically reviewed by student directors and during supervised sessions with our chief faculty adviser.

Finally, with growing interest among the student body, accommodating all interested students has been difficult. During their RWJMS orientation, approximately two-thirds (120 students) of the first-year class expressed interest in participating. Only 33 could be accommodated, leaving a significant number unable to participate. We are working diligently to increase opportunities for involvement, including educational workshops for clients designed and taught by students.

Discussion

Health care institutions can play a role in addressing the unmet health needs of a community.[12] Collaboration among medical students, residents, and faculty can help provide increased access to care[13] and a rich learning experience for participating students.[14,15] The Promise Clinic demonstrates collaboration between an academic medical center and a social service provider. The community benefits from the talent and resources available through an academic medical center. The academic medical center benefits from the wisdom and energy of the community. Such endeavors, where the needs of patient and community come first, can increase access and improve outcomes for populations in need,[16] allowing deficiencies in health care delivery and medical education to be met simultaneously.

The Promise Clinic began with a needs assessment. As a result, we were able to create a clinic specifically designed to overcome health care barriers identified by this patient population, including the need for evening clinic hours, medication cost coverage, and effective communication between health care and social service providers. Although further investigation is warranted, we see the success of the Promise Clinic as preliminary evidence that collaborative clinics can make a significant contribution to the improvement of health care access in similar populations.

The student-doctor team model provides rich learning opportunities and exposure to continuity of care for students at all levels of training. This is important in light of the recommendation that medical schools should present students with early experiences that stress viewing the patient as a person, a member of a family, and a member of the community.[17] The Promise Clinic student-doctor team model also affords students an opportunity to gain longitudinal continuity of care experience that is difficult to obtain in traditional curricula. Continuity experiences can provide valuable lessons, including observation of the course and treatment of disease and formation of relationships with patients (rather than with complaints or disease).[18] Such long-term interactions can create powerful bonds between a patient and a student.

After several years of operation, the Promise Clinic continues to grow. Our focus has shifted from implementing to maintaining, improving, and evaluating a successful clinic. The Promise Clinic demonstrates the possibility of partnership between medical students, academic faculty, and a local social services organization to provide increased access to primary care and a service-learning experience for students. We encourage our colleagues at other medical schools to develop similar programs.

Acknowledgments

We would like to thank several individuals who have been integral to the development and sustainability of the Promise Clinic. First and foremost we wish to thank our patients, who have entrusted us with their care. Lisanne Finston, executive director of Elijah's Promise; Yvette Molina, director of social services at Elijah's Promise; Susan Giordano, program coordinator of HIPHOP; Denise Rodgers, MD, former senior associate dean of community health at UMDNJ-RWJMS; the staff and administration of Catholic Charities of Metuchen St. Johns Family Health Center; the current student leadership of HIPHOP and the Promise Clinic; and all past and current student doctors and faculty preceptors.

Notes

1. Association of American Medical Colleges. Report I: learning objectives for medical student education—guidelines for medical schools. Available at http://www.aamc.org/meded/msop/msop1.pdf.

2. Swick HM, Szenas P, Danoff D, et al. Teaching professionalism in undergraduate medical education. JAMA. 1999 Sep 1;282(9):830–2.

3. O'Toole TP, Kathuria N, Mishra M, et al. Teaching professionalism within a community context: perspectives from a national demonstration project. Acad Med. 2005 Apr;80(4):339–43.

4. U.S. Census Bureau. Census 2000 Demographic Profile Highlights: New Brunswick City, New Jersey. Washington, DC: U.S. Census Bureau, 2000.

5. City of New Brunswick, New Jersey. New Brunswick Census Demographics. New Brunswick, NJ: City of New Brunswick, 2007. Available at http://newbrunswick.com/content.php ?content=Demographics_block%20.

6. United States Department of Health and Human Services, Agency for Healthcare Research and Quality (AHRQ). Medical expenditure panel survey. Rockville, MD: AHRQ, 2006. Available at http://www.ahrq.gov/.

7. Buchanan D, Witlen R. Balancing service and education: ethical management of student-run clinics. J Health Care Poor Underserved. 2006 Aug;17(3):477–85.

8. Beck E. The UCSD Student-Run Free Clinic Project: transdisciplinary health professional education. J Health Care Poor Underserved. 2005 May;16(2):207–19.

9. Bennard B, Wilson JL, Ferguson KP, et al. A student-run outreach clinic for rural communities in Appalachia. Acad Med. 2004 Jul;79(7):666–71.

10. Campos-Outcalt DE. Specialties chosen by medical students who participated in a student-run, community-based free clinic. Am J Prev Med. 1985 Jul–Aug;1(4):50–1.

11. Davenport BA. Witnessing and the medical gaze: how medical students learn to see at a free clinic for the homeless. Med Anthropol Q. 2000 Sep;14(3):310–27.

12. Tallia AF, Micek-Galinat L, Formica PE. Academic-community linkages: community-based training for family physicians. Fam Med. 1996 Oct;28(9):618–23.

13. Haq CL, Cleeland L, Gjerde CL, et al. Student and faculty collaboration in a clinic for the medically underserved. Fam Med. 1996 Sep;28(8):570–4.

14. Fournier AM, Perez-Stable A, Greer PJ Jr. Lessons from a clinic for the homeless. The Camillus Health Concern. JAMA. 1993 Dec 8;270(22):2721–4.

15. Clark DL, Melillo A, Wallace D, et al. A multidisciplinary, learner-centered, student-run clinic for the homeless. Fam Med. 2003 Jun;35(6):394–7.

16. Michener JL, Champagne MT, Yaggy D, et al. Making a home in the community for the academic medical center. Acad Med. 2005 Jan;80(1):57–61.

17. American Association of Medical Colleges Ad Hoc Committee of Deans. Educating doctors to provide high quality medical care: a vision for medical education in the United States. Washington, DC: American Association of Medical Colleges, 2004 July.

18. Vogt HB, Lindemann JC, Hearns VL. Teaching medical students about continuity of patient care. Acad Med. 2000 Jan;75(1):58.

Chapter 24
Engaging Student Health Organizations in Reducing Health Disparities in Underserved Communities through Volunteerism: Developing a Student Health Corps

Vickie M. Mays
Lichin Ly
Erica Allen
Sophia Young

The 2000 U.S. Census indicates that underrepresented minorities (URMs) (African Americans, Hispanics, and Native Americans/Alaskan Indians) and Asian/ Pacific Islanders account for nearly a third of the U.S. population, with the projection that these racial/ethnic populations will constitute the majority in the United States by 2050.[1] Despite improvement in overall life expectancy in the United States, racial/ethnic minorities have not shown the same progress and continue to have poorer health outcomes from preventive and treatable conditions such as cancer, cardiovascular disease, diabetes, IIIV/AIDS, infant mortality, and asthma compared with whites.[2-5] As the U.S. population grows more racially and ethnically diverse, so grows the need to address health disparities that account for poorer health outcomes and premature deaths and disease among racial/ethnic minorities.[6-9] Furthermore, the current U.S. health care workforce lacks the growing diversity of the overall population: URMs continue to be underrepresented in the health profession fields of medicine (6%),[10] nursing (6.7%),[11] dentistry (7%),[12] and pharmacy (12%).[13] This lack of diversity is important, because research indicates that underrepresented minorities are more likely to practice and provide culturally competent care in underserved, racial/ethnic minority communities.[14-16] Some studies also show that minorities tend to seek care from physicians who share their ethnicity and that these patients rate satisfaction, quality of overall

Vickie M. Mays, PhD, MSPH, is a professor in the Department of Psychology and in the Department of Health Services at UCLA and is the director of the UCLA Center on Research, Education, Training and Strategic Communication on Minority Health Disparities (MHD). *Lichin Ly, MPH,* works at the UCLA Center for Research, Education, Training and Strategic Communication on Minority Health Disparities. *Erica Allen, MD, MPH,* is employed by the Mid-Atlantic Kaiser Permanente Medical Group. *Sophia Young, MPH,* is affiliated with the Yale University School of Public Health.

care, and health outcomes more highly than do those receiving care from physicians of other ethnicities.[17-19]

As the population of racial/ethnic minority groups increases, so too does the need for health care providers who speak the languages of the group served, whose ethnicities match the preferences of the group being served, and who are willing to practice in underserved communities. One population that can contribute to increasing a diverse health care workforce is racial/ethnic minority undergraduate students majoring in health. When these students engage in community-based health activities in multicultural or poor urban settings, they have been found to rate these experiences positively and to be more inclined to develop their clinical practices with these underserved populations.[20-22]

Despite these findings, little research has explored ways to leverage the volunteer efforts of undergraduate college students as a strategy to eliminate health disparities, while also increasing the likelihood that these students will pursue clinical practice and/or research in underserved racial/ethnic minority communities.[23,24] In recent years there has been a movement, especially in public universities, to engage undergraduate students in service learning and volunteer efforts within communities.[25-28] In the area of reducing health disparities, one underutilized source of volunteers undergraduate volunteer-run student health organizations that conduct health outreach, education, and preventive health screenings in underserved communities. Although not a substitute for affordable comprehensive health care, health fairs can play a beneficial role in providing preventative services to medically underserved populations who face an array of financial, linguistic, and cultural barriers to receiving such services.[29-33]

The goal of this study was to examine preventive health-screening activities conducted by volunteer undergraduate students in health organizations and determine the type and extent of their outreach health services to underserved racial/ethnic communities. We also assessed the training of these volunteers in order to examine the adequacy of the services provided and determine if there are ways to improve their volunteer efforts toward reducing health disparities in racial/ethnic minority and underserved communities.

Methods

Undergraduate volunteer student health organizations at a major public land grant university in Southern California involved in conducting health outreach in racial/ethnic minority communities were identified and their officers asked to participate in a needs assessment about the work of their organizations. Thirteen of the groups were volunteer health groups targeting specific underserved racial/ethnic minorities; the remaining group (a chapter of SHOUT [Student Health OUTreach]) enrolled underserved families and children in federally funded health insurance programs. This group typically participates in the health fairs organized by the other 13 predominantly minority student health organizations.

A needs assessment was developed with the help of the project director, a third-year medical student, the faculty principal investigator, and several undergraduate volunteer students, many of whom served as health fair directors for the various student health organizations. The needs assessment included questions on the membership of the student health organization, characteristics of the populations they served, the type of preventive screenings provided, frequency of their outreach efforts, identification and evaluation of the training they received, and their views on what additional resources would be helpful to them in expanding their efforts and providing culturally competent screening and health education in racial/ethnic minority communities. The needs assessment was pretested for length, clarity, and coverage of issues important to the student-run organizations. It was decided that the outgoing presidents and any officers of the student organizations were the best candidates for completing the surveys due to their years of experience in the organizations, as well as their management and oversight of their group's activities and its membership.

Data collection procedures

The student health organization presidents were contacted by either the project director or an undergraduate student member of our health fair team. They were given the needs assessment to complete with a promise that a $5.00 Starbucks gift card would be given to them and to each member of their organization who assisted them in completing the surveys. Reminders were sent to each of the student group presidents about completing the needs assessment. Finally, when student health presidents indicated that the survey was completed, our health fair project director or an undergraduate health fair team member (all were also health organization participants) met with them and reviewed the survey to ensure that all questions relevant to the activities of the organization were completed. There was a 100% completion rate as all 14 of the student health organizations thoroughly completed the needs assessment. (Some questions were not answered by some organizations because they were not relevant to the activities of those particular organizations.)

Data analysis and data synthesis

Questions with predetermined responses were tabulated. Undergraduate health volunteers entered the data using Excel and analyzed it with Stata 10.[34] Open-ended data were coded and viewed by two additional raters for agreement on the coding categories. Inter-rater reliability among the three coders was 0.97.

Results

Volunteer undergraduate organization student-run health fairs

Undergraduate health organizations vary in size of active membership (defined as students who participate in community health outreach activities), with the smallest group having 12 members (Black Pre Health) to the largest having over 200 members (Chicanos for Community Medicine). Most of the groups (*n*=9/14) conducted one to two health fairs annually, with each health fair taking, on average, three months to plan. For each health fair, on average, 14 students per organization volunteered to work at a particular event with assistance from approximately 13 students from other student-run health groups. The number of volunteers needed to plan and conduct a health fair also varied with the size of the fair. Student volunteers ranged from 4 to 38 members from the primary health organization in charge of organizing the fair to an additional 0 to 55 students from other student groups.

Services provided

The majority of the respondents (n=9/14) indicated that their group offered various types of preventive screenings at health fairs (data not shown). Health fair screenings/exams focused on general health conditions (blood pressure, cholesterol, and anemia) and risk factors for diabetes, obesity, and cardiovascular diseases, but few to no screenings were offered on a regular basis for other chronic or debilitating diseases prevalent in racial/ethnic communities (e.g., breast, cervical, or prostate cancer; HIV/AIDS and other sexually transmitted infections [STIs]; asthma) or behavioral health factors (e.g., alcohol, drugs, tobacco, physical fitness/activity, domestic violence, seat belt or bicycle helmet compliance). Brochures were distributed that contained information on general health conditions, such as high blood pressure, cholesterol, and anemia. At least five of the student health organizations indicated that their group provided glucose and blood pressure checks, performed either by students or professional medical volunteers (physicians or nurses). Two organizations indicated that they provided anemia and cholesterol tests in addition to the aforementioned screenings. Dental and optometric services were sometimes provided at the health fairs by two volunteer student groups, with the assistance of dental students, undergraduate optometry students, and a volunteer optometrist. The following professionals are ranked in the order of being most often present to least often present at the student health fairs: health educators, dental students, physicians, medical students, and dentists.

On average, a student volunteer spent 14.6 minutes speaking with participants after their screenings to discuss their results. Respondents indicated that they provided educational presentations or consultations on various health-related topics, such as organ donation, insurance enrollment, monitoring of chronic health conditions, weight management, fitness, nutrition, contraception use, stress reduction, domestic violence, substance abuse, child health, HIV/AIDS, and STIs. Free or low-cost primary care clinic referrals were provided by all seven student organizations for whom this question was relevant (see table 24.1). Observations at various health fairs revealed that actual incidents of counseling and health education for behavioral topics were brief. Students focused more on test results and their relationship to changing behaviors to lower diabetes and cardiovascular disease (CVD) levels.

Populations served

The undergraduate organizations provided services to a diverse population reflective of the racial/ethnic diversity of Los Angeles County. Health fairs were conducted in seven of the eight Los Angeles County Service Planning Areas

Table 24.1

Types of referrals provided by student organizations at health outreach activities or health fairs

Types of referrals provided	# of organizations' affirmative responses / organizations responding (%)
Free or low-cost primary care clinics (*n*=7)	7/7 (100%)
Free mental health services (*n*=6)	1/6 (17%)
Dental clinics (*n*=8)	4/8 (50%)
Optometry services (*n*=6)	2/6 (33%)
Nutrition services (*n*=7)	2/7 (29%)
Substance abuse programs (*n*=6)	0/6 (0%)
Smoking cessation programs (*n*=6)	1/6 (17%)
Domestic violence programs (*n*=5)	1/5 (20%)
Legal service agencies (*n*=7)	0/7 (0%)
Homeless shelters (*n*=7)	1/7 (14%)
Health insurance programs (*n*=6)	1/6 (17%)
Health care providers who speak their languages (*n*=7)	3/7 (43%)
Social service agencies who service people who speak their languages (*n*=6)	2/6 (33%)
Other types of referrals provided (*n*=5)	0/5 (0%)

(SPAs, or health districts), which comprise more than 9 million people from a wide array of racial, ethnic, and immigrant subpopulations.[35] Most of the student-run health fairs were held in SPA 3 (San Gabriel), which has over 1.7 million residents, the majority of whom belong to racial/ethnic minority groups (43.6% Hispanic, 22.7% Asian Pacific Islander, and 4.7% African American).[36] The second most frequently served area (SPA 5, West Los Angeles) comprises neighborhoods surrounding the public land grant institution that the students attended. This area had 650,000 residents, with a racial/ethnic minority distribution of 18% Hispanic, 12% Asian Pacific Islander, and 7% African American.[37]

The total number of health fair attendees served annually was estimated by the 14 groups as 12,425 people (67% Hispanic, 25% African American, and 6.33% Asian Pacific Islander; see table 24.2). The majority of student health organizations (*n*=12/14) indicated that their health fairs served a diverse set of groups, including Chinese, Southeast Asian Indians, Pacific Islanders, South Asians, African Americans/Afro Caribbeans, Latinos, and American Indians. Eleven student health organizations indicated that in addition to the groups above, they also provided services to whites and Middle Easterners (e.g., Armenians, Persians, Arabs), ten groups to Africans, and one group indicated provision of services to Cambodians, Laotians, Thai, and Vietnamese.

Approximately 138 people, on average, attended an organization's health fair or health outreach activity, with a range of 30 to 310 per event (*n*=9/14). The average

Table 24.2

Racial/ethnic populations typically served by student health organizations at health outreach activities or health fairs

Racial/ethnic population	# of student organizations serving population	For student organizations serving the population, mean percentage of individuals served who belong to that population (*n* varies)
African	6	7
Asian	6	2.5
South East Asian	5	3
Pacific Islander	5	0
Indian / South Asian	6	0.83
African American	7	25
Latino	7	67
Caucasian	5	2.5
American Indian / Alaskan Native	5	0
Southwest Asian / Middle Eastern	6	0.83

number of people served in a year by members of each organization was 1,035, with a range from 5 to 5,000. Most of the student groups focused their efforts on particular racial/ethnic populations or communities, such as Hispanics, Asians, Pacific Islanders, or African Americans. The two most commonly spoken languages by health fair attendees were English and Spanish. Other languages spoken by attendees included Amharic (by the Ethiopians), Thai, Mandarin, Cantonese, Arabic, Armenian, and Hindi. Not every student health organization was able to provide the subgroup designations of their community participants. Furthermore, attendees who spoke, for example, Spanish could have been Mexican, Afro Caribbean, Belizean, or from another Spanish-speaking country of Central or South America.

Assessment of underserved community heath needs

We assessed student organizations' methods of determining health needs of the communities they selected for outreach. Over half of the groups ($n=6/11$) searched Internet sites for information, but fewer ($n=5/13$) used online fact sheets or statistics supplied by the local county health department. Most groups ($n=11/12$) attempted to address the health needs of their target populations using personal experience and knowledge from the previous year's organization officers. When asked whether research articles and Los Angeles County Health Department SPA statistics on racial/ethnic demographics and prevalence of diseases would be useful for increasing the effectiveness of health screenings, the majority of the organizations ($n=9/12$) indicated they would find these very useful. The majority of the organizations ($n=10/11$) indicated that their active members needed to learn more about the health status and/or health issues of their target population.

The research team reviewed literature for health-related activities that should be assessed in the surveys.[38–55] Based on their health fair experiences, the organization officers identified several health needs of attendees. These included health care services such as screening for hypertension or diabetes, immunizations/vaccinations, and access to dental care. No organization respondent mentioned screening for nonchronic conditions, such as bacterial or viral infections, unintentional injuries or child safety (e.g., seat belt and helmet compliance), or skin diseases (sun screen protection, skin self-exams). Information about social services (concerning such things as health insurance, domestic violence, STIs and safer sex, weight management, nutrition, and physical activity) was also identified as needed ($n=6/14$).

Trainings

At the start of each academic year, student volunteer groups organized training sessions so that their members could obtain the technical skills needed to provide preventive screenings at the health fairs. Ten of the groups surveyed indicated that they provided members with specific training activities. Training sessions were conducted by the group's leadership board or health professionals, such as emergency medical technicians, registered nurses, physicians, or Red Cross or Planned Parenthood representatives, and involved presentations as well as a distribution of study materials. Some organizations required their volunteers to complete written and/or practical exams to demonstrate proficiency. One organization utilized an academic course as part of the training, for which students conducted screenings at health fairs. In this case, proficiency was assessed via exams, course grade, and practical evaluations.

Despite efforts to achieve screening competency, only a few of the student organization respondents ($n=3/7$) felt their trainer was extremely knowledgeable about the health conditions that their organizations were being trained to detect. Of nine student organization officers, only two believed their sessions were effective in training volunteers to discuss health-related behavioral change issues with health fair attendees. Only half of the groups that engaged in training ($n=5/10$) had methods in place to maintain the skills of their volunteers, and fewer ($n=3/10$) performed ongoing competency evaluations of their student health fair workers. Officers from several groups mentioned that while training sessions were helpful, much of the experience acquired by student volunteers came from on-site experiences. In addition, nine of ten groups indicated a need for the development of a health fair assessment tool that would enable them to better evaluate the efficacy of their fairs (through collecting and analyzing data on all aspects of their events). All of the student organization respondents ($n=10/10$) stated that they would like to learn about methods for evaluating their health fairs and health outreach activities.

Barriers and limitations

Student health organization respondents indicated that there were barriers that hindered the planning and implementation of health fairs. The predominant complaint was inadequate funding for supplies (e.g., blood pressure cuffs, glucose testing machines), which limited the number of events they were able to conduct. Another cost barrier was the expense of paying trainers (e.g., Red Cross). Another problem was the linguistic barrier that sometimes arose between volunteers and health fair attendees due to insufficient numbers of Spanish-speaking staff. This made information dissemination difficult and limited the efficacy of service delivery. The last difficulty identified was limited knowledge of the health needs of the community in which the fair was being hosted, coupled with insufficient publicity to ensure large-scale community participation.

Discussion

Findings from this study strongly support that the volunteer efforts of student health organizations that provide health screenings and health education programs in underserved areas,[56–59] as well as other community health activities,[23,24,60] can play a significant role in reducing and eliminating health disparities. In this study, we found that student health organizations, acting in a volunteer capacity, provided much-needed health services to thousands of racial/ethnic minority group members (Hispanics, African Americans, and Asian Pacific Islanders). The undergraduate volunteer student health organizations in our study were predominantly racial/ethnic minority organizations that forged relationships with minority populations in the community that continued from year to year through the provision of health fairs. These volunteer activities formed an avenue for delivering preventive screenings to people who traditionally face social, economic, and linguistic barriers to such services.[31,32] Many underserved communities and those with a large number of uninsured residents have come to depend on volunteer-provided health services to monitor their blood pressure, conduct mammograms, and provide a number of other services.[30] The area where most of the student organization health fairs occurred (SPA 3) had a population that was more than 37% foreign born and more than 57% foreign language speaking;[35] and a third of the Latino population in SPA 5 (the second most-served area) met federal poverty guidelines.[36]

While our results indicate that preventive screening needs of these populations can be addressed in part through volunteer undergraduate student activities, the results also indicate that these services could be improved by consistent, affordable training coupled with accurate data on the health needs and conditions of the populations served. In addition, the efforts of the students to serve large numbers of individuals were limited due to a lack of funding to purchase supplies essential to screening efforts. If student volunteers are to extend preventive health services, help identify much-needed health care interventions, and enroll the uninsured in health care coverage, attention must be paid to identification of sources of financial resources for supplies as well as training.

Cardiovascular disease and diabetes in African Americans, Hispanics, and Asians/Pacific Islanders are among the leading causes of death and disability in the SPAs served by the student volunteers.[61] The student health fairs provided services to reduce or eliminate these health disparities through blood pressure and glucometer checks, as well as health promotion education for nutrition, fitness, and weight management. The student organizations, in general, did not provide detailed assessments or health information on behavioral risk factors or injury prevention. Training to increase their activities regarding alcohol, drug, and tobacco use, as well as injury prevention (e.g., seat belt use, helmet use, bicycle safety), could be especially useful, as these are also significant contributors to health disparities in racial/ethnic populations.[41] The presence of a SHOUT chapter, a student organization with a mission to decrease disparities in health insurance, was an excellent vehicle for ensuring that community participants could be enrolled on site in federal, state, and county programs designed to increase their access to health services. Access to health services and health care is integral to reducing and eliminating health disparities. In 2002–2003 in Los Angeles County, 6 out of 10 low-income uninsured children had difficulty accessing necessary medical care.[62] Volunteer student health organizations' efforts to enroll underserved community members who qualify into state and federal health coverage programs can be useful in closing the gap in access to health services.

This study also suggests that undergraduate student volunteer health organizations need assistance in developing (a) more effective training tools to improve volunteers' proficiency in conducting screenings, (b) language skills to communicate findings to all participants, and (c) understanding of the health status and needs of their target population as derived from credible resources. This will help volunteers enable health fair attendees to use screening data to change their health habits and health status, thereby contributing to the reduction of health disparities in underserved communities.[63] Students also need assistance in developing evaluation measures to assess proficiency of volunteers, effects of screening and health education on health behavior change, patient satisfaction, and accessibility of services to the community.[64] Almost all organizations indicated that their members would benefit from the development of health fair assessment tools (such as surveys and other data collection methods). The DHHS Office of Minority Health has issued a similar call for better tools for community health assessments that can be used by community organizations to monitor and identify health disparities.[65,66] As one remedy, we developed an online health fair guide (www.minorityhealthdisparities.org) that provides this information as well as tools to conduct behavioral health education and health promotion (e.g., helmet safety, infant car seat usage, violence prevention), health promotion materials in several languages, and health fair activities for children.

Another way of ensuring adequate and up-to-date screening and health promotion competencies of undergraduate student health volunteers is by means of (credit or noncredit) academic courses offering university-based community service–learning experiences. Studies have shown that health science departments, such as schools of medicine and nursing, have the capability and expertise to offer undergraduates knowledge of health education and health promotion, as well as skill-based trainings, under the guidance of faculty, staff, health educators, or clinical providers.[56,67,68]

Finally, a national, state, or local initiative might take the form of a volunteer health corps of undergraduate students. Commissioned health corps have existed in our nation's history to respond to large-scale public health crises such as national disasters, disease outbreaks, and terrorist attacks.[69] The continuing gaps evident in health disparities combined with the loss of community-based hospitals and clinics requires a large-scale public health solution.[70-72] Student health corps on college and university campuses, which can be organized through campus health-affairs or student-affairs offices or through schools of nursing and medicine, can assist local and national efforts to reduce health disparities among the medically underserved through federal leadership or university-based civic engagement.[73] While such corps can help provide needed health screening, health education, and health promotion services in underserved racial/ethnic and poor communities, a corps of this nature can also increase the number of individuals who will commit their clinical, research, and policy careers in health to addressing health disparities. Such a health corps could not only engage students from health majors but also non-health disciplines. In particular, students who major in a foreign language are much needed as translators during health outreach group activities in monolingual communities. An additional group of students who would be helpful are math and statistics majors, who might help conduct evaluations, analyze data, and predict utilization of services to better anticipate staffing needs and supplies for health fair efforts.

Engaging minority students, especially URMs, in service to underserved communities where health disparities persist is a vital step in developing a culturally competent and diverse health workforce. A study conducted by Blue et al. demonstrated that medical students' community service involvement correlated with the number of different types of organizations they served and the length of their involvement prior to entering medical school.[74] In addition, studies have shown that students report a strong preference for working in underserved minority communities after they graduate based on personal volunteer or work experience within the community.[20-22] Further research is needed to explore ways to create or enhance health-related community service experiences of undergraduates as a way of increasing their likelihood of pursuing clinical practice and or research careers in underserved communities, and thereby help reduce health disparities among ethnic groups. Colleges and universities would be ideal partners in state or federal efforts to organize health corps to respond to the crisis of reducing health disparities and providing the personnel for a diverse health care workforce. Important to these efforts are ensuring that volunteers, particularly undergraduate volunteers, are provided with the necessary training and supervision by appropriate personnel to engage in health screenings. However, in some communities where liability concerns result in insurance costs beyond what many community- and student-based organizations can afford, "Good Samaritan" laws that protect against the threat of lawsuits are also needed as part of a policy overhaul. If we are to tap into the rich volunteerism of undergraduate students within the context of a civic engagement model, policies requiring adequate instruction and supervision by health professionals along with liability protections will need to be addressed. It is important that the medically underserved receive high-quality, evidenced-based screening services, including community outreach efforts such as health fairs, if we are to be successful at reducing, and ultimately eliminating, health disparities.

As U.S. president Barack Obama calls on the nation to help overcome difficulties faced in the United States to address adequate health care for all, instituting a student health corps structured much like our Public Health Services Corps, in partnership with universities' and colleges' civic engagement activities, could be a significant factor in the reduction or elimination of health disparities. This fits well with the president's proposed $4,000 tuition credit for 100 hours of service.[75] Not only would the development of a health corps bring preventive services to underserved areas, but it could have the effect of increasing the numbers of individuals who eventually, as health professionals, deliver research in these underserved areas. Results of our work indicate that students are eager to be trained and to render services in underserved racial/ethnic minority communities.

Acknowledgments

This study was supported by a grant from the National Center on Minority Health and Health Disparities (MD000508). We acknowledge the contributions of Laurel Methot, Sharetta Garrett, Winnie Shu, and several other undergraduate minority health disparity scholars and volunteers (www.minorityhealthdisparities) for their invaluable assistance with this project. The views expressed here are those of the authors and may not be attributed to the National Institutes of Health. No financial conflict of interest.

Notes

1.   U.S. Census Bureau. U.S. Census population of the United States by race and Hispanic origin: 2000 to 2050. Washington, DC: U.S. Census Bureau, 2004.

2.   Betancourt JR, Maina AW. The Institute of Medicine report "Unequal Treatment": implications for academic health centers. Mt Sinai J Med. 2004 Oct;71(5):314–21.

3.   Satcher D. The Initiative to Eliminate Racial and Ethnic Health Disparities is moving forward. Public Health Rep. 1999 May–Jun;114(3):283–7.

4.   Agency for Health Care Research and Quality. National health care disparities report. Rockville, MD: U.S. Department of Health and Human Services, Agency for Health care Research and Quality, 2003. Available at http://www.ahrq.gov/qual/nhdr03/nhdr2003.pdf.

5.   Walker B, Mays VM, Warren R. The changing landscape for the elimination of racial/ethnic health status disparities. J Health Care Poor Underserved. 2004 Nov;15(4):506–21.

6.   Lurie N, Dubowitz T. Health disparities and access to health. JAMA. 2007 Mar 14;297(10):1118–21.

7.   Frist WH. Overcoming disparities in U.S. health care. Health Aff (Millwood). 2005 Mar–Apr; 24(2):445–51.

8.   Betancourt JR, Green AR, Carrillo JE, et al. Cultural competence and health care disparities: key perspectives and trends. Health Aff (Millwood). 2005 Mar–Apr;24(2):499–505.

9.   Mays VM, Cochran SD, Barnes NW. Race, race-based discrimination, and health outcomes among African Americans. Annu Rev Psychol. 2007; 58:201–25.

10.   The Sullivan Commission. Missing persons: minorities in the health professions. Atlanta, GA: The Sullivan Commission on Diversity in the Healthcare Workforce, 2004. Available at http://www.aacn.nche.edu/Media/pdf/SullivanReport.pdf.

11.   Health Resources and Services Administration. The registered nurse population: findings from the March 2004 National Sample Survey of registered nurses. Rockville, MD: U.S. Department of Health and Human Services, Health Resources and Services Administration, 2004. Available at ftp://ftp.hrsa.gov/bhpr/workforce/0306rnss.pdf.

12.   Valachovic RW, Weaver RG, Sinkford JC, et al. Trends in dentistry and dental education. J Dent Educ. 2001;65(6):539–61.

13.   Pharmacy Education and the University of California. Final report of the Health Sciences Committee—April 2004. Los Angeles, CA: Pharmacy Education and the University of California, 2004. Available at http://www.ucop.edu/hss/documents/ pharmacy.pdf.

14.   Cantor JC, Miles EL, Baker LC, et al. Physician service to the underserved: implications for affirmative action in medical education. Inquiry. 1996 Summer;33(2):167–80.

15.   Komaromy M, Grumbach K, Drake M, et al. The role of black and Hispanic physicians in providing health care for underserved populations. N Engl J Med. 1996 May 16;334(20):1305–10.

16.   Moy E, Bartman BA. Physician race and care of minority and medically indigent patients. JAMA. 1995 May 17;273(19):1515–20.

17.   Saha S, Taggart SH, Komaromy M, et al. Do patients choose physicians of their own race? Health Aff (Millwood). 2000 Jul–Aug;19(4):76–83.

18.   Saha S, Komaromy M, Koepsell TD, et al. Patient-physician racial concordance and the perceived quality and use of health care. Arch Intern Med. 1999 May 10;159(9):997–1004.

19.   Cooper-Patrick L, Gallo JJ, Gonzales JJ, et al. Race, gender, and partnership in the patient-physician relationship. JAMA. 1999 Aug 11;282(6):583–9.

20.   Ramsey AH, Haq C, Gjerde CL, et al. Career influence of an international health experience during medical school. Fam Med. 2004 Jun;36(6):412–6.

21.   O'Toole TP, Hanusa BH, Gibbon JL, et al. Experiences and attitudes of residents and students influence voluntary service with homeless populations. J Gen Intern Med. 1999 Apr; 14(4):211–6.

22.   Weissman JS, Campbell EG, Gokhale M, et al. Residents' preferences and preparation for caring for underserved populations. J Urban Health. 2001 Sep;78(3):535–49.

23.   Brosnan CA, Upchurch SL, Meininger JC, et al. Students nurses participate in public health research and practice through a school-based screening program. Public Health Nurs. 2005;22(3):260–6.

24.   Mohan CP, Mohan A. HealthSTAT: a student approach to building skills needed to serve poor communities. J Health Care Poor Underserved. 2007 Aug;18(3):523–31.

25.   Ostrander SA. Democracy, civic participation, and the university: a comparative study of civic engagement on five campuses. Nonprofit and Voluntary Sector Quarterly. 2004;33(1):74–93.

26.   Marullo S, Edwards B. Editors' introduction: service-learning pedagogy as universities' response to troubled times. Am Behav Sci. 2000;43(5):746–55.

27.   Checkoway B. Renewing the civic mission of the American research university. J Higher Educ. 2001 Mar–Apr;72(2):125–47.

28.   Gronski R, Pigg K. University and community collaboration: experimental learning in human services. Am Behav Sci. 2000 Feb;43(5):781–92.

29.   Melland R, Mauntel B, Contreras P. C.A.R.E. Fair: one-stop shopping for an underserved population. Am J Public Health. 1994 Aug;84(8):1337–8.

30.   Dulin MK, Olive KE, Florence JA, et al. The financial value of services provided by a rural community health fair. J Health Care Poor Underserved. 2006 Nov;17(4):821–9.

31. Macias EP, Morales LS. Utilization of health care services among adults attending a health fair in South Los Angeles County. J Community Health. 2000 Feb;25(1):35–46.

32. Aponte J, Nickitas DM. Community as client: reaching an underserved urban community and meeting unmet primary health care needs. J Community Health Nurs. 2007 Fall;24(3):177–90.

33. Ponce NA, Cochran SD, Mays VM, et al. Health coverage of low-income citizen and noncitizen wage earners: sources and disparities. J Immigr Minor Health. 2008 Apr;10(2):167–76.

34. StataCorp. Stata statistical software, release 10. College Station, TX: StataCorp, 2007.

35. County of Los Angeles. Estimated population of the 88 cities in the County of Los Angeles. Los Angeles, CA: County of Los Angeles, 2007. Available at http://ceo.lacounty.gov/forms/Population%20Pg_Color.pdf.

36. Los Angeles County Children's Planning Council. Population profile 2000—Service Planning Area 3; San Gabriel. Los Angeles, CA: Los Angeles County Children's Planning Council, 2000. Available at http://www.lapublichealth.org/childpc/spas/spa3/demog_3.pdf.

37. West Service Planning Area, Los Angeles Public Health. The health of the residents in the West Service Planning Area of Los Angeles County. Los Angeles, CA: West Service Planning Area, Los Angeles Public Health, 2007. Available at http://lapublichealth.org/wwwfiles/ph/chs/spa5/5-NARATIVE-all.pdf.

38. Murray CJL, Lopez AD, Mathers CD, et al. The global burden of disease 2000 project: aims, methods and data sources. Geneva, Switzerland: World Health Organization, 2001. Available at http://www.who.int/healthinfo/paper36.pdf.

39. Krieger J, Higgins DL. Housing and health: time again for public health action. Am J Public Health. 2002 May;92(5):758–68.

40. Ailinger RL, Lasus H, Dear M. Americans' knowledge and perceived risk of tuberculosis. Public Health Nurs. 2003 May–Jun;20(3):211–5.

41. Briggs NC, Schlundt DG, Levine RS, et al. Seat belt law enforcement and racial disparities in seat belt use. Am J Prev Med. 2006 Aug;31(2):135–41.

42. Garcia AN, Patel KV, Guralnik JM. Seat belt use among American Indians/Alaska Natives and non-Hispanic Whites. Am J Prev Med. 2007 Sep;33(3):200–6.

43. Briggs NC, Schlundt DG, Levine RS, et al. Seat belt use among Hispanic ethnic subgroups of national origin. Inj Prev. 2006 Dec;12(6):421–6.

44. Bernard SJ, Paulozzi LJ, Wallace DL. Fatal injuries among children by race and ethnicity—United States, 1999–2002. MMWR Surveill Summ. 2007 May 18;56(5):1–16.

45. Briley JJ Jr, Lynfield YL, Chavda K. Sunscreen use and usefulness in African-Americans. J Drugs Dermatol. 2007 Jan;6(1):19–22.

46. Cokkinides VE, Weinstock MA, Cardinez CJ, et al. Sun-safe practices in U.S. youth and their parents: role of caregiver on youth sunscreen use. Am J Prev Med. 2004 Feb;26(2):147–51.

47. Pichon LC, Mayer JA, Slymen DJ, et al. Ethnoracial differences among outdoor workers in key sun-safety behaviors. Am J Prev Med. 2005 May;28(4):374–8.

48. Helfand M, Mahon SM, Eden KB, et al. Screening for skin cancer. Am J Prev Med. 2001 Apr;20(3 Suppl):47–58.

49. Ferrini RL, Perlman M, Hill L. American College of Preventive Medicine policy statement: screening for skin cancer. Am J Prev Med. 1998 Jan;14(1):80–2.

50. Greenberg JS, Howard D, Desmond S. A community-campus partnership for health: the Seat Pleasant–University of Maryland health partnership. Health Promot Pract. 2003 Oct;4(4):393–401.

51. Gielen AC, O'Campo PJ, Campbell JC, et al. Women's opinions about domestic violence screening and mandatory reporting. Am J Prev Med. 2000 Nov;19(4):279–85.

52. Smith MU, DiClemente RJ. STAND: a peer educator training curriculum for sexual risk reduction in the rural South. Students Together Against Negative Decisions. Prev Med. 2000 Jun;30(6):441–9.

53. Wilson LF. Adolescents' attitudes about obesity and what they want in obesity prevention programs. J Sch Nurs. 2007 Aug;23(4):229–38.

54. Reger B, Wootan MG, Booth-Butterfield S. A comparison of different approaches to promote community-wide dietary change. Am J Prev Med. 2000 May;18(4):271–5.

55. Green LW, Orleans CT, Ottoson JM, et al. Inferring strategies for disseminating physical activity policies, programs, and practices from the successes of tobacco control. Am J Prev Med. 2006 Oct;31(4 Suppl):S66–81.

56. Maltby H. Use of health fairs to develop public health nursing competencies. Public Health Nurs. 2006 Mar–Apr;23(2):183–9.

57. Levy K, Lehna C. A service-oriented teaching and learning project. Pediatr Nurs. 2002 May–Jun;28(3):219–21.

58. Simpson SA, Long JA. Medical student-run health clinics: important contributors to patient care and medical education. J Gen Intern Med. 2007 Mar;22(3):352–6.

59. Cadzow RB, Servoss TJ, Fox CH. The health status of patients of a student-run free medical clinic in inner-city Buffalo, NY. J Am Board Fam Med. 2007 Nov–Dec;20(6):572–80.

60. Gaines C, Jenkins S, Ashe W. Empowering nursing faculty and students for community service. J Nurs Educ. 2005 Nov;44(11):522–5.

61. Los Angeles County Department of Health Services and UCLA Center for Health Policy Research. The burden of disease in Los Angeles County: a study of the patterns of morbidity and mortality in the county population. Los Angeles, CA: The Los Angeles County Department of Health Services & The UCLA Center for Health Policy Research, 2000. Available at http://www.lapublichealth.org/epi/reports/dburden.pdf.

62. Kenney GM, McFeeters J, Yee J. Access gaps among uninsured children in Los Angeles County: baseline findings from the 2002/2003 Los Angeles County Health Survey. Los Angeles, CA: Urban Institute, 2006. Available at http://www.urban.org/UploadedPDF/411463_uninsured_children.pdf.

63. Mays VM, Ly L. Health fair resource guide 2008. Los Angeles, CA: UCLA Center for Research, Education, Training, and Strategic Communication on Minority Health Disparities, 2008. Available at http://cretscmhd.psych.ucla.edu/healthfair/HF%20 Mainpage/HFmain page.htm.

64. Hecker EJ. Feria de Salud: implementation and evaluation of a communitywide health fair. Public Health Nurs. 2000 Jul–Aug;17(4):247–56.

65. Graham GN, Leath B, Payne K, et al. Perceived versus actual risk for hypertension and diabetes in the African American community. Health Promot Pract. 2006 Jan;7(1):34–46.

66. Graham GN, Kim S, James B, et al. Benefits of standardized diabetes and hypertension screening forms at community screening events. Health Promot Pract. 2006 Jan;7(1):26–33.

67. Steinbach A, Swartzberg J, Carbone V. The Berkeley Suitcase Clinic: homeless services by undergraduate and medical student teams. Acad Med. 2001 May;76(5):524.

68. Albritton TA, Wagner PJ. Linking cultural competency and community service: a partnership between students, faculty, and the community. Acad Med. 2002 Jul;77(7):738–9.

69. U.S. Public Health Services Commissioned Corp. History about the Commissioned Corps. Rockville, MD: U.S. Public Health Services Commissioned Corp, 2008. Available at http://www.usphs.gov/aboutus/history.aspx.

70. Holmes GM, Slifkin RT, Randolph RK, et al. The effect of rural hospital closures on community economic health. Health Serv Res. 2006 Apr;41(2):467–85.

71. Reif SS, DesHarnais S, Bernard S. Community perceptions of the effects of rural hospital closure on access to care. J Rural Health. 1999 Spring;15(2):202–9.

72. Buchmueller TC, Jacobson M, Wold C. How far to the hospital? The effect of hospital closures on access to care. J Health Econ. 2006 Jul;25(4):740–61. Epub 2005 Dec 13.

73. Mays VM, Ly L. Report on the outreach and academic preparation of undergraduate student health organization of the University of California and comparison public universities. In preparation.

74. Blue AV, Basco WT Jr, Geesey ME, et al. How does pre-admission community service compare with community service during medical school? Teach Learn Med. 2005 Fall;17(4):316–21.

75. Muskegon Chronicle. Obama says he will offer $4,000 tuition tax credit. Muskegon, MI: Muskegon Chronicle, 2008 Jun 17. Available at http://blog.mlive.com/ chronicle/2008/06 /obama_says_he_will_offer_4000.html.

Chapter 25
HealthSTAT: A Student Approach to Building Skills Needed to Serve Poor Communities

Carmen Patrick Mohan
Arun Mohan

A growing number of health professionals argue that community service, advocacy, and leadership constitute core professional responsibilities with important implications for responsibly serving poor communities.[1-4] Yet, few schools' curricula address the skills required to fulfill those responsibilities. Such skills include community partnership, public speaking, fundraising, consensus building, organizational management, community organizing, team building, and interprofessional collaboration.[5-8] When courses are offered that address these skills, they are often didactic and, in our experience as medical students, marginalized in the curriculum and by our classmates.[9]

Throughout the last five decades, students who felt unprepared to serve poor communities by their formal education searched for alternative ways to gain the requisite skills, work across professional lines, and initiate change.[10-12] With the notable exception of student-run health clinics (such as those described in this book), student-initiated efforts are only rarely documented in the literature, and little is known about how these programs originate, how they are sustained, and what schools can do to facilitate this kind of leadership and creativity.[10,11,16,17] Here, we address these questions by describing one extracurricular organization through which students in Georgia have taught each other the skills needed to work on behalf of underserved communities: Health Students Taking Action Together (HealthSTAT). We also discuss challenges intrinsic to this learning modality, including limited time and rapid leadership turnover.

About HealthSTAT

HealthSTAT is a student-led, Georgia-focused, nonprofit organization that emphasizes peer-to-peer learning in medically underserved communities. Students from each of the state's four medical schools volunteer, along with students from

Carmen Patrick Mohan, MD, is an instructor of medicine at Emory University School of Medicine, Atlanta, Georgia. *Arun Mohan, MD, MBA,* is a practicing hospitalist at Emory University Hospital and an associate vice chair for information technology (IT) in the Emory Department of Medicine.

several nursing, public health, and undergraduate institutions. Although medical students represent the largest proportion of volunteers, HealthSTAT is represented at various Georgia professional schools: Emory University schools of medicine, nursing, public health, law, and business; Georgia State University Department of Nutrition; Medical College of Georgia schools of medicine and nursing; Mercer University schools of medicine and nursing; and Morehouse schools of medicine and public health. A minority of our volunteers are undergraduates attending the University of Georgia, Emory University, or Morehouse College.

History

HealthSTAT began at an informal meeting of five students from Emory and Morehouse schools of medicine who were concerned about the uninsured, a topic they felt was not sufficiently addressed in their classrooms. They convened monthly to teach each other about the issue. Through their conversations, these students came to recognize that just as health students learn clinical skills in real clinical settings, learning community health requires action on real issues.

They used e-mail to place an online call for students interested in organizing a candlelight vigil for uninsured Georgians. Nine students from a variety of health professional schools responded. Featured on local television, the event became the 2002 Candlelight Vigil for Uninsured Georgians, was supported by three community partners, and attended by nearly 150 students from 4 of the state's health professional schools. The vigil is now in its fourth year. Figure 25.1 shows a poster used to advertise the 2005 vigil.

Buoyed by this enthusiastic response, these students opted to incorporate HealthSTAT in July 2002 as a 501c3 nonprofit organization. Since then, HealthSTAT has expanded its issue-based agenda to include (1) reducing Georgia's uninsured, (2) preventing childhood overweight, and (3) preventing HIV/AIDS. As students' collective interests and community needs change, HealthSTAT's agenda changes. For example, the board recently adopted *increasing access to care* as an issue area that includes reducing the number of uninsured and improving access to care for the state's immigrant community.

Program initiation and management

As HealthSTAT's organizational history suggests, passionate student leaders were involved at all stages of its development. The role of passionate leaders continues today. Here, we have attempted to categorize pivotal events and roles captured within the HealthSTAT model.

The cornerstone of the model is interprofessional and interinstitutional team-based leadership. Responsibilities are distributed in three ways: programmatically, organizationally, and administratively. Student volunteers hold all positions, unless otherwise noted.

Programmatic

When HealthSTAT launches an issue area, it provides students with a framework structured around the school calendar to study the issue, work with com-

Figure 25.1 Flyer advertising 2005 candlelight vigil for Georgia's uninsured children.

munity partners to develop solutions, and implement a plan working toward that solution. In the fall, HealthSTAT highlights the new issue by organizing a Leadership Symposium that brings together 30–40 students for two days to meet with community leaders to study the problem and compose a white paper outlining ways that students might address the issue. Interested students are invited to join a working group of 5–7 students facilitated by an issue coordinator. Over the winter, this working group plans spring programs that include lectures, direct-service projects, and advocacy. The summer is used to reflect. As mentioned previously, HealthSTAT has launched three issues in this way. HealthSTAT invests heavily in the launch phases and then secures funding for work on each issue to continue in subsequent years. For examples of HealthSTAT's programs, see figure 25.2.

Once an issue area has been established, working groups manage programs and add components as needed. They recruit additional volunteers to coordinate programs and participants. HealthSTAT's president ensures that activities are in line with organizational strategy, leverages synergy between issues, and secures funding for the upcoming school year. To coordinate geographically dispersed individuals, working groups communicate using the HealthSTAT website (www.health statgeorgia.org), electronic surveys, and conference calls. In addition, the HealthSTAT president leads semiannual one-day workshops for working group members that focus on project planning, teamwork, and reflection.

Organizational

A board of directors reflecting the interprofessional background of program participants governs HealthSTAT. In 2005–2006, there were 16 directors (7 from medicine, 3 nursing, 3 public health, and 1 each from law, business, and nutrition). All but 3 of these directors were students, while the rest were recent alumni, younger than 30 years old. A board of advisors comprising recognized community leaders supports the directors.

A board chairperson facilitates all board activities, including an annual board retreat, quarterly meetings, strategic planning, fundraising, and elections of issue coordinators and the four officers who constitute the executive committee (president, board chairperson, treasurer, and secretary). While directors make larger decisions that influence the organization's long-term trajectory, the executive committee makes week-to-week decisions regarding program execution.

Administrative

Day-to-day administrative tasks are performed by paid staff, including a managing director, two work-study students, and as many as four summer interns per year. The staff assists students in making connections within the community, researching funders and issues, and evaluating programs. The staff also enhances the richness of student experiences by relieving students of secretarial work, logistics, and bookkeeping.

Students are involved in every facet of HealthSTAT's work, from the administrative to the programmatic. Even formalized trainings on such topics as media relations, fundraising, lobbying, and team-based leadership are developed by students. Most learning is not didactic. For example, as students are required to recruit other student volunteers, form strategies, plan a project budget, and execute an implementation plan, they are simultaneously learning, practicing, and modeling such skills as public speaking, consensus building, organizational management, and teamwork. Figure 25.3 shows HealthSTAT's organizational chart.

	Event Type	Number of Years	Avg # Participants Per Year	Approx. Total Participant Hours
Advocacy	**Candlelight Vigil for Uninsured Georgians***			
	Annual	4	150	2,400
	Campaign to Prevent Cuts to PeachCare for Kids: *Year-long campaign that educated students about proposed cuts to GA sCHIP through lectures.*			
	Annual	2	1,307	1,307
	Campaign to Preserve Immigrant Access to Healthcare*: *Year-long campaign focused on educating students about proposed restrictions to immigrant access to healthcare.*			
	Annual	1	93	186
Peer-to-Peer Education	**Leadership Symposium*:** *Brings together student leaders to develop a position paper on a pressing health related issue.*			
	Annual	4	38	2,280
	Political Leadership Institute*: *Teaches policy advocacy skills.*			
	Annual	3	25	525
	HIV/AIDS Prevention and Policy Workshop*			
	Annual	2	29	406
	Oral History Project*: *Pairs students with patients living with HIV/AIDS to understand the story.*			
	Ongoing	2	45	234
	Voter Education Guide: *Provides candidates' positions on health issues students are concerned with.*			
	Annual	2	-	1,000 Guides Distributed
	Introduction to Health Policy Workshop*			
	Annual	1	49	196
	Context*: *Nation's first, peer-reviewed, online journal dedicated to student engagement in communities.*			
	Ongoing	1	-	-
	Curbside Consult*: *Monthly podcast providing student perspective on issues related to public health.*			
	Monthly	1	4,787	2,872
Service	**PeachCare Registration Drives:** *Door-door canvassing event to assist*			
	Annual	1	61	244
	POWERPLAY*: *Pairs health students with overweight teens for structured intervention focused on healthy lifestyle.*			
	Weekly	2	20	250
	Stepping for Health*: *Pairs health students and fraternities for health related intervention at local elementary schools.*			
	Weekly	1	54	150
Leadership	**Board Retreat*:** *Provides space for reflection, planning, evaluation.*			
	Annual	3	13	780
	Fundraising Training*			
	Annual	2	6	96
	Builiding United Invested Leadership Teams*: *Day-long workshop to train working groups in teamwork and leadership.*			
	Annual	2	16	256
	TOTAL PARTICPANT HOURS			**12,182**

Figure 25.2 HealthSTAT programs and participation from 2002 to 2005.
*Denotes current program for 2005–2006 school year. Total participant hours do not include planning hours for paid staff and volunteers.

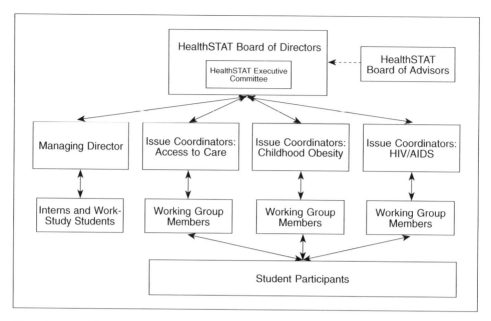

Figure 25.3 HealthSTAT organizational chart.

Accomplishments

The quality of HealthSTAT's work can be assessed on three scales: (1) the extent to which students become involved in communities, (2) skills that students gain, and (3) the community impact of work done. HealthSTAT has not yet had the organizational lifespan to measure the community impact of its programs. However, some measure of HealthSTAT's success can be seen in its ability to engage diverse students in programs that range broadly in scope and to garner financial support for those programs. Future evaluation will focus on the quality of these programs and their community impact.

Student Engagement

HealthSTAT's effectiveness in engaging students can be measured in number of participant-hours per year (average = 4,060 hours/year), variety of programs (17 programs), number of self-publications (3 position papers), and funds garnered (more than $300,000 over 4 years). Since HealthSTAT's incorporation, over 1,500 students from 11 schools have participated in its activities, totaling 12,182 participant-hours. The cost to HealthSTAT per participant-hour is $18. As shown in figure 25.2, HealthSTAT has organized programs that span advocacy, education, service, and leadership.

Community impact

Student impact on the community is difficult to gauge; we share the following story as one example of how HealthSTAT has successfully created processes that support students with administration, funding, training, and social capital. In campaigning against 2006 legislation that would have restricted undocumented immigrants' access to public health services, student leaders already active on the issue relied on HealthSTAT for access to a statewide network of volunteers, mentors from various disciplines, a neutral place to meet, media relations, and funding. The legislation that was ultimately passed excluded most health restrictions. Although many groups were involved in the political process, student involvement was cited as instrumental by representatives and lobbyists central to the legislation's opposition and was highlighted in three publications and on two local television stations.[13-15]

Funding

HealthSTAT is supported by foundations, participants' schools, registration fees, individuals, and fundraising events. Healthcare Georgia Foundation seeded Health-STAT with a grant of $35,000 in 2003. Since then, HealthSTAT has raised $185,000 from national and local foundations, including the Robert Wood Johnson Foundation and the W. K. Kellogg Foundation. Though students are involved in direct solicitations and proposal writing, development staff has played a key part in securing these funds. Figure 23.4 shows HealthSTAT's expanding financial resources.

Key Success Factors

As demonstrated by our study of barriers to student community service in 2004, the major challenge to greater student community involvement is time constraints.[9]

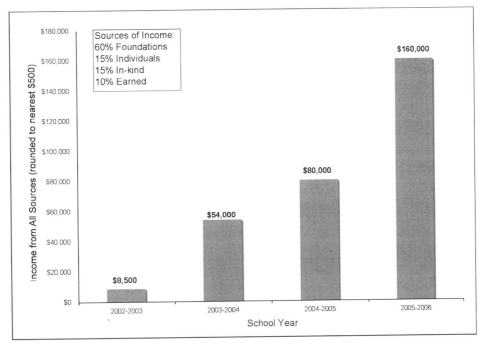

Figure 25.4 HealthSTAT's financial resources allow steady organizational growth. HealthSTAT relies heavily on foundation support but has begun to diversify funding streams.

HealthSTAT reduces this barrier by promoting team-based leadership and staff support.

Team-based leadership

With team-based leadership, HealthSTAT encourages shared responsibility to overcome time constraints and facilitate leadership development. Team-based projects are effective ways to advance the work even as exam schedules and clinical responsibilities escalate. This is especially true of interprofessional and interinstitutional teams, as the schedules are unlikely to overlap.

Staff accountability, to students

The HealthSTAT paid staff assists students with fundraising plans, public relations, and making key community contacts. Importantly, staff is hired by and accountable to students, who conduct performance evaluations twice yearly. Selecting, managing, and retaining staff provides yet another opportunity for students to grow professionally.

HealthSTAT volunteers are with the organization for one to four years, meaning rapid turnover of leadership could negatively affect the fragile relationships that underserved communities have with student organizations. Our team-based approach and support staff not only foster a smooth transition and retain institutional memory, but also provide consistent commitment to Georgia's underserved.

Statewide scope

Students involved with HealthSTAT cite their success serving poor communities as a key motivator. When students see the broader implications of their work, their commitment to community-oriented action is sustained. In HealthSTAT's experience, success is more readily apparent at the state rather than national level. Moving beyond the local community forces students to reach out to a broad range of professions and institutions. This, together with the dearth of student organizations working at this level, is why HealthSTAT remains a Georgia-focused organization.

Continuing Challenges

General challenges moving forward include funding and the continuing support of our institutions. Challenges unique to HealthSTAT include increasing student diversity, deepening the level of student participation, and developing a pipeline for health professionals training to serve poor communities. Maintaining institutional, professional, and racial diversity requires vigilance, relationship building, and investment in infrastructure to bridge geographic divides. These challenges are complex for any organization and will require that HealthSTAT continue to make diversity a high priority as we move forward with our work.

Conclusion

Student-generated models such as HealthSTAT must be further studied so that their successful strategies may be incorporated into formal health professional education. HealthSTAT demonstrates that when students are provided with infrastructure and administrative assistance, they create ways to learn skills necessary to serve poor communities. HealthSTAT offers an interactive way to cultivate skills needed to assume the core professional responsibilities of service, leadership, and advocacy. Team-based leadership and staff support can maximize the contributions students make to communities, enhancing (rather than detracting from) their clinical and research experiences.

Acknowledgments

We wish to acknowledge the students whose contributions make HealthSTAT possible, especially Rebecca Bedingfield, MPH; Matthew Coldiron, MPH; AJ Khaw, MD; Kamilah Pickett, MPH; Nishant Shah, MD, MPH; Perry Sheffield, MD; Larissa Thomas; Emile Toufighian, MSN; and Dorothy Wadsworth. We also wish to acknowledge HealthSTAT's first executive director, Dana Lee, MPH. Finally, thanks to David Wilkinson, JD; Daniel Blumenthal, MD; and Henry Khan, MD, for their constructive feedback regarding this chapter and their continuing support of HealthSTAT's work.

Research for this report is supported in part by a grant from the Paul and Daisy Soros Fellowships for New Americans. The program is not responsible for the views expressed here.

Notes

1. Maurana CA, Wolff M, Beck BJ, et. al. Working with our communities: moving from service to scholarship in the health professions. Educ Health (Abingdon). 2001;14(2):207–20.

2. Recreating health professional practice for a new century: the fourth report of the Pew Health Professions Commission. San Francisco, CA: UCSF Center for the Health Professions, 1998. Available at http://www.futurehealth.ucsf.edu/pdf_files/rept4.pdf.

3. Godkin MA. Community advocacy, physician roles, and medical education. Fam Med. 1993 Mar;25(3):170–1.

4. Gruen R, Pearson SD, Brennan TA. Physician-citizens—public roles and professional obligations. JAMA. 2004 Jan 7;291(1):94–8.

5. Treadwell H, ed. Healthcare partnerships: meeting the needs of underserved populations. Battlecreek, MI: W.K. Kellogg Foundation, 2000 Jul: 37–40.

6. Pew Health Professions Commission. Health America: practitioners for 2005. An agenda for action for U.S. health professional schools. San Francisco: Pew Health Professions Commission, 1991.

7. D'Amour D, Ferrada-Videla M, San Martin Rodriguez L, et al. The conceptual basis for interprofessional collaboration: core concepts and theoretical frameworks. J Interprof Care. 2005 May;19 (Suppl 1):116–31.

8. Paine R, Sachs R, Krause T, et al. Educating medical students and residents as health protectors and patient advocates. Am J Prev Med. 1993 Mar–Apr;9(2):117–21.

9.   Davidson RA. Community-based education and problem solving: the Community Health Scholars Program at the University of Florida. Teach Learn Med. 2002 Summer; 14(3):178–81.

10. Eckenfels EJ. Contemporary medical students' quest for self-fulfillment through community service. Acad Med. 1997 Dec;72(12):1043–50.

11. Grande D, Srinivas S. Student leadership and activism for social change in the US. Educ Health (Abingdon). 2001;14(2):198–206.

12. Madison DL. American medical student activism. N C Med J. 1988 Sep;49(9):457–64.

13. Ramage S. Chicken soup for the pols. Atlanta Sunday Paper. 2006 Feb 19:2–3.

14. Guthrie P. Doctors demand services for illegals. Atlanta Journal-Constitution. 2006 Feb 14.

15. Abkowitz A. Students want to be docs, not immigrations refs. Atlanta: Creative Loafing Atlanta, 2006 Feb 15. Available at http://atlanta.creativeloafing.com/ gyrobase/Content? oid=oid%3A20913.

16. Beck E. The UCSD Student-Run Free Clinic Project: transdisciplinary health professional education. J Health Care Poor Underserved. 2005 May;16(2):207–19.

17. Buchanan D, Witlen R. Balancing service and education: ethical management of student-run clinics. J Health Care Poor Underserved. 2006 Aug;17(3):477–85.

Index